GOETHE
WILHELM MEISTER'S
APPRENTICESHIP

GOETHE

Collected Works in 12 Volumes

Goethe's Collected Works, Volume 9

Johann Wolfgang von
GOETHE

Wilhelm Meister's Apprenticeship

Edited and Translated by Eric A. Blackall
in cooperation with Victor Lange

Princeton University Press
Princeton, New Jersey

Published by Princeton University Press, 41 William Street,
Princeton, New Jersey 08540
In the United Kingdom by Princeton University Press, Chichester, West Sussex
Copyright © 1989 Suhrkamp Publishers, New York, Inc.

Reprinted in paperback by arrangement with Suhrkamp Verlag

Library of Congress Cataloging-in-Publication Data

Goethe, Johann Wolfgang von, 1749–1832.
[Wilhelm Meister's Lehrjahre. English]
Wilhelm Meister's apprenticeship / Johann Wolfgang von Goethe ;
edited and translated by Eric A. Blackall in cooperation with Victor Lange.
p. cm. -- (Princeton paperbacks)
Originally published: New York : Suhrkamp, 1989. (Goethe's
collected works ; v. 9
ISBN 0-691-04344-2
I. Blackall, Eric A. (Eric Albert) II. Lange, Victor, 1908–.
III. Title. IV. Series: Goethe, Johann Wolfgang von, 1749–1832.
Works. English. 1994 ; v. 9
PT2026.A1C94 1994 Vol. 9
[PT2027.W5]

831'.6—dc20   94–39893
[833'.6]

First Princeton Paperback printing, 1995

© for the poems "Who never with hot tears ate his bread," "Know you the land where
lemon blossoms blow," "Only they know my pain who know my yearning," and "Do not
sing in tones depressing" 1989 by Hal Draper. Used with permission.

Printed in the United States of America

3 5 7 9 10 8 6 4

Contents

GOETHE
WILHELM MEISTER'S
APPRENTICESHIP

Book One

Chapter One

The play lasted for a very long time. Old Barbara went to the window several times to see if the coaches had already started leaving the theater. She was waiting for Mariane, her pretty mistress who was that night delighting the audience as a young officer in the epilogue—waiting for her with more impatience than usual, when she merely had a simple supper ready. For this time a surprise package had come in the mail from a wealthy young merchant named Norberg, to show that even when he was away, he was still thinking of his beloved. A trusty servant, companion, adviser, go-between and house-keeper, Barbara had every right to open the package. And this evening she could not resist, for the favors of this generous lover meant even more to her than they did to Mariane. To her great delight she found in the package not only fine muslin and elegant ribbons for Mariane, but for herself a length of cotton material, scarves and a roll of coins. She thought of the absent Norberg with great affection and gratitude, and eagerly resolved to praise him to Mariane, to remind her of what she owed him, and of his hopes and expectations that she would be faithful to him.

The muslin, brightened by the color of the half-unrolled ribbons, lay like a Christmas present on the table, and the light of the candles added a special luster to the gift. Everything was in place as she heard Mariane's footsteps on the stairs and she hastened to meet her. But how surprised she was when this female officer disregarded her affectionate greeting, and, pushing past her, rushed into the room, dropped the sword and plumed hat with unusual haste, walked restlessly up and down and never noticed the festive candles.

"What is it, my dear?" asked the old woman, puzzled. "For heaven's sake, girl, what's wrong? Look at these presents. Who could they be from but your loving friend? Norberg has sent you a length of muslin for a nightgown. He'll soon be here, and seems more eager and generous than usual."

Barbara was about to show Mariane the gifts that she too had received from him when Mariane, turning away from the gifts, cried out: "No! No! I don't want to hear any more about all this. I did what you wanted, so be it! When

Norberg comes back, I'll be his again, I'll be yours—do with me what you will. But until then, I want to be myself. If you had a thousand tongues, you couldn't change my mind. I am going to give all of myself to the one who loves me and whom I love. Don't make such faces! I am going to love him with everything I have as if it could last forever."

The old woman had counterarguments enough. But when the exchange began to get violent and bitter, Mariane jumped up and grabbed her. The old woman only laughed uproariously and said, "If I am to be sure of my life, I have to see to it that you are soon in a long dress again. Go and change! I hope that you will apologize, as a girl, for the harm you did me as a flighty officer: off with that coat and with everything underneath it. It's an uncomfortable costume, and dangerous for you, I see. The epaulettes have gone to your head."

Barbara tried to hold her but Mariane broke free. "Not so fast!" she said, "I'm expecting a visitor tonight."

"That's not good," the old woman replied. "Surely not that young, lovesick, unfledged merchant's son?" "Exactly! Him!" said Mariane.

"Magnanimity seems now to be your ruling passion," the old woman scornfully replied. "You exert yourself for those who are either immature or poor. It must be nice to be adored as an unselfish benefactress."

"Make fun of me if you like! I love him! I love him! Oh, how happy I am to say this, for the first time in my life. This is the passion I have acted on the stage and yet never really known. I will throw myself at him, embrace him as if I would hold him forever. I shall show him all my love and enjoy all of his!"

"Calm down! Calm down," said the old woman quietly. "I must interrupt your joy with the news that Norberg will be here in two weeks. Here is his letter, which came with the presents."

"The dawn may take my lover away, but I won't think about that now. Fourteen days! That's an eternity! Just think what can happen, what can change, in two weeks."

Wilhelm entered the room. How eagerly she rushed towards him! And how passionately he embraced that red uniform and the white satin vest. Who would dare to describe, who has the right to describe, the bliss of two lovers. The old womanservant went off muttering, and we, too, leave the happy couple to themselves.

Chapter Two

When Wilhelm greeted his mother the next morning, she told him that his father was very angry and would soon forbid those regular visits to the theater. "I, too, like to go to the theater sometimes," she continued, "but I am often annoyed at the way our domestic peace and quiet are disturbed by your wild addiction to this pleasure. Your father is always saying, 'What's the use of this? Why waste one's time in the theater?'"

"I've often heard him say that," said Wilhelm, "and I may have answered him too rudely; but for goodness' sake, Mother, why is everything useless that doesn't bring in money or enlarge our property? Didn't we have enough room in the old house? Was it necessary to build a new one? Doesn't my father spend a sizable amount of his profits every year in decorating these rooms? All these silk wallpapers and this English furniture, do we need all that? Couldn't we do with less? These striped walls, with their endless rows of flowers, their scrolls and baskets and figures, seem so unpleasant, like a stage curtain in our own house. It's different in a real theater where you know that the curtain will go up and reveal all sorts of things to entertain, enlighten and elevate us."

"Don't overdo it!" said his mother. "Your father likes to have his own fun of an evening. Moreover, he believes that it only distracts you, and in the end I'll be blamed when he gets cross. How often have I been reproached for giving you that wretched puppet theater for Christmas twelve years ago. It gave you that taste for the theater!"

"Don't blame the puppet theater, don't regret that token of your love and care for me. Those were my first happy moments in the new and empty house. I can still remember it, that moment of wonder: after we had received our usual presents, we were told to sit down in front of a door to an adjacent room, which then opened, not just to let us in or out, but for some unexpected festive event, with a great gate closed by a mystic curtain. We watched this from a distance and then, as we were dying to know what was twinkling and rattling behind the half-transparent curtain, we were told to draw up our chairs and to wait.

"So, we all sat quietly until a whistle blew, the curtain rolled up and revealed, in bright red, a view into a temple. Samuel, the High Priest, appeared with Jonathan, and their curious exchange of voices sounded very dignified. Then Saul came on the scene, annoyed by the pompous and heavily armored warrior who had challenged him and his followers to battle. I was glad when the dwarf-like son of Jesse leaped forward with his shepherd's crook, bag and slingshot and said, 'Almighty King and Master! Let no man's heart fail because of him. If Your Majesty will permit me, I will go and fight this mighty giant.' That was the end of the first act, and the audience was eager to see what would happen next. Everyone wished the music would stop. Then the curtain rose again. David was consecrating the giant's flesh to the birds of the air and the beasts of the field. The Philistine vented his scorn, stamped both feet, then fell down like a log and put the matter to a glorious end. And then the maidens sang: 'Saul hath slain his thousands, and David his ten thousands!' The head of the giant was carried in before the tiny victor and he won the hand of the king's daughter. But I, for all my delight, was annoyed by the fact that this lucky prince was fashioned like a dwarf, for 'little David' and 'big Goliath' had really been presented true to life. But Mother, where are those puppets now? I promised to show them to a friend who was amused by what I told him recently of these childhood games."

"I am not surprised that you remember these things so vividly, you were so interested in them from the beginning! I remember how you sneaked the text away from me and then learned the whole play by heart. I noticed that one evening, when you made a David and Goliath out of wax, let them talk to each other, gave the giant a whack, stuck his shapeless head onto a big pin and put it in little David's hand. Your mother was so delighted at your good memory and the fine speeches, that she decided to give you the whole company of wooden puppets on the spot. Little did I know what trouble that would give me."

"Don't grieve over that," Wilhelm replied. "Those playthings have given us both so many pleasant hours." He then asked for the keys for the room where the puppets were kept, rushed off, found the puppets and for a moment was transported back to the time when he thought they were real, live creatures, when he thought he could bring them alive by his own lively voice and the movements of his own hands. He took them up to his room and guarded them carefully.

Chapter Three

If, as is often said, first love is the best that any heart can experience early or late, our hero must be considered thrice blest for being able to enjoy these supreme moments in full measure. Few of us are so favored, for in our early years our feelings often take us through a hard school and, after a few paltry indulgences, we must forgo our highest wishes and learn forever to do without what we once dreamed of as utter bliss.

It was on the wings of imagination that Wilhelm's desire for this charming girl soared. He won her affection after a short acquaintance and soon found himself in possession of someone he both loved and worshipped. She had first appeared in the flattering light of a theatrical performance, and his own passion for the stage was closely connected with his first love for a woman. Being young, he could fully enjoy the offered pleasures which were sustained and intensified by the poetry of her world. And her own ambiguous situation, her fear that he might discover all too soon what her position was—this gave her a pleasing semblance of modesty and anxiety, which only enhanced his fondness for her. As she loved him so dearly, her uneasiness only increased her tenderness. In his arms she was the most adorable creature.

When he awoke from the first frenzy of joy, and thought about his life and his circumstances, everything seemed different—his duties more compelling, his pastimes more absorbing, his knowledge clearer, his talents much stronger, his purposes more definite. It was therefore easy for him to avoid his father's reproaches, to pacify his mother, and to enjoy Mariane's love undisturbed. He performed his daily tasks promptly, stopped going to the theater regularly and made sure to be pleasant at supper; but when everyone had gone to bed, he put on his cloak, crept quietly into the garden and hurried straight to his beloved, his heart beating fast like that of a young lover in a play.

"What did you bring?" asked Mariane one evening when he arrived with a parcel, which Barbara, hoping for a nice present, scrutinized closely. "You'll never guess," said Wilhelm.

Mariane was amazed (and Barbara dismayed) when what he unwrapped turned out to be a jumbled pile of miniature puppets. Mariane laughed as he untangled the wires and proudly displayed each figure. Barbara slunk off, displeased.

Not much is needed to amuse two lovers; they had a wonderful evening. The little band of puppets was paraded, every figure carefully examined and laughed over. Mariane did not like King Saul in his black velvet gown and gold crown: she thought him much too stiff and pedantic. She preferred Jonathan's smooth chin, his yellow and red costume and his turban; she moved him nicely by the wires and made him bow and declare his love. But she wouldn't pay any attention to the prophet Samuel, although Wilhelm proudly pointed to his breastplate and told her that the taffeta of his gown was from one of his grandmother's old dresses. David was too small for her, and Goliath too big. It was Jonathan she loved. Him she treated with particular delicacy, and in the end transferred her cherishing embraces from the puppet to Wilhelm. And so, once again, a little game became the preliminary for hours of bliss.

They were interrupted in their sweet dreams of love by a noise in the street. Mariane called to the old woman, who was busy as usual altering Mariane's costumes for the next play. Barbara reported that some merrymakers were just leaving the tavern nearby where they had been treating themselves to fresh oysters (which had just come in) and champagne.

"A pity we didn't think of that earlier," said Mariane. "We could have done ourselves a bit of good, too."

"It's not too late," Wilhelm replied, and gave Barbara a gold coin. "Go and get what we want; and you can have some with us."

The old woman hurried off, and in no time a well arranged collation was set out before the lovers. Barbara had to join them. They ate, drank—and were merry.

On such occasions there is never any lack of entertainment. Mariane took out her Jonathan, and the old woman steered the conversation to Wilhelm's favorite subject: "You once told us," she said, "about the first performance of your puppet theater one Christmas Eve. It was very amusing, and you were interrupted just when your ballet was about to begin. But now we have met with the distinguished cast that produced such splendid effects."

"Yes," said Mariane, "do tell us more, and what your feelings were at the time."

"It is always pleasant, my dear, to remember old times and our past, but harmless, mistakes. Especially when this occurs as we feel we have achieved a high point from which we can now look about and reflect on the path that brought us to this lofty view. It is pleasant and satisfying to remember the obstacles that we sadly thought were insurmountable, and then compare what we, as mature persons, have now developed into, with what we were then, in our immaturity. I cannot tell you how happy I am now that I can talk to you about the past—now that I gaze out towards the joyous landscape that we shall travel hand in hand."

"Well—how was that ballet?" interrupted the old woman. "I fear that it didn't turn out as well as it should have."

"Oh, yes, it did," said Wilhelm. "It was just fine! Those marvelous leaps of the Moors, the shepherds and the dwarves—little men and women—have remained something like a dim memory through all my later life. The curtain came down, the door closed and we all went off to bed, dizzy and drunk with delight—but I couldn't sleep. I wanted to know more, and was still so eager to ask questions that I didn't want the nursemaid who put us to bed to leave.

"Next morning that magic structure had vanished, the mystic curtain was gone and you could once again move without hindrance from one room to the next. All the enchantment had disappeared and left no trace. My sisters and brothers ran about with their toys, but I crept around silent and alone. It seemed impossible that there should be just two doorposts where the night before there had been such wonders. No one, not even if he were looking for a lost love, could have been more unhappy than I seemed to be."

His glance at Mariane, filled with joy, convinced her that he had no fear of ever being in such an unhappy state.

Chapter Four

"My only wish," Wilhelm continued, "was to see a second performance. I talked to my mother, and when the moment seemed right, she tried to persuade my father; but all her efforts were fruitless. He insisted that if a pleasure was to have any value, it must be infrequent, and that young and old don't appreciate the good things that come their way every day.

"We would have had to wait a long time, perhaps till the following Christmas, if the maker and secret director of the theater had not himself wanted to repeat the performance and in an epilogue introduced a clown he had just made.

"A young soldier from the artillery, who had all sorts of talents and especially great mechanical skill, had helped my father considerably in the building of our house and been handsomely rewarded for this; but he wanted to show his special gratitude to the family at Christmastime, and made us a present of this fully equipped theater which he had put together and painted in his free time. He was the one who, with the help of a servant, had animated the puppets and recited the various parts in different tones of voice. It was not hard for him to persuade my father, who gladly granted to a friend the favor he as a matter of principle had refused his own children. So, the theater was set up again, some children invited from the neighborhood, and the play was repeated.

"The first time I had the joy of surprise and astonishment; at the second performance I was intensely curious and observant. This time I wanted to find out exactly how everything was done. I had decided on that first evening that it couldn't be the puppets themselves that were speaking, I had even suspected that they could not move by themselves. But why it was all so agreeable, and why the puppets themselves seemed to speak and move, and where the lights were, and the people who operated all this — these mysteries disturbed me so much that I wanted to be both among the enchanted and the enchanters, somehow secretly to have a hand in it, and at the same time, as a spectator, be able to enjoy the pleasure of the illusion.

"The play came to an end, and preparations were being made for the epilogue. The audience stood up and chatted. I made my way to the door and from the clatter that was going on inside, realized that they were clearing up. I lifted the lower curtain, and looked through the framework. My mother noticed me and pulled me back; but I had already seen how my friends and foes, Saul and Goliath, and whoever all the others were, were being put away in a drawer. This was fresh nourishment for my half-satisfied curiosity. To my great astonishment I saw the lieutenant busy in this sanctuary. And as a result the clown in the epilogue, despite his heel-clattering, had no appeal for me. I was lost in thought, and after this discovery seemed both calmer and more restless than before. Having discovered something, I felt that I didn't really know anything, and I was right: for what I lacked was a sense of the enterprise as a whole, and that after all is the most important thing."

Chapter Five

"Children in well-established and well-organized homes feel rather like rats and mice: They seek out cracks and crannies to find their way to forbidden dainties. The furtive and intense fear with which they indulge in this search is one of the joys of childhood.

"I noticed more quickly than any of my sisters or brothers when a key was left in a lock. Much as I respected those closed doors, when I had to walk past them week after week or month after month, I would peek in unobserved when my mother opened that sanctuary to get something out, and I was quick to use the brief moments which the negligent housekeeper sometimes provided.

"As could be expected it was the pantry door that drew my sharpest attention. Few joys of anticipation matched those when my mother called me in to help her carry something and, whether by her kindness or my cunning, I managed to pick up some dried prunes. Those piles of wonderful things filled my imagination with a sense of abundance, and the marvelous smell of all the spices had such a mouth-watering effect on me that I never failed to breathe in deeply when I was nearby. One Sunday morning this special key was left in the keyhole as my mother was caught unawares by the bells ringing for the church service and the rest of the house was wrapped in sabbath stillness. As soon as I noticed it, I crept gingerly along the wall, moved quietly to the door, opened it, and with one stride was in the midst of so many long-desired delights. I rapidly scrutinized all the chests, sacks, boxes, cases and jars and, wondering what to take, I finally picked up some of my beloved prunes, some dried apples and some preserved pomegranate skin, and was about to slip out with my loot when I noticed some boxes with wires and hooks hanging out of the lids, which had not been properly closed. I had an idea what these might be, fell upon them and discovered to my delight that here packed away was the whole world of my joys and my heroes. I tried to pick up the ones on top to look at them, and then those underneath, but soon I had tangled up all the wires and got very upset and frightened, especially since I heard the cook moving in the adjoining kitchen. I stuffed everything back as quickly as I could and closed the drawer, taking with me only a handwritten little book, the play of David and Goliath, which had been lying on top, and with my booty escaped to the attic.

"From this time on I spent every hour that I could have by myself in reading over and over 'my' play, learning it by heart, and imagining how wonderful it would be if with my own fingers I could bring the figures to life. I felt myself becoming David and Goliath. I absorbed the play by studying it wherever I could find a corner—in the attic, the stable or the garden—I took each part and memorized it thoroughly, except that I caught myself taking the parts of the main characters and imagining the others trotting along like attendants. The grandiose speeches of David, in which he challenged the boastful Goliath, filled my mind day and night; I muttered them to myself, but no one paid attention except my father who sometimes noticed one of my exclamations and secretly praised the good memory of his son, who seemed to have retained so much after so little listening. As a result I became bolder and one evening recited almost the whole play to my mother, making actors out of lumps of wax. She seemed surprised and wanted an explanation— and I confessed.

"Fortunately all this occurred just when the lieutenant had proposed to initiate me into the secrets of the performance. My mother told him about my unexpected talent, and the lieutenant managed to get permission to use some rooms on the top floor of the house, which were usually empty: one for the spectators and one for the actors, with the doorway between as proscenium. My father allowed his friend to do all this, pretended not to be aware of it, as he was convinced that one ought not to let children see how much one loves them, or else they will ever ask for more. One should appear stern while they are enjoying themselves, and sometimes spoil their pleasures so that they do not become too easily satisfied—and impertinent."

Chapter Six

"The lieutenant set up the theater and looked after everything else. I had noticed him several times during the week coming into the house at an unusual hour, and suspected what was going on. My eagerness increased amazingly, as I knew I couldn't take part in what was being prepared until the following Saturday. But at last the longed-for day arrived, and at five o'clock the lieutenant took me upstairs. Trembling with joy I entered the room and saw the puppets hanging on both sides of the stage, in the order they were to appear. I studied them carefully, and then climbed on the step which set me above the stage, so that I seemed suspended above this miniature world. With a sense of awe, I looked down between the boards, because I remembered how splendid it had all seemed from the outside, and realized that I was now being initiated into the inner mysteries. We made a trial run and everything worked beautifully.

"The next day, in a performance before a group of children we had invited, we managed well, except that in the heat of the moment I dropped my Jonathan and had to reach down with my hand to pick him up — an accident which destroyed the illusion, provoked much laughter, and upset me greatly. My father seemed pleased by this slip-up, for very wisely he kept his pride in my skill to himself and, when the play was over, rather concentrated on the mistakes, and said that it would have been nice if only this or that hadn't gone wrong.

"I was deeply hurt and was miserable all evening, but by next morning had slept off my irritation and was now happy at the thought that, apart from one mishap, I had done very well. The applauding spectators had all agreed that though the lieutenant used coarse and refined tones of voice to good effect, his speech had on the whole been too artificial and stiff, whereas the new helper spoke his David and Jonathan to perfection. My mother praised especially the straightforward way in which I had summoned Goliath to battle and later presented the modest victor to the King.

"To my great joy, the theater remained set up and when spring arrived and we could do without a fire, I spent all my free time in my room playing with the puppets. Often enough I invited my brothers and sisters as well as friends; and if they didn't want to come, I played alone, my imagination brooding over that little world, which soon began to take on a different shape.

"After I had several times performed that first play for which theater and actors had been set up, I began to lose interest in it. But among my grandfather's books I found the collection of plays by Professor Gottsched called 'The German Stage,' and texts of several operas in German and Italian, in which I immersed myself, and, having counted up the characters at the beginning of the text, proceeded to perform the play. As a result King Saul in his black velvet robe now had to stand for some tyrant, or for Darius, or Cato. Usually it was not the whole play but only the fifth act, where the stabbing to death took place, that was performed.

"It was quite natural that the operas with their constant changes of scene and ever new adventures should appeal to me most. For they had everything—storms at sea, gods descending in clouds and, what I especially liked, thunder and lightning. Using cardboard, paper and paint, I provided an excellent night sky: The lightning was fearsome, though the thunder didn't always work. But that didn't matter much. There were also more opportunities to make use of my David and Goliath in the operas than in regular plays. I became more and more attached to that little room where so much pleasure had come my way; and I must admit that the smell of the larder, which still clung to the puppets, added considerably to my delight.

"The scenery for my theater was now pretty well complete, for I had always had a knack for using compasses, cutting up cardboard and making sketches. Now I was all the more disappointed that the limited number of available puppets should prevent me from performing more demanding plays.

"When I saw my sisters dressing and undressing their dolls, I had the idea of getting exchangeable clothes for my heroes. The costumes were taken off in small sections, and I recombined them as well as I could. I saved some money, bought ribbons and finery, begged bits of taffeta, and little by little assembled a whole collection of stage costumes, not forgetting hooped skirts for the ladies.

"I now had enough costumes for even the longest play and, one would have thought that other plays would surely follow. But what often happens with children happened to me. They think up grand schemes and make elaborate preparations, perhaps even a trial run, but ultimately nothing materializes. I made the same mistake. My greatest pleasure was in inventing and imagining. A play interested me only because of a particular scene, for which I immediately had new costumes made. As a result the original costumes got into a state of complete disorder, some had disappeared, so that we could not do even the first of our full-length plays again. I was living entirely in my imagination, trying out this or that, always planning, building a thousand castles in the air, but not realizing that I had destroyed the very foundations of this small world."

During this long recital, Mariane had been at pains to conceal her sleepiness by mustering all her affection toward Wilhelm. Amusing as the whole business might seem in one sense, she found it all too simple, and Wilhelm's commentary too ponderous. She would tenderly place her foot on his, and gave what appeared to be signs of attentiveness and approval. She drank from his glass, and Wilhelm was persuaded that not a word of his narration had been lost.

After a while he said: "Now it is your turn, Mariane, to tell me about the first joys of your childhood. We have been much too busy with the present to be concerned about the past. Tell me, how were you brought up and what early impressions do you remember?"

These questions might have been embarrassing for Mariane, if the old woman had not come to her aid. "Do you really believe," she said sensibly, "that we took so much notice of what happened to us earlier in life, that we have such pleasant things to tell as you have, and even if we did, that we could describe them so cleverly?"

"As if that were necessary!" Wilhelm exclaimed. "I love this tender, sweet, good, lovely girl so much that I would regret every moment of my life that I spent without her. Let me at least share, in my imagination, in your past life. Tell me all about it and I will tell you about mine. Let's use our imagination as much as possible, and try to recover those past times that were lost to our love."

"If you insist, we can certainly satisfy you on that score," said old Barbara. "But you tell us first how your love of the theater grew, how you rehearsed so that you are now quite a good performer. Surely there must have been some amusing incidents. It's not worth going to bed now; I have another bottle in reserve, and who knows when we shall be together again like this, so relaxed and content."

Mariane looked at her with a melancholy glance, but Wilhelm did not notice it and continued with his story.

Chapter Seven

"The distractions of youth began to take their toll of the solitary pleasures, especially when the circle of my friends grew larger. I was huntsman, foot-soldier, cavalryman, as our games demanded; but I always had a slight edge over the others, because I could provide the necessary properties for these occasions: The swords were mostly from my workshop, it was I who decorated and gilded the sleds, and some curious instinct made me transform our whole militia into Romans. We made helmets and topped them with paper plumes; we made shields, even suits of armor, and many a needle was broken by those of our servants who knew how to sew or make clothes. Some of my young comrades were now well armed, the rest were gradually, though not quite so elaborately, equipped, and soon we were a respectable army. We marched into courtyards and gardens, knocking against each other's shields and heads; there were occasional fights, but these were settled easily enough.

"These games, which much appealed to my friends, very soon ceased to please me. The sight of all those armed figures only intensified visions of knights and knighthood which, since I had taken to reading old romances, had recently been filling my mind.

"A translation of Tasso's *Jerusalem Delivered* that I happened to find gave my rambling thoughts a definite direction. I could, of course, not read the whole poem, but there were passages in it that I soon knew by heart and whose images haunted me. Especially Clorinda, in all that she did, fascinated me. Her almost masculine femininity, the serenefulness of her being had a stronger effect on my developing mind than the artificial charms of Armida, however much I was captivated by her 'Bower of Bliss.'

"Time and again in the evening I walked on the balcony between the gables, looking out over the landscape that was illuminated by the last quivering gleam of the setting sun on the horizon, the first stars coming out. As darkness descended from every depth and corner and crickets chirped through the solemn stillness, I recited to myself the sad story of that final combat between Tancred and Clorinda.

"Although I was quite properly on the side of the Christians, my whole heart stood by the heathen Clorinda as she was about to set fire to the tower of the besiegers. And when at night Tancred came upon the supposed warrior, the combat began under cover of darkness and they fought so fiercely, I could never, without tears coming to my eyes, utter the words:

> But now the measure of Clorinda's days is full
> The hour draws near, the hour when she must die.

My tears flowed freely as the unhappy lover plunged his sword into her breast, loosened her helmet, recognized who it was, and trembling, fetched water to baptize her. And how my heart overflowed when Tancred's sword struck the tree in the enchanted wood, blood spurted out and a voice resounded in his ears, telling him that he had wounded Clorinda again, that he was destined unwittingly to harm everything he ever loved!

"My imagination was so enthralled by this story, and everything that I had read in the poem began to form some kind of whole in my mind that I longed somehow to perform it on the stage. I wanted to play both Tancred and Rinaldo, and found two suits of armor that I had made which were quite suitable for these characters. One, made of dark-grey paper with scales, would do for the sober Tancred, the other, gold and silver, for the dazzling Rinaldo. Excited by the whole idea, I told my friends the entire story; they were thrilled, but wondered how all this could be performed, and by them.

"I easily dispelled their hesitation. I decided to take over a few rooms in the neighboring house of one of my friends, without considering that the old lady would on no account let us have them. And I had no clear notion of how to set up a stage, except that it must rest on beams, and we would use folding screens for scenery and a big sheet for the backdrop. But where the materials and tools to make all this were to come from, I had absolutely no idea.

"We found a good way to produce a forest by persuading a fellow who had been a servant in one of the households and was now a forester, to find us some young birches and spruces, which, as a matter of fact, arrived sooner than we had expected. Now the problem was how to put on the play before the trees withered. We sorely needed advice, for we had no room, no stage, no curtain—only the folding screens.

In this predicament we once again approached the lieutenant, giving him an elaborate account of all the splendor that was in the offing. Though he scarcely understood what we were really about, he did help us by pushing together in the little room all the tables we could find, setting up the side walls on these and making a backdrop of green curtains; the trees were placed in a row.

"Evening came, the candles were lit, children and maidservants settled in their places, the company of warriors were all decked out in their costumes and the play was about to begin. Suddenly it dawned on us for the first time that we didn't know what we were going to say. My imagination was so excited by the whole enterprise that I had completely forgotten that everyone should know what and when he had to speak. The others, so thrilled to be performing, hadn't thought about it either. They imagined that all they had to do was to present themselves as heroes and that it would be easy to act and speak like the characters in the world I had told them about. Now they all stood in astonishment, wondering what was to happen next, and having from the beginning thought of myself as Tancred, I came on alone and began to recite some of Tancred's words from the poem. But since the passage soon turned into a narration where I was referred to in the third person, and Godfrey was mentioned without actually appearing on the stage, I had to withdraw, much to the amusement of the spectators—a mishap which grieved me greatly. The whole show turned out to be a failure.

"The audience sat there waiting to see something; and as anyway we were all in our costumes, I pulled myself together and decided to play David and Goliath instead. My fellow actors had seen this at the puppet theater many times, some had even assisted me. We divided up the parts, everyone promised to do his best, and a funny little fellow painted a black beard on his chin so that he could come on as a clown if there was any unforeseen hitch in the performance. I did not like to do this, for I thought it would detract from the solemnity of the play. But I swore that once I was out of this fix, I would never again put on a play without a great deal more thought."

Chapter Eight

Mariane, overcome by sleep, had put her head on her lover's shoulder. He held her tight while he continued his narration; Barbara finished off in a leisurely fashion what remained of the wine.

"The embarrassment of having tried to perform a nonexistent play was soon forgotten. My passionate determination to turn any novel that I read, any story that I heard from my teachers, into a play was not to be diminished by even the most unsuitable subject matter. I was convinced that any story that appealed to me would be still more effective on the stage, where I could actually see it happening before my eyes. When we were taught world history at school, I reflected in great detail on the particular way in which a personage was stabbed or poisoned; my imagination leapt over exposition and development, and hurried to the much more interesting fifth act. And so I actually started to compose a few plays from the ending and working back to the beginning. At the same time, both on my own impulse and at the instigation of like-minded friends, I read my way through a whole stack of plays—whatever happened to come to hand. I was at that happy age when one delights in all sorts of things, when plenty and variety satisfy. My judgment was warped in still another way: My preference was for plays in which I thought I would myself have particular success, and I read few plays where I did not feel this would be the case. My lively imagination, by which I could put myself into any part, misled me into thinking that I could successfully act them all. As I distributed the parts, I gave myself roles for which I was not at all suited and, if possible, gave myself more than one.

"When children play, they can make something out of anything: A stick becomes a gun, a piece of wood a sword, any old bundle a doll, and any corner a hut. This is how our little theater came about. Totally unaware of our limited abilities, we embarked on anything and everything; we never realized that we sometimes confused one character with another, and assumed that everyone would take us for what we claimed to be. The results were so ordinary and uninteresting that I don't have even one amusing piece of silliness to report. First we performed the few plays that had only male characters. After that some of us dressed up as women, using what costumes we had. And finally we persuaded our sisters to join in. A few of our families thought that what we were doing was useful enough, and invited some friends. And our lieutenant did not leave us in the lurch. He showed us how to enter and exit, how to declaim, how to use gestures. But he got little thanks for his pains, for we were sure that we knew more about acting than he did.

"We started with tragedies, because we had heard—and believed it—that it is easier to write and perform a tragedy than to excel in comedy. We really felt in our element when we tried our hand at tragedy, representing high social station and nobility of character by a certain stiffness and affectation. We thought we really amounted to something. But we weren't completely happy until we could rant, stamp our feet, and in rage and desperation, throw ourselves on the ground.

"It was not long before natural instincts began to stir in boys and girls, and the company divided up into little love affairs—plays within plays. In the wings, the couples held hands tenderly, idealizing each other in their beribboned finery, while the disappointed rivals, eaten up with envy and spite, embarked on all sorts of mischief.

"Yet, all this playacting, though it lacked both understanding and direction, was not without its usefulness. We trained our memory, exercised our bodies, achieved greater ease in speaking and greater refinement in behavior than children at that age usually acquire. Certainly, now, for me that time was a turning point, because as a result my whole being was directed towards the theater and from then on I knew no greater pleasure than reading, writing and performing plays.

"At school, lessons with my teachers continued, and since it had been decided that I should go in for commerce, I was assigned to work in a neighbor's firm. But at the same time, my whole being rebelled violently against what I could only consider a base occupation. I wanted to devote myself entirely to the stage, there to find my happiness and satisfaction.

"I remember writing a poem, which must still be somewhere among my papers, in which the Muse of Tragedy and another female figure respresenting Commerce were struggling for possession of my worthy self. The whole idea is, of course, trivial and I don't remember whether the verse was any good, but you should have seen it, if only to get an idea of the fear and horror, the love and passion that I put into it. How timid was my portrayal of the old housewife with her keys and distaff, spectacles on her nose, always busy and bustling, quarrelsome and domestic, petty and pompous! How pitiful my account of those who had to submit to her and perform their menial duties in the sweat of their brow.

"And how different the other figure! What a vision for an oppressed spirit! Noble of stature, she was in every ounce of her being and behavior the true daughter of freedom. Her sense of herself gave her dignity and pride. Her garments suited her perfectly, the wide folds of her dress moved like echoes of the graceful movements of a divine creature. What a contrast between the two! You can well imagine which way my inclination turned. And my muse had all the accoutrements—crowns and daggers, chains and masks—that our literary predecessors had given their muses. The altercation between these two females was heated, their speeches, in the usual black-and-white of a fourteen-year-old, suitably contrasted. The old woman talked like one who had to pick up and save every pin, and the other as though she were distributing kingdoms. The warnings and threats of the old woman were treated with scorn; I turned my back on the riches she promised me, and, naked and disinherited, I gave myself to the muse who lent me her golden veil to cover my nakedness.

"If only I could have imagined," Wilhelm exclaimed as he pressed Mariane close to him, "that another and more lovely goddess would confirm me in my resolve and accompany me on my path—my poem would have turned out much better and achieved a far more interesting ending! But life in your arms is no poem—it is reality. Let us savor the sweet joy in full consciousness."

His voice was so loud and his grasp so tight that Mariane suddenly woke up. She tried to conceal her embarrassment by carressing him, for she had not heard one single word of the last part of his narration; it is to be hoped that in the future our hero will find more attentive listeners for his favorite stories.

Chapter Nine

And so Wilhelm spent his nights in the intimate pleasures of love and his days in anticipation of further hours of bliss. Earlier, when he had set his desire and hopes on winning Mariane, he had begun to feel a different person. Now that he was joined to her, the satisfaction of his desires became a pleasant habitual occupation. His heart strove to ennoble the object of his affections, and his mind to lift them both on to a higher plane. He was always thinking of her when for a short time she was not with him. She had been important to him before — now she was indispensable, because he was bound to her by every fiber of his being, and his mind felt, in all its unclouded innocence, that she was half — more than half — of himself. He was grateful, and absolutely devoted, to her.

Mariane, too, was able to deceive herself for a while, because she shared his feeling of intense joy, despite the cold reproaches that sometimes passed over her heart and from which she was never entirely free even in his embraces and the exhilaration of his love. When she was alone and had descended from the heights to which his passion had transported her back into a true sense of her position, she was indeed to be pitied. Her natural frivolity sustained her as long as she lived thoughtlessly, not realizing or even knowing the situation she was really in, she would take this or that incident as just part of a total picture, and cheerfully alternate between pleasure and displeasure, humiliation and pride, deprivation and momentary abundance, accepting necessity and habituation as a justifiable law of living, and shaking off any feeling of unpleasantness from one moment to the next. But now, when for moments this poor girl felt herself transported to a better world and looked down from all this sunshine and joy to the drab emptiness of her ordinary life, aware of the wretchedness of not being able to inspire love and respect as well as arousing desire, and therefore no better off than she was before, she found nothing in herself to help her rise above this state of mind, for her mind was empty and her heart had no resistance. The sadder she felt, the more she clung to her passion for her beloved, which grew stronger from day to day, as the danger of losing him loomed ever larger.

But Wilhelm soared happily in loftier regions. For him, too, a new world had opened up, a world with vistas of endless delight. The full measure of his initial joy was succeeded by a clear realization of what had obscurely moved him before: "She is yours! She has given herself to you who loved, sought and adored her — given herself in faith and trust to you, and not to someone who is ungrateful." He talked to himself, no matter where he was. His heart was full to the brim and he recited to himself the loftiest of sentiments in the most grandiloquent phrases. Fate, he decided, was extending its helping hand to him, through Mariane, to draw him out of that stifling, draggle-tailed middle-class existence he had so long desired to escape. It seemed to him the easiest thing in the world to leave his family and his father's house. He was young and inexperienced in the ways of the world, eager to seek happiness and contentment anywhere, and elated by love. That his future lay in the theater had now become quite clear to him, and the high goal that he envisioned for himself seemed nearer to realization as he aspired to the hand of Mariane. In self-satisfied modesty he saw in himself the great actor, the founder of a future

National Theater that he heard various people pining for. Everything that had been dormant in the recesses of his heart suddenly came alive. From all these thoughts and aspirations he painted, with colors from the palette of love, a picture against a misty background; the fact that the figures in the picture were not easily distinguishable made the general effect all the more pleasing.

Chapter Ten

He now sat at home, rummaging amongst his papers and preparing for his departure. What smacked of earlier intentions was put aside, for he did not want to take anything with him on his journey into the wide world that might arouse unpleasant memories. Only works embodying good taste, poets and critics, were admitted as trusty friends to the company of the Elect. Up to now he had not spent much time on critics, and so he looked through his books in search of enlightenment but found that the theoretical works were still mostly uncut. He had acquired many such works in the full conviction that they would be essential to him; yet, with the best will in the world, he had never succeeded in getting further than halfway into any of them. But he had zealously read model texts, and tried his hand at writing in those styles he had become familiar with.

Werner came in, and seeing his friend busied with his manuscripts, said: "Are you poring over those things again? I bet you don't intend to finish any of them. You'll just look through them again and again — and then start something new."

"It is not the business of a pupil to finish a thing. He should try his hand at everything."

"But surely he should finish them as best he can."

"But you can also consider it promising if a young man does not continue with something that he feels is clumsily done, and refuses to spend more time and effort on something that can never have any value."

"I know that you were never concerned with bringing something to completion; you were always tired of it before it was half done. When you were directing our puppet theater, new costumes always had to be made for our little company and new sets constructed. First one tragedy was to be performed, then another, and the most you ever put on was the fifth act where everything got confusing and people stabbed each other."

"Since you are talking about those days, tell me: Who was responsible for taking apart the costumes we had fitted to our puppets, and setting up a large and useless wardrobe? Wasn't it you who was always trying to sell us some new ribbon or other, and you who encouraged this hobby of mine to your own advantage?"

Werner laughed, and said: "I still remember with delight how I profited from your theatrical forays, like suppliers from the wars. While you were preparing to deliver Jerusalem, I made a handsome profit, much as the Venetians did on a similar occasion. I think there is nothing in life more sensible than making profit out of the follies of others."

"I would think it a nobler pleasure to cure people of their follies."

"That might be a fruitless undertaking, judging from the people I know. It takes some effort to be smart and become rich, and that usually happens at the cost of others."

"I have just found that poem I wrote called 'The Youth at the Crossroads,'" said Wilhelm, pulling out a copybook. "That *was* finished, such as it was."

"Throw it out! Burn it!" said Werner. "As a piece of artistic invention it was not remarkable. It irritated me at the time and displeased your father. The verses were pretty enough but the whole presentation was absolutely wrong. I well remember your personification of commerce as a miserable, shrivelled-up old witch. You must have filched that portrait from some old junk shop. At the time you had no idea what the world of business is really like. The mind of a true businessman is more wide-ranging than that of all other men—has to be so. What an overview we gain by the orderly fashion in which we conduct business. It permits us to survey the whole without being confused by the parts. What tremendous advantages accrue to the businessman by double bookkeeping. This is one of the finest inventions of the human mind, and every serious manager should introduce it into his business."

"Forgive me," said Wilhelm with a smile, "but you are treating form as though it were substance, and in all your adding up and balancing of accounts you usually ignore the true sum total of life."

"Unfortunately, my friend, you don't seem to understand that in this case form and substance are identical, in that the one cannot exist without the other. Order and clarity increase the desire to save and to acquire. A man who doesn't keep good accounts, who doesn't reckon up what he owes, easily finds himself in a foggy state, whereas a good manager knows no greater pleasure than watching his fortunes mounting daily. A setback may be an unpleasant surprise for him, but it does not scare him; he can balance this out with the gains he has made elsewhere. I am convinced, my friend, that if you could only acquire some lively interest in our affairs, you would convince yourself that many faculties of the mind are freely involved in such matters."

"Maybe the journey I am about to undertake will make me change my opinions!"

"Surely it will. Believe me, all you need is to see for yourself some big enterprise, and you will feel yourself one of us. And when you come back you will be glad to join those who know how, by speculating and the transmission of goods, to acquire part of the money and prosperity that must always circulate in the world. Just look at the natural and artificial products of every country and see how, now the one, now the other, have become necessities. What a pleasant exercise of careful ingenuity it is to find out what is most wanted at a given moment and is therefore bound to be in short supply and difficult to get. You can quickly and easily provide everyone with what is needed by building up stocks in advance, and reaping the advantages of wide circulation. That, it seems to me, should appeal greatly to anyone who has a head on his shoulders."

Wilhelm seemed not to disapprove, and so Werner went on: "First visit a few big trading centers, a few seaports, and you will certainly be fascinated. When you see how many people are occupied, and how many things come in and go out, you will surely enjoy seeing them pass through your own hands. You will see the smallest commodity in relation to trade in general, and as a result you will not consider anything insignificant because everything increases the circulation from which your life too receives its nourishment."

Werner, who had sharpened his own mind by his contact with Wilhelm, had come to think of his trade and business activities in terms of spiritual elevation, and always believed that he did so with greater justification than his otherwise sensible and respected friend who placed such high value, indeed the whole weight of his soul, on what seemed to Werner the most unreal thing in the world. He sometimes thought that such false enthusiasm could not fail to be overcome and this good fellow be brought back on to the right path. And so, with such hopes, he continued: "The mighty of this world have seized the earth and live in luxury and splendor. Every small corner of this earth is already taken possession of, every property firmly established. Official positions do not bring in much in remuneration. What other regular occupation, what more reasonable means of aggrandizement is there than trade? The princes of this world control the rivers, roads and harbors and make good profits from what goes through them or past them. Why shouldn't we also relish the opportunity of extracting by our labors custom duties on those articles made indispensable by the requirements and caprices of men and women? And I can assure you that if you would but engage your poetic imagination, you could establish *my* Goddess as the undoubted victor over yours. She bears the olive branch rather than the sword, has no daggers and chains, but she does distribute crowns to her favorites, which, it can be said without demeaning that other woman in your poem, are of pure gold from mountain streams and gleaming with pearls fetched from the depths of the ocean by her always industrious helpers."

Wilhelm was somewhat peeved by this outburst, but concealed his irritation, for he remembered that Werner used to listen to his speeches without losing his composure. He was also reasonable enough to be pleased when people spoke so warmly about their occupations—but they should not demean his own, which he had espoused with such fervor.

"And since you take such an interest in human affairs," Werner exclaimed, "what a spectacle it will be for you to see what joy accompanies bold enterprises for those who take part in them! What could be more pleasing than the sight of a ship returning from a successful journey, a trawler returning early with a good catch! Everyone is excited—relatives, friends, associates, even complete strangers—when the shipbound sailor leaps joyfully on land even before his boat touches it, feeling free once more and ready to entrust to solid land what he has extracted from the treacherous water. Profit is not just a matter of figures, my friend—Fortune is the sovereign goddess of all living things, and, to experience her favors fully, one must *live* and see people who exert their powers and enjoy their senses."

Chapter Eleven

It is high time that we become better acquainted with the fathers of these two friends. They were two very different temperaments but of one mind in that they regarded commerce as the noblest of all occupations and were attentive to every advantage to be gained by speculation. Wilhelm's father had, on the death of his own father, sold a valuable collection of paintings, drawings, etchings and antiques, had remodelled and refurnished his house from the ground up, all in the newest taste. He used what remained of his capital in various profitable ways, investing a considerable part of it in the business of Werner's father, who was respected for his initiative and for his speculative ventures, which usually turned out to his advantage. What he desired above all else was to impart to his son Wilhelm the qualities that he himself lacked, and to leave to his children those possessions which he particularly valued. He had indeed a certain penchant for sumptuousness, for what was impressive and yet had real lasting value. Everything had to be solid and massive in his house— plentiful provisions, heavy silver, costly china—but there were few guests, for every party turned into a celebration which, owing to cost and inconvenience, could not be repeated very often. His household was characterized by calm and monotony, and any change or innovation was always in those things which gave no one any pleasure.

Old Werner led a totally different life in his dark and gloomy house. Once he had finished his day's work at his decrepit old desk in his poky office, all he wanted to do was to eat well and, if possible, drink even better. He did not like to enjoy good things by himself, and so he wanted, beside his close family, to have all his friends, even strangers who had any sort of connection with his business, at his table. The chairs were very old but every day he invited someone to sit on them. The guests were so much attracted by the good quality of the food that they never noticed that it was served in very ordinary dishes. His cellar did not contain much wine, but when a bottle was finished it was usually replaced by a better one.

This is how they lived, these two fathers who often consulted each other on business matters, and this very day they had decided to send Wilhelm on a commercial journey.

"Let him see the world," said old Meister, "and at the same time do business for us in various places. There is nothing better one can do for a young man than introduce him early to his future career. Your son profited so much from his expedition and conducted his affairs so well, that I am curious to see how my son makes out, but I fear he will need more money than yours did." He had a high opinion of his son's ability, and so, in saying this, had hoped that the other would contradict him and emphasize Wilhelm's excellent qualities. But he was mistaken, for old Werner, who in practical matters trusted no one that he had not himself tested, calmly added: "One should try everything. We could send him on the same route and give him instructions to follow. There are debts to be collected, old acquaintanceships to be renewed and new ones to be made. He could also help to advance the venture I talked to you about recently, for we can do little unless we gather exact information on the spot."

"Let him get ready then, and leave as soon as possible," said Wilhelm's father. "But where shall we get a suitable horse for him?"

"We won't have to look far for that. There is a shopkeeper in H . . . who still owes us money, a good fellow who has offered me a horse in lieu of payment. My son has seen it; it seems to be perfectly acceptable."

"Well, let him go and get it. If he takes the postchaise he can be back in good time the day after tomorrow, and in the meantime we can get his bag ready and the letters he is to deliver, so that he could leave early next week."

They called Wilhelm and told him of their decision. He was absolutely delighted that the means to achieve his purpose were being provided for him without his having to find them for himself. He was so passionately convinced that he was doing the right thing in escaping from the burden of his present form of life by embarking on a new and nobler course that he did not have the least pangs of conscience or anxiety: Indeed, he felt that this deception was somehow sanctioned by Heaven. He was sure that his parents and relations would eventually approve the step he was about to take. He perceived in this concatenation of circumstances the guiding hand of Fate.

How time dragged till nightfall, when he would be able to see his beloved again! He sat in his room, thinking over his travel plans, like a crafty thief or magician in prison, easing his feet out of the shackles that bind him in order to persuade himself that liberation is not only possible, but nearer than his imperceptive goalers imagine. But at last the longed-for hour arrived, he left the house and, shaking off all sense of oppression, he walked through the quiet streets, raising his hands to Heaven on the open square, disembarrassed, discarding everything, imagining himself in Mariane's arms, then alongside her in the bright lights of the theater, transported in a welter of hopes and anticipations, until the voice of the night watchman sounding the hours reminded him that he was still on this earth.

She met him on the stairs, and how beautiful, how lovely, she was. She was wearing her new white negligé, and he thought she had never looked so charming. For the first time she wore the gift of her absent lover in the arms of her present one, showering him passionately with natural affection and studied caresses, and—need we ask whether he was blissfully happy? He told her what had happened, and gave her a general idea of his plans and desires. He would look for somewhere to live and then send for her; he hoped she would not refuse him her hand in marriage. The poor girl said nothing, suppressing her tears and clasping him to her breast. He interpreted her silence favorably, though he would have liked an answer, especially since he had recently asked her in all modesty, and in the gentlest terms, whether he was not about to become a father, to which she had only replied with a sigh, and a kiss.

Chapter Twelve

Next morning Mariane awoke once more in a sad state. She felt very much alone, did not want to begin the day, stayed in bed, and wept. The old woman sat by her and tried to talk to her and console her, but she did not succeed in healing this wounded heart so quickly. The moment was fast approaching which the poor girl had been dreading as if it were to be her last. Can one imagine a more anxious state than that she was in? The man she really loved was leaving, an unwelcome admirer was due to arrive any moment and it would be a real calamity if, which was perfectly possible, they were to encounter each other.

"Don't get upset, my dear, don't spoil your pretty eyes by weeping," said Barbara. "Is it such a misfortune to have two lovers? Even if you only love the one, you can always be grateful to the other who, by the way he looks after you, deserves to be called a friend."

But Mariane tearfully replied: "My dear Wilhelm sensed somehow that we would part; a dream told him what I had so carefully tried to conceal from him. He was sleeping so peacefully beside me, when suddenly I heard him murmuring barely audibly. I was frightened, and woke him up. How tenderly, how lovingly, how passionately he embraced me. 'Oh Mariane!' he said, 'What a frightful situation you rescued me from! How can I thank you for freeing me from such hell? I was dreaming that I was far away from you in some strange part of the country, but your image hovered before me and I saw you standing on a beautiful hilltop in the sunlight. How charming you looked! But it didn't last long: your image floated down from the hill, down and down, and I stretched out my arms to you, yet couldn't reach you. You were slipping towards a big lake at the foot of the hill, more of a swamp than a lake, when suddenly some man took your hand. He seemed to be wanting to lead you back up, but in fact led you off to the side, trying to drag you towards him. I called out, since I myself couldn't reach you, to warn you. When I tried to move, the ground held me fast, and when I could move, the water blocked me and even my cries were stifled in my anxious breast.' —That's what the poor fellow told me as he was recovering from his fright on my breast, happy at finding such a terrifying dream dispelled by blissful reality."

The old woman did her best in her own sober prose to bring Mariane from her flights of poetry down to everyday reality, using the tricks of birdcatchers, who imitate on a tin whistle the song of those they wish to catch in their nets. So she praised Wilhelm—his figure, his eyes, his affection—and the unfortunate Mariane listened with approval, then got up, dressed and seemed calmer. "I don't want to worry or offend you, or rob you of your happiness, my child," the old woman said, ingratiatingly. "Don't you understand what I have in mind? Don't you know that I have always been more concerned for you than for myself? Just tell me what you want to do, and we'll see how to bring it about."

"How can I do anything?" Mariane replied. "I am miserable, and shall be miserable for the rest of my life. I love him, he loves me, and yet I see that I must part from him and don't know how I can survive this. Norberg will come. We owe our whole existence to him. We cannot do without him. Wilhelm's means are very limited. He cannot do anything for me."

"Yes indeed, he is unfortunately one of those lovers who have nothing to give but their heart and are therefore the most demanding."

"Don't make fun of him! Unfortunately he intends to leave home, go on the stage, and offer me his hand."

"We already have four empty hands between us, you and me."

"I have no choice," Mariane went on. "So why don't *you* decide? Push me this way or that, but let me tell you one thing: I most likely carry a pledge within me that should bind us even closer together. Think of that, and decide: whom should I leave and whom should I follow?"

The old woman fell silent, then said: "Why do young people always think in terms of irreconcilable opposites? What could be more natural than to combine pleasure and profit? Why not love the one, and let the other pay? It's only a question of our being smart enough to keep them apart."

"Do as you like," said Mariane. "I can't think anymore. But I'll do what you want."

"The Director's stubborn insistence on maintaining the good morals of his actors can be used to our advantage. Both your lovers are accustomed to go to work secretly and cautiously. I'll arrange time and place, but you play the part I assign you. Who knows what circumstances might not assist us. If only Norberg would come now when Wilhelm is away! And who is to prevent you from thinking of the one when you are in the arms of the other? I hope you have a son. He shall have a rich father."

Such thoughts did not encourage Mariane for long, for she could not reconcile her feelings or her conviction with her present situation, the misery of which she longed to forget, but a thousand small matters reminded her of it at every turn.

Chapter Thirteen

In the meantime Wilhelm had completed his short journey and delivered his letter of recommendation to the wife of the business associate to whom he had been sent, for the husband was not at home. She was not able to give much of an answer to his questions, because she was much perturbed and the whole house was in a state of confusion.

However, she did not take long to inform him confidentially of something that could not be kept secret, namely that her stepdaughter had gone off with an actor, a creature who had recently left a small theatrical company, stayed for a while in this place, and given French lessons. The girl's father, beside himself with distress and irritation, had run to the authorities to have the fugitives pursued. The wife expressed her anger at the girl and her scorn of the lover with such vigor that nothing remained to be said in favor of either of them, and she vociferously bewailed the scandal that had befallen the family; she put Wilhelm in considerable embarrassment at finding his future, secret plans reviled and rejected by this sibyl, as if by some prophetic voice. But he was even more deeply affected by the deep sorrow and the half-uttered words of the father when he returned, and told his wife about his expedition to the authorities. He was unable to conceal his distraction and bewilderment; he read the letter and had the horse fetched for Wilhelm.

Wilhelm fully intended to mount his horse and leave this house where, under the circumstances, he could not possibly feel at ease, but the good man would not let the son of someone to whom he was so indebted leave without showing him due hospitality, and put him up for the night.

So our friend partook of a sad supper, spent a restless night, and left hurriedly next morning, to escape these people who by their tales and utterances had unwittingly so tormented him.

He was riding slowly and pensively down the street, when he saw a group of armed men crossing a field. From their long, baggy coats, wide lapels, shapeless hats and clumsy firearms, and their stolid gait and relaxed posture, he recognized them as a detachment of the local militia. They halted beneath an old oak tree, put down their flintlocks and settled comfortably on the grass to smoke a pipe. Wilhelm joined them and got into conversation with a young man who rode up on a horse. And so he had once again to hear the familiar story of the two fugitives, but this time laced with comments that were not especially favorable either to the young people or the parents. He also learned that the militiamen had come to take the young people, who had been stopped and apprehended in the neighboring town, into safe custody. Soon they saw a wagon drawing up, which was guarded in a fashion more ridiculous than terrifying. An unofficial looking town clerk rode ahead and exchanged compliments at the town limits with an actuary on the other side (the same young man that Wilhelm had been talking to), punctiliously and accompanied by fantastic gestures such as a magacian and a spirit, the one inside and the other outside the magic circle, might well use during some ominous nocturnal operations.

Meanwhile all eyes were fixed on the farm-wagon; and the poor fugitives, who were sitting together on bundles of straw and gazing at each other lovingly and almost unaware of the bystanders, were observed with sympathy. It

so happened that they had had to be transported in this unsuitable way from
the last village, because the old coach in which the girl had been placed had
broken down. As a result she asked to be with her friend, who, because they
believed him guilty of a capital crime, had been made to walk beside the
coach, in heavy chains. The sight of this loving pair was made even more
appealing by these chains, especially since the young man handled them
gracefully as he repeatedly kissed his beloved's hands.

"We are very unhappy," she cried out, "but not so guilty as we may seem.
This is how cruel people reward true love, and parents utterly neglectful of
their children's happiness tear them away from the joy that is theirs after so
much sadness."

The bystanders expressed their sympathy in various ways while the authorities went through their ceremonial actions. The wagon moved on, and
Wilhelm, very concerned about the fate of the lovers, hurried ahead on a foot-
path to make the acquaintance of the magistrate before the others arrived.
But just before he reached the courthouse where everyone was busily preparing for the arrival of the fugitives, the actuary caught up with him and gave
him a detailed account of all that had happened, and expansively praised his
horse which he had got from some Jew the day before—which prevented any
further conversation.

The unfortunate couple had been set down in the adjoining garden at the side
of the building, and then led quietly into the courthouse. Wilhelm expressed
to the actuary his appreciation of this consideration, though the actuary had
simply wanted to play a trick on the people assembled in front of the courthouse by depriving them of the pleasing spectacle of a humiliated towns-
woman.

The magistrate was not especially fond of such unusual cases as this,
because he usually made some mistake or other and, for all his good will,
earned a harsh reproof from the government. He walked stolidly toward the
courtroom where the actuary, Wilhelm and some of the respected citizens
joined him.

The girl was the first to be led into the room. She showed respect as she came
in, and a true sense of what she was. The way she was dressed and the nature
of her behavior showed that she was indeed a self-respecting girl, and she
began, without being asked, to talk about her situation in a seemly manner.

The actuary told her to be silent and held his pen over his opened sheaf of
paper. The magistrate settled himself, looked at the actuary, cleared his throat,
and then asked the girl what her name was, and how old she was.

"Well, sir," she replied, "it seems very odd that you ask for my name and my
age, since you know very well who I am and that I am of the same age as your
eldest son. I will gladly tell you without beating about the bush what you wish
to know from me, and what you are required to find out.

"Since my father's second marriage I have not been at all well treated at
home. I could have made several attractive matches if my stepmother had not

ruined everything by worrying about my dowry. And when I became acquainted with young Melina, I fell in love with him, and since we foresaw the obstacles that would be placed in our way, we decided to seek together the happiness in the world at large that seemed not likely to be granted to us at home. I have taken nothing with me that was not my own. We did not run off like thieves and robbers. And my friend has not deserved to be dragged around in chains and fetters. Our prince is just; he will not approve of such harshness. If we are guilty, we are not guilty in a way to justify such treatment."

The old magistrate became doubly—and trebly—embarrassed at this. The prince's reprimands were already buzzing in his head, and the girl's fluent speech had completely wrecked his ideas on how to write up the case. His distress grew even worse when she repeatedly refused to say anything more and steadfastly insisted on what she had already maintained.

"I am not a criminal," she said. "Yet, I was in shame brought here on bundles of straw. But there is a higher justice that will restore our honor."

The actuary had in the meantime been writing down what she said and whispered to the magistrate that he should just continue. A formal protocol could easily be drawn up later. The old man was encouraged by this and began to enquire in plain terms and conventional dry phrases about the sweet secrets of love.

Wilhelm turned red at this, and the charming criminal herself blushed with shame. She maintained silence until her embarrassment finally gave her courage to speak. "Be assured," she declared, "that I would not flinch at telling the truth, even if it meant discrediting myself, but in this case, when the truth does me honor, why should I hesitate and refuse to speak? Yes indeed, from the moment that I was convinced of his affection and loyalty, I thought of him as my husband. I gladly gave him everything that love demands and a heart that is sure of itself cannot deny. Do with me what you will. If I hesitated for a moment to confess all this, the reason was simply that I feared some evil consequences for my beloved."

Having heard her confession, Wilhelm formed a high opinion of the girl's character, whereas the officials treated her as a brazen hussy, and the good burghers in the courtroom were thankful that nothing like this had happened in their families—or at least was not public knowledge.

Wilhelm pictured his Mariane being thus brought to judgment, put even finer words in her mouth, and let her appear even more heartfelt in her sincerity and nobler in her confession. He was seized by the most passionate desire to help these two young lovers, and not concealing this, he quietly urged the magistrate to bring matters to a speedy conclusion, for everything was as clear as daylight and needed no further investigation. This helped, in the sense that the girl was told to step down; but the young man was ordered to come in, once they had removed his chains at the door. He seemed more concerned about his fate than she. His answers were more composed, and although in some ways he seemed less heroic than the girl, he made a good impression by the precision and orderliness of his statements. After his examination, which coincided in every point with hers except that, to spare the girl, he resolutely denied what she had already admitted, she was brought in again, and there followed a scene which entirely won them Wilhelm's affection. For what usually happens only in plays and novels, was now played out before his very eyes in this wretched courtroom—generosity of each toward the other, the strength of love in misfortune.

"Is it then true," he said to himself, "that bashful affection, which shuns the light of day and only displays itself in extreme seclusion and deep secrecy, when it is dragged out into the open by hostile circumstance, reveals itself to be stronger, bolder, more courageous than the most raging, grandiloquent of passions?"

Much to his relief the whole affair was settled very quickly. The young people were placed in minimum confinement, and if it had been possible he would have returned the girl to her parents that very evening. For he decided to act as a mediator and help to bring about a happy and respectable union of these two young people. So he asked permission of the magistrate to talk with Melina alone, which was granted him without further ado.

Chapter Fourteen

Their conversation soon became quite friendly and lively. For when Wilhelm told the downcast youth about his acquaintance with the girl's parents, when he had offered to act as intermediary and expressed the fondest hopes, the mournful and troubled spirit of the prisoner revived, he felt he was free again, reconciled with his parents-in-law—and the conversation moved on to considerations of what they should live on and where.

"But that should not be a problem for you," said Wilhelm, "for you both seem by nature well equipped to achieve success in the profession you have chosen. A good figure, a melodious voice, a heart full of feeling—what more do actors need? If I could help you with some introductions, I would be very happy to do so."

"I thank you from the bottom of my heart," said Melina, "but I could hardly make use of them, because I shall most likely not return to the theater."

"That would be a great mistake," said Wilhelm, after a pause to recover from his surprise, for he had assumed that, once freed with his young wife, the actor would resume his work in the theater. This seemed to him as natural and necessary as water to a frog. He had not doubted this for a moment, and so was astonished to find that he was mistaken.

"No, I do not intend to return to acting," said the young man. "I would rather find some occupation like other townsfolk have, whatever it may be—if only I can find it." "I cannot say I approve of such a strange decision," said Wilhelm. "For it is never a good idea to change the life one has chosen, except for a really good reason. Also I cannot think of any profession that is as attractive and offers such agreeable prospects as that of an actor." "That shows that you have never been one yourself," said Melina; to which Wilhelm replied: "But sir — rarely is a man satisfied with the conditions in which he finds himself! He is always wishing he had those of his neighbor, and the neighbor is equally eager to change his." "But there is a difference between bad and worse," said Melina. "It is experience, not impatience, that makes me decide as I have. Is there any livelihood in the whole world more meager, insecure and tedious? One might just as well be a beggar in the street. What one has to put up with from the jealousy of colleagues, the favoritism of managers, and the fickleness of the public! You have to be really thick-skinned, like a bear on a chain, beaten with a stick in the company of dogs and apes, to dance to the bagpipes before children and riff-raff."

Wilhelm was having all sorts of thoughts that he did not dare voice to this worthy fellow. What he did say had a certain detachment about it, whereas Melina talked more and more volubly and openly. "Shouldn't every theater manager beseech the town council to allow more money to circulate for four weeks during the annual trade fair? I have often felt sorry for our manager, for he is quite a good fellow, even though at times he has given me cause for dissatisfaction. A good actor profits him, but the bad ones he can't get rid of, and if he tries to make his takes more or less keep pace with his expenses, that's too much for the public, the theater is empty and, so as not to fold entirely, we have to play at a loss. No, sir, if, as you say, you want to take our part, then I beg you to talk seriously to her parents and get them to provide for us here and find me some small job as a copyist or tax collector. Then I shall feel happy."

After some further exchange between them Wilhelm went off, with the promise that he would go to her parents early next day and see what he could do. Once he was alone, he vented his feelings in a series of exclamatory outbursts: "O, unhappy Melina, the misery that oppresses you, lies not in your profession but in yourself! What man in the whole world would not find his situation intolerable if he chooses a craft, an art, indeed any form of life, without experiencing an inner calling? Whoever is born with a talent, or to a talent, must surely find in that the most pleasing of occupations! Everything on this earth has its difficult sides! Only some inner drive — pleasure — love — can help us overcome obstacles, prepare a path, and lift us out of the narrow circle in which others tread out their anguished, miserable existences! The stage is for you, Melina, just a set of boards, and your roles are nothing more than school assignments! You view the spectators as they see themselves — part of the daily grind! It would be just the same for you if you were sitting over ledgers at a desk, recording interest payments and worming our arrears from people. You never feel that sense of a conglomerate, inflammable whole that can only be created, comprehended and executed by the mind. You have never felt that there is a brighter spark in man which, if it receives no nourishment, if it is not allowed to ignite, becomes covered ever more deeply by the ashes of daily needs and indifference, and yet is never entirely extinguished—or only very late. You don't feel any strength within you to ignite it, no riches in your heart to give it sustenance. You are driven by hunger, inconveniences upset you, and you are quite unaware that such adversaries lurk in every human soul, no matter what it is engaged in, and that only by joyfulness of spirit and evenness of purpose can they be vanquished. You do well to long for the limitations of some vulgar occupation, for how could you fulfil the obligations of one that demands courage and spirit! Transfer your sentiments to any soldier, any statesman, any priest, and he too would complain with equal justification about the miseries of his station. Have there not been men, so deprived of any feeling for life, that they considered all human life worthless, a pitiable existence of dust? If the examples of active men were always present to your mind, if your bosom were inflamed by a desire to participate, if your whole being were enveloped in some feeling that came from your inmost self, if the sounds of your voice, the words of your mouth were pleasing to listen to, if you felt that strength of self, you would surely look for places and opportunities where you might feel your own strength in other people."

With such fine words and thoughts our hero undressed and went to bed with a feeling of inmost satisfaction. In his mind a whole romance began to develop around what he would do next day in the place of this unworthy fellow. Pleasant fantasies led him to sleep and delivered him up to dreams which received him with open arms and surrounded him with images of heaven.

Next morning he awoke and began thinking of the business at hand. He returned to the house of the girl's parents, who received him with some surprise. In a few simple words he told them what he had to propose, and encountered both more and less opposition than he had expected. For what had happened, had happened; and although people with firm and strict opinions usually tend to voice vigorous disapproval of what has already irrevocably taken place, and thereby increase their misfortune, the fact that it *has* already happened works on them irresistibly and what had seemed unthinkable has become part of their everyday experience. It was therefore soon settled that Melina should marry their daughter, but that, because of her behavior, she should receive no dowry, and leave the inheritance she had from an aunt in her father's hands for a few years, receiving only a modest interest from it. This second point—the matter of financial provision for her—encountered considerable difficulties. For they did not wish to set eyes on their errant child, nor materially advance this union of a vagrant with a member of a highly respectable family (which even counted a Superintendent among its members), and as for an official position for the husband—there was little prospect of that. Both parents were vigorously opposed to it, and though Wilhelm spoke strongly in favor of the idea (because he agreed that this man, of whom he had no high opinion, was not worthy to return to the delights of the stage), he could not, despite all his arguments, move them in his direction. If he had only known their true motives he would not even have tried to persuade them. The father wanted to keep his daughter at home, and hated the young man because his own wife had cast a favorable eye on him, and that meant that she would never have welcomed a rival in her stepdaughter. And so Melina was obliged to leave in a few days with his young bride (who wanted more than he to see the world and be seen by it) in order to find a position in some other theatrical company.

Chapter Fifteen

Happy youth, happy those first gropings for love, when we converse readily with ourselves, delighting in echoes of our own conversation and satisfied when our invisible partner merely repeats the last syllables of what we have just uttered!

Wilhelm was in this state during the first days of his love for Mariane—and even more so later, when he began to shower her with all the wealth of his feelings and to regard himself as a beggar living from what she gave him in return. And as a landscape is always, or indeed only, pleasing when the sun shines upon it, so everything that surrounded her, everything she touched, was beautified and glorified by her presence.

He would often stand in the wings, once he had been allowed this privilege by the manager, and although the illusion disappeared from this perspective, the far greater magic of love began to operate. He would stand for hours alongside the grubby cart on which the lights were fixed, breathing in the smell of tallow, and looking to see his beloved who, when she finally came on stage, would gaze at him lovingly and transport him into a realm of bliss amidst the skeletal framework of slats and crossbeams. The stuffed lambkins, glittering cloth waterfalls, cardboard rosebushes and thatched cottages with only one side to them aroused in him pleasing poetic images of a distant pastoral world. Even the dancers, so ugly at close quarters, did not displease him, for they were on one and the same stage with his dearly beloved. The love needed to bring life to rosebushes, myrtle groves and moonlight can certainly also endow woodchips and paper snippers with a degree of real live existence. Such seasoning is so potent that it can give flavor to the blandest or most distasteful concoction.

Some such seasoning was needed to make the usual state of Mariane's dressing room, and even sometimes her own appearance, palatable to him. For he had been brought up in a superior middle-class household, where cleanliness and order were the very air he breathed; and since he had inherited something of his father's love of finery, he had, even as a boy, arranged his room like a small kingdom. The curtains of his bed were gathered in folds and fastened with tassels, the way one imagines thrones to be. He had put a rug in the middle of the room, and a coverlet, of finer quality, on his table, with his books and other objects arranged on it, so meticulously that a Dutch painter could have made a still life from them. A white cap would be fastened on his head like a turban, and he turned up the sleeves of his dressing gown in oriental fashion, asserting that the long sleeves got in his way when he was writing. Of an evening, when he was alone and without fear of being disturbed, he would girdle himself with a silk sash, and sometimes stick a dagger in, which he had got from some old junk room, and, thus accoutred, rehearse the tragic roles that he had assigned to himself. He even knelt on the carpet to say his prayers.

How fortunate, he used to think, were actors in former days, when—so he imagined—they had magnificent costumes, suits of armor and weapons and always presented a model of noble behavior, their minds reflecting the noblest and best in attitudes, sentiments, and emotions. He pictured the domestic life of such an actor as a sequence of worthy actions and occupations of which his appearances in the theater were the climax—like silver, long treated in the refiner's fire and then finally emerging, free of all base elements, in all its resplendent brilliance.

How startled he was when, emerging from such a haze of beautiful fancies, he first looked at the chairs and tables in his beloved idol's dressing room! The remains of some momentary false adornment lay scattered around in complete disorder, like the glittering coat of a descaled fish. The instruments of human hygiene, such as combs, soap and washcloths, were there for anyone to see. Music, shoes, dirty laundry, artificial flowers, little boxes, hairpins, makeup jars, ribbons, books and straw hats lay in unabashed proximity to each other, covered with a uniform layer of powder and dust. But since Wilhelm, when he was in her presence, noticed little but her and even everything associated with her, everything she touched, was necessarily dear to him, he discovered a certain charm in this household of disorder such as he had never experienced in the splendor of his own room. When he removed her corset to get to the piano, or put her petticoats on the bed so that he could have a place to sit, or when she did not put away certain objects that she would normally have concealed from others out of a sense of decorum but had no scruples at leaving around when he was there, he felt that he was drawing closer to her all the time and invisible bonds were strengthening their union.

It was not so easy for him to relate to his idealized concept of their calling the behavior of the other actors that he sometimes met when he called on her the first few times. Busy at idling, they never seemed to be concerned about their profession and calling. He never heard them discussing the poetic merit of a play or criticizing it (rightly or wrongly). All they talked about was: "How much will it make? Will it be a hit? How long will it run? How many performances will we give? . . ." and such like. Then they usually went on to attack the manager: that he was too stingy with salaries, and unjust to one or the other of them; that the public seldom applauded the right man, that the German theater was getting better every day, that the actors were more and more appreciated for their merits and should be more respected. There was a lot of talk about coffeehouses and wine restaurants, and what had happened there, how much one of them was in debt, how much his salary had been docked, the inadequacy of their weekly wages, and the intrigues of one group against the other. Finally there was some consideration given to the importance of having an attentive audience; and the influence of the theater on the cultural level of the nation, indeed of the world, was not overlooked.

All these matters, which had caused Wilhelm much uneasiness, returned vividly to his mind as his horse carried him slowly toward home and he reflected on the various events he had witnessed. He had observed at first hand the disturbance that the flight of one girl had created in a good middle-class family and indeed a whole town. He recalled those scenes on the road and in the courthouse, the opinions expressed by Melina, and all that had resulted filled his mind, always eager to press on, with such uneasiness that he spurred on his horse and hurried toward the town.

But in so doing he ran into new unpleasantness. For Werner, his friend and presumptive brother-in-law, was waiting to have a serious and unexpected talk with him.

Werner was one of those who, having settled into a particular mode of existence, are usually taken to be cold, because they never flare up quickly or visibly. His relationship with Wilhelm was one of continual conflict, which, however, brought them ever closer together, for despite their different attitudes, each of them profited from the other. Werner gave himself credit for being able to restrain in some degree Wilhelm's lively, but occasionally overenthusiastic, spirit, and Wilhelm, for his part, had a sense of real triumph when in the heat of his emotion he was able to carry his sober-minded friend with him. The one tried himself out on the other, they saw each other almost every day, and one could have said that their desire to discover each other through their conversations was only increased by the impossibility of making themselves mutually understood. Basically, however, they were both good men, and both working towards one and the same goal, separately and together, and yet never able to understand why the one could not reduce the other to his way of thinking.

Werner had been aware for some time that Wilhelm's visits were becoming less frequent, that he was curt and inattentive when he got on to his favorite topics, and that he no longer plunged so intensely into the active elaboration of unusual ideas; it seemed to Werner that Wilhelm, in his own mind, was seeking peace and contentment in the presence of his friend. Werner, cautious and careful by disposition, assumed at first that the fault was his, until some town gossip gave him the clue, and certain indiscretions of Wilhelm's confirmed his suspicions. He started to investigate and soon found out that some time ago Wilhelm had been visiting an actress, had spoken with her at the theater and even taken her home. He would have been desolate if he had known about the nocturnal meetings, for he heard that Mariane was a seductive girl who was probably after his friend's money, and in addition to that, was kept by a worthless lover.

Having satisfied himself as far as possible of the truth of his suspicions, he decided to make an assault on Wilhelm, and was fully prepared for this, when Wilhelm returned in a bad humor from his journey.

On that very evening Werner told him all he knew, quite calmly at first but then with all the intense earnestness of a well-meaning friend, leaving nothing imprecise and making him taste to the full all the bitterness that calm people in their vindictive virtuousness lavish on passionate lovers. But as might be expected, he achieved little. Wilhelm responded with irritation but quite firmly: "You don't know the girl. Appearances may be against her, but I am as sure of her loyalty and virtue as I am of my own love."

Werner, however, persisted in his accusations and offered to provide evidence and witnesses. But Wilhelm rejected all this and left his friend in a disturbed and vexed frame of mind, like someone having a defective but firmly rooted tooth grasped by a clumsy dentist, who vainly tries to dislodge it.

Wilhelm was ill at ease to find his shining image of Mariane becoming tarnished and almost distorted by the vagaries of his journey and Werner's unkind words. So he decided on the best means of restoring it to its pristine clarity and beauty—and hastened that very night to go and see her by the usual route. She greeted him cheerfully and eagerly. She had earlier the day seen him ride by, and so was waiting for him at night. One can well imagine that all his doubts were soon dispelled, for her tenderness restored his confidence in her, and he told her how other people, including his friend Werner, had been maligning her.

Many a lively conversation led them back to the beginning of their relationship, the memory of which always remains a favorite subject for lovers. The first steps into the maze of love are always so delightful, our first prospects so bewitching that we always like to recall them. And each of the two claims precedence over the other, each claims to have been the first in his or her unselfish affection, and each would rather be proved wrong than the opposite.

Wilhelm told Mariane once again what she had heard so often, namely that she had soon distracted his attention from the play so that he was entirely taken up with her, and had been captivated by her figure, her acting, her voice, and finally only went to the plays that she was performing in, and even crept onto the stage and stood alongside her without her noticing. And he remembered that blissfully happy evening when he had the occasion to do her some small service and thereby start a conversation. Mariane for her part would not agree that it was so long before she noticed him. She had often seen him out walking, she said, and could describe the clothes he was wearing that day, for even at that time she had liked him better than all the rest, and she had wanted to make his acquaintance.

How pleased Wilhelm was to believe all this, pleased to be persuaded that she had come to him as he to her, both led by some irresistible force to each other—that she had purposely come up beside him in the wings, so that she might look at him from close by and get to know him, and that finally, since his shyness and reserve seemed impossible to overcome, she herself had given him the opening by almost forcing him to bring her a glass of lemonade.

Time passed quickly in this lovers' competition, for they followed through every moment in the course of their short romance, and Wilhelm left her with his mind completely at peace, and the firm determination to put his plan into action immediately.

Chapter Sixteen

Wilhelm's parents had got together everything that he would need for his journey, but there were still a few items lacking, and that delayed his departure for several days. He used the time to write a letter to Mariane in order to bring out into the open the matter that she had always avoided discussing. This is how the letter ran:

"Wrapped in the beloved cloak of night, which usually covers me in your arms, I sit and think and write to you. And what I think and what I do is all for you. O Mariane, I am the happiest of men, and feel like a bridegroom who senses a whole new world opening up for him and through him when he stands on the festive carpet and is transported during the sacred ceremony in lusting thoughts towards those dark curtains of mystery behind which the joys of love enticingly rustle. I have steeled myself to not seeing you for a few days. This was not so difficult because I am hoping to make up for this loss by being with you always, by being all yours. Must I tell you once more what I desire? I feel that I must; for it seems that so far you have not understood me.

"How often have I, with a few words of loving trust, fearing to lose what I have by saying more, ventured to question your feelings about a lasting union between us. You must have understood me, for in your heart the same wish must have grown, you heard me in every kiss, in the nestling peace of all our happy evenings together. I have got to know your modesty, and this has but increased my love for you. Whereas any other girl would have used every artifice and by spreading excessive sunshine to bring to fruition a decision in her lover's heart, elicited a declaration that would harden into a promise, you have always withdrawn, closed the half-bared breast of your beloved and tried by seeming indifference to conceal your approval. But I understand—and what a miserable creature I would be if I did not recognize in these signs the purity of your unselfish love, your concern for your dear friend! Trust me and do not be anxious! We belong together and neither of us will forgo anything when we live for each other.

"Take my hand, take it solemnly as a further sign of my love. We have tasted all the joys of love but new blessings are in store for us once we decide on a lasting relationship. Don't ask how, and don't worry. Fate takes care of love, and all the more so, since love is its own reward.

"In my mind I have long left my parents' home, in order to be in spirit with you on the stage. O, my beloved, was ever a man so fortunate in combining his desires as I? My eyes are closed in sleep, for your love and your happiness keep appearing before me, the dawn of a new life.

"I can hardly stop myself from rushing to you and wresting from you your approval, and then off next morning early into the wide world to work towards the goal I have in mind. But I must control myself, I should not rush fool-hardily and impatiently, for I have thought out a plan of action and must pursue it circumspectly.

"I am acquainted with a theater manager named Serlo, and will go straight to him. About a year ago he urged his people to develop my enthusiasm for the theater and wished they had something of the same. He will certainly be glad to see me. I would not like to join your company, for various reasons. And Serlo's company is playing at such a distance from here that I can initially conceal this step. I'll find somewhere decent to stay, look around at what the audiences are like, get to know the actors—and then send for you to join me there.

"You see, Mariane, how I can conquer my desire in order to get you for sure. For not to see you a long time, knowing you are somewhere or other out there in the world, that I do not dare to think about! But then when I think of your love—that will sustain me, if you meet my request and, before we part, give me your hand before the priest, I will go in peace. It will only be a formality for us, but a lovely one, to have the blessing of Heaven as well as that of the earth. It can be done quite quietly and secretly here in the neighborhood, I have enough money to start with. We can divide it up, there will be sufficient for us both. And when that is used up, Heaven will provide.

"You see, my dear, I am not at all worried. What started so joyfully, must end happily, I have never had any doubts that one can make one's way in the world, so long as one is serious. And I am determined enough to find ample support for two, even for more. 'The world is ungrateful,' people say, but I have never found it so, if one knows what to do for the world, and how my whole soul is aglow with the thought of at last being on the stage and telling men's hearts what they have long been yearning to hear. Convinced as I am of the glory of the stage, I have many times been distressed watching wretched actors imagining that they could speak noble words to our eager hearts, whereas what they produce is worse than a squeaky falsetto, and a coarse clumsiness that is beneath contempt.

"The theater has often found itself in conflict with the church, but this should not be so. How desirable it would be if both would glorify God and Nature through the mouths of noble human beings. These are not dreams, Mariane! I have felt your heart and know that you are in love. Likewise I believe in my brilliant idea, and say—better perhaps not say, but hope—that someday we will appear together, a pair of noble spirits, opening up the hearts of men, touching their souls, and offering them heavenly delights. I believe this because the joys of being with you were always heavenly delights, because we were lifted beyond ourselves, and felt above ourselves.

"I can't finish. I have already said too much, and yet do not know if I told you all that you should know. For no words are adequate to express the movement of the wheel that turns within my heart.

"Yet keep this letter, my dear. I have read it again and feel I should start once more at the beginning. But it does contain everything that you should know, to prepare you for my joyful return to your loving breast. I feel like a prisoner in his cell, listening as he files off his shackles. I bid my blissfully sleeping parents goodnight! — Farewell, my beloved, farewell. I will stop now. My eyes have already closed two or three times. For it is very late at night."

Chapter Seventeen

The day would not end when Wilhelm, his letter nicely folded in his pocket, longed to be with Mariane. Although it was hardly dark, he made his way to her lodging, with the idea of announcing his return at nightfall and leaving the letter in her hands before he absented himself for a while, intending to return at night to get her answer, receive her approval or, if need be, force it from her by the passion of his caresses. He flew into her arms and could hardly control himself as he clasped her to him. The intensity of his feelings was such that he did not at first notice that she failed to respond as warmly as usual. But she could not conceal her anxiety for long, claiming she was not feeling well, had a headache and did not welcome his coming back that night. He did not suspect anything, and did not press her, but felt this was not the right moment to give her the letter. So he kept it in his pocket, and since several words and gestures of hers politely indicated to him that she wished him to leave, he grabbed one of her scarves in the heat of his unsatisfied emotion, stuck it in his pocket, unwillingly tore himself away from her lips and left her. He walked slowly home, but could not stay there for more than a short while. He changed his clothes and went out again to get some fresh air.

He walked around the streets, and then a stranger approached him and asked him the way to a certain inn. Wilhelm offered to take him there. The stranger asked the name of the street, and those of the owners of several large houses that they passed, enquired after certain local police regulations, and by the time they reached the door of the inn the two men found themselves involved in a very interesting conversation. The stranger persuaded his guide to step inside and have a glass of punch with him. He told Wilhelm his name and place of birth, and the nature of the business that had brought him here, urging Wilhelm to be equally communicative. So Wilhelm began by telling him his name and where he lived.

"Aren't you a grandson of old Meister who had such a fine art collection?" the stranger asked. "Yes, I am," said Wilhelm. "But my grandfather died when

I was ten, and I was very grieved to see those lovely things sold." "But your father got a great sum of money for them." "How do you know that?" "Oh, I saw those treasures when they were still in your house. Your grandfather was not just a collector, he knew a great deal about art. He had been in Italy in earlier and happier times, and brought back with him treasures such as could now not be bought at any price. He possessed marvelous paintings by the best artists, and you could hardly believe your eyes when you looked through his collection of drawings. He had various priceless fragments of sculpture and an instructive array of bronzes. His coins were collected with regard to art as well as history, his precious stones, few though they were, were of the highest quality. And everything was well arranged, even though the rooms in the old house were not designed symmetrically."

"Then you can imagine what a loss we children felt when all these things were taken down and packed," said Wilhelm. "Those were the first sad days of my life. I remember how empty the rooms seemed, as we watched one thing after the other disappear, things that we had enjoyed since childhood, things which had seemed to us as permanent as the house itself or the town we lived in."

"If I am not mistaken," said the stranger, "your father invested the proceeds in a neighbor's business and formed a sort of company with him?"

"Right! And their business has worked out very well. In those twelve years they have substantially increased their capital and both are all the more concerned now with increasing it even further. And old Werner has a son who is much better suited to this sort of thing than I am."

"I am sorry that this town should have lost such a treasure as your grandfather's collection. I saw it shortly before it was sold, and I can honestly say that I was the instigator of the sale. A rich nobleman and great connoisseur, who, however, did not trust his own judgment in so large a deal, sent me here so that I might give him my advice. I examined the collection for six whole days, and on the seventh I advised my friend to pay the asking price without questioning it. I remember you then as a bright boy, always at my side, telling me what the paintings were about and making quite good comments on the collection."

"I remember such a person being there, but I wouldn't have recognized you."

"Well, it was quite a while ago and we all change to some degree. I seem to remember that you had a favorite picture from which you were unwilling to let me move on."

"Yes, indeed. It was the picture of a sick prince consumed by passion for his father's bride."

"It wasn't exactly the best painting in the collection: the composition was not good, the colors were nothing special, and the execution was mannered."

"I didn't understand that, and still don't understand it: The subject is what appeals to me in a painting, not the artistry."

"Your grandfather seemed to think otherwise, for the major part of his collection consisted of excellent things in which one always admired the merits of the painter without reference to the subject. And that particular picture was hanging in an anteroom to show that he did not value it highly."

"That was where we children were allowed to play," said Wilhelm, "and where that particular picture made such an indelible impression on me which not even your criticism (which, on the whole, I have great respect for) could obliterate if we were standing before it now. How distressed I was—and still am—that a young man should have to keep bottled up in himself those sweet feelings, the best that Nature gives him, and must hide those fires which should warm him and others, so that his soul is consumed with pain and suffering! And how I pity an unhappy woman being joined to someone other than the one her heart felt worthy of her true, pure love!"

"Such emotion is certainly far removed from the way an art lover looks at the work of great artists. But if the paintings had remained in your home, you would probably have developed more understanding for the works themselves, instead of always putting yourself and your feelings into them."

"I always regretted the sale of the pictures and missed them often even when I was older. But when I consider that it was necessary, so to speak, in order that I myself could develop a passion, and talent, of my own which will affect my life more than all those dead pictures ever did, then I accept the fact and respect it as a stroke of fate which opened up the best in me, as it does in others."

"I am sorry to hear the word 'fate' used once again by a young man at a time in his life when passionate inclinations are all too often interpreted as the workings of higher forces," said the stranger.

"But don't you believe in fate, some power which rules over us and guides everything to our advantage?" Wilhelm asked.

"It is not a matter of believing, or trying to make sense out of what is otherwise incomprehensible, but simply of deciding which way of looking at things suits us best. The texture of this world is made up of necessity and chance. Human reason holds the balance between them, treating necessity as the basis of existence, but manipulating and directing chance, and using it. Only if our reason is unshakeable, does man deserve to be called a god of the earth. Woe to him who, from youth on, is prone to find arbitrariness in necessity and ascribes a certain reasonableness to chance and accepts this religiously. For that amounts to denying one's rational self and giving free play to one's feelings. We think we are god-fearing people if we saunter through life without much thought, we let ourselves be carried along by happy chance, and then finally declare that our wavering existence was a life governed by divine guidance."

"But have you never experienced a situation where some small circumstance made you take a certain path on which a favorable opportunity soon presented itself to you, and a whole series of unexpected occurrences brought you to a goal you had yourself hardly envisioned? Shouldn't that encourage you to trust in fate and its guidance?"

"With such opinions no girl would keep her virtue and no man his money, for there are enough opportunities to lose them both. But I can be really happy only with a person who knows what is useful to him and others, and works at controlling his own arbitrariness. Everyone holds his fortune in his own hands, like a sculptor the raw material he will fashion into a figure. But it's the same with that type of artistic activity as with all others. Only the ability to do it, only the capability, is inborn in us, it must be learned and attentively cultivated."

They went on discussing this and many other things, and finally parted, without seeming to have convinced each other, but they agreed on a place to meet again next day.

Wilhelm walked up and down the streets. He heard clarinets, horns and bassoons and was delighted at their sound. Some travelling musicians were giving a pleasant serenade. He spoke with them and paid them to follow him to where Mariane lived. He positioned the singers under the tall trees before the house, lay down on a bench some distance away and abandoned himself entirely to the soaring sounds that floated around him in the soothing night. Stretched out beneath the beauty of the stars he felt that his whole existence was one golden dream. "She can hear these melodies," he said to himself. "She will know in her heart whose thoughts and sounds of love are resounding through the night. Even at a distance we are bound together by such music with all its delicate sounds. For two loving hearts are like a pair of magnetic compasses: when the one moves, the other moves with it, for only one thing is at work, one force permeates them both. When I am in her arms, how can I possibly imagine being separated from her? And yet I will be far from her, seeking a sanctuary for our love, and she will therefore always be with me.

"How often has it happened that, being away from her, or lost in thoughts of her, I touched a book or some garment, and thought it was her hand I felt, so absorbed was I in her presence, and remembered those precious moments which shunned the light of day as if it were some icy interloper, those moments to enjoy which gods would gladly abandon their state of bliss. But how can one talk of remembering—as if one could ever relive that frenzied intoxication which enslaves with heavenly bonds all our senses—and her figure. . . ." He lost himself in thoughts of her, thoughts that soon changed to desire, embraced a tree, cooled his cheek on the bark, and breathed out his excitement into the night air that was all too ready to receive it. He tried to find the scarf that he had taken from her room, but he had left it in his other suit. His lips were burning and his limbs quivering with desire.

The music stopped, and he felt as if he had fallen down from the heights scaled by his soaring emotions. His restlessness increased, now that his feelings were no longer being nourished and tempered by the sweetness of the music. He sat down on the steps of her house and became somewhat calmer. He kissed the ring on the brass knocker, kissed the theshold of the door she went in and out of, warming it at the fire in his heart. Then he sat still for a a while, thinking of her up there behind the curtains, sleeping in her white nightgown with the red ribbon round her head, and imagined himself so close to her as to make her dream of him. His thoughts were as lovely as twilight spirits, sometimes peaceful and sometimes eager. Love's quivering hand passed over every string in his soul. He felt as if the music of the spheres had halted to listen to the melodies of his heart.

If he had had the key on him which usually let him into her house, he would not have hesitated to enter the temple of love. But since he had not, he slowly and dreamily sauntered along beneath the trees, in the direction of his own home but always turning back, until finally he reached the corner and, looking once more, thought he saw Mariane's door open and a dark figure emerge. He was too far away to see clearly, but by the time he collected himself and looked, the shadow was lost in the night, though he thought he could perceive it far off against a white wall. He stood and blinked, and before he could pull himself together and hurry after it, the figure had disappeared. Where should he look? What street had swallowed up that person, if it was a person?

His eyes and his emotions were confused like those of a man unable to find his way again when he has just been blinded by the sudden illumination of an area nearby. And like a ghost at midnight that scares the wits out of us, and when we regain our composure seems the product of our own anxiety and leaves us with doubts whether in fact we ever saw it, a great uneasiness came over Wilhelm as he stood leaning against the corner of a wall, unaware that day was breaking and the cocks were crowing. Tradesmen began to go about their morning rounds, and that drove him home.

By the time he got back he had more or less found reasons to dismiss the surprising phantom from his mind; but all the beauty of the night, which now seemed equally unreal, was gone as well. And so to assuage his heart and put a seal on his returning faith in his beloved, he took out her scarf from the pocket of the suit he had been wearing earlier. As he raised it to his lips a piece of paper fell out. He picked it up, and read: "Well, my little rogue and loved one, what was the matter with you yesterday? I'll come tonight. I can well understand that you will be sorry to leave here. But be patient, I'll follow you to the fair. And listen, don't wear that black, green and brown jacket. It makes you look like the Witch of Endor. Didn't I send you that white negligé, so that I could hold a white lamb in my arms? Always send me your messages by the old harridan, for she's the devil's own messenger."

Book Two

Chapter One

Anyone whom we observe striving with all his powers to attain some goal, can be assured of our sympathy, whether we approve of the goal or not. But once the matter is decided, we turn our attention elsewhere, for when something is completed or resolved our concern with it diminishes, especially if we have, from the start, foreseen an unsatisfactory outcome. So we will not treat our readers to a detailed account of the woes and sorrows of our unfortunate friend when he saw his hopes and desires so unexpectedly shattered, but rather jump over a few years and join him again where we shall hope to find him more pleasurably occupied. But before that we must fill in with what is necessary for our story to make sense.

Plague and high fever take a firmer and quicker hold on healthy and vigorous persons than on others, and Wilhelm had been so unexpectedly struck down by misfortune that his whole being was instantaneously disorganized. When a firework catches light unexpectedly and all those carefully shaped and filled rockets, which were intended to eject balls of colored fire in predetermined succession, suddenly start hissing and crackling, ominously and without any pretense of order, this was not unlike the tumult of disorder into which all his hopes and joys, all his dreams and realities collapsed. In such moments of utter desolation the friend who hastens to help, stands petrified, and the person affected is fortunate if his sensitivities are numbed.

Days of repeated, and constantly revived, pain followed, days when nature was working beneficially in Wilhelm. For during this time he had not yet lost his beloved entirely, and his sorrow was a series of insistently renewed attempts to hold on to the happiness that had left him, recapture it in his imagination and prolong for a little while those joys that had gone forever. A body is not entirely dead while the process of decay is still underway and its various powers are working themselves off by systematically destroying those members that they normally activate. Only when everything has worn away everything else and reduced the whole to indifferent dust, only then are we invaded by that wretched sense of emptiness that we call death, a state that can only be quickened by the breath of eternal life.

There was so much to disrupt, to destroy, to kill off in this young, loving spirit, that the healing powers of youth merely stoked the fires of sorrow. What had happened, had struck at the roots of his whole existence. Werner, of necessity the only person that Wilhelm could confide in, did all he could to pour fire and flame onto this hateful passion, the dragon in his entrails. The occasion was so apposite, the evidence was so everpresent, that he made use of everything he had heard in the way of rumors and stories. He did this so systematically and with such vehemence and savagery that he did not leave his friend one consoling moment of illusion, one escape hatch from his despair. And so nature, determined not to lose a favorite son, afflicted him with sickness, so that he had, in his own way, time to breathe.

A raging fever, and what followed—medication, overexcitement and lassitude, ministrations from the family, affection from his acquaintances that showed itself only now that he really needed it—these were distractions in changed circumstances and meager occupations for his mind. When he felt better—that is to say when all his energies were exhausted—he gazed in horror down into the empty abyss of torment and misery that opened up before him, barren like the burnt-out hollow crater of a volcano.

He now began to reproach himself bitterly when, having lost so much, he could enjoy a moment of calm, painless reflection. He despised his very heart, and longed again for the refreshment of tears and misery. To restore this he would persistently recall every moment, every scene of his past happiness. He recreated them in the brightest colors, thought himself back into them, and when he had worked himself up to the point where the sunshine of past days was beginning to warm his body and spirit, he would look back at the ghastly abyss, feast his eyes on the dizzying depths, and then hurl himself into them and exact from nature all the torments of bitter pain. And so he tore himself to pieces in repeated accesses of savagery, for youth, so rich in hidden powers, never knows what it is robbing itself of when it joins trumped-up sorrows to the pain of a real loss, as if this were necessary to impart real significance to the pain of what has been foregone. Also, he was so convinced that this would be the only loss, the first and the last, that he would ever experience, that he despised any consolation that might suggest such sorrow as his could not last forever.

Chapter Two

Accustomed as he was to torment himself in this way, he began also to pour savage criticism onto what, apart from his love, had been his greatest hope and joy—his abilities as a poet and an actor. His own compositions now seemed to him mere sterile imitations of conventional models, with no life of their own—school exercises, totally devoid of any trace of reality, truth or inspiration. His poems were rhythmically monotonous, held together by wretched rhymes, with commonplace thoughts and feelings ponderously expressed. There was no longer any pleasure or expectation of recovery for him from this quarter. Nor was there from his acting talent. He reproached himself for not having understood earlier that vanity was at the bottom of that, and nothing more. He reconsidered his figure, his movements, his gestures and declamation, and decided that they had no particular merit or distinction, were nothing above the ordinary. This merely increased his silent desperation. Hard as it is to abandon one's love of a woman, it is equally painful to desert the company of the muses because one feels unworthy of their company, and to forego those delightful rounds of applause at one's person, one's demeanor and one's voice.

And so our friend resigned himself fully to active participation in the world of business. To the astonishment of Werner and to the great delight of his father, no one was more industrious than Wilhelm in the countinghouse, on the exchange, in the office or the warehouse. He dealt with correspondence and bills and everything else assigned to him with the greatest efficiency. Not indeed with that joyful eagerness which is its own reward when one executes in an orderly fashion what one is born to do, but with a certain quiet sense of duty, based on solid foundations and sustained by conviction, self-rewarding on the whole. But sometimes he was unable to suppress a sigh even when his best qualities were being engaged.

Wilhelm went on living in this way for quite a time, industrious and convinced that the hard school of fate was working to his advantage. He was glad to see that he had been warned in time, though rather unpleasantly, and that others would not later have to pay heavily for the errors of his youthful self-satisfaction. For usually a man resists, as long as he can, having to admit that he is a fool at heart, that he has made a big mistake. Men are unwilling to admit a truth that may drive them to despair.

Determined as he was to give up his dearest aspirations, it took some time for him to be convinced of his misfortune. But finally he had so completely eradicated, and with convincing arguments, every hope of love, of poetic creativity and acting in himself, that he found the necessary courage to wipe out every trace of his former folly, everything that might possibly remind him of it. One chilly evening he lit a fire and got out a box of keepsakes, in which there were all sorts of things he had received or snatched from Mariane in certain memorable moments. There were dried flowers to remind him of the time when they were fresh in her hair, little notes inviting him to hours of bliss, ribbons from her lovely bosom where he had rested his heart. Did not these souvenirs serve to renew every feeling he had thought dead, revive every passion that he thought he had mastered, now that he was separated from her? For we never notice how sad and unpleasant a gloomy day is, until a ray of sunshine suddenly breaks through and presents the brightening gleam of a joyful hour.

He was not unmoved as he watched these treasures go up in smoke that he had preserved for so long. Once or twice he hesitated, and he still had a string of beads and a flowered scarf left when he decided to stoke the fire with the poetic efforts of his youth. Up to now he had carefully preserved everything that had flowed from his pen since his mind began to develop. His writings were tied up in bundles which he had packed in the trunk he had hoped to take with him on his journey. How different was his frame of mind now as he opened them from when he had bundled them together.

When we open a letter that we once wrote and sealed on a particular occasion but which never reached the friend it was sent to, and was returned to us, we have a strange feeling as we break the seal, our own seal, and converse with our different self as with a third person. Just such a feeling it was that gripped our hero as he opened the first packet and threw the various sheets into the fire, which burned up brightly. At this moment Werner came into the room, was surprised at the blazing fire and asked Wilhelm what he was up to.

"I'm giving you a proof," said Wilhelm, "that I'm serious about abandoning an occupation I wasn't born to," and with these words he threw the second package into the flames. Werner tried to prevent him, but he was too late.

"I don't see why you should go to such extremes," he said. "Why should these pieces of work, imperfect though they may be, be completely destroyed?"

"Because a poem should either be perfect or not exist at all. Anyone without the ability to produce the very best, should not engage in artistic activity and should resist any temptation to do so. Of course there is a vague longing in all of us to imitate what we see, but that does not prove that one has the power to achieve what one aims at. Look how boys who have seen acrobats performing, walk up and down trying to balance on planks and beams till some other pastime attracts them. Haven't you seen that amongst our own friends? When we hear a virtuoso performer, there are always some of us who start learning the instrument. And how many falter on the way! Happy he who realizes early enough that desire is no indication of ability!"

Werner didn't agree. The conversation became heated, and Wilhelm found himself using against his friend the same passionate arguments that he had been tormenting himself with. Werner insisted that it was ridiculous to abandon a talent he had exercised with pleasure and some skill, simply because he would never achieve perfection through it. There were always those dull hours that could be filled up in this way, and something would gradually emerge that would give pleasure to us and to others.

Our hero, whose opinion was quite different, cut in and exclaimed vehemently: "How wrong you are, my friend, in thinking that a work, the first concept of which must fill one's whole soul, can possibly be produced in odd spots of snatched time. Oh no, a poet must live *entirely* for himself and in his beloved subjects! Endowed by heaven with a fund of inner riches, he must labor to increase this by living, happy and undisturbed, with his own treasure. No man can acquire such happiness by the mere amassing of riches. Just look at how men rush after fortune and pleasure, driven on restlessly by money, effort and desire, but to what end? To the same state that the poet has received by nature:

to enjoyment of the world, the sense of being a part of a community, harmonious coexistence with many different things that often seem irreconcilable with each other.

"What troubles most people is that they are unable to reconcile their ideas with reality, pleasure evades them, wishes are fulfilled too late, and what they do achieve does not give them the pleasure they had expected in anticipation. Fate has placed the poet above all this—like a god. He sees the whirlpool of passions, the fruitless activity of families and nations, the serious problems born of misunderstandings, fraught with dangerous consequences, that a single word could often dispel. He experiences in himself all the joys and sorrows of human existence. And whereas men of the world either consume their time in melancholy brooding over losses, or embrace their fate with unbridled joy, the poet with his receptive and fluid mind moves like the sun from night to day, tuning his harp with gentle transitions from joy to pain. The flower of wisdom grows naturally out of the soil of his heart, and whereas others, when they dream in waking life, are frightened by the images that arise from their senses, the poet lives out the dream of life in constant wakefulness, and integrates even the most extraordinary occurrence into both past and future. The poet is teacher, prophet, friend of gods and men. How can you expect him to lower himself to some miserable trade or occupation? Built like a bird to soar above the earth, nest in high trees, nourish himself from buds and fruits, moving easily from branch to branch—how can he at the same time be an ox pulling a plough, a hound trained to follow a scent, or a watchdog on a chain in a farmyard, barking to ward off intruders?"

Werner listened to all this, as one can well imagine, with some astonishment, and then said: "If only men were made like birds and, instead of laboring away, could spend their days in a state of blissful pleasure! If only, when winter comes, they could escape to faraway climes, and avoid all dearth and cold!"

"That is indeed how poets lived when true value was better recognized, and so they should always live," Wilhelm declared. "Inwardly they are so well provided for, that they need little sustenance from outside. The gift that they have of presenting to men glorious feelings and wondrous images in sweet words and melodies that clothe every object, has always captivated the world and secured them a rich inheritance. They were listened to at the courts of kings, the tables of the rich, and the doors of lovers, while eyes and minds were closed to all else, just as the song of the nightingale strongly affects us from out of the dark thickets through which we wander, and we stand still and listen, enraptured and grateful. They found a world that was always open to them, and their seemingly humble station increased the respect that was paid to them. Heroes listened to their songs and conquerors revered them, because, without the poet's songs, their mighty presence would vanish like the wind. Lovers wished to experience their desires and joys as strongly and harmoniously as the poet described them. Even rich men could not see the value of their treasured possessions as clearly as when these were transfigured and enriched by the poet's sense of values. Who but the poet, one might say, fashioned gods, lifted us up to them, and brought them down to us?"

"My dear Wilhelm, I have often regretted your strenuous attempts to banish from your mind what you feel so strongly," said Werner after some thought. "If I am not mistaken, you might better try to achieve some reconciliation with yourself, instead of working yourself up into a state of irritation at the magnitude of your loss. Why deprive yourself of all other pleasures because of the loss of the joys of innocence?"

"Don't think me ridiculous," Wilhelm replied, "when I tell you that I am still pursued by the images of those joys, however much I try to banish them from my thoughts, and all those former desires are still firmly implanted in my heart—even more so than before. For what else is left for me in my misery? If anyone had ever told me that the arms of my spirit, with which I reached out into infinity and hoped to grasp great things, would so soon be broken, I would have been utterly despondent. And now that judgment has been passed on me and I have lost her who, instead of a god, was to lead me towards the fulfilment of all my desires, what is left for me but resignation to pain and bitterness? I must admit, Werner, that, in all my secret plans, she was the foundation block on which my rope ladder was secured. Hopefully courting dangers this adventurous spirit of mine floated in the air, but the foundation broke and it fell to the ground, shattered at the base of its aspirations. There is no hope or consolation for me anymore! I will not keep any of these wretched papers." With these words he jumped up, grabbed a few more bundles, tore them open and threw them in the fire. Werner tried to stop him, but in vain. "Let me be!" said Wilhelm, "what's the use of these wretched scribblings—they are not a stage toward anything, nor encouragement for anything anymore—are they to remain to torment me till the end of my days, a mockery instead of arousing sympathy or wonder? What a wretched state I am in, what a miserable fate is mine! Now I understand at last the laments of those poets, who achieved wisdom through suffering. I used to think I was indestructible, invulnerable, but now I see that an early but deep wound will never, never heal. I feel that I will take it with me into the grave. The pain will not leave me all my life. It will finally kill me. And the memory of her, worthless as she was, will stay with me always, live and die with me.—But, my friend, if I am to speak truthfully, she was not entirely worthless. Her profession, her experiences have absolved her a thousand times in my mind. I was too cruel. You yourself savagely imbued me with your own coldness and harshness. You fettered my distracted feelings, prevented me from doing for her and me what I owed to us both. Who knows what state she is in now, all because of me—what despair and helplessness I have abandoned her to—all this is gradually beginning to weigh on my conscience! Isn't it possible, perhaps, that she could have given me some explanation? Isn't that possible? Misunderstandings can create such confusion, circumstances can so often pardon mistakes! I picture her so often, sitting alone in the quiet, resting her head on her elbows, and saying: 'So this is the troth he swore, the love he promised me! How could he so cruelly destroy the beautiful life we were sharing!'" Wilhelm burst into a flood of tears, sank his head onto the table, and covered the remaining papers with his tears.

Werner stood beside him in acute embarrassment. He had not expected such a wild outburst of passion. Several times he tried to interrupt and change the course of the conversation, but always without success. He was quite unable to halt the flow. But his long-lasting friendship with Wilhelm took control of the situation, and as Wilhelm poured out his misery, he showed his deep and sincere concern by maintaining silence. And so they spent that evening: Wilhelm still immersed in sorrowful reflection, and Werner alarmed by this new outbreak of a passion that he thought he had long since curbed in his friend by what he thought was good advice and active encouragement.

Chapter Three

After such setbacks Wilhelm usually devoted himself all the more vigorously to business affairs, and this was indeed the best way for him to flee the labyrinth that was once again opening up enticingly before him. His easy manner with strangers and his ability to conduct correspondence in almost all languages gave his father and his associates increased hope, and compensated for the break in their plans due to the sickness of which they did not know the cause. So they decided once again to dispatch him on a business trip, and we catch up with him riding along on his horse, his clothes in a saddlebag—stimulated by the good fresh air and by the thought of going somewhere. He was proceeding in the direction of a mountainous area where he had some business to attend to.

He passed through valleys and hills with a feeling of extreme pleasure, seeing for the first time in his life overhanging cliffs, deep ravines, raging streams and tree-clad slopes, though such landscapes had haunted his dreams from his earliest days. In fact, he felt young again. All the pain he had suffered was washed away from his thoughts, and he began joyfully to recite passages from certain poems, especially from the *Pastor Fido* of Guarini, which crowded in on his mind in these isolated spots. He even recalled certain passages from his own poems and declaimed these with particular satisfaction. He was filling the world around him with figures from the past, and every step forward was accompanied by a sense of important actions he was destined to perform, and noteworthy events that would occur.

Several persons, coming up from behind him, greeted him and then hurried on ahead up the steep footpaths through the mountains, interrupting the silent course of his meditation without, however, his paying much attention to them. But finally a talkative fellow told him the reason why all these people were going this way. "At Hochdorf," the man said, "there is to be a play tonight and people from all around are going to see it." "Are you telling me," said Wilhelm, "that the art of the theater has penetrated these dense woods and built a temple, and that I am on my way to celebrate there?" "You will be even more surprised when you learn who the actors are. There is a large factory in the neighborhood, which employs many people. The owner, living as he does apart from all human society, knows no better way of occupying his workers in winter, than encouraging them to perform plays, for he will not countenance card playing and other coarse amusements. So this is how they spend their long evenings; and today being the old man's birthday, they are putting on a special performance."

So Wilhelm went to Hochdorf, where he had planned to spend the night anyway. He dismounted at the factory whose owner was on his list of creditors. When he gave his name, the old man expressed his delight at seeing him: "So you, sir," he said, "are the son of that worthy man to whom I owe so much thanks, and still some money. Your father has been very patient with me, and I would really be an utter rascal if I did not pay up promptly and gladly. You have arrived at just the right time to see that I mean what I say." He called in his wife, who was just as pleased to see Wilhelm as he was, said how like his father he was and regretted that, because of the many visitors, she could not put him up for the night. The business matter was soon settled, and Wilhelm put the small roll of gold in his pocket, hoping that all his other transactions would be so easily completed.

The hour was approaching when the play was due to begin. They were still waiting for the head forester, who eventually arrived, accompanied by several hunters, and was greeted with the greatest respect. The assembled company was then led into the barn alongside the garden, which was to serve as the theater. The whole place had been made pleasant and cheerful, though without any particular signs of good taste. One of the painters at the factory, who had worked for a time at the court theater, had produced some sort of forest, street and interior to serve as backdrops. The text of the play had been borrowed from a travelling company of actors and adapted to the needs of the present performers. And such as it was, it was entertaining enough. The plot, in which two lovers try to steal a girl from her guardian and then from each other, produced all sorts of interesting situations. This was the first play that Wilhelm had seen for a long time, and he engaged in various reflections as a result. It was full of action but lacking in real character portrayal. It amused and delighted, like all primitive forms of drama. For simple people are satisfied by seeing plenty of action, whereas a more cultured spectator will have his feelings engaged as well, and only a truly cultured person wants to reflect on a play. Wilhelm would gladly have helped the actors a bit here and there, for little would have been needed to improve the performance considerably.

He was disturbed in his silent musings by the tobacco smoke, which got thicker and thicker. The forester lit his pipe soon after the play started, and gradually several others took the same liberty. The big dogs were also a troublesome nuisance. They had indeed been left outside, but they soon found their way through a back door into the theater, ran onto the stage and into the actors, then jumped over the pit to their master who was sitting in the front row.

As an epilogue they offered a tribute. A portrait of the old man in his wedding clothes had been placed on an altar and decked out with flowers. All the actors paid homage to it in appropriate postures of respect. The youngest child, dressed in white, stepped up and delivered a speech in verse, by which the whole family and the forester, who was thinking of his own children, were moved to tears. And so the play ended, and Wilhelm could not refrain from stepping onto the stage to look at the actresses at closer range, praising their performance, and giving them advice for the future.

He attended to his other business obligations, in various mountain places, but not all of them were absolved so easily or pleasantly as here in Hochdorf. Some of the creditors asked for further time, some were plain rude, and some even denied that they owed any money. According to the instructions that had been given him, Wilhelm was required to start proceedings against some of them—which meant finding a lawyer, briefing him, appearing in court, and engaging in various other tiresome duties. It was just as aggravating when people tried to show him their respect. He found few who could give him information, few with whom he could hope to enter into a useful business relationship. In addition there were unfortunately several rainy days, and journeying on horseback in this sort of country became extremely arduous. He was therefore relieved when he came into flat country again, and found a pleasant little country town at the foot of a hill, on a beautiful fertile plain beside a gentle river, all bathed in sunshine. He had no business to transact in this particular place, but decided to stay there for a few days to give himself some rest, and some respite for his horse, which had suffered from the bad roads.

Chapter Four

Wilhelm stopped off at the inn on the marketplace. Inside things were very lively indeed and everyone seemed to be having a good time. A company of acrobats, jugglers and tightrope dancers had just moved in with their families, and there was even a strong man amongst them. They were preparing for a public performance, and occupied themselves in the meantime with all sorts of pranks. They argued with the landlord, then quarrelled amongst themselves. The subjects of their disputes were certainly not worth quarrelling about, and the way they expressed their satisfaction was absolutely insufferable. So Wilhelm hesitated whether to stay there or not, as he stood by the entrance watching the workmen assembling a platform on the square.

A young girl came up selling roses and other flowers from a basket, he bought a nice bouquet, tied it up to his satisfaction, and was contemplating his handiwork with pleasure, when the window of another inn on the other side of the square was opened and an attractive woman appeared in it. He could see, despite the distance, that her face had a pleasant gaiety. Her blond hair fell loosely around her neck, and she seemed to turn and look at him. Shortly afterward a boy wearing a barber's apron and a white jacket came out and greeted him with the message that "the lady at the window ventured to ask if he would give her some of his beautiful flowers." — "She may have them all," said Wilhelm, giving the boy the whole bunch, and with it his compliments to the lovely lady, who responded to his message with a friendly greeting and then retired from the window.

Reflecting on this pleasant episode, he was going upstairs to his room when a young creature jumped out at him and immediately attracted his attention. The child was neatly dressed in a short silk bodice with slashed Spanish sleeves and puffed-out long slim trousers. Its long black hair was curled and wound in locks and braids on its head. He looked at the figure with amazement, uncertain whether it was a boy or a girl. But he finally decided in favor of the latter and stopped her as she was rushing past, wished her goodday, and asked to whom she belonged, although he could easily see that she must be a member of the group of acrobats and dancers. With a dark and penetrating sidelong glance she broke loose and rushed into the kitchen, without saying a word.

Further up the stairs there was a broad landing on which two men were practicing fencing, trying out their skill on each other. One of them obviously belonged to the troupe, the other had a somewhat less savage appearance. Wilhelm watched them and had cause to admire them both, and when the wilder one, who was husky and had a black beard, left the scene, the other one offered Wilhelm his rapier, with a gesture of great courtesy. "If you are prepared to take on a pupil," said Wilhelm, "I would be glad to try a few passes with you." They fenced together, and although the other was far superior to Wilhelm, he was polite enough to say that it was all a matter of practice, and Wilhelm had shown he had been taught by a good, solid, German fencing master.

Their conversation was interrupted by the hubbub created by the troupe leaving the inn in order to inform the townsfolk of the forthcoming spectacle and thereby arouse their interest in the performance. First came a drummer, and behind him the manager on horseback, and then, mounted on an equally skinny nag, a female dancer, holding a child decked out in ribbons and finery. The rest of the troupe came on foot, some of them carrying children in fantastic positions comfortably on their shoulders, and amongst these Wilhelm noticed again the dark, somber-looking young girl. A clown was running around in the gathering crowd, handing out playbills as he kissed a girl or smacked a little boy, all the time making jokes, which were so easy to grasp that everybody felt drawn towards him and eager to get to know him better. The playbills underscored the many different skills of the performers, especially those of a Monsieur Narcisse and Mademoiselle Landrinette, who, as principals, were wise enough to absent themselves from the procession, in order to give themselves a higher status and arouse more curiosity.

During the parade the lovely woman in the neighboring inn reappeared at the window, and Wilhelm lost no time in enquiring about her from his fencing partner, whom we shall call Laertes. He offered to take Wilhelm over to meet her. "She and I," said Laertes with a smile, "are the remains of a company of actors which was disbanded here recently. We liked the place so much that we decided to stay here for a while and use up our little remaining cash, while a friend has gone off to find a place for himself and us."

Laertes accompanied his new acquaintance to the door of Philine's room, where he left him for a moment while he went to buy candy in a nearby store. "You will certainly be grateful to me," he said on his return, "for providing you with this delightful acquaintance." The girl came out to meet them, wearing a pair of light slippers with high heels. She had thrown a black mantilla over her white negligé which, because it was not quite clean, gave her a domestic, relaxed appearance; and her short skirt revealed a pair of the tiniest feet imaginable.

"I am glad to see you," she called out to Wilhelm, "and thank you so much for the lovely flowers." She led him into the room with one hand while she pressed the flowers to her bosom with the other. When they had sat down and were engaged in some casual conversation to which she managed to give a charming twist, Laertes shook into her lap some burnt almonds which she immediately began to nibble. "Just look what a baby this young fellow is," she said: "He will try to persuade you that I am a passionate sweet eater, but actually he's the one who can't exist without eating something sweet." "Well," said Laertes in reply, "let us agree that in this as in so much else we like to keep each other company. For example, today is such a nice day. I would suggest that we ride out and have lunch at the mill." "Good idea," said Philine. "We must provide our new friend with a change of scene."

Laertes ran off (he never walked) and Wilhelm wanted to go back for a moment to his room to fix his hair, which was still a bit untidy from the journey. "You can do that here," said Philine, calling her young servant boy, and persuaded Wilhelm very sweetly to take off his coat, put on her smock and let the boy fix his hair right there in her presence. "One can't waste time," she said, "for one never knows how long one will be together."

The boy did not do his job very well, more because of his surly indifference than because he lacked the necessary skill. He kept pulling Wilhelm's hair and it seemed he would never be finished. Philine reproved him several times for his ill-mannered behavior, and finally lost her patience, shoved him aside and threw him out. She then took things into her own hands and curled Wilhelm's hair very efficiently and elegantly. She didn't hurry over this, kept changing her mind on what she was doing, and couldn't avoid her knees touching his, and her bouquet and bosom getting so close to his lips that he was more than once tempted to give her a kiss.

When Wilhelm had removed some powder from his forehead with a knife that she had for this purpose, she said: "Keep that in remembrance of me." It was a pretty little knife with a handle of inlaid steel on which were engraved the words: "Remember me." Wilhelm put it in his pocket, thanked her, and asked her permission to give her something in exchange.

Now they were all ready. Laertes had found a coach, and off they went on a very pleasant excursion. Philine threw something or other out of the window to every beggar, with a few kind and cheerful words. They came to the mill and had just ordered something to eat, when musicians started playing in front of the building. They were miners, singing pleasant songs in loud, shrill voices to the accompaniment of a zither and triangle. They were soon surrounded by people who came up to listen, and guests applauded them from the windows of the mill. Noticing this extra attention the musicians spread out in preparation, so it seemed, for something really special. After a short pause, a miner stepped forward with a hoe, and made digging motions whilst the others played a solemn melody. After this, up came a farmer from the crowd and made threatening gestures at the miner, indicating that he should remove himself from here. The spectators were puzzled by this, and only when the "farmer" opened his mouth to reprove the other man for digging in his field, did they realize that he was a miner dressed as a peasant. The first man calmly told the other that he had every right to start digging here, and began to explain the basic elements of mining. The farmer, who didn't understand the strange terminology, asked all sorts of stupid questions at which the spectators, feeling superior, burst into laughter. The miner tried to explain to the farmer the advantages he would gain, once he had dug up the treasures that lay beneath the earth; and the farmer's threatening attitude became gradually modified, and they parted as good friends. But the miner had won the argument.

"This little dialogue," said Wilhelm as they sat at table, "shows quite clearly how useful the theater could be for all classes of society, and what profit the state could derive from displaying on the stage the best side of human occupations, vocations and undertakings, those aspects that the state must itself respect and support. Nowadays all we seem to see is the ridiculous side of things; the writer of comedies has become a sort of malicious monitor of human follies, always on the lookout for some new one to register on his list, and jubilant when he finds one. Wouldn't it be a satisfying and worthy occupation for any statesman to survey the influence of the various classes of society on each other, and thereby give support to a writer with a real sense of humor? I am convinced that in this way many useful as well as entertaining plays could be produced."

"So far as I have been able to observe in my own travels," said Laertes, "there is more discouragement than the opposite, more refusals, denials and rejection than permission, encouragement and rewards. Everything is allowed to go on until it becomes harmful; and then it is angrily and violently terminated."

"Let's stop talking about the state and statesmen," said Philine. "They always suggest full-bottomed wigs to me, and it doesn't matter who is wearing a wig,

I have a twitchy feeling in my fingers and long to pull them off the venerable gentlemen, and dance around in the room laughing at their bald pates."

She cut off the conversation with some lively songs, which she performed very prettily, and pressed for a speedy return to the town, so that they should not miss the evening performance by the acrobats and tightrope dancers. Comical almost to the point of eccentricity, she continued to show her generosity to the wayside beggars on the return journey, and, since she and both the men had run out of money, she threw her hat out of the window to a young girl, and her scarf to an old woman.

Philine invited her two companions to her quarters, saying that there would be a better view of the performance from her windows than from the other inn.

When they arrived, they found the platform already set up and carpets hung up to make a colorful background for the show. The springboards were already in place, the slack rope fastened to the posts, and the tightrope pulled over the blocks. The square was filled mostly with the common people, and the windows with persons of quality. The clown began to put the audience in a good mood and capture their attention with some silly tricks, and these, as always, were greeted with laughter. Then several children, executing the weirdest contortions with their bodies, aroused both horror and amazement; and Wilhelm was filled with deep pity when he saw amongst them the same child that had so interested him earlier, striving to achieve these abnormal postures. But then came the merry acrobats who delighted everybody by twisting and turning in the air, first alone, then one after another, and finally all together. At this there was vigorous clapping and shouts of joy from all the spectators.

And then all eyes were fixed on something quite different. One after another the children stepped onto the tightrope. First came those who were still learning the art, so that the performance would be prolonged and the difficulties of this particular skill amply demonstrated. Then came the men and women who showed only a moderate amount of skill—but not yet Monsieur Narcisse or Mademoiselle Landrinette. Finally these two appeared from behind the red curtains of a sort of tent, and fulfilled every expectation of the eager spectators by their attractive figures and elegant costumes. He was a lively young man of medium height with black eyes and a heavy pigtail; she was equally attractive and looked just as strong. They followed each other on the tightrope, executing steps and leaps with the greatest ease and maintaining unusual postures. Her lightness, his boldness, and the precision with which both of them carried out their artistic feats, increased the enthusiasm of the spectators at every new twist or turn. The easy grace with which they conducted themselves, as compared with the apparent strain and effort of the others, gave them such an air of superiority, that they might well have been the lord and master of the entire troupe; indeed everyone thought they deserved such an important position.

The enthusiasm of the people at the windows was just as great as that of the people down on the square, for the ladies had their eyes fixed on Narcisse and the gentlemen on Landrinette. The people on the square yelled with delight;

the more refined watchers at the windows expressed their approval by clapping their hands, but they did not laugh at the clown, as those down below did. Only a few of those on the square slunk away when members of the troupe came through the crowd with pewter plates to collect money.

"It seems to me that they did very well," said Wilhelm to Philine, who was with him at the window. "I admire their ability to make even quite small feats have a really telling effect by bringing them on in succession, each at the appropriate moment; and also how they managed to combine the clumsiness of the children and the virtuosity of their star performers into a total effect which held our attention and pleasantly diverted us."

The people on the square had gradually dispersed, leaving it empty, and meanwhile Philine and Laertes were arguing about the relative quality of the figures and skills of Narcisse and Landrinette, and teasing each other. Wilhelm saw the strange girl standing alongside children playing on the street, and drew this to the attention of Philine, who called and beckoned to the child with her usual vivacity. But since the child seemed unwilling to come to her, she went to fetch it herself, singing as she clattered down the stairs on her high-heeled slippers.

"Here's our mystery," she said, drawing the child into the room. But the girl standing in the doorway, as if eager to slip away, placed her right hand on her chest and her left on her temple, and made a deep bow. "Don't be afraid, little one," said Wilhelm, walking up to her. She looked at him with an expression of uncertainty, and stepped forward a few paces. "What is your name?" he asked. "They call me Mignon." "How old are you?" "Nobody has counted." "Who was your father?" "The big devil is dead."

"Well, that's all very odd!" said Philine. They asked her a few more questions, which she answered in broken German and a strange, formal manner, bowing deeply each time and placing her hands as before on her chest and temple.

Wilhelm could not take his eyes off her; her whole appearance and the mystery that surrounded her completely absorbed his mind and feelings. He thought she was probably twelve or thirteen years old. She was well built, but her limbs suggested further development to come, which possibly had been arrested. Her features were not regular, but striking: her forehead seemed to veil some secret, her nose was unusually beautiful, her mouth, though too tight-lipped for her age and inclined to twitch at times on one side, had a certain winsome charm about it. The grease paint almost obscured her dark complexion. Wilhelm was so absorbed in contemplating her, that he lapsed into silence and became completely oblivious of the others. But Philine roused him out of his daze by offering the child some of the candy she had left over, and then gave the girl a sign that she should leave, which she did, with her usual bow, and in a flash ran out of the door.

The time came for the other three to separate for the evening, but before doing so they agreed to embark next day on another excursion. They decided to go out again for lunch, but this time to a different place, a nearby hunting lodge. Wilhelm spent much of the evening praising Philine to Laertes, to which the latter reacted lightheartedly and curtly.

The next morning, after an hour's fencing practice, they went to Philine's inn, having earlier seen the rented coach. But Wilhelm was surprised to find that the coach had left and Philine was nowhere to be found. They were told that she had driven off with two strangers who had arrived that very morning. He had been looking forward to a pleasant time in her company and could not conceal his irritation. Laertes, on the other hand, just laughed, and said: "That's what I like about her! That's exactly how she is! But let's go straight to the hunting lodge, and let's not give up our excursion on her account, wherever she may have taken herself off to."

On the way Wilhelm expressed his disapproval of such fickle behavior, but Laertes replied that he did not think it was fickle to remain true to character. "When Philine agrees to something, or gives someone a promise, she does so on the unspoken condition that it will suit her when the time comes. She likes to make gifts, but one must always be prepared to give them back."

"What a strange character!" said Wilhelm. "Not strange at all," Laertes replied, "and in no wise hypocritical. I love her for it, and am her friend, because she represents in all its true colors the sex that I have such good reason to hate. She is the real Eve, the progenitrix of the whole female race. They're all like her, though they won't admit it."

The conversation continued in this vein, with Laertes venting his wrath against the whole female sex but without giving any reasons. Wilhelm was depressed by what Laertes had been saying, because it reminded him all too vividly of his own experience with Mariane. They entered a forest, and what should they find but Philine sitting alone at a stone table beside a spring shaded by a group of fine old trees. She greeted them with a cheerful song and when Laertes asked what had happened to her companions, she said: "I led them a real dance, and fooled them. That's just what they deserved. On the way here I tested their generosity, and when I found out they were skinflints I decided to punish them. When we arrived, they asked the waiter what there was to eat, and with usual glibness of tongue he recited a list of everything they had, and other things too. I saw their embarrassment: they looked at each other, dithered a bit, and then asked the prices. 'Why should you concern yourselves with all that?' I said. 'It's the business of the lady to decide on the menu. Let me take care of it.' So I ordered the craziest lunch, some of which had to be brought from elsewhere in the neighborhood. The waiter, after some grimacing on my part, had become my ally in all this and gave me good solid help, and we scared them both so much at the thought of the sumptuous banquet we had ordered, that they decided to take a walk in the woods, and I doubt whether they will come back! I laughed and laughed for full fifteen minutes, and I shall go on laughing whenever I recall the expression on their faces." Laertes regaled them at table with similar stories, and they all entertained each other with tales of misunderstandings and hoodwink-ings of one kind and another.

A young man whom they knew from the town came walking through the woods with a book in his hand, sat down beside them and praised the beauty of the place. He directed their attention to the rustling spring, the movement of the branches, the light effects and the song of the birds. At this Philine sang a song about a cuckoo, which seemed to displease the newcomer, and he soon left.

"I don't want to hear another word about Nature and all its beauties," said Philine, once he had gone. "There is nothing more insufferable than having one's pleasure analyzed while one is enjoying it. When the weather's fine, you go for a walk; when the music starts, you dance. But who wants to *think* about the fine weather or the music? It's the dancers that interest us, not the music; and to look into a pair of beautiful dark eyes doesn't do a pair of blue eyes any harm. Compared with that, what's the use of rustling springs and old worm-eaten lime trees?" As she said this, she was gazing into Wilhelm's eyes, and her glance could not but penetrate to the gates of his heart. "You're quite right," he said, with some embarrassment. "People are what's most interesting, and perhaps that's all we should be interested in. For everything else around us is either the atmosphere in which we live, or instruments that we use for our-selves. The more we occupy ourselves with our environment, the more we think about it or partake of it, the less alive is our sense of our own value and of belonging to a community of fellow men. People who attach great impor-tance to gardens, buildings, clothes, jewels or possessions of any kind, are not very sociable and not very agreeable. They lose sight of other people, and few of them succeed in entertaining them and amusing them. Don't we see that in the theater? A good actor can make us forget a wretched decor, but a fine theater simply makes us more aware of the poverty of the acting."

When they had finished eating, Philine ensconced herself in the tall, shady grass. Her two companions had to bring her flowers in quantity. She made a single wreath out of these and set it on her head, which made her look unbelievably charming. There were enough flowers left for her to make another wreath, which she did while the two men sat down beside her. When after much joking and innuendo she had it finished, she lowered it delicately onto Wilhelm's head, and kept rearranging it till she had it just right. "Am I then to go empty-handed?" asked Laertes. "Not at all," replied Philine. "You shall have no cause for complaint"; and with that she took the wreath off her own head and put it on his. "If we were rivals in love, we could have a fierce argument as to whom you are favoring more," said Laertes. "In that case," she replied, "you would be silly fools." She leaned over him, offering her mouth to be kissed and turned immediately to put her arm around Wilhelm and plant a passionate kiss on his lips. "Which tasted better?" she said, teasingly. "Mar-velous!" said Laertes. "It seems that something like that could never taste of wormwood." "As little as any present enjoyed without envy or pride. But now," she said, "I would like to dance for an hour or so, and then we should go back to our acrobats."

They went into the house, and there they found music. Philine, who was a good dancer, cheered them both up. Wilhelm was not clumsy, but he lacked experience in dancing; so Philine and Laertes decided to give him a few lessons.

By now it was getting late, and when they arrived back, the rope dancers had already begun the show. There were still many spectators on the market-square, but a good number of them had gone over to the door of the inn where Wilhelm was staying, because, as our three friends noticed when they got out of the coach, there was some kind of trouble there. Wilhelm rushed over and pushed his way through the crowd to see what was happening, and, to his horror, saw the manager of the troupe dragging the mysterious child by the hair out of the building and beating her frail body mercilessly with the handle of a whip.

Wilhelm tore over to the man and seized him by the chest. "Let go of that child!" he cried, yelling like a maniac, "or one of us will be dead!" With that, inflamed with anger, he grabbed the man by the throat so fiercely that the fellow thought he was going to choke, let go of the girl, and tried to defend himself. Some of the bystanders, equally concerned about the child but unwilling to start a fight, now grabbed his arms, took away the whip, threatened him and poured abuse on him. The man himself, his only weapon now being his mouth, began to threaten and curse abominably, and said that this useless, lazy creature wouldn't do what she was supposed to, refusing to perform the egg dance that he had promised the public. He was going to kill her, and no one would stop him. He then tried to break loose to find the child who was hiding in the crowd. But Wilhelm held him back and said: "You shall not see or touch that child until you explain to the magistrate where you stole her from. I will go to any length; you will not escape me." These words, which Wilhelm uttered in the heat of his anger, trusting some deep dark feeling (or inspiration, if you like) but without much thought or intention, brought the infuriated fellow to his senses. "What should I do with such a creature?" he said: "She's utterly useless to me. Just pay me what her clothes cost and then you can keep her. But let's settle the matter this very evening." With this he rushed off to continue the show and appease the spectators with a few worthwhile artistic feats.

When things had quieted down, Wilhelm looked around for the child, but couldn't find her anywhere. Some people said they had seen her in the attic, some on the roofs of neighboring houses. But after searching everywhere they decided to wait and see if she would turn up again of her own accord.

Meanwhile Narcisse had come back and Wilhelm questioned him about the child and where it came from. He did not know anything about this, for he had only recently joined the troupe. Instead, he went on to tell Wilhelm volubly and very amusingly about his own experiences. When Wilhelm congratulated him on his success with the public, he seemed quite indifferent. "We are used to being laughed at and being admired, but all this approval doesn't improve our lot. The manager pays us, and has to make his profit." He then was about to take his leave and hurry away, when Wilhelm asked him where he was off to in such a hurry. The young man smiled, and admitted that his figure and his talents aroused elsewhere more solid approval than he got from the public. Several women had sent messages that they were eager to know him better, and he was afraid that, with all the visits that he had to pay, he would hardly get through by midnight. He went on to enumerate very frankly all his assignations, and would have given names and street numbers if Wilhelm had not disdained such indiscretion and politely dismissed him.

While this was going on, Laertes had been entertaining Landrinette and assuring her that she was fully deserving of being a woman and remaining one.

The negotiations with the manager began, and the child was transferred to Wilhelm's keeping for the sum of thirty thalers. The black-bearded, intemperate Italian gave up all his rights to her, but would say nothing about her origins, except that he had acquired her on the death of his brother who, because of his extraordinary performing skills, had been known as the Big Devil.

Most of the next morning was spent in trying to find the child. Every corner of the house, every inch of the neighborhood was searched—but with no results. She had disappeared; and it was feared that she might have drowned herself, or done herself harm in some other way.

Even the charms of Philine could not distract Wilhelm from his anxiety. He spent a mournful day, just brooding. Even the performance that night, when acrobats and dancers exerted all their powers to make the very best impression, did not cheer or divert his heavy mind.

The number of spectators was so greatly increased by those from neighboring villages that the applause snowballed in intensity. The leaps over swords and through the paper bottom of a cask created a great sensation. The strong man, to everyone's horror and amazement, stretched himself out across the space between two chairs and then lifted an anvil onto his arched stomach and had two husky smiths forge a horseshoe on it. To end the show, there was the so-called Hercules Tower, never before seen in these parts, in which a row of men stood on the shoulders of another row, and on top of them women and youths, so that a living pyramid was built, with a child standing on its head at the top as the pinnacle and weather vane. Narcisse and Landrinette were carried in sedan chairs on the shoulders of the others, through the best streets of the town, which was greeted by the populace with shouts of delight. They were showered with ribbons, flowers and silks, and everyone pressed forward to get a closer look at them, happy to see them and to be honored by a glance from them.

"What actor, writer, or indeed what human being would not feel he had reached the summit of his desires when, by some noble word or deed, he produced such a universal impression? What a rich experience it would be to disseminate worthy human feelings so quickly—like electricity—through the ranks of the common people, such as these people did by the display of their bodily skill—to impart a sense of common humanity to the masses, inflame and disturb them with a display of all our pleasures and misfortunes, wisdom and follies, stupidity and idiocy, and release their sullen minds into a state of active, vigorous, unimpeded freedom!" Thus spoke Wilhelm, but since neither Philine nor Laertes seemed inclined to continue such a discourse, he was obliged to articulate to himself these favorite reflections of his, as he walked through the streets far into the night, and indulge once more in his passionate desire to incorporate into drama all that was great, noble and good. And he could do so now in the full vigor and freedom of his unfettered imagination.

Chapter Five

The next day, as soon as the tightrope artists had departed with a great deal of noise, Mignon appeared and stepped up to Wilhelm and Laertes who had resumed their fencing practice. "Where have you been hiding?" Wilhelm asked her gently. "We were very worried about you." The child looked at him, but said nothing. "Now you are ours," said Laertes. "We have bought you." "How much did you pay?" she asked curtly. "A hundred ducats," said Laertes. "And when you pay us back, you may go free." "That's a lot, isn't it?" the child asked. "Yes indeed, so just see that you behave well." "I'll be your servant," she replied.

From that moment on, she watched carefully to see what services the waiter had performed for the two friends, and would not let him enter the room anymore. She wanted to do everything herself and performed her various services, though slowly and sometimes awkwardly, but correctly and very attentively.

She would often take a vessel of water and wash her face so vigorously and thoroughly that she almost rubbed her cheeks raw. Laertes teased her about this, but found out that she was trying to get rid of the paint on her cheeks and thought that the red patches she had caused by her vigorous rubbing, were particularly stubborn paint. They explained this to her, and once she stopped what she had been doing, a fine brown complexion, brightened by only a hint of red, was revealed.

Attracted more than he cared to admit to himself both by the wanton charms of Philine and the mystery surrounding the child, Wilhelm spent several days in this strange company. He justified this by diligent practice in fencing and dancing, since he might not so easily have an opportunity to indulge in these two occupations.

One day, to his surprise and delight, he saw Melina and his wife arriving. Once they had greeted him, they enquired about the actors, and were dismayed to learn that the director had long since left, and the actors, except for very few, had also gone off to various other places. Since getting married—in which, as we have seen, Wilhelm had been helpful—the young couple had been looking in various places for a job, but so far without success. They had been advised to try here: several people they met on the way reported that they had seen good theater. Philine took a dislike to Madame Melina, and the lively Laertes to her husband. They would gladly have gotten rid of the newcomers immediately, and Wilhelm was not able to change their unfavorable opinion despite his repeated assertions that they were really quite decent people.

This addition to the company disturbed in several ways the happy-go-lucky existence of the adventurous spirits of Philine, Laertes and Wilhelm. They found a room in the inn where Philine was staying, and Melina began immediately to haggle and complain, demanding better quarters, more copious meals and faster service for less money. In a very short time he had the innkeeper and the waiters scowling; and whereas the others, intent on enjoying life, accepted what was served and paid promptly in order not to think about what they had been eating, Melina criticized every meal and then went over it again afterwards, so that Philine had no hesitation in declaring that he chewed over everything.

Madame Melina was even more distasteful to the vivacious Philine, for although she was not uneducated she was totally lacking in mind and soul. She recited quite well, but was always reciting, and just words, emphasizing particular passages but without expressing the spirit of the whole. She was by no means unpleasant to people—especially not to men, and those she associated with usually felt that she had a fine mind. For she knew how to adopt the feelings of others. She would feel her way into the respect of a friend by agreeing with his ideas until she was out of her depth, and then wax ecstatic at what was new to her. She knew when to talk and when to keep quiet, and although she was not malicious, she knew how to find someone's weak spot.

Chapter Six

Melina spent his time discovering what was still left of the properties which had belonged to the troupe. The scenery and costumes had been left as securities with some local merchants, and a lawyer had the authority of the previous director to sell these, under certain conditions, if anybody turned up who wanted them. Melina wanted to see what there was, and took Wilhelm along. Although he would not admit it, Wilhelm felt a certain attraction towards these things when they entered the rooms where they were stored. Although the scenery was all spotty and in bad shape, and the costumes—turkish, saracen, grotesque, and cowls for wizards, jews or priests—were no longer very convincing, he could not resist the feeling that it was admidst such junk as this that he had spent the happiest moments of his life. If Melina could have gazed into his heart, he would have urged him even more strongly to provide a sum of money to redeem these scattered remnants and put them together again into a living whole. "How happy I would be if I had two hundred thalers to secure these basic theatrical materials," exclaimed Melina; "I could soon get a play together that would provide for us in this town." Wilhelm said nothing. The precious things were locked up again. And they left, both of them deep in thought.

From now on Melina talked of nothing else but plans and proposals for setting up a theater and making a profit. He tried to interest Philine and Laertes in this, and it was suggested to Wilhelm that he should advance some money and act as security. But this matter only made Wilhelm realize that he should not have spent so long in this town. He excused himself, saying that he really must think about continuing on his journey.

But the person and character of Mignon attracted him more and more. There was something strange about everything she did. She never walked up or down stairs, she always ran. She climbed up on to banisters, and before one knew it, there she was on top of a closet, sitting quite still. Wilhelm also noticed that she had a different greeting for everybody. For some time now she had been greeting him with arms folded on her breast. Some days she would be completely silent; on others she would answer certain questions, but always strangely so that it was difficult to decide whether it was a joke or her German mixed with French and Italian was intentional or simply the result of an imperfect knowledge of German. She was tireless in Wilhelm's service, getting up at sunrise but retiring early to rest on the bare floor of one of the rooms. Nothing could persuade her to sleep in a bed or on a straw mattress. He often found her washing herself. Her clothes were clean though heavily patched. Wilhelm was also told that early every morning she went to mass, and once he followed her and saw her kneeling in a corner of the church, piously saying her rosary. She did not see him, and he went home full of thoughts about this strange creature and unable to make up his mind about her.

When Melina pressed him further for money to buy the theater properties, Wilhelm became even more determined to move on. He decided that very day to write to his family, who had had no news of him for quite a while, and even began a letter to Werner. He had got quite far in the account of his various adventures—often straying from the truth without noticing it—when he discovered on the other side of the sheet some lines he had been copying for Madame Melina from his own notebook. So he tore up the sheet in a fit of displeasure, and put off writing his letters to the next post day.

Chapter Seven

One day they were all together as usual, when Philine, who was observing every horse and scrutinizing every carriage that passed, suddenly shouted: "Look! There's our dear old pedant! I wonder whom he has with him in the carriage!" She called to him, waving from her window, and the carriage stopped. A pitiful old fellow who, with his shabby, greyish-brown coat and soiled linen, looked like a musty old schoolman, got out of the carriage and respectfully took off his hat to Philine, revealing a badly powdered and very stiff wig. Philine blew him a multitude of kisses. For though there were always men she loved and whose love she enjoyed, she took almost equal delight, and that as often as possible, in teasing those she was not in love with at the moment.

The noise with which Philine greeted her old acquaintance and the confusion which that created, was such that they neglected to look at the other persons with him. These were an oldish man with two women. Wilhelm had the feeling that he had met them somewhere before, and it soon turned out that this was indeed the case. Several years previously he had seen all three of them take part in a theatrical performance in his hometown. The two daughters had changed a lot in the meantime, but not their father. He usually played those good-natured, garrulous old men that German drama is full of and whom you can often encounter in everyday life. Since it seems to be a part of our national character to do good without ostentation, we seldom reflect on the fact that it is also possible to do what is right with some degree of graciousness and style, and as a result we tend all too easily to be cross-grained in order to emphasize by contrast the sweetness of our virtues. It was these roles that this actor played so well. He played them so often, indeed so exclusively, that he began to take on the same character in real life.

Wilhelm, once he had recognized him, became very perturbed, for he remembered having often seen him playing alongside his beloved Mariane. He could still hear him scolding and the gentle voice with which she had to counter his brusqueness in so many plays.

The first question addressed to these newcomers was an eager inquiry whether there was any hope of finding employment elsewhere, but they said that they had approached various theater troupes only to be told that there were no vacancies. Some of these companies were even concerned that the threat of approaching war might cause them to disband. The old man and his two daughters had just given up a favorable engagement because they were bored and wanted a change, and had hired a carriage together with the "schoolmaster," or "pedant" as Philine always called him, whom they had met on the road, in order to come to this particular town. But the opportunity they had hoped to find here was obviously not forthcoming.

While all the others were discussing their affairs, Wilhelm was deep in thought. He would have liked to talk to the old man privately. He wanted to hear about Mariane, but was also afraid of what he might learn; and so he was in a state of extreme uneasiness.

The two young women were very pleasant to him but even this did not rouse him from his brooding, until one particular exchange of words claimed his full attention. Friedrich, the blond boy who had been performing various services for Philine, suddenly refused to lay the table and get the meal. "I agreed to serve you," he said to Philine with some heat, "but not to wait on all sorts of other people." At this, there was a violent argument. Philine insisted that he must do his job, but he stubbornly refused. So she told him he could leave, and go wherever he pleased. "Do you think I can't leave you, if I want to?" he said, with an air of defiance. He packed up his things and hurriedly left the house. "Go and get us what we want, Mignon!" said Philine. "Tell the waiter, and help him serve!"

At this point Mignon came up to Wilhelm and asked, in her usual laconic fashion: "Shall I? May I?" "Yes, my child," said Wilhelm. "Do what Mademoiselle requests." So she took care of everything and waited very attentively on the guests at table. After dinner Wilhelm found the opportunity to take a walk alone with the old man, and after various questions about how life had been treating him, he succeded in turning the conversation on to the troupe he had been part of, and finally ventured to ask after Mariane.

"Don't mention that despicable creature!" the old man exclaimed. "I have vowed never to think of her again." Wilhelm was shocked, and even more discomfited by the way the old man went on to upbraid her for her frivolity and wantonness. He would gladly have terminated the conversation, but he had to suffer through the garrulous effusions of this strange man.

"I am ashamed that I was so fond of her. But if you had known her well, you would have pardoned me for that. She was so nice, so natural and good, so pleasing in her manner, so thoroughly agreeable. I would never have imagined that insolence and ingratitude were so deeply ingrained in her character."

Wilhelm had by now become resigned to hearing nothing but the very worst, when he suddenly noticed with astonishment that the old man's tone was changing. He became more gentle, and finally the words stuck in his throat, and he took out a handkerchief to dry his tears. "What is the matter?" said Wilhelm. "What makes you suddenly feel so differently? Do tell me. I am more concerned about this girl than you know. But do tell me everything."

"I have little more to say," the old man replied, lapsing back into that earlier tone of petulant severity. "I will never forgive her for what she made me suffer. She always had a certain trust in me. I loved her like a daughter and, while my wife was still living, I had decided to take her into my family in order to get her out of the clutches of the old man from whose protection I saw no possible benefits for her. But my wife died, and the whole plan came to nothing.

"Towards the end of our stay in your home town, I noticed a certain sadness about her. That would be about three years ago. I asked her about this, but she evaded my questions. Then we got ready to leave. She rode with me in the same coach and I noticed something which she herself soon confirmed: namely, that she was pregnant. She was terribly afraid that the manager would dismiss her. And indeed he soon did, cancelling her contract (which was only for six weeks anyway), and totally unconcerned about the appearances she was engaged for. He paid out what he owed her, and left her in a wretched inn in a small town.

"To Hell with all such lewd whores," said the old man, full of anger, "and especially this one. For she has ruined so much of my life. Why should I spend my time telling you how attentive I was to her needs, even when she was away

from us. I would rather throw my money into a pond and spend my time training mangy dogs than ever again devote my attentions to such a creature. For
what happened? At first I got some letters of thanks, with news of various
places where she had stayed; but in the end not a word, not even thanks for the
money I sent her for her confinement. Dissemblance and wantonness combine in women to provide them with a comfortable life and honest fellows like
me with hours of sorrow!"

Chapter Eight

Imagine Wilhelm's state of mind as he returned home from this conversation!
All the old wounds had been torn open, and the feeling that she had not been
quite unworthy of his love came over him again. For her whole loveable nature
had come through the old man's account of his attentions to her and what he
had said, albeit grudgingly, in her praise. Even his most violent denunciations
of her had contained nothing to discredit her in Wilhelm's eyes, because he
himself felt that he shared responsibility for her misdeeds, and her ultimate
silence seemed to him not something to reproach her with, but something that
filled him with anxious thoughts of what she must have been through. First the
confinement, then as a mother, having to wander around the world, without
anyone to assist her, wandering about with a child that was probably his—all
this distressed him greatly.

Mignon had waited up for him, with a light to guide him up the stairs. When
she had put down the candle, she asked his permission to give a performance
for his benefit that evening. He would rather have said no, for he did not know
what this might turn out to be. But he could not refuse this good-hearted creature anything. She came back into the room after a little while, carrying under
one arm a carpet which she spread out on the floor. Wilhelm let her continue.
She brought four lighted candles and put one at each corner of the carpet.
When she next fetched a basket of eggs, her intentions became clearer. With
the measured steps of an artist she paced back and forth on the carpet, distributing the eggs in definite groups. Then she called in a servant who played
the violin. He stood with his instrument in one corner. She blindfolded herself, gave a sign for the music to begin, and started to move like a wound-up
mechanism, beating the time of the melody with the clap of her castanets.

Nimbly and lightly she executed the dance with rapid precision, stepping so
briskly and firmly between and beside the eggs that at any moment one
thought she would crush one of them or dislodge it by the swiftness of her
twistings and turnings. But she never touched an egg despite the variety of her
steps, now short, now long, including some leaps. She finally wound her way
through the rows in a half-kneeling position. She pursued her course relentlessly like clockwork and the strange music gave a new twist to the movement
of the rousing dance every time it started up again. Wilhelm was absolutely

transported by this strange spectacle; forgetting all his cares, he followed every step of the beloved creature, amazed to see how completely her character was manifested in the dance. Severe, sharp, dry and violent—all this she certainly was; and in her quieter movements there was solemnity rather than grace. He suddenly realized what he had been feeling about her all this time. He wanted to take this abandoned creature to his bosom as his own child, caress her and by a father's love awaken to her the joys of life.

The dance came to an end. With her feet she rolled the eggs into a pile, not overlooking or breaking one of them. Then she stood beside the pile of eggs, took off her blindfold, and terminated the performance with a bow. Wilhelm thanked her for so pleasantly and unexpectedly executing for him alone the dance that he had so much wanted to see. He stroked her cheeks and said how sorry he was that she had been treated so harshly. He promised her a new suit of clothes, whereupon she exclaimed: "In your color." He agreed to this, though he was not quite sure what she meant. She gathered up the eggs and the carpet, asked if he had any further orders, and leapt out of the room.

Wilhelm learnt from the musician that she had spent much time and effort singing the tune of the dance to him, which was a fandango, until he could play it himself; and that she had offered him money for his pains, which he had refused.

Chapter Nine

Wilhelm spent a restless night, partly wide awake and partly harried by disturbing dreams in which he saw Mariane at one moment in all her beauty, then in pitiful shape, first with the child in her arms and then without it. Dawn was just breaking, when in came Mignon with a tailor. She brought with her some grey cloth and blue taffeta, saying, in her own peculiar way, that she wanted a new jacket and sailor pants, such as she had seen on boys in the town, with blue ribbons and lapels.

Wilhelm had not worn any bright colors since losing Mariane, and had accustomed himself to grey, as the color of shades, except that he had somewhat livened up this somber garb by a light blue lining or a little collar of the same hue. Mignon, eager to wear his colors, put pressure on the tailor, who promised to deliver the suit in a short while.

That day, the dancing and fencing lessons with Laertes did not turn out too well; they were interrupted by Melina, who expatiated on the fact that they now had assembled a little company of actors that could put on plenty of plays. He renewed his request that Wilhelm should put down some money to get things started, but Wilhelm still hesitated.

Philine and the two girls came in laughing and shouting. They had worked out a plan for another outing, always eager to have a change of place and new things to look at. What they desired most, was to eat in a different place every

day. This time it seemed to be a river trip. The Pedant had already found a boat
to take them down the winding course of the river, and urged on by Philine,
the whole company fell in with the idea and were soon on board.

"So—what shall we do now?" said Philine when they had all found somewhere to sit. "The simplest thing would be to extemporize a play," said Laertes.
"Let everyone pick a role that suits his character, and we'll see how it turns
out."

"Excellent idea!" said Wilhelm. "If people don't dissemble at all but simply
act according to their own impulses, harmony and contentment will not be
theirs for long; and never, if they dissemble all the time. It will not be a bad
idea if we assume a personality at the beginning and then show as much as we
wish of the real self hidden beneath the mask."

"Yes," said Laertes. "That's why women are so agreeable, for at first they
never show their true colors."

"That's because they're not as vain as men," said Madame Melina. "Men
always think they are quite attractive enough as nature made them."

All this time they were moving past delightful hills and woods, gardens and
vineyards, and the young women showed their enthusiasm over the landscape.
Especially Madame Melina, who began ceremoniously to recite a pretty poem
in the descriptive mode on a similar scene. But she was interrupted by Philine,
who now proposed a rule that no one be allowed to talk about inanimate
objects. She returned to the idea of extemporizing a play, supporting it
vigorously. The blustering old man should be a pensioned officer, Laertes a
travelling fencing master, the Pedant a Jew, and she herself a Tyrolean girl.
The others could be what they wanted. They should pretend they were meeting each other for the first time on a boat going to some market town. She herself began to play her part with the Jew, and general merriment broke out.

After a while the skipper asked them whether he might take on another pas-
senger, for a man was standing on the shore, waving. "Just what we need," said
Philine. "What we need is a stowaway." An attractive man stepped on board,
and from his clothing and dignified appearance he looked as though he might
be a clergyman. He greeted the assembled company, which thanked him and
then told him about the little amusement they were planning. He took on the
role of a country parson, and to their amazement played it extremely well,
admonishing at one moment and telling yarns at the next, revealing certain
weaknesses but always maintaining an air of respectfulness.

Anyone who failed to act in accordance with his or her role had to pay a forfeit. Philine gathered these conscientiously and threatened particularly to
shower the clergyman with kisses when the forfeits had to be redeemed. But
he always remained true to character. Melina, on the other hand, was stripped
of buttons, buckles and anything else that was detachable. He had chosen to
represent a travelling Englishman, but could not really get into the part.

The time passed very pleasantly, with everybody exerting their wits and
imagination, embroidering their parts with all sorts of quips and sallies. They

arrived at the place where they intended to spend the day, and Wilhelm, taking a walk with the clergyman (let's call him such because of his appearance and the role he was playing), found himself involved in a most interesting conversation.

"I think this kind of exercise amongst actors, especially when in the company of friends or acquaintances, is extremely useful," said the stranger. "It is the very best way to take people out of themselves and, by way of a detour, return them to themselves. It should be introduced in all theatrical companies. They should practice in this way, and the public would surely profit greatly if every month or so an unwritten play were performed, though the actors would have to prepare for this by several rehearsals."

"But an extemporized play should not be made up on the spur of the moment," Wilhelm objected. "The general plan, action and division of scenes should have been decided on, and the actors left to work out the presentation."

"Yes, indeed," said the stranger. "And once the actors were in the swing, the presentation should benefit by this procedure. Not so much the verbal presentation, for the words must be the product of the author's considered reflection, but the gestures, facial expressions, cries and the like, all that belongs to miming and what is partially articulated—an art which seems to be disappearing from our stage. There are certainly still actors in Germany whose bodies show what they are thinking and feeling, who can work up to a speech by silences, hesitations, slight and delicate movements, and can fill out pauses between speeches with appropriate gestures, connecting these pauses with the rest into a coherent whole. This use of mime to complement an actor's natural talent and to make him equal to the playwright's use of words, is however not so widespread as it should be for the benefit of those who come to the theater."

"But," said Wilhelm, "shouldn't natural talent be all that an actor, like any other artist, or indeed any human being, needs to enable him to reach the high goal he has set himself?"

"That should certainly be, and continue to be, the alpha and omega, beginning and end; but in between he will be deficient if he does not somehow cultivate what he has, and what he is to be, and that quite early on. It could be that those considered geniuses are worse off than those with ordinary abilities, for a genius can more easily than ordinary men be distorted and go astray."

"And yet," said Wilhelm, "will not a genius be able to save himself, to heal the wounds that he has inflicted on himself?"

"Not at all," said the stranger. "Or if so, then not very effectively. Nobody should ever believe that one's first youthful impressions can be counteracted. If a person is brought up in great freedom, surrounded by fine and beautiful objects, exposed to the company of good people, taught by excellent teachers to understand what he must first know in order to appreciate everything else, if he has learned what he will never need to unlearn, if his first actions are so guided that he will later be able to accomplish good things more easily and readily, without having to disaccustom himself from past tendencies, then he

will live a happier, better life than someone who expended his youthful energies in resistance and error. So much is talked and written about education;
and yet I see very few people who understand what that simple, noble, all-
embracing concept means, and who can translate it into action."

"That may well be true," said Wilhelm. "We are all so limited in our thinking,
that all we want is to make the other person exactly like ourselves. Happy are
those who are educated by Fate, each in his own way."

"Fate is a distinguished but costly tutor," the other replied with a smile. "I
would rather entrust myself to the reason of a human tutor. Fate, for whose
wisdom I have indeed the greatest respect, may well have in Chance a very
clumsy means through which to operate. For Chance rarely seems to bring
about exactly what Fate has decided."

"That seems to me a very strange way of thinking," Wilhelm replied.

"Nonsense!" said the stranger. "Almost everything that happens in the
world, will confirm what I am saying. Doesn't many a train of events begin by
displaying some lofty purpose and then end in sheer stupidity?"

"Surely, you're joking," said Wilhelm.

But the stranger continued: "And isn't the same true of the course of
individual experience? Let's suppose that Fate has destined someone to
become a good actor (and why shouldn't Fate provide us with good actors?),
but unfortunately chance has it that as a child this young man became so
addicted to the absurdities of the puppet theater that he finds stupidity not
only tolerable but even interesting, and cannot regard these childish impressions, which never fade and continue to attract, from the proper perspective."

"What got you on to the puppet theater?" asked Wilhelm in a state of some
alarm.

"It was just an arbitrary example. If you don't like it, we can take another.
Suppose Fate has destined a man to be a great painter and chance has it that
he spends his early years in dirty cottages, stables and barns: do you believe
that he would ever rise to purity, nobility and freedom of soul? The more
vigorously he took hold of all that was impure in his youth and tried to ennoble
it, the more this would take its toll of him in later life. For while he was trying
to eradicate these impurities, the hold that they exercised over him would
become ever stronger. If a man has spent his early years in base company, he
may later wish for better associates and yet yearn for those earlier companions, whose influence on him will always be colored by the recollection of the
youthful pleasures which can rarely be regained."

The rest of the company had dispersed while this conversation was going
on. Philine in particular had taken herself off right at the start. The two men
took a side path and rejoined the others. Philine produced the forfeits which
were redeemed in various ways, and while this was going on, the stranger
delighted the company, and particularly the ladies, with the most amusing
stories and his unabashed participation in the proceedings. And so the hours
passed most pleasantly in joking, singing, kissing and other sorts of light-
hearted amusements.

Chapter Ten

When they were about to start back, they looked around for the clergyman, but he had disappeared and was nowhere to be found. "That's not very nice of the man, who seemed otherwise to have such good manners, to leave people who have welcomed him so warmly, without even so much as saying goodbye," said Madame Melina. "I, for my part," said Laertes, "have been wondering all the time where I had seen that strange man before; and I meant to ask him, when we said goodbye." "I've had the same feeling," said Wilhelm, "and I certainly would not have let him go off without his telling us more about who and what he was. I must be very mistaken if I haven't spoken to him somewhere before." "And yet you could actually be wrong," said Philine. "This man gives one the impression of being someone familiar because he looks like a real person, not just anyone." "What does that mean?" said Laertes, "don't we also look like real persons?" "I know what I'm talking about," Philine replied, "and if you don't understand what I mean, then let it be. I'm not going to explain."

Two coaches drove up. Laertes was complimented for his thoughtfulness in ordering them. Philine took a seat next to Madame Melina, opposite Wilhelm, and the others fitted in where they could. Wilhelm's horse had been brought along too, so Laertes rode it back to town.

Once Philine had sat down, she started singing pretty little songs and switched the conversation to subjects which she insisted would make good plays. By this skillful maneuver she soon had our friend in the best of moods, and from his vast store of imaginative material he put together a whole play with acts, scenes, characters, and twists and turns of plot. It was decided to include some arias and songs and the words for these were composed. Philine, who was joining in everything, used some well-known melodies and sang them without further ado. She was having one of her best, her very best, days. She cheered up our friend by constant teasing, and he felt better than he had for a long time.

Since that cruel discovery which had torn him away from Mariane, Wilhelm had remained true to his vow to avoid the traps of all female embraces, to shun the fickle sex and keep his sorrow as well as his yearning and desire locked up in his own bosom. The conscientiousness with which he stuck to this resolve provided him with secret nourishment, but since his heart could not remain entirely unaffected, some kind of loving communication became a pressing need for him. So he went about once more in a youthful daze, joyfully watching every attractive object, and tolerant in his judgment of every pleasing person that met his eyes. It is easy to understand how dangerous such a frolicsome creature as Philine was bound to be for a man in his state of mind.

When they returned home, they found Wilhelm's room all set up for a reading, a table in the middle for the punch bowl.

At that time the latest thing in the theater was plays that were attracting great attention and approval from the public about medieval German knights. The old Blusterer had brought one of these, and it was decided that this should be the subject of the reading. They all took their seats, and Wilhelm began to read. The knights in armor with their ancient fortresses, the honesty, loyalty, righteousness and especially the solid independence of the characters—all these were received with great acclaim. The reader gave of his very best, and the assembled company were transported by what they heard. Between the second and third acts the punch arrived in a huge bowl, and since there was a great deal of toasting and drinking in the play, what could be more natural than that the audience each time joined the heroes in clinking their classes and singing the praises of the most favored personages in the play.

Everyone was enflamed by national fervor. Being Germans they were delighted to indulge poetically in a piece that expressed their own national character and played on their native soil. The vaults and cellars, ruined castles, moss, hollow trees, and especially the nocturnal gypsy scenes and secret tribunals had a stunning effect. Every one of the actors began to see himself in a helmet and cuirass, and the actresses envisioned themselves in big stiff collars proclaiming their Germanness to the public. Each of them decided immediately to assume a name from the play or from German history, and Madame Melina, who was pregnant, swore that if she bore a son, his name should be Adelbert, or if it were a daughter, she should be christened Mechthilde.

The applause grew louder and louder as the fifth act got underway, and toward the end, when the hero finally escaped his oppressor and the tyrant was punished, spirits were running so high that they all declared that they had never spent a better evening. Melina, excited by drink, was the most vociferous, and when the second punch bowl was emptied and midnight was approaching, Laertes swore full heartily that the lips of no other human being were worthy of drinking from these glasses, and with this assertion, threw his glass over his shoulder through the window on to the street. The others followed suit and despite the protestations of the innkeeper, who came running up, the punch bowl itself was broken into a thousand pieces so that, after such a festival, it should never be descrated by base liquor. Philine, apparently not so intoxicated as the others (the two girls were stretched out in dubious positions on the sofa) took a malicious pleasure in instigating the others to make even more noise. Madame Melina recited a few sublime verses, and her husband, rather unpleasant while in his cups, began to criticize the poor preparation of the punch—he had quite different ideas on how to give a party. When Laertes told him to be quiet, he became more and more obnoxious and noisy, and finally Laertes threw the remains of the punch bowl at his head, which merely increased the general tumult and hubbub.

Meanwhile the night watch had arrived and insisted on being let into the house. Wilhelm, who had drunk little but was excited by his reading, had his work cut out, by words and money, and with some assistance from the innkeeper, to quieten people down and get the rest of the group home, despite the miserable state they were in. When he himself got back, he fell into his bed without bothering to undress, overcome by sleepiness and in a thoroughly bad mood. Next morning when he opened his eyes and gloomily surveyed the mess and destruction of the previous evening, he felt thoroughly depressed at the sad results which a stimulating, spirited and well-intentioned work of literature had produced.

Chapter Eleven

After short reflection Wilhelm summoned the innkeeper and had the cost of the party and the damage put on his account. At the same time he was annoyed to learn that his horse had been so badly treated by Laertes, when he rode it home the previous day, that it was probably, as they say, "ill-shod," and the smith thought that there was little hope of making it serviceable again. On the other hand a greeting from Philine, who waved to him from her window, restored his spirits, and he went immediately to the nearest store to buy her a present to compensate for the powder knife she had given him. We must admit that he did not limit himself to equal compensation. For not only did he buy her a pair of delicate earrings, but also a hat, a scarf and various other things like those she had that first day thrown out of the carriage.

Madame Melina, who came to see him just when he was delivering these presents, found an occasion before dinner to speak to him seriously about his feelings for the girl, and he was utterly astonished at being, as he thought, so unjustly reproached. He declared most emphatically that it had never entered his head to start something with Philine, of whose mode of living he was well aware. He excused himself, as well as he could, for his friendly behavior to her, but this did not satisfy Madame Melina. On the contrary, she became increasingly ill-tempered when she noticed (as indeed she had to) that the flattery with which she herself had gained some degree of attention from Wilhelm, was insufficient to ward off the attacks of this younger, livelier creature who was more pleasantly endowed with nature's gifts.

At table they found Melina in a bad frame of mind, and Wilhelm was beginning to charge him with various pettinesses, when the host entered and announced that a harper was in the house. "You will certainly take pleasure in his playing and his songs: no one who hears him can fail to admire him and give him some reward."

"Let's not bother with him," replied Melina. "I'm not in the mood to listen to a droning musician and there are plenty of singers amongst us who are eager to earn a little." He accompanied these words with a malicious sidelong glance at Philine. She got the point, and decided to annoy Melina by favoring the musician. So she turned to Wilhelm and said: "Why can't we listen to the man? Are we to do nothing to escape this miserable boredom?" Melina was about to answer and a vigorous quarrel would probably have ensued if Wilhelm had not welcomed the man as he entered the room, and beckoned him towards them.

The strange appearance of the harper so astonished the company that he had already taken his seat before anyone had the heart to ask him anything or make some appropriate remark. His bald head was wreathed by a few grey hairs, and his large blue eyes peered gently from beneath heavy white eyebrows. He had a finely shaped nose, and a long white beard which, however, left his kindly mouth uncovered. His slender body was clothed from head to foot in a dark brown garment. He began to let his fingers glide gently over the strings of the harp, and the pleasing sounds he produced, immediately delighted the group.

"You sing, too, my dear old man, don't you?" said Philine.

"Give us something to please heart and mind," said Wilhelm. "An instrument should be just an accompaniment for the voice. Melodies, runs and passages without words and meaning seem to me like butterflies or colorful birds that swirl around before our eyes as we try to catch them and hold them. Whereas singing is like an airy spirit leading us heavenward and inducing our better self to follow."

The old man first looked at Wilhelm, then cast his eyes upward, plucked the strings a few times, and began to sing. The ballad paid tribute to the art of song and praised the work of singers, urging all to respect and honor them. He presented the song with such vigor and sincerity, that he seemed to have composed it at that moment specially for this occasion. Wilhelm could hardly resist throwing his arms around him, but the fear of being laughed at kept him in his seat; the others were already muttering silly remarks and arguing whether the old man was a priest or a Jew.

When they asked him who had written the song, he gave an evasive answer. He did, however, assure them that he knew a large number of songs which he hoped might please them. Most of the company were in a cheerful mood, and even Melina was receptive in his own way. So while they were all gossiping and joking with each other, the harper intoned a splendid song in praise of the pleasures of being together. He sang of harmony and grace in limpid, mellifluous phrases; but, suddenly, the music became harsh, discordant and troubled when he expressed his disapproval of acrimonious indifference, short-sighted enmities and the dangers of strife—shackles of the mind that everyone listening was all too ready to cast off as the melody of his song soared upwards into praise of all peacemakers and of men's joys at rediscovering each other.

When he had finished, Wilhelm exclaimed: "Whoever you may be, you have come into our midst bestowing blessings and new life on us, like a protective spirit. Please accept in return my thanks and respect. Be assured of our admiration; and be sure to tell us if you need anything."

The old man fell silent, letting his fingers glide gently over the strings of the harp, then plucked them firmly, and sang this song:

"What do I hear outside the gate,
Resounding on the drawbridge?
Bring your song into the hall
That we may hear it better!"
Thus spake the king, the page-boy ran,
The boy returned, the king cried out:
"Bring the old man within here!"

"My greetings to you, noble lords,
My greetings, beauteous ladies!
The sky is studded full with stars,
And who can name them rightly?
Inside this splendid noble hall
Close up, o eyes; this is no time
To gape and feast on wonders."

The singer pressed his eyelids close
And rich full tones he struck.
The knights looked proud and sternly on
The ladies bowed attentive heads.
The king took pleasure in the song,
And wishing to reward the bard,
A golden chain had straightway brought.

"O give me not that golden chain,
Bestow it on your warriors
Before whose bold and fierce visage
The enemy lances splinter.
Or give it to your chancellor,
That he may add its golden weight
To all his other burdens.

"My song soars freely like the bird's
That sounds from out the branches.
And music coming from the throat
Rewards itself right richly.
If I may but one gift entreat,
Then bring me now of your best wine
A draught in purest goblet."

The wine was brought; he drank it up,
The drink of sweet refreshment.
Thrice blessed he declared a house
Where gifts like this were trifles.
"And if you flourish, think of me,
And render unto God like thanks
As I for what you gave me."

When the singer, having finished, grasped a glass of wine that had been poured for him and drank it down with a grateful glance at his benefactors, general delight spread throughout the company. They applauded and expressed the wish that the wine would be good for his health and strengthen his aged limbs. He sang a few more ballads and the mood of all those present became even livelier.

"Do you know the tune to 'The Shepherd Dressed Himself for the Dance,' old man?" asked Philine. "Yes, I do," he said. "If you would sing and act it, I will be glad to do my part."

Philine stood up and was ready. The old man began playing the melody and Philine sang the song—which we cannot repeat for our readers because they might well think it in bad taste, or even indecent.

Meanwhile they were all getting merrier and merrier, drinking more and more wine, and beginning to make a lot of noise. Since the bad effect of such behavior was still all too vividly present in our friend's mind, he tried to break up the proceedings, giving the old man a handsome recompense for his labors. The others contributed something as well, and let him go and rest, looking forward to that same evening and the pleasure of another demonstration of his skill.

After the Harper had left, Wilhelm said to Philine: "Your favorite song didn't seem to me to have either poetic or moral distinction. But if you were ever to perform something that was decent, with the same freshness, originality and charm, you would certainly be applauded."

"Yes," said Philine. "It must be quite pleasant to warm oneself on ice."

"Moreover," said Wilhelm, "this fellow puts many an actor to shame. Did you notice how perfect his dramatic expression was in those romances? There was more live presence in his singing than in our stiff stage personages. Many plays are performed as if they were simply being narrated, whereas music that tells stories really touches us."

"You are unfair," Laertes objected. "I don't pretend to be a great actor or a great singer. But this I do know: when music accompanies bodily movements, enlivening and at the same time controlling them, and the manner of delivery and the expression needed are indicated to me by the musical composer, then I am a totally different person from when I have to create these for myself, as I have to in spoken drama, inventing my own tempo, my own manner of speaking, and always liable to be disturbed in this by my fellow actors."

"For my part," said Melina, "I must say that in one respect this fellow has put us all to shame, and in a most important respect. The strength of his talent is shown by the use he puts it to. Whereas people like us may be uncertain where the next meal is coming from, he persuades us to share our meal with him. He knows how to extract from us the money that we might well use to improve our lot—and all that for one little song. It seems such a nice thing, to squander the money that could have been used to give us and others a stable livelihood."

This remark was not exactly a pleasant turn. Wilhelm, who was the real target of the reproach, answered with some heat, and Melina, who was by no means the subtlest of persons, was reduced to repeating his objections in harsh and direct terms. "Two whole weeks have gone by," he said, "since we looked at those props and costumes. We could have bought them for a modest amount. You gave me reason to hope that you would advance the necessary sum, but I cannot see that you have given the matter any further thought, let alone come to a decision. If you had taken action, we would already be in business. You said you intended to leave on a journey, but you haven't done so; and you don't seem to have been sparing of your money lately. At least there are certain persons who are apparently all too ready to provide you with opportunities of getting rid of it faster."

This reproach, which was not totally unjustified, hit home. Wilhelm made some rejoinder, with some passion, even vehemence, and took the occasion to leave, just as the company was about to break up, explaining in no uncertain terms that he did not wish to stay longer with such unfriendly and ungrateful people. He hurried away in a bad humor, and took himself off to a stone bench in front of the inn, not noticing that, partly for pleasure and partly from irritation, he had drunk more than usual.

Chapter Twelve

After a short while, as he sat there racked by disturbing thoughts, and staring straight in front of him, Philine came sauntering through the door singing, and sat down beside him, or rather on him, for she edged up so close, laid her head on his shoulders, played with his curly hair, stroked him and talked in the sweetest manner. She urged him to stay, not to leave her alone with the others who bored her to death; she simply could not continue to exist under the same roof with Melina and had therefore moved over to the inn where Wilhelm was staying.

He tried in vain to get rid of her, and make her understand that he could and would not stay here any longer. She continued her entreaties and unexpectedly put her arm around his neck and kissed him fervently.

"Are you crazy, Philine?" he said, trying to break loose. "Making a public street a witness to caresses that I have in no wise deserved! Let me go. I cannot and I will not remain here."

"I will keep hold of you and kiss you here in public until you give me your word that you will do what I want. I'm just dying with laughter," she went on. "After these intimacies people will think we've been married just four weeks, and husbands who observe this tender scene will praise me to their wives as a model of childlike, unabashed affection."

At that moment some people passed by, and she caressed him so tenderly that he was obliged, in order to avoid a scandal, to play the role of the patient husband. Philine made faces at these people behind their backs and behaved so outrageously that he finally had to agree to stay on for today, tomorrow, and the next day.

"You're a regular stick-in-the-mud!" she said, letting go of him, "And I am a silly fool to waste such affection on you." She got up and sulkily walked away; then turned back laughing, and said: "But I suppose that's because I'm so crazy about you. I'm just going to fetch my knitting, so that I have something to do. Stay here, and let me find the stone man sitting on the same stone bench when I return."

Actually she was this time being quite unjust to him; for much as he tried to keep away from her, he would probably not have failed to respond to her caresses, if he had been alone with her in some leafy arbor. She for her part went into the house, darting a roguish glance at him as she left. He felt no particular compulsion to follow her; indeed her recent behavior had again been quite distasteful to him. And yet he got up from the bench, without really knowing why, and went after her.

He had just reached the door of the inn, when up came Melina, spoke to him in modest terms and apologized for those rather harsh words he had uttered during their recent dispute. "Don't think ill of me," he went on to say, "if in the state I'm in, I seem rather worried; but my concern for a wife, and perhaps soon for a child as well, prevents me from going on quietly from day to day, displaying pleasant emotions, as you are still able to do. Think it over, and if it is at all possible, do let me acquire those props. I won't be your debtor for long. And I will be eternally grateful to you."

Wilhelm, unwilling at that moment to be held up on the threshold when some irresistible attraction was impelling him towards Philine, spoke to him in a state of surprised distractedness and hasty generosity, saying: "If I can make you contented and happy, then I will not hesitate any longer. Go and arrange everything as seems fit. I am prepared to pay the money tonight or tomorrow morning." A handshake confirmed his promise, and he was delighted to see Melina hurry away down the street. But unfortunately he was prevented for a second time from entering the house, and this time in a more unpleasant manner.

A young man with a bundle on his back came rushing down the street towards Wilhelm who immediately recognized him as Friedrich. "I'm back!" he said, merrily rolling his big blue eyes and looking up at all the windows. "Where's Mademoiselle? Devil take me if I can live a day longer without seeing her!" The innkeeper, coming up, told him she was upstairs, and he leapt up the steps, leaving Wilhelm rooted to the spot. He would gladly have pulled the boy back by his hair, but fierce jealously cramped the flow of his spirits and of his thinking, and once he had recovered from this paralysis he felt more uneasy and more uncomfortable than ever before.

He went to his room, and there found Mignon occupied in writing. The child had for some time been applying herself diligently to writing down everything that she knew by heart, and giving it to her friend and master to correct. She was tireless at what she was doing, and did it quite well except that the letters were uneven and the lines not straight. In this too her body seemed to be at variance with her mind. Wilhelm, who, when he was at peace with himself, took great pleasure in the child's attentiveness, paid on this occasion little attention to what she showed him. She felt this and was especially distressed because she thought that this time she had done her work quite well.

Wilhelm was so restless that he walked up and down the corridors and back to the door of the house. A horseman came riding up, good-looking and sprightly, though quite mature in years. The innkeeper rushed up and greeted him as an old friend, saying: "Well, Mr. Stablemaster, are we once more to have the pleasure of your company?" "I'm just stopping here to feed my horses, then I really must ride to the estate to see that things are in order. Time is pressing, because the count is arriving tomorrow with his wife and they will be staying for a while in order to receive the Prince of *** and entertain him as best they can. The prince will probably set up headquarters in this neighborhood." "What a pity that you can't stay with us," said the innkeeper, "for we have interesting people in the house." A groom came and took the stablemaster's horse, while he was conversing with the innkeeper in the doorway and casting sidelong glances at Wilhelm.

When Wilhelm noticed that they were talking about him, he left and walked up and down the nearby streets.

Chapter Thirteen

Wilhelm was so restless and ill-tempered that he decided to look up the Harper in the hope that his music might dispel the evil spirits. He inquired where he lived and was directed to a shabby inn in a remote part of the town, and then up a flight of stairs to an attic room from which came the sweet sounds of the harp. The somber, deeply moving music was accompanied by anguished melancholy singing. Wilhelm crept up to the door. The old man was rhapsodizing, repeating stanzas, half singing, half reciting, and then, after a short while, Wilhelm heard something like this:

> Who never with hot tears ate his bread,
> Who never through the nighttime hours
> Sat weeping in sorrow on his bed,
> He does not know you, Heavenly Powers.
>
> You lead us into life, ordain
> That wretches pile up guilt from birth,
> And then you yield them up to pain;
> For all guilt is atoned on earth.

This mournful, heartfelt lament affected the listener deeply. It seemed to him as if the old man was at times prevented by tears from continuing to sing, and the strings of the harp resounded until the voice came in again, softly and with broken sounds. Wilhelm stood by the door, deeply moved, his own constricted heart opened up by the immense grief of the stranger. He was overcome by such fellow feeling that he did not, could not, restrain the tears brought to his eyes by the old man's bitter lamentation. The sorrows oppressing his heart all came out into the open. He abandoned himself completely to them, pushed open the door, and stood facing the old man who was sitting on his wretched bed, the only piece of furniture in the miserable room.

"Oh what feelings you have aroused in me, good old man!" he cried. "You have released everything that was hidden in my heart. But don't let me disturb you. Go on—and while you are soothing your own pains, you will make a friend happy." The old man was about to stand up and say something, but Wilhelm kept him from doing this. He had noticed at noon that the Harper did not speak readily. Instead Wilhelm sat down beside him on the straw sack that was his bed.

The old man dried his tears and asked with a friendly smile: "Why did you come? I was intending to see you this evening." "It's quieter here," Wilhelm replied. "Sing me whatever you have a mind to, whatever you're in a mood for—and just pretend I'm not here. It seems to me that today nothing can go wrong for you. I think you are very fortunate to be able to occupy yourself so pleasantly in your solitude, and, since you are a stranger everywhere, to find your dearest friend in your own heart."

The old man looked down at the strings of his harp, his fingers gliding softly over them, and then started to sing:

He who turns to solitude
Is soon, alas! alone.
Life comes to each, love comes to each,
And leaves him to his pain.
Oh leave me to my torment here,
And if I dwell in solitude
I'll never be alone.

A lover softly creeps and listens
Whether she is alone.
And so come creeping, day and night,
My sorrow and my pain
To me in all my solitude,
And in my solitary grave
At last leave me alone.

We could expend a great number of words and still not be able to convey the charm of the extraordinary conversation which our friend had with the curious stranger. The old man responded, as though agreeing with everything the young man said, by producing music that evoked all sorts of similar feelings and opened up the full range of the imagination.

Anyone who has been present at an assembly of pious people seeking a degree of purer, richer, more spiritual edification than is to be found within the church, will have some idea of the nature of this encounter. He will recall how the leader will adapt to what he is saying the verse of some hymn which directs the mind to where he himself is tending in his homily. Then someone in the group will break in with a different tune, a verse from another hymn. Then a third person will add something from still another hymn, with the result that the community of ideas in these various hymns is evoked, and each individual passage by reason of these associations takes on a new light, as if it had just been composed. A new synthesis is evolved out of familiar ideas and hymns and verses for this particular audience, in the enjoyment of which they are edified, quickened and fortified. In a similar way the old man wove together for his guest well known and unknown songs and snatches, and thereby set moving a complex of recent or more remote feelings, waking and slumbering, pleasant and painful emotions, from which only good could be expected for our friend in his present state.

Chapter Fourteen

On his way back Wilhelm did indeed begin to reflect more deeply on his present situation, and by the time he reached home, he had resolved to extricate himself from it. The innkeeper told him in confidence that Philine had made a new conquest in the person of the duke's stablemaster, and, having attended to his duties at the estate, this man had returned very quickly and up in her room was enjoying a good dinner with Philine.

At this very moment Melina arrived with a notary, and both went to Wilhelm's room, where Wilhelm somewhat reluctantly fulfilled his promise to Melina. He gave him a draft in the amount of three hundred thalers, which Melina immediately handed to the notary, receiving in exchange a document confirming the sale of all the theatrical effects which would early next day be handed over to Melina.

Just after the others had left, Wilhelm heard a terrible cry from somewhere in the house. It was a young person's voice, angry and threatening, and constantly interrupted by weeping and moaning. Then down the stairs it came, past his room, out on to the square. Curiosity impelled him to go downstairs and look: he found Friedrich in a state of frenzy. The boy was weeping, stamping, grinding his teeth, clenching his fists, and almost beside himself with anger and dismay. Mignon stood looking at him with amazement, and the innkeeper offered some sort of an explanation.

He said that on his return the boy had been cheerful and content, since Philine treated him well, and had gone around singing and dancing until the time when the stablemaster made her acquaintance. Since then—half boy and half man that he was—he had shown outbursts of temper by slamming doors and running up and down stairs. Philine had ordered him to wait at the table that evening, and at this he became even more sulky and defiant, so that finally instead of putting a dish of stew on the table he threw it between Mademoiselle and her guest, who were sitting quite close to each other. Whereupon the man gave him a couple of mighty clouts and threw him out. The innkeeper himself had been obliged to clean up the two; their clothes were in a sorry state.

When the boy saw the results of his revenge he burst out laughing while tears continued to roll down his cheeks. For a time he was intensely happy, but when he remembered the insult he had suffered from someone bigger than himself, he started howling again and threatening.

Pensively and somewhat disconcertedly Wilhelm observed this whole scene. What he saw was an exaggerated display of his own self, for he too had been consumed by fierce jealousy, and if his sense of propriety had not prevented him, he too would have indulged his wildest fancies, gleefully and maliciously harmed his beloved, and challenged his rival. He would gladly have obliterated everybody who seemed to be there just to exasperate him.

Laertes joined them, having also heard what had happened. He was rogue enough to encourage Friedrich when the angry boy asserted that the stablemaster would have to fight a duel with him, for he, Friedrich, had never taken insults. And if the fellow refused, he would take his revenge in some other way. Laertes was really in his element. He solemnly went upstairs and challenged the stablemaster in the boy's name. "That's amusing," said the man, "I hadn't expected such entertainment this evening." They went downstairs, Philine following them. "My boy," said the stablemaster to Friedrich, "you're a fine fellow and I won't refuse to fight with you. But since our ages and skills are so unequal that the whole affair will be somewhat bizarre, I propose rapiers instead of other weapons. Let's mark the buttons with chalk and whoever scores the most hits on the other's jacket shall be declared the winner and be treated to the best wine in town."

Laertes decided to accept this proposal, and Friedrich abode by his master's decision. The rapiers were brought. Philine sat down with her knitting, watching the two combatants with complete composure.

The stablemaster, who was a very good fencer, was obliging enough to spare his opponent by letting him achieve several chalk marks on his jacket, whereupon they embraced and the wine was brought in. The man wanted to know about Friedrich's home and his life, and Friedrich for his part spun a tale he had often told, which we will reserve for some other occasion.

The duel was for Wilhelm an additional externalization of his own feelings. He couldn't deny that he himself would have liked to direct a rapier, or still better, a sword, at the stablemaster, although he soon observed that the man was a far better fencer than he was. But he did not deign to cast on Philine a single glance, avoided anything that might betray his feelings, and once he had drunk several times to the health of the combatants, he hurried up to his room. There he was overcome by a host of unpleasant thoughts.

He recalled the time when his spirit was uplifted by an eager surge of boundless activity, full of hope and promise, a striving that knew no limits, swimming in the enjoyment of everything. But now, as he realized, he had fallen into a state of continual floundering, sipping at life instead of drinking deeply as before. He could not perceive clearly that there was an irresistible yearning which nature had imposed on him as a law of his being, and that this was being stimulated, but only half satisfied, and ultimately frustrated by circumstance.

It was therefore not surprising, whenever he considered his condition and his desire to work himself out of it, that he became completely confused. It was not right that, because of his friendship with Laertes, his attraction to Philine and his concern for Mignon, he should stay longer than was reasonable with these people in a place where he could foster his prime desire, fulfil it, so to speak, on the side, and still go on dreaming as before, without really setting himself a definite goal. He had thought to have enough strength to break loose from this situation, and leave. But now just a few moments ago he had entered on a business deal with Melina and had come to know the mysterious harper whose secret he was so anxious to discover. But, after much thinking, he decided that not even this should stop him from leaving—or at least he thought he had so decided. "I must leave," he cried out. "I want to leave." In a state of great agitation he threw himself into a chair. Mignon came into the room and asked if she might fix his hair for him. She came in very quietly; his curtness to her earlier that day had hurt her deeply.

There is nothing more moving than when a secretly nourished love and silently strengthened devotion suddenly finds itself face to face with the object that has hitherto been unworthy of its affection, but now at least realizes it. The bud that had been tightly closed for so long was ready to open, and Wilhelm's heart was ready to receive it.

She stood before him and saw his unrest.—"Master!" she said, "If you are unhappy, what shall become of Mignon?" "Dear creature," he said, grasping her hands, "you too are part of my sorrow. I must leave this place."—She looked into his eyes, which were dimmed with tears, and then threw herself on her knees before him. He held her hands; she laid her head on his knees and stayed quite still. He stroked her hair like a friend. She did not move. Suddenly he felt her twitching, a movement which began quite gently and then increased, spreading through all her limbs. "What is it, Mignon?" he cried. "What is the matter with you?" She raised her head, looked at him, then put her hand to her heart as if to stop some pain. He lifted her up and she fell onto his lap. He pressed her to him and kissed her. She did not respond, neither with her hands nor with any other movement. She kept clutching her heart and suddenly let out a cry which was accompanied by convulsive movements of her body. She jumped up, and then immediately fell down in front of him, as if every limb of her body were broken. It was a terrifying sight. "My child," he said, lifting her up and gripping her with his arms, "what is it?" — But the convulsions persisted, spreading from the heart into her dangling limbs. She was just hanging in his arms. He clasped her to his heart and covered her with tears. Suddenly she seemed taut again, like someone experiencing great bodily pain. All her limbs became alive again, and with renewed strength she threw herself around his neck, like a lock that springs shut, while a deep cleft opened up inside her and a flood of tears poured from her closed eyes on to his breast. He held her close. She wept tears such as no tongue can describe. Her long hair hung loosely around her as she wept, and her whole being seemed to be dissolving into a steady flood of tears. Her rigid limbs unfroze, her whole inner self poured itself out, and in the confusion of the moment Wilhelm feared that she might melt away in his arms so that nothing of her would remain. He grasped her more and more firmly to himself. "My child!" he cried, "My child! You are mine. Let that console you. You are mine! I will keep you. I will never leave you!" — Her tears continued. Finally she raised her head, and a gentle serenity lit up her face. — "My father!" she cried. "You will never leave me! You will be my father! — I am your child!"

From outside the door came the soft sounds of the harp. The old man was singing his most heartfelt songs, as an evening offering to his friend who, holding his child ever closer in his arms, experienced a feeling of the most perfect, indescribable bliss.

Book Three

Chapter One

Know you the land where lemon blossoms blow,
And through dark leaves the golden oranges glow,
A gentle breeze wafts from an azure sky,
The myrtle's still, the laurel tree grows high—
You know it, yes? Oh there, oh there
With you, O my beloved, would I fare.

Know you the house? Roof pillars over it,
The chambers shining and the hall bright-lit,
The marble figures gaze at me in rue:
"You poor poor child, what have they done to you?"
You know it, yes? Oh there, oh there,
With you, O my protector, would I fare.

Know you the mountain and its cloudy trails?
The mule picks out its path through misty veils,
The dragon's ancient brood haunts caverns here,
The cliff drops straight, the stream above falls sheer.
You know it, yes? Oh there, oh there
Our path goes on! There, Father, let us fare!

When Wilhelm looked around for Mignon the next morning he could not find her; but he heard that she had gone out early with Melina, who had left to fetch the costumes and other props.

Some hours later he recognized music outside his door, and assumed at first that this was the Harper; but he then heard the sound of a zither and the voice that began to sing was Mignon's. He opened the door for Mignon who came in and sang the song we have just communicated. The melody and the expression pleased Wilhelm greatly, though he could not make out all the words. So he asked her to repeat it, and explain it; then he wrote it down and translated it into German. He found, however, that he could not even approximate the originality of the phrases, and the childlike innocence of the style was lost when the broken language was smoothed over and the disconnectedness removed. The charm of the melody was also quite unique.

She intoned each verse with a certain solemn grandeur, as if she were draw-ing attention to something unusual and imparting something of importance. When she reached the third line, the melody became more somber; the words "You know it, yes?" were given weightiness and mystery, the "Oh there, oh there!" was suffused with longing, and she modified the phrase "Let us fare!" each time it was repeated, so that one time it was entreating and urging, the next time pressing and full of promise.

When she had finished the song a second time she paused, looked straight at Wilhelm, and asked: "Do you know that land?" "It must be Italy," Wilhelm replied. "Where did you get the song?" "Italy!" said Mignon in a meaningful tone; "if you go to Italy, take me with you. I'm freezing here." "Have you ever been there?" asked Wilhelm; but the child kept silent and not one word more could be elicited from her.

Melina, who came in, saw the zither and was delighted that it had been put into such good shape. It had been part of the props. Mignon had asked for it that morning, the Harper had restrung it, and the child showed a talent that they had not known about.

Melina had already taken possession of the whole wardrobe. Some members of the town council promised to get him a permit to put on performances. He was overjoyed and his face shone when he returned. He seemed a different person: gentle, polite to everyone, even obliging and considerate. He hoped he would be lucky as he was now able to give work to his friends who had been idle for quite a while and at a loss what to do. He could give them a fixed engagement for a time, though he regretted that at first he could not pay those excellent actors that fate had brought his way in a manner consonant with their ability and talents; he first had to settle his debt to their generous friend Wilhelm.

"I cannot tell you what a display of friendship this is on your part that ena-bles me to become the director of a theater. For when I first met you, I was in a very strange position. You will recall that at our first meeting I expressed my strong antipathy to the theater, but when I got married, I had to look around for an engagement, out of love for my wife who hoped thereby to find satisfac-tion and appreciation. I couldn't find anything, at least nothing lasting, but I did have the good fortune to meet several officials who sometimes could use someone who knew how to wield a pen, understood French and was experienced in bookkeeping. And so for a while things went quite well for me. I was fairly well paid, bought various things and my standard of living was quite respectable. But the commissions I had from my employers began to peter out, there was no hope of permanent support, and my wife was so desperately anxious to go onto the stage—unfortunately at a time when, because of her pregnancy, she could not expect to make the best impression on the public. But now I hope that the company which, thanks to your help, I am to direct, will be a good start for me and mine, and to you I will owe my future fortune, whatever it may turn out to be."

Wilhelm listened to these words with satisfaction, and all the actors were fairly content with what their new director had said, were secretly delighted at having secured an engagement so soon, and inclined to make do for the start with a small wage. Most of them considered what they were so unexpectedly being offered as a supplement they could not have counted on. Melina used this situation to talk to each of them individually, and to use every argument to persuade them that it was in their interests to sign their contracts without delay. As a result they gave little thought to this new arrangement, feeling sufficiently safeguarded by being able to terminate it any time at six weeks' notice.

The conditions of the agreement were then spelled out in proper form, and Melina was already thinking about what plays should be put on first in order to capture the public's interest. At this very moment a messenger came for the stablemaster, announcing the impending arrival of the count and countess and that he had been told to bring out the horses that he had in his charge.

Soon a heavily loaded carriage drew up in front of the inn. Two servants jumped down from the box of the coach, and Philine, true to character, was the first to be at hand in the doorway. "Who is that?" asked the countess as she went into the inn. "An actress, and at your Grace's service," the roguish girl replied, putting on a sober face, curtseying modestly, and kissing the lady's skirt. The count saw several people standing around, who also claimed to be actors and inquired how large the company was, where they had last performed, and who their director was. "If they are French," he said to his wife, "we might delight the prince with an unexpected pleasure by providing his favorite form of entertainment in our own house."

"Even if these people are unfortunately only Germans," said the countess, "we still might seriously think of letting them perform at the castle while the prince is there. They must have acquired some skill. The best way of entertaining a large number of people is to have some theater, and the baron will coach them."

With these words they went up the stairs and Melina introduced himself as the director. "Call your people together and present them to me," said the count, "so that I can see what they're like. I also want to see a list of the plays they would be ready to do."

Melina made a deep bow, hurried out of the room and came back with the actors. They pushed and shoved each other in all directions, some presenting themselves poorly as they hoped to please, and others no better because they adopted a silly manner. Philine showed great respect to the countess, who was extremely gracious and friendly, and the count took a good look at the others. He asked all of them what their specialties were, and told Melina that he should insist on maintaining set roles, an opinion that Melina accepted with the greatest respect.

The count then told each of them what he or she should particularly work at, what needed improvement in figure and posture, instructing them in what

Germans always lack and thereby revealing such unusual knowledge of these matters, that they all stood there in deep humility before such a distinguished connoisseur and lofty patron, hardly daring to breathe in his presence.

"Who's that fellow over there in the corner?" the count asked, staring at someone who had not yet been presented to him, and a thin man in a shabby coat with patches on the elbows and a wretched wig on this humble fellow's head came over to him. This was the man, familiar to us from the previous Book as Philine's favorite, who usually played pedants, teachers and poets, and took on those roles where someone has to be beaten or doused with water. He had acquired a rather unctuous, nervous, ridiculous manner of bowing, and his halting speech, so well suited to the roles he played, always made the spectators laugh, so that he was still considered a useful member of the troupe, and was always ready to take on an assignment and to please. He came up to the count, bowed in his own special way, and answered all his questions about the gestures that he employed in his roles. The count observed him with pleasure and attention, and then, after some reflection, he said to his wife: "Just look at that man, my dear. I guarantee he's a good actor, or could become one." The fellow was so overjoyed at this that he made the stupidest bow and the count just burst out laughing, and said: "This man is excellent. I bet he could play anything he has a mind to, and it's a shame that he hasn't been given better parts."

It was rather irritating for the others that the Pedant should be singled out, but Melina did not take it to heart. He agreed wholeheartedly with the count, and added in a tone of the greatest respect: "Yes, indeed. All he and some of the others have lacked, is the encouragement of someone as knowledgeable as your Excellency."

"Is this the whole company?" the count asked. "A few of them aren't here just now," Melina shrewdly replied, "but we could soon get some others from nearby to make up the complement, if we had the necessary funds." Meanwhile Philine was saying to the countess: "There's quite a handsome young man upstairs who would do well as *jeune premier*." "Why can't we see him?" the countess asked. "I'll go fetch him," said Philine and hurried out of the door.

She found Wilhelm still occupied with Mignon, but she persuaded him to go downstairs with her. He followed her somewhat unwillingly, but with some curiosity, for having heard mention of persons of high station, he was anxious to become acquainted with them. He walked into the room and his eyes immediately encountered those of the countess directed at him. Philine took him to the lady whilst the count was busy with the others. Wilhelm bowed to the countess and answered with some confusion the questions this charming lady addressed to him. Her beauty, her youthful grace, her elegance and refinement of manner made the most pleasing impression on him, all the more so because a certain shyness—even embarrassment—was in her words and gestures. He was also introduced to the count, who paid little attention to him, and instead walked up to the window with his wife and seemed to be asking her about something. It was apparent that her opinion was entirely in agreement with his. She seemed to be urging him eagerly to follow his own inclinations.

He came back to the group and said: "I can't stay here any longer at the moment, but I will send a friend of mine to you, and if you make reasonable conditions and work really hard, I am disposed to let you play at the castle." They all expressed their delight at this, especially Philine, who ardently kissed the hands of the countess. "Now listen, little one," the lady said, patting the cheeks of the flighty girl, "Listen, my child. You come back to me, and I will keep my promise. But you must be better dressed." Philine apologized for having so little to spend on her wardrobe, and the countess immediately ordered one of her ladies-in-waiting to bring up an English hat and a silk scarf, which could easily be taken out from the luggage. The countess began to dress up Philine, who continued behaving delightfully with a hypocritical expression of innocence on her face.

The count escorted his wife down the stairs. She greeted the whole company in passing, turning again to Wilhelm, and finally saying, in the most gracious manner: "We'll see each other again soon."

These favorable prospects brought new life to the whole company. Everyone began to talk about his or her hopes and wishes, the ideas each had in his head, the roles they would play and the applause they would receive. Melina began to think of how he could quickly make some money by a few performances to the townsfolk, which would at the same time get the actors in trim. Others went into the kitchen to order a better meal than they had been used to.

Chapter Two

A few days later the baron arrived and was received by Melina with some trepidation. The count had described him as a connoisseur, and it was to be feared that he would soon discover the deficiencies of the little company and realize that this was not an organized troupe, because they could hardly get together an adequate cast for any play. But both the director and the other members were relieved to discover in the baron a man with great affection for the native theater, a man for whom every actor and any company was a source of welcome pleasure. He greeted them all ceremoniously, and expressed his delight at having the good fortune to come so unexpectedly into contact with German theater and being able to introduce the national muses into the castle of his relatives. Thereupon he drew from out of his pocket a notebook from which Melina hoped to learn the terms of their engagement; but it turned out to be something quite different. For the baron asked them to listen carefully to a play he had himself composed and wished them to perform. They gathered round, delighted at the prospect of winning the favor of such an important person at such little cost, although, noticing the length of the manuscript, they feared they were in for quite a long sitting. Which indeed it turned out to be. The play was in five acts and was one of those which seem never to end.

The hero was a noble, virtuous, generous but unappreciated and persecuted man, who finally won out over his adversaries, dispensing the finest poetic justice, but not pardoning them immediately.

During the reading of the play all of the actors had ample opportunity to think about themselves and move from inadequacy into a state of jubilant self-satisfaction and radiant future prospects. Those who did not find in it a suitable role for themselves, decided that it was a bad play, and its author untalented; others, noticing a passage which would earn them acclaim, to the great satisfaction of the author, followed the reading with appreciation.

The business end of things was soon settled. Melina succeeded in negotiating with the baron a contract that was favorable to him, and did not reveal its terms to the other actors.

He spoke to the baron in passing about Wilhelm, saying that he was well suited to be a writer of plays and had no mean acting talent. The baron treated Wilhelm immediately as a colleague, and Wilhelm recited for him some brief pieces that, with a few other relics, had by chance survived from the conflagration that had consumed most of his manuscripts. The baron praised the plays and Wilhelm's delivery, taking for granted that Wilhelm would come to the castle with the others, and promising them all, as he left, the best reception, comfortable accommodation, good food, appreciation and rewards; and Melina guaranteed them a fixed amount of pocket money.

It is easy to imagine the good mood that prevailed amongst the actors after this visit. Instead of an anxious, lowly existence, they saw themselves about to enter on a life of honor and comfort. They amused themselves by calculating all this in advance, and dismissed as improper the idea of keeping any money in their pockets.

Wilhelm considered whether he should go with them to the castle or not, and decided that there were several good reasons to do so. Melina hoped by this advantageous engagement to repay part of what he had borrowed, and Wilhelm, always eager to meet people, did not wish to forego the opportunity of getting to know the "world" from which he hoped to derive insights on life, on himself and on art. Also he did not dare admit how much he wished to become better acquainted with the beautiful countess. He tried to persuade himself of the great advantages that would accrue to him by closer contact with the world of sophistication and wealth. He thought about the count and countess and the baron, the confidence, grace, and ease of their manner, and, once he was alone, he broke out into words of rapture: "Thrice happy and praiseworthy are those whose high birth elevates them above the lower classes of humanity. They never—not even occasionally—need to labor under conditions which afflict so many good people with constant anxiety their whole life long. From their higher position, their view must be clear-sighted, and every step they take in life light-footed. By their birth they are, so to speak, in a ship that, in the journey we all must undertake, can profit from favorable winds and can wait till unfavorable ones have passed, whereas we others swim, struggling for our lives, without much help from favorable winds, and perishing in rapidly exhausted energy. What comfort and ease an inherited income provides! How well a business flourishes if it is based on fixed capital, so that every faulty transaction need not result in inactivity! Who can judge the value or lack of value of earthly goods better than someone who has been able to enjoy these from early years! Who can apply his mind earlier to what is necessary, useful and true than he who becomes aware of errors at an age when he still has sufficient energy to begin a new life."

Thus did our friend ascribe good fortune to those who dwell high up; but also to those who approach such lofty realms, and find sustenance there. He praised his guiding spirit for leading him upward on this path.

Meanwhile Melina, having racked his brains to distribute type roles to the various members of the company (as the count wanted and he himself believed desirable), and specifying to each of them what their particular contribution would be, was very satisfied to discover, when he had finally worked this out, that every member of the little company was prepared to take on this or that role. Laertes usually took the part of lovers and Philine that of the maids. The two young girls divided the innocent and the sentimental sweethearts between them, and the old Blusterer played himself and that was best of all. Melina thought he could play the part of the gentleman; his wife, to her great chagrin, had to take on the young women's parts, even that of the affectionate mothers. And because there were not many pedants or poets ridiculed in modern plays the count's favorite had to play presidents and ministers because these were usually represented as wicked and in the fifth act came to a bad end. As chamberlain or such like Melina gladly suffered the insults that trusty German gentlemen were subjected to in many popular plays of the time, because in such scenes he could dress up and affect the airs of a courtier, which he believed he had at his command.

Before long, more actors began to arrive from different parts of the country, and were taken on without much testing and without any special conditions. Several times Melina tried in vain to persuade Wilhelm to play the *jeune premier*. Wilhelm took great interest in all the preparations, although the new director did not give him much credit for his trouble. Melina believed that, with his honorific position he had assumed greater powers of insight. One of his favorite occupations was to make cuts to reduce all plays to a suitable length, without any other considerations. He was encouraged in this by the fact that the public was well satisfied, and those with taste declared that the theater at the court was nothing like as well established as theirs.

Chapter Three

The time finally came to move to the count's castle. Coaches and carriages were awaited to transport the whole company. Various arguments ensued as to who should ride with whom and where everybody should sit. The order and arrangement was eventually worked out with some difficulty but little effect. Fewer vehicles than had been expected came at the appointed hour, and everyone had to make do. The baron, following on horseback, said the reason was that at the castle everything was in a state of confusion, not merely because the prince was to arrive several days early, but also because unexpected visitors had already arrived. They were getting short of space, so the actors could not be so well housed as they had been promised, the baron was sorry about that.

They distributed themselves as best they could in the carriages, and since the weather was passable and the castle was not a great distance away, the sprightlier ones preferred to walk rather than wait for the coaches to come back to fetch them. The caravan left with shouts of joy and for the first time not worrying how the innkeeper was to be paid. The count's castle hovered before their minds like a fairy palace, they were the happiest and luckiest people on earth, and everyone associated this day in his thoughts with what he conceived to be fortune, honor and well-being.

Even unexpected heavy rain did not divert their minds from such pleasant thoughts; but when it kept up and got steadily worse, many of them did feel a certain discomfort. Night began to fall and nothing was more welcome than the sight of the count's residence, with lights on every floor, gleaming towards them from a hill, so that they could count the windows. As they came nearer they could see that even the side-tracts were brightly illuminated. Each of them wondered which would be his quarters, and most of them would have been quite satisfied with a small room under the roof or on the side.

They drove through the village past an inn. Wilhelm called a halt so that he could alight, but was told that there was absolutely no room at all there. The count had taken over the whole inn because those unexpected guests had arrived, and at every door the name of the guest occupying it, was written in chalk. And so our friend was obliged, against his will, to drive with the others into the castle courtyard.

They saw cooks busy around the kitchen fires in one of the side-buildings, and this cheered them up considerably. Servants bearing lighted candles came running up to the staircase of the main building, and our travelers' spirits bubbled over in anticipation. But how amazed were they when this reception dissolved into a torrent of abuse! The servants yelled at the coachmen for coming in on this side; they should turn around and go to the old part of the castle — there was no room here for guests! This unfriendly and unexpected reception was accompanied by jeering remarks; they laughed to see the newcomers exposed once again to the rain because of this mistake. It was still pouring, there were no stars in the sky, and the whole company was now dragged down a bumpy road between two walls into the old castle, which had stood unoccupied since the count's father had built the new one. The carriages came to a halt in the courtyard or in the long arched gateway, and the drivers from the village unharnessed the horses and rode home.

Since no one came forward to welcome them, they all got out, called for assistance, then went to look for it, but without any results. Everything remained dark and silent. The wind blew through the open gate, and the old turrets and courts, hardly visible in the darkness, made a gruesome effect. Everybody was freezing and shuddering, the women trembling, the children crying. Their impatience was mounting with every moment, for this sudden change of fortune had caught them quite unawares and completely robbed them of their composure.

They continued to wait for someone to open the doors for them, mistaking the sound of the rain and the wind for the steps of an approaching steward, and there they stayed for quite a long time, losing their tempers but doing nothing about their situation. It never occurred to any of them to go over to the new castle and ask for help from some sympathetic soul. They could not understand where their friend the baron was and were in an exceedingly troublesome state.

At last some people did arrive, and were recognized by their voices as those who had followed the carriages on foot. They reported that the baron had fallen from his horse and seriously hurt his foot. They too had gone first to the new castle and been angrily told to come here.

The whole company was completely perplexed; discussed what to do and came to no decision. At last a light approached from a distance, and they gave a sign of relief; but their hopes of deliverance were soon dashed when they saw that this was the count's stablemaster with a groom holding a lantern to light his path. The stablemaster inquired eagerly after Mademoiselle Philine; she detached herself from the others, and he offered to escort her to the new castle, where a place was reserved for her with the countess's ladies-in-waiting. Without a moment's hesitation she accepted his offer, grasped his arm and, leaving her trunk in the care of the others, was about to rush off with him, when their path was barred and the stablemaster bombarded with questions and requests, so that, in order to escape with his beloved, he had to promise them everything and assured them that the castle would soon be opened up and they themselves well lodged. They watched his lantern disappear from sight, and waited a long time for another light and new hope to appear; but nothing came. Then finally, after much waiting, grumbling and cursing, they saw it coming, and were again consoled and hopeful.

An old servant opened the door of the old building, and they all rushed inside. Each attended to his own possessions, unloading them and bringing them into the house. Most of the things, like the owners themselves, were soaked through. There was only one light, so things went very slowly, with a good deal of shoving, stumbling and falling down. They asked for more lights, they asked for a fire. The uncommunicative servant was obliged to leave his lantern for them, went away, and did not come back.

Then they began to search through the house. The doors of all the rooms were standing open. There were massive stoves, tapestry wallcoverings and inlaid floors as reminders of past splendor, but no ordinary household furniture, no tables, no chairs, no mirrors, just a few huge empty bedsteads, stripped of necessities as well as decoration. So they used their wet boxes and knapsacks as seats; some of our tired wanderers even stretched out on the floor. Wilhelm seated himself on some steps, with Mignon's head on his knees. She was restless, and when he asked her what was wrong, she said, "I'm hungry!" He found that he had nothing to give her, and the rest of the company had already used up their provisions; so he had to leave the poor creature hungry. He had been uninvolved in what was going on and meditative, vexed and angry that he had not stuck to his own intention and stayed at the inn, even if he had to sleep on the attic floor.

The others all behaved in accordance with their character. Some of them brought down a pile of old wood, lugged it into one of the huge fireplaces in the room, and set it alight with shouts of glee. But unfortunately their hope of drying and warming themselves was to be frustrated by the fact that this particular fireplace was purely ornamental and the chimney had been bricked up, so that the smoke came pouring back into the rooms, while the wood was so dry that it crackled into flames and shot out into the room, fanned by the draught through the broken windowpanes and darting hither and thither, so that it was feared that the whole castle might catch on fire. They separated the burning wood, stamped on it, doused it, and that made even more smoke. The whole situation became unbearable and everyone was by now quite desperate.

Wilhelm had retreated from the smoke into a distant room. Mignon followed him, bringing with her a well-dressed servant carrying a brightly burning pair of candles who turned to Wilhelm and said, handing him a fine porcelain dish of fruit and sweetmeats: "The young lady over there sends you these with the request that you join the company." He then added somewhat frivolously: "She asked me to tell you that everything is fine with her, and that she would like to share her satisfaction with her friends." Nothing could have surprised Wilhelm more than this message: since the episode on the stone bench he had treated Philine with open scorn, quite determined never to have anything more to do with her. He was just about to return the gift when he caught an imploring expression on Mignon's face; so he sent back his thanks on Mignon's behalf, but for himself firmly declined the invitation. He asked the servingman to pay some attention to the needs of the others, and inquired after the baron. He was told that the baron was confined to his bed, and, so far as he knew, had given orders to someone else to look after the needs of the actors who were so miserably housed.

The man went away, leaving Wilhelm one of his candles which, for lack of a chandelier, he had to fix on one of the windowsills, so that at least all four walls of the room were illuminated as he pursued his various thoughts. But it still took a long time before arrangements were made so that the guests could go to their rest. More candles were brought in, though without snuffers, then some chairs, then, one hour later, blankets, then pillows (all wet), and it was long past midnight when finally mattresses and sacks of straw were brought in, which, if these had been provided first, would have been most welcome.

Meanwhile some food and drink was delivered, which was consumed with few objections, although it looked like an untidy mess of leftovers instead of an indication of the respect usually paid to guests.

Chapter Four

The ill manners and impertinence of some in the company added to the restlessness and discomfort of that night. They teased one another, woke each other up, and played all sorts of tricks between them. The next morning everyone complained about their "good friend" the baron for having misled them and giving them such a false picture of the orderliness and comfort which was to be theirs. But to their amazement and consolation the count himself came to see them quite early, accompanied by several servants, and inquired after their circumstances. He was very angry when he learned how badly they had been treated. The baron, limping, blamed the steward for not carrying out his orders and gave him what he thought was a real dressing down.

The count immediately gave orders that while he was still there, everything should be done to ensure the greatest possible comfort for his guests. Up came several officers who straightway made the acquaintance of the actresses, and the count had the whole company introduced to him, calling each by his or her name and leavening the interviews with some jocular remarks, so that everybody was simply delighted with such a gracious lord. Wilhelm was the last to be presented, with Mignon clutching him. He apologized as best he could for being so bold, but the count seemed to accept his being there as a foregone conclusion.

There was one man standing near the count, whom they thought was an officer, though he was not wearing a uniform. He was engaged in conversation with Wilhelm, and seemed somehow superior to the others. He had big blue eyes gleaming from beneath a high forehead, and blond hair loosely combed back. His medium height gave him a sturdy, firm and rather stolid appearance. His questions were pointed, and he seemed to have considerable understanding of what he inquired about.

Wilhelm asked the baron about this man, but the baron had little good to say about him. He was referred to as the major, was really the prince's favorite, attended to his most private business and was considered his right arm. There was even reason to believe that he was the prince's natural son. He had been with embassies in France, England and Italy, and was treated everywhere as a person of distinction, which made him conceited. He professed to know German literature through and through, and indulged in constant shallow mockery of it. The baron for his part had given up all contact with him, and thought that Wilhelm would do well to maintain a certain distance, for ultimately he did harm to everybody. He was known as Jarno, but no one knew what to make of such a name. Wilhelm had nothing to say, for, although the man had something cold and repellent about him, he felt a certain attraction toward him.

The actors now all had their separate quarters in the castle, and Melina gave strict orders that they should behave properly, the women keep to themselves, and everybody apply themselves to their roles and concentrate their thoughts on art. He posted rules and regulations, each consisting of several points, on all the doors. Fines were fixed and had to be deposited in a communal box.

Little attention was paid to these strictures. Young officers strolled in and out, joking with the actresses in what was certainly not the most refined manner, played tricks on the actors, and created havoc with Melina's attempts at policing his company before these had had time to establish themselves. People raced through the rooms, disguising themselves and hiding from each other. Melina, who had at first shown some seriousness, was soon driven to distraction by all this mischief, and when the count summoned him to see the place where the stage was to be set up, everything became worse. The young gentlemen, egged on by some of the actors, began to engage in stupid pranks which got coarser and coarser, so that it seemed as if the whole castle had been occupied by a frenzied troop of soldiers. The noise and confusion continued until mealtime.

The count had taken Melina into a large hall which was still part of the old building but connected to the new castle by a gallery. In this room a small stage could very well be set up, and the knowledgeable lord of the house explained how he wanted everything arranged.

Work was begun at great speed. The frame of the theater was set up and decorated, and the sets put together from what they had in their baggage that was usable; what they still needed was assembled with the help of some resourceful members of the count's entourage. Wilhelm took part in all this, making sure the perspectives were right, measuring distances, and generally concerned that nothing should look clumsy. The count, who often looked in, was very satisfied, explained how they should do some particular thing— rather than the way they were doing it—and showed remarkable artistic sense.

Then the rehearsals began in earnest. They would have had plenty of time and space, if they had not been constantly interrupted by the many strangers. More and more such guests kept arriving daily, and every one of them wanted to take a look at the company of actors.

Chapter Five

For some days the baron had been holding out to Wilhelm the hope of being personally presented to the countess. "I have told this excellent lady so much about your intelligent and very moving plays," he said, "that she is very eager to talk with you and hear you read one or the other of them. So be prepared, at the first signal from her, to come right over, for she will certainly be sending for you when she next has a morning that is not taken up with other things." Wilhelm should read the epilogue first, in order to make a particularly favorable impression. The lady had said how much she regretted that Wilhelm had come at such a busy time and that he had been obliged to make do with the rest of the troupe in the old part of the castle with such poor lodging.

Wilhelm took great pains choosing the play with which he should make his debut in the world of the great. "Up till now," he said to himself, "you have labored away quietly for yourself, and the approval you have received was only from a few personal friends. For a time you were in a state of complete despair as to whether you had any talent at all; and you are still deeply concerned whether you are on the right path and whether you have as much talent for the theater as you have liking for it. What you are about to attempt, in a private room where no theatrical illusion is possible and before experienced listeners, is a much riskier enterprise than it would be elsewhere, and yet I would not willingly forego the pleasure of regaining contact with previous joys and expanding my hopes for the future."

He read through several of his plays with close attention, making corrections here and there, then read them aloud in order to get the right tone and expression, and slipped into his pocket the one he had worked at most and hoped to gain most respect for, when one morning he was summoned in to the presence of the countess.

The baron had assured him that she would be there with one other lady who was one of her best friends. As he entered the room the Baroness von C** came towards him, expressed her pleasure at meeting him and presented him to the countess, who was just having her hair done and received him with friendly words and glances. Unfortunately, however, he saw Philine kneeling beside the countess's chair and engaged in all sorts of nonsense. "This dear child," said the baroness, "has been singing us a variety of songs. Do finish the one you have just started," she said to Philine, "so that we don't miss any of it."

Wilhelm listened very patiently to Philine's ditty, wishing the while that the hairdresser would leave before he began his reading. He was offered a cup of chocolate, and the baroness herself brought him a biscuit, but he took no pleasure in this, being too eager to recite to the lovely countess something that might interest her, and earn him her good graces. Philine was also very much in his way, for as a listener she had often been a nuisance. Anxiously he watched the hands of the hairdresser, hoping that his creation would any moment be completed.

Meanwhile the count had come into the room to inform them of the guests who would be arriving that day, and how the day should be divided up. He also mentioned various domestic matters that were liable to come up. After he had left, several of the officers sent a message asking the countess's permission to pay their respects at this time, because they would have to ride off before she went to table. Her valet de chambre having by now finished doing her hair, she asked the officers to come in.

Meanwhile the baroness was doing all she could to keep our friend entertained, and giving him her whole attention, to which he responded respectfully, albeit somewhat distractedly. Every now and again he would finger the manuscript in his pocket, hoping for the blessed moment to arrive, and almost losing his patience when a peddler was admitted to the room, who infuriatingly proceeded to open up all his boxes, chests and cases one after the other, displaying all his merchandise with the importunateness common in those of his trade.

More and more people came into the room. The baroness looked at Wilhelm and then to the countess. He noticed this, without appreciating the reason. This became clear to him only when he arrived back in his room after a fruitless hour of nervous waiting, and found a beautiful English wallet, which the baroness had managed to slip into his pocket. Soon after this the little moorish servant of the countess brought him a handsomely embroidered vest, without clearly indicating where it came from.

Chapter Six

The rest of that day was spoilt for Wilhelm by mixed feelings of irritation and gratitude, until the evening brought him a new task when Melina informed him that the count had spoken about a prologue to extol the prince on the day of his arrival. In it the qualities of this great hero and friend of humanity were to be personified. His various virtues should appear side by side praising him and proclaiming the honor of this noble personage; finally, his bust should be crowned with wreaths of laurel and flowers, and his decorated initials should shine forth from beneath a coronet. The count had entrusted Melina with providing the necessary verses as well as everything else that would be needed, and Melina hoped that Wilhelm would help him in what ought to be something that came quite easily to him.

"What!" said Wilhelm petulantly, "Are we to have nothing but portraits, illuminated initials and allegorical figures to honor a prince who, to my mind, deserves quite a different demonstration of acclaim. How can an intelligent man be flattered by seeing himself displayed in effigy and his name glittering on oiled paper! My fear is that, with our restricted range of costumes, the allegory might give rise to inappropriate jokes. If you want to do this or have it done for you, I have no objections; but I must ask you to leave me out of it."

Melina apologized, saying that the count had only given rough instructions, and it was entirely left to them to arrange the whole affair as they thought fit. "I will be very glad," said Wilhelm after hearing this, "to contribute to the pleasure of our noble lord, and my muse has never had so pleasing an assignment as to speak out, even hesitantly, in praise of such a worthy prince. I will think the matter over, and perhaps I may succeed in getting our little company to put on something that will make an impression."

From this moment on Wilhelm seriously pondered the task that was facing him. And before he went to sleep that night, he had it all fairly well sketched out. The next morning he got up early, completed the plan, worked out the individual scenes and even set down on paper some of the more imposing passages and the verses for the songs.

Wilhelm hastened to see the baron in order to ask him about certain details and lay before him his plan. The baron was well pleased, but somewhat perplexed, for, the evening before, he had heard the count talking about quite a different play which he had said was to be turned into verse.

"I do not believe it is the count's intention to have the play exactly as he described it to Melina," said Wilhelm. "Unless I am mistaken, all he was trying to do was to give us a hint as to the right type of thing. A connoisseur and man of taste indicates to an artist what he wants, but leaves it up to him how it should be produced."

"You're quite wrong," said the baron. "The count will insist that the play be performed exactly as he indicated. Your work does indeed have a remote resemblance to what he had in mind, and if we are to succeed in deflecting him from his first intentions, then we shall need the help of the ladies. The baroness in particular is superb at such operations; but the question will be whether your plan appeals to her sufficiently for her to espouse it. If it does, then everything will be all right."

"We need the assistance of the ladies anyway," said Wilhelm, "for our performers and costumes will hardly suffice for this performance. I am reckoning on the assistance of several pretty young children I have seen running about the house, who seem to belong to the valet and the steward."

He asked the baron to make the ladies acquainted with his plan. The baron returned soon afterwards with the news that the ladies would like that evening to talk to Wilhelm in private. They would pretend to be indisposed and retire to their chamber when the gentlemen sat down to cards, which would be a more serious affair than usual because of the arrival of a general. Wilhelm would be conducted there by way of a secret staircase, and then be in the best position to given account of his project. The element of furtiveness made the whole occasion into a doubly attractive prospect, especially for the baroness who was as excited as a child at the thought of this clandestine meeting arranged without the approval of the count.

Toward evening Wilhelm was fetched at the appointed time and cautiously led up to the ladies' apartment. The manner in which the baroness received him in the small anteroom reminded him of former happy occasions. She conducted him to the countess's room, and there then began a whole series of questions. He put forward his plan with so much enthusiasm and vigor that the ladies were immediately taken by it. And our readers will surely allow us to acquaint them with it.

The play was to begin with a pastoral scene in which children performed a dance representing a game of changing places. This should be followed by an exchange of pleasantries and culminate in a round dance to a merry song. Then the Harper and Mignon would come on, and the countryfolk gather round them, attracted by their strange appearance. The old man would sing songs about peace, repose and happiness and then Mignon would perform the egg dance. This atmosphere of innocent joy should be disrupted by the sounds of martial music, and the whole company set upon by a troop of soldiers, with the men trying to defend themselves but being captured, and the women fleeing and being brought back. Just when everything seems to be collapsing into disorder, a certain person appears—the author had not finally decided who this should be—and announces that the leader of the army is approaching, and order is restored. The character of this heroic leader would now be described in all its finest features, safety from every attack will be assured, and arrogance and violence put an end to. Then should follow a general celebration in honor of the magnanimous captain of the army.

The ladies were well satisfied with all this, but maintained that there must be something allegorical in the play to be acceptable to the count. The baron proposed that the leader of the attacking soldiers should be presented as the spirit of discord and violence, and that Minerva should restrain him with shackles toward the end, announce the arrival of the hero, and proclaim his praises. The baroness assumed the responsibility for persuading the count that the plan he had suggested would be adhered to with only a few minor alterations; but she insisted that the bust, initials and coronet must appear at the end of the play, or else the whole performance would have lost its raison d'être.

Wilhelm, who had already sketched the fine words that he would place in Minerva's mouth in praise of his hero, objected for a while to what the baroness was insisting on, but finally gave way, because he felt pleasantly compelled to do so. The beautiful eyes of the countess and her charming manner would quite easily have persuaded him to abandon his most cherished ideas, the unity of the composition together with every contributing detail that he so much desired, and to act against all his poetic convictions. He faced a real struggle with his middle-class state of mind when, during the casting, the ladies insisted that he himself should play one of the roles.

Laertes was given the role of the mighty god of war. Wilhelm should play the leader of the countryfolk, who had some very nice and impassioned lines to speak. He objected at first, but finally had to give in, having no excuse after the baroness had explained to him that theater at this castle was really only a social affair in which she too would be happy to participate, if they could find

a proper way to include her. The ladies then dismissed him with many signs
of their friendly feelings toward him. The baroness assured him that he was a
most exceptional person, and accompanied him back to the staircase, wishing
him goodnight with a clasp of the hands.

Chapter Seven

Wilhelm was fired up by the sincere interest shown by the ladies and his own
description of the action of the play; the whole structure now became clear to
him, and he spent most of the night and next morning carefully composing dialogue and songs. He was almost finished, when he received a summons to go
to the new part of the castle where the count, having just finished breakfast,
wished to speak to him. He entered the hall, and once again it was the baroness
who came to meet him, and, under the pretext of wishing him a good morning,
whispered in his ear: "Don't tell him anything about the play, except in answer
to his questions."

"I am told," said the count, "that you are busily working at my prologue in
honor of the prince. I approve of the idea of bringing in Minerva, but I have
been wondering how she should be costumed so as not to arouse offense. I
have therefore asked that all the books in my library which include a picture
of her should be brought here." And at that very moment in came several
servingmen with huge baskets containing books of all shapes and sizes.

Montfaucon's *Antiquity Illustrated*, catalogues of Roman sculptures, gems
and coins, together with all kinds of treatises on mythology were consulted
and the representations of Minerva compared with each other. But even that
did not satisfy the count, whose excellent memory recalled all sorts of
Minervas from title pages, vignettes and other places. And so one tome after
another had to be fetched from the libary, and the count was soon surrounded
by piles and piles of books. Finally, when he could not think of any more
Minervas, he exclaimed with a laugh: "I bet there isn't a single Minerva left in
my library, and this must be the very first time that a collection of books completely lacks a true representation of their presiding goddess."

Everyone was amused at this, and Jarno laughed the hardest, for it was he
who had been urging the count to have more and more books brought in.

"Well," said the count, turning to Wilhelm, "is it really important which goddess? Minerva or Pallas? The goddess of war, or the goddess of the arts?"

"Wouldn't it be best, your Excellency, not to be specific on that point?" Wilhelm suggested. "Why not present her in the double character which she had
in mythology? She announces the arrival of a fighter, but only to bring peace
to the populace. She praises a hero for his humaneness. She forcibly restrains
force and thereby restores peace and quiet."

The baroness, afraid that Wilhelm might give himself away, cut this short by
pushing forward the countess's tailor, who simply had to give his opinion on

how a Roman garment could best be created. This man, experienced in providing costumes for masquerades, knew the easiest way to make things, and since Madame Melina, despite her advanced pregnancy, was to play the role of Minerva, he was instructed to measure her. The countess had to decide, much to the chagrin of her maids, which of her dresses was to be cut up for the purpose.

The baroness slyly drew Wilhelm aside and told him that she had taken care of everything else. She sent him the director of the count's orchestra, so that he could start composing the necessary music or find suitable melodies from the stock of music in the castle. Everything was proceeding satisfactorily, the count made no further inquiries about the play, being mainly occupied with the transparent decoration at the end, which was to be a real surprise. His own inventiveness combined with the producer's skill did indeed achieve a very pleasing effect. On his journeys the count had seen big festivities of this kind, and had collected innumerable engravings and drawings. He really knew what was needed, and he had good taste.

Meanwhile, Wilhelm had finished the text of the play, gave everyone his part, took on his own, and the music director, who was equally knowledgeable about dance, arranged the ballet; everything was going along splendidly.

But then there occurred an unexpected obstacle, which threatened to make a big gap in all his well-laid plans. He had reckoned that Mignon's egg dance would make the strongest impression, and was therefore absolutely stupefied when with her usual curtness she refused to dance at all, saying she was now his and would never again appear on the stage. He tried every possible argument to persuade her, and did not give in until the poor child began to weep bitterly, fell at his feet, and cried: "Oh, Father, you stay away from it too!" He did not respond to this. Instead he began thinking of some other means of making the scene interesting.

Philine, who was to be one of the country maidens and sing the solo in the round dance, with the chorus taking up what she sang, was overjoyed at this prospect. She had everything she desired: her own room, constant proximity to the countess whom she entertained with her foolery and was daily rewarded for this, a costume for the play made specially for her, and, since she was the sort of person who delights in imitating others, she soon observed from being with the ladies as much decorum as she could comfortably assume, and in a very short time developed good manners and real savoir vivre. The attentions of the stablemaster increased rather than diminished, and since the officers were also constantly currying her favors, she found herself with an excess of riches, and decided for once to play the prude, using all her wits to affect an air of sophisticated superiority. This cool refinement enabled her to discover within a very few days all the weak spots in the company at the castle, and, if she had really wanted to, she could have made her fortune by this means. But in this too she only used her advantage to amuse herself, to give herself a pleasant day, and to be impertinent when she saw it was safe to be so.

When the actors had all memorized their parts, a full rehearsal was set. The count wanted to be present and his wife began to be nervous about his reactions. The baroness summoned Wilhelm privately, and the nearer the time for the rehearsal approached, the more embarrassed they all became, for absolutely nothing of the count's original idea remained in the play. Jarno, who happened just then to come in, was let in on the secret, and was delighted. He felt inclined to offer his services to the two ladies. "It would be unfortunate if you could not by your own efforts extricate yourself from this situation," he said to the countess. "But I will be lying in wait for any eventuality." The baroness then told him that she had talked to the count about the whole play, but only in bits and pieces and those not in any particular order so that he would be prepared for the details. But he still thought that the plan of the whole would conform with his original idea. "I will sit next to him this evening at the rehearsal," she said, "and try to distract him. I have also suggested to the decorator that he do the decorations at the end really well, but make sure that some little thing is not quite right."

"I know a court where we could use such active and intelligent people as you," said Jarno. "And if for some reason your skills are not producing the desired results, then just give me a sign and I will get the count out of the rehearsal and not let him back again until Minerva has made her appearance; the illuminations can be depended on to carry the day. For several days now I have had something to tell him concerning his cousin, which, for one reason or another, I have kept putting off. That will be a distraction for him, though certainly not the pleasantest."

Various business matters prevented the count from being there at the start of the rehearsal. Then he was entertained by the baroness. Jarno's help was never needed. For since the count found plenty to put right, to improve and to insist on, he totally forgot everything else, and since Madame Melina spoke her lines exactly as he would have wanted them, and the final tableau turned out well, he seemed completely satisfied. It was only when the prologue was over and they went on to the play itself, that he began to notice things and to wonder whether this play was really what he had thought up. At this point Jarno did come out of his ambush position, and the evening passed with the news of the prince's arrival being confirmed, and various people riding out to see the vanguard of the prince's entourage encamped in the neighborhood. The whole house was full of noise and commotion, and our actors, who had not always been loooked after properly by the surly servingmen, were obliged to spend the time waiting and practicing in the old part of the castle without anyone paying any particular attention to them.

Chapter Eight

The prince finally arrived. The generals, staff officers and the rest of his attendants who arrived with them, and all those who visited them or came on business—all these turned the castle into a regular beehive. Everyone was pushing and shoving to catch a glimpse of the illustrious prince, everyone admired his affable condescension, everyone was astonished to find that this great hero, this noble commander, was the smoothest of courtiers.

The household staff had been ordered by the count to be at their posts when the prince arrived, but none of the actors was to be visible because the count wanted to surprise the prince with the festivities that were being prepared. The prince, when he was escorted that evening into the handsomely lit great hall decorated with wall coverings from the previous century, seemed in no wise to be expecting a theatrical presentation, let alone a prologue in his honor. Everything went off splendidly, and when the performance was over all the actors had to appear before the prince, who graciously asked a question of every one of them, or had something pleasant to say to them. Wilhelm, as the author, had to step forward separately, and he too received his share of appreciation.

Nobody had anything much to say about the prologue, and in a few days it was if there had been no performance at all, except that Jarno occasionally talked to Wilhelm about it, and praised it, showing real understanding. But he added: "It is a pity that you play for empty nuts with empty nuts." Wilhelm pondered this expression for several days, not knowing how to interpret it or what he should make of it.

Every evening the troupe performed and exerted every effort to capture the audience's attention. Applause, barely deserved, encouraged them to think that it was on their account that the guests came pouring in here, just in order to be present at the performances, which were the center of attraction for all the guests at the castle. Wilhelm, however, realized to his regret that this was not the case. For although the prince sat through the first performances and followed them conscientiously from start to finish, he soon seemed to find good reasons to absent himself. The very people who from their conversation had seemed to Wilhelm to be the most intelligent, above all Jarno, only spent fleeting moments in the room where the stage was set up, and preferred to sit in the anteroom playing cards or talking about business.

He was disappointed that, despite persistent effort, he had failed to receive the amount of approval he thought he had earned. He assisted Melina in selecting the plays and copying the parts, he was always at hand during the frequent rehearsals and when anything else needed attention. Melina, secretly conscious of his own inadequacy, eventually accepted his help. Wilhelm meticulously memorized his parts and performed with feeling and vigor and as much style as his self-education allowed him.

The continued interest of the baron in their undertaking removed any doubts that the rest of the actors might have had, for he assured them that they were very successful and would be even more so especially if they were to perform one of his own plays. But he was sorry to say that the prince's taste was exclusively for French drama, and that some of his acquaintances, foremost among them Jarno, had a passionate preference for those monstrous productions of the English stage.

The artistry of our actors may not have been adequately observed and respected; but as for their persons they were certainly not greeted with indifference by the spectators, both male and female. We have already reported that the actresses had from the start attracted the attention of the young officers. As time went on things went even better for them, and they made some important conquests. But let us not go into that, noting only that Wilhelm was becoming more interesting every day to the countess, and an unavowed affection for her was beginning to blossom in him. When he was on stage she could not take her eyes off him, and he soon seemed to be acting and speaking only for her. It was an indescribable delight for them just to look at each other, and they abandoned themselves to this harmless pleasure without nourishing stronger desires or worrying about what might happen. They exchanged glances despite what separated them as to birth and station, just like two outposts of opposing armies, facing each other across a river, and engaging in lighthearted talk without any thought of war—both entirely trusting their own feelings.

The baroness for her part had sought out Laertes, whose lusty vigor appealed to her, and he, despite his avowed hatred of women, was not averse to a passing adventure; this time he would have been really captivated against his will by the vivaciousness and attractions of the baroness, if the baron had not had occasion to do him a good, or perhaps bad, service by making him better acquainted with her sentiments. For one day when Laertes was singing her praises as the best of all women, the baron jokingly observed: "I see where matters stand. Our friend has secured another one for her stables." This unfortunate choice of metaphor, referring all too clearly to the blandishments of Circe, made Laertes extremely angry, and he was annoyed to hear the baron go on to say pitilessly: "Every newcomer believes he is the first to deserve such attentions, but he is utterly mistaken, for we have all, at one time or another, been led up the garden like this. Man, youth or boy—no matter who it is—every one of us has devoted himself to her for a time and striven to gain her favors."

Nothing is more dispiriting to a happy man who, entering the gardens of a sorceress, finds himself surrounded by the joys of an artificial spring, but, while listening for the song of the nightingale, finds his ears invaded by the grunts of some transformed predecessor.

Laertes was heartily ashamed after this disclosure that he had once more been led astray by his vanity to think well of a woman. So he avoided her from now on, consorting instead with the stablemaster, with whom he fenced vigorously and went hunting, but treating the whole matter as insignificant when he was rehearsing or performing on stage.

Sometimes of a morning the count and countess would summon members of the troupe, and on these occasions all had reason to envy Philine's undeserved good fortune. While he was dressing, the count often had his favorite actor, the Pedant, at hand, sometimes for hours on end. The fellow was gradually decked out from head to toe, equipped even with a watch and snuffbox. Sometimes after dinner the entire company were bidden to appear before the lord and lady; they considered this a singular honor, not realizing that at the same time a whole pack of dogs were brought in by huntsmen and servants, and the horses being readied in the courtyard.

Wilhelm had been advised to praise Racine, the prince's favorite dramatist, when an appropriate opportunity presented itself, and thereby put himself in the prince's good graces. He found such an occasion one afternoon, when he had been summoned to appear with the others, and the prince asked him whether he too had studied the great French dramatists. Wilhelm said that he had. He did not notice that the prince had already turned to speak to someone else, without waiting for his answer. Almost interposing himself, he claimed the prince's attention by declaring that he had indeed a very high opinion of French drama and had read its masterpieces with great appreciation; and he had been delighted to hear that the prince paid great respect to the talents of a man like Racine: "I can well imagine," he went on to say, "that persons of noble station will appreciate an author who portrays so excellently and correctly the circumstances of high social rank. Corneille, if I may put it thus, portrays great people, but Racine portrays persons of quality. As I read his plays I can always picture a poet residing at a brilliant court, with a great king before his eyes, surrounded by all that is best, who can penetrate to the secrets of men which are concealed behind richly woven hangings. Whenever I study his *Britannicus* or his *Bérénice*, I have the sense of being at court myself, of being privy to things great and small in these dwellings of the gods of this earth, and through the eyes of a sensitive Frenchman I perceive kings adored by whole nations, courtiers envied by multitudes, all in their natural shape with all their defects and sorrows. The report that Racine died of grief because Louis XIV showed his dissatisfaction by no longer looking at him — that to me is the key to all his works. It was impossible for such a talented writer, whose whole life, and his death, depended on the eyes of a king, not to write plays worthy of the admiration of a king — and of a prince."

Jarno had joined them and listened with amazement to what Wilhelm said. The prince, who never answered but signified approval only by an appropriate glance, turned away. Wilhelm, still unaware that it was not seemly in such circumstances to prolong a conversation and try to exhaust a topic completely, would gladly have gone on talking and proved to the prince that he had read the prince's favorite poet with profit and emotional involvement.

Taking him aside, Jarno asked him: "Have you never seen a play by Shakespeare?" "No," Wilhelm replied, "for since his plays have become better known in Germany, I have not been close to the theater; and I don't know whether I should be pleased that mere chance has reawakened in me a passion which in my youth occupied me intensely. But I must say that what I have heard about his plays has not made me eager to know more about such strange monstrosities which transcend all probability and overstep all propriety."

"I would nevertheless advise you take a look at them," said Jarno. "It can't do anyone any harm to observe with one's own eyes something that is strange. I will lend you a few samples, and you could not employ your time better than by disassociating yourself from everything else and, in the solitude of your own room, peering into the kaleidoscope of this unknown world. It is a sinful waste of time for you to spend it in dressing up these apes as humans and in teaching these dogs to dance. But one thing I would insist on in advance: don't take offense at the form of what you read. As for the rest—that I can leave to your own true judgment."

The horses were standing ready outside the door, and Jarno swung himself into the saddle to entertain himself by hunting with some of the other courtiers. Wilhelm followed him sadly with his eyes. He would have liked to talk about many things with this man who, though not in a very friendly fashion, had nevertheless given him new ideas, ideas that he needed to think about.

When a man approaches the point at which his powers, capabilities and concepts are about to develop decisively, he often finds himself in a state of uncertainty, which some good friend could easily help him overcome. He is like a traveler who falls into the water close to the shelter that he seeks. If someone comes to his aid right away and drags him on to dry land, then he only has to put up with getting wet, whereas if he has to get himself out of the water onto the other bank, he still has to take a big, tiresome detour to reach his destination.

Wilhelm was beginning to feel that things work out differently in the world from what he had imagined. He was now observing at close range the life, full of importance and significance, of those in high station, the great of this world, and he was surprised at the easiness of manner which he had acquired thereby. An army on the march, with a princely hero at its head, surrounded by so many active soldiers and so many eager admirers—all this gave wings to his imagination. It was in this state of mind that he received the books that Jarno had promised him. And in a very short while, he was seized, as one would expect, by the torrent of a great genius which swept toward a limitless ocean in which he completely lost and forgot his own self.

Chapter Nine

The baron's relationship with the actors had gone through various modifications since their arrival at the castle. At first it had been one of mutual satisfaction. For since the baron, for the first time in his life, had one of his own plays, which up to then had only been social entertainment for amateurs, in the hands of real actors, with the prospect of a reasonably good performance, he was in the best of moods and full of generosity, purchasing little gifts for the actresses from various peddlers who appeared and many a bottle of champagne for the actors. They in return took great pains over his works, and Wilhelm spared no effort in memorizing every detail of the lofty speeches of the illustrious hero the portrayal of whom was entrusted to him.

But gradually certain disagreement arose: the baron's preference for certain of the actors became more noticeable every day, and that naturally displeased the other members of the company. His praise was reserved exclusively for his favorites, and this aroused jealousy and discord in the troupe. Melina, who never knew what to do in such cases of dissension, found himself in a very unpleasant situation. Those who received praise were not particularly grateful for it, and those who did not indicated their displeasure in all sorts of ways and made things uncomfortable for their erstwhile respected benefactor. Their malicious attitude toward him was encouraged by a certain poem, of unknown authorship, which circulated in the castle. There had always been gossip about the baron's relations with the actors, with all sorts of tales told and certain events improved in the telling to make them amusing and more interesting. All this had been done in a relatively subtle way. But now the assertion was made that professional envy had broken out between him and some of the actors who fancied themselves as writers; and this was the basis for the poem we spoke of, which ran as follows:

O Baron, how I envy you
Your high place in society.
Poor wretch I am, and would that I
Were near to thrones, and had such land,
Proud castle as your father has,
With hunting and with shooting.

O Baron, how you envy me,
Poor wretched me; for so it seems,
That Mother Nature cared for me
And wished me well from childhood on
With easy heart and easy head,
I'm poor, but not in brains or wit.

So I would think it best if we,
Dear Baron, leave things as they are.
You stay your father's own true son
And I'll remain my mother's child.
Let's live without distrust and hate,
And neither grudge the other's title,
You on Parnassus seek no place
And I none with their lordships.

Opinions on this poem, which was circulating in several not very legible copies, were sharply divided, but no one could hazard a guess as to who had written it. When people began to take a malicious delight in it, Wilhelm declared himself very much against this.

"We Germans," he exclaimed, "have fully deserved that our muses are still suffering from the disdain in which they have languished for so long, if we are not able to respect men of station who occupy themselves in one way or another with our literature. There is no contradiction between birth, station and wealth on the one hand, and genius and taste on the other. Foreign countries have taught us that, for amongst their best minds are many who belong to the aristocracy. So far it has been a miracle if anyone of our German nobility has devoted himself to learning, and few famous names owe their fame to their interest in art and learning, whereas others have emerged from obscurity and appeared as unknown stars on the horizon. But this will not always be so, and unless I am much mistaken, the uppermost class of our nation is in the process of employing its advantageous condition to gain in future the laurel wreath of the muses. Nothing is more distasteful to me than to hear not only members of the middle classes making fun of aristocrats who set store by the muses, but also those persons of quality, who with ill-considered frivolity and despicable malice watch others of their own station being scared away from a path that would bring honor and gratification to everyone."

This last utterance seemed to be directed at the count, for Wilhelm had heard that he thought the poem was really good. The count was of course accustomed to joke in his own particular style with the baron, and so he had welcomed this opportunity to tease him in various ways. Everyone had his own conjectures regarding the authorship of the poem, and the count, not willing to be proven less perspicacious, lighted on an idea that he swore must be the truth, namely that the author of the poem was his own Pedant, who was a really fine fellow and in whom he had long observed some signs of poetic genius. So to provide himself with good entertainment he sent for the man one morning and made him read the poem aloud in the presence of the countess, the baroness and Jarno, which the Pedant did in his own special way; he earned praise, applause, and a present for his efforts. He cleverly evaded answering the count's questions whether he had poems that he had written earlier. And so the Pedant gained the reputation of being a poet and a wit, but, in the opinion of those who were well disposed toward the baron, of a lampooner and a bad character. The count applauded him more and more, no matter how he played his roles, so that the poor fellow became quite puffed up, in fact almost crazy, and even thought of taking a room in the castle, like Philine.

If he had done this immediately, a most unfortunate accident might have been avoided. Late one night, when he was going to the old part of the castle and fumbling about in a narrow dark passage, he was set upon by several persons who held him fast while others rained blows on him and beat him up so badly that he could hardly drag himself to his feet. But he managed to creep upstairs to his companions who, although pretending to be outraged, felt some inward pleasure at the occurrence and had to laugh at seeing him so thoroughly pummelled, his new brown coat covered with white dust as if he had had a fight with some millers.

The count, as soon as he got news of this, was absolutely furious. He treated the incident as a serious offense, an incursion on his jurisdiction, and instituted through his marshal a thoroughgoing inquiry. The spattered coat was to be the major evidence. Everybody in the castle having anything to do with powder or flour was drawn into the investigation. But all in vain.

The baron swore on his honor that although the kind of joke to which he had been subjected was not at all to his liking, and the count's own behavior had not been of the kindest, he had got over all that, and had in no wise been implicated in the misfortune that had befallen the poet or lampooner, whatever he should be called.

The activities of the guests and the general commotion in the castle led to the whole incident being quickly forgotten, and the count's unfortunate favorite had to pay dearly for his brief pleasure of wearing borrowed plumes.

The troupe performed every evening and was on the whole well looked after, but the better things went, the more demands they made, soon claiming that food, drink, service and accommodation were inadequate. They urged their protector, the baron, to see that they were better provided for and finally given the pleasures and comforts that he had promised them. Their complaints became more and more insistent, and the baron's efforts to satisfy them, ever more fruitless.

Wilhelm was less and less visible except at rehearsals and performances. Shut up in one of the back rooms, which only Mignon and the Harper were allowed to enter, he lived and moved in the world of Shakespeare, entirely oblivious of all that was going on outside.

There are said to be certain sorcerers who by magic can entice a host of different spirits into their chamber. The conjurations are so powerful that the whole room is filled and the spirits, jostled up to the tiny magic circle that the wizard has drawn, swirl around it and float above his head, constantly changing and increasing in number. Every corner is crammed full, every shelf occupied, eggs keep expanding, and gigantic shapes shrink to toadstools. But unfortunately the necromancer has forgotten the magic word to make this flood of spirits subside. As Wilhelm sat there reading, hosts of feelings and urges arose within him of which he had previously no conception or intimation. Nothing deflected him from this state of total absorption, and he was most impatient when someone came to tell him what was going on outside.

Hence he hardly paid any attention when he heard that some public punishment was about to take place in the castle yard and a boy be whipped, who was under suspicion of breaking into the castle at night. Since he was wearing a wigmaker's coat, he might well have been one of the baron's assailants. The boy categorically denied this and could not therefore be formally punished, but the intention was to accuse him of vagrancy and send him packing, because he had been wandering around the neighborhood for several days, spending the nights in mills, and had finally placed a ladder against a garden wall and climbed over.

Wilhelm did not think there was anything remarkable about this, but then Mignon came rushing in and told him the boy was Friedrich who, since his dispute with the stablemaster, had been lost from sight, both for the actors and us readers.

Wilhelm, who took an interest in this boy, hurried down to the courtyard where preparations for the occasion were already underway. For the count loved ceremony, even in small matters like this. The boy was brought in, but Wilhelm intervened on his behalf, asking for a delay because he knew the boy and had various things concerning him to report. He had some difficulty in making his point, but was finally given permission to speak privately with the delinquent. Friedrich assured him that he was in no wise implicated in the maltreatment of an actor. He had been strolling around the castle and had crept in at night to visit Philine, for he had spied out the location of her bedroom and would certainly have got to it if he had not been apprehended.

Wilhelm, not anxious to reveal this relationship (which might affect the good reputation of the company), rushed off to see the stablemaster, and asked him, in view of his acquaintance with the person involved and those at the castle, to act as an intermediary and get the boy released. With Wilhelm's help the whimsical fellow thought up quite a tale: the boy had once belonged to the troupe, then run away, then wanted to join it again, and so had decided to visit some of his previous associates at night, in order to win their good graces. Everyone said that he had always behaved well, the ladies too gave their opinion, and he was set free.

Wilhelm took charge of him, and so Friedrich became the third member of the strange family that for some time Wilhelm had considered his own. The Harper and Mignon were pleased to see Friedrich again, and all three of them were now determined to be attentive to the needs of their friend and protector, and to provide him with what pleasure they could.

Chapter Ten

As each day passed, Philine discovered more and more how to ingratiate herself with the ladies. When they were alone together she would move the conversation on to the subject of the men who had been around, and Wilhelm was not the last to be talked about. She was bright enough to be aware that he had made a great impression on the countess's feelings; and so she told her what she knew (and didn't know) about him, carefully avoiding anything that might be to his disadvantage, and praising his nobility of character, his generosity, and especially his moral behavior toward women. All other questions that were addressed to her she answered prudently, and when the baroness noticed the countess's increasing emotional attachment, she was delighted at the discovery. For her own relationships with various men, and most recently with Jarno, were not unknown to the countess, whose pure soul could not possibly observe such frivolity without disapproval and gentle reproach.

The baroness and Philine, therefore, had, each in her own way, a special interest in bringing Wilhelm and the countess closer together. Philine hoped in addition to regain his favor and to operate to her own advantage when such opportunity should arise.

One day, when the count had gone off hunting with the rest of the company and the men were not expected back till the following morning, the baroness thought up an amusement of the sort she particularly favored. She liked to dress up and was always appearing, in order to surprise everybody, as a peasant girl, or a page boy, or a huntsman. She acquired thereby a sort of faery reputation, flitting hither and thither and emerging where she was least expected. She was simply delighted when she was able to wait at table, or mingle with the guests without being recognized, only to reveal her identity in some humorous fashion.

That evening she summoned Wilhelm to her room, and since she had something else to do first, Philine was told to prepare him for what was to come. He arrived, and was surprised to find the flighty girl there instead of the noble ladies. She received him with an air of decorous ease, which she had worked at perfecting, and thereby made him likewise adopt a stance of politeness. First she referred jocularly and in general terms to the good fortune that attended him and that, as she well observed, had brought him here at this very moment. Then she reproached him gently for his behavior toward her, which had so tormented her. She blamed herself for this as she had deserved his attentions; she vividly described what she called her former condition, and added that she would despise herself if she were unable to change and make herself worthy of his friendship.

Wilhelm was astounded by this speech. He had too little experience of the world to know that irreparably frivolous persons are often those who demean themselves most, admit their faults most openly, and deplore them, although they do not possess the slightest ability to abandon the course which their strong natures have impelled them to take hitherto. He therefore could not be unkind to the winsome sinner, engaged in conversation with her and learnt the plan for an unusual masquerade which was intended to be a surprise for the beautiful countess.

He had some misgivings, which he voiced to Philine. Yet when the baroness came in, she left him no time to express further doubts, but carried him off, and said the hour had come. It was already dark. She led him into the count's dressing room and made him take off his coat; Wilhelm slipped into the count's silk dressing gown, and she put the count's red-ribboned nightcap on his head. She then took him into the count's sitting room, told him to settle himself in the big armchair with a book, lit the reading lamp in front of him, and instructed him on what kind of role he was to play.

The countess, she said, would be told that the count had returned unexpectedly and was in a bad mood. She would then come in, walk up and down, seat
herself on the arm of the chair and say a few words. He should continue playing the role of the husband as long and as well as he possibly could; and if at
last he had to reveal his identity he should be courteous and gallant.

Wilhelm felt very uncomfortable in this strange disguise. The whole idea
had astonished him, and its execution was proceeding before he had time to
think about it. The baroness had already left him before he realized how dangerous the position in which he had put himself really was. He could not deny
that the countess's beauty, youth and grace had made a considerable impression on him, but he was by nature in no sense inclined to empty shows of
gallantry; yet his principles did not induce him to undertake anything more
serious. So he was in a state of some perturbation—afraid of displeasing the
countess and yet equally concerned not to please her too much.

His imagination recalled all those occasions when female charms had
affected him. Mariane in her white négligé was there, begging him to remember her. Philine's amiability, her lovely hair and her ingratiating behavior had
worked on him once again when he saw her just now. But all this receded into
the distance when he thought of the noble, radiant countess, whose arm he
should feel on his neck in a few moments and whose innocent caresses he was
called upon to return.

He could however never have guessed the strange manner in which he would
be relieved of his discomfort. How astonished and frightened he was when
he heard the door open behind him, and a quick look in the mirror showed
him quite clearly that it was the count entering with a candle in his hand!
His hesitation what to do now, whether to remain seated or get up, run away,
confess, prevaricate or ask for forgiveness, all that lasted only a few moments.
For the count, who had stood motionless in the doorway, turned back, gently
closing the door behind him. At that very moment the baroness rushed in
through a side door, extinguished the lamp, dragged Wilhelm out of the chair
and pulled him into the dressing room, where he discarded the count's dressing gown, putting it back in its usual place. She then hung Wilhelm's coat
over her arm, and hurried away with him through various rooms, passageways and box rooms until they reached her own room. There she told him,
once she had recovered, that she had gone to the countess to spin the yarn
that the count had arrived earlier than expected. "But I know that already,"
the countess had said. "What can have happened? I've just seen him riding
through the side gate." So the baroness in fright had rushed to the count's room
to fetch Wilhelm.

"Unfortunately you came too late!" said Wilhelm. "The count had just come
into the room, and he saw me sitting there."

"Did he recognize you?"

"I don't know. He saw me in the mirror, as I did him, and before I knew
whether it was a ghost or he himself, he went out again and closed the door
behind him."

The baroness became even more disconcerted when a servant called her and said the count was with his wife. She went there, crestfallen, and found the count sitting quietly brooding; when he spoke he was gentler and kinder than usual. She did not know what to make of this. They talked about what had happened on the hunt and why he had come back earlier. The conversation soon petered out. The count fell silent, and the baroness was particularly struck by the fact that he inquired after Wilhelm and expressed the wish that he should be asked to come and read to them.

Wilhelm, who meanwhile in the baroness's room had dressed and recovered himself somewhat, obeyed the summons with some trepidation. The count handed him a book from which with a certain uneasiness he read them an adventure story. His voice had something unsteady about it, something quivering that, thank goodness, was appropriate to the content of the story. From time to time the count signalled his approval, and when he finally let him go, he praised the expressiveness with which Wilhelm had been reading.

Chapter Eleven

Wilhelm had read but a few of the plays of Shakespeare, when he found that he had to stop because they affected him so deeply. His mind was in a state of ferment. He sought out an opportunity to speak with Jarno and told him that he could not thank him enough for providing him with such an experience.

"I foresaw that you would not be insensitive to the great merits of this most extraordinary and marvelous of writers," said Jarno. "Yes indeed," said Wilhelm, "I cannot remember a book, a person, or an event that has affected me as deeply as these wonderful plays that you so kindly brought to my attention. They seem to be the work of some spirit from heaven that comes down to men and gently makes them more acquainted with themselves. They are not fictions! One seems to be standing before the huge open folios of Fate in which the storm winds of life in all their turbulence are raging, blowing the pages back and forth. I am so astonished by the forcefulness and tenderness, the violence and the control of it all, that I am completely beside myself and long for the time when I will be able to continue reading." "Bravo!" said Jarno, clasping our friend's hand, "that's just what I wanted; and the results that I hoped for will not be long in coming."

"I wish," said Wilhelm, "that I could describe to you all that is going on in my mind. Presentiments that I have had from youth on, without being aware of them, about human beings and their destinies, all these I have found confirmed and enlarged in Shakespeare's plays. He seems to reveal all the mysteries without our being able to point to the magic word that unlocked the secret. His personages seem to be ordinary men and women, and yet they are not. Mysterious composite creatures of nature act out their lives before us in his plays, like clocks with faces and movements of crystal, showing the passage of time in accordance with their regulated progression; at the same time one can perceive the springs and wheels that make them go. The few glances that I have cast into Shakespeare's world have impelled me more than anything else to take more resolute steps into the real world, to plunge into the flood of destinies that hangs over the world and someday, if fortune favors me, to cull several drafts from the great ocean of living nature and distribute these from the stage to the thirsting public of my native land."

"I am pleased at the state of mind you are in," said Jarno, clapping his hand on the impassioned youth's shoulder. "Don't give up your intention of embarking on an active life, and be quick to take full advantage of the good years that are given you. If I can assist you in any way, I will gladly do so with all my heart. I have never asked you how you came to be in this company of actors, to which you were neither born nor trained. What I would hope is that you will want to get yourself out of this situation; and I see that you do. I know nothing of your origins or your domestic circumstances, but you can entrust me with as much as you are willing for me to know. This much I would say to you now: that this present war can bring about rapid changes of fortune, and if you are prepared to put your talents and abilities at our service, and do not shy away from hard work, perhaps danger if needs be, then I would have an opportunity to put you in a position which you will not regret having occupied for a time." Wilhelm, extremely grateful for this, now felt in the mood to tell his friend and benefactor his whole life story.

While they were talking, they strayed into the middle of the park and came to the road that ran right through it. Jarno stood still for a moment, then said: "Think over my proposal, make your decision, give me your answer in a few days, and have confidence in me. I assure you that I have found it totally incomprehensible that you should have joined forces with such people as these. I have been distressed, indeed disgusted, that, in order to have some experience of life, you should have given your heart to an itinerant ballad singer and a silly androgynous creature."

He was about to continue, when an officer came riding up in haste, followed by a groom leading another horse. Jarno gave him a warm welcome. The officer dismounted and the two of them embraced each other, then started a conversation while Wilhelm, dismayed at Jarno's last words, stood to the side, deep in thought. Jarno looked through some papers the officer had brought him, and this man went up to Wilhelm, extended his hand to him and said with emphasis: "I find you in worthy company. Take your friend's advice, and fulfil the desires of someone unknown to you who nevertheless is deeply concerned about you." As he said this, he embraced Wilhelm, pressing him warmly to his breast. Then Jarno came up and said to the stranger: "The best thing would be for me to accompany you. You can get the necessary orders and ride off before nightfall." They both got on their horses and left our astonished friend to his own reflections.

Those last words of Jarno's were still ringing in his ears. He could not bear to have these two human beings who had so innocently gained his affection, debased by a man whom he respected so highly. The strange embrace of the officer whom he did not know, affected him little, merely arousing his curiosity and stirring his imagination for a brief moment; but Jarno's words had struck deeply, he felt wounded by them, and recoiling he reproached himself for having temporarily ignored and forgotten that icy harshness of Jarno that was apparent in his every glance and motion. "No, no!" he shouted, "you insensitive man-of-the-world, you only imagine that you can be someone's friend. Nothing you have to offer me can outweigh the affection which binds me to these two unfortunate creatures. What luck that I should have found out in good time what to expect from you."

Mignon came to meet him and he clasped her in his arms, saying: "Nothing shall part us, good little creature! The seeming wisdom of the world shall not persuade me to leave you, or to forget what I owe to you."

The girl, whose passionate embraces he usually warded off, was delighted by this unexpected outburst of affection, and clung so close to him that he had difficulty in loosening her hold.

From that time on he was more attentive to Jarno's actions, not all of which seemed laudable to him, and some he utterly disapproved of. He had, for instance, a strong suspicion that the poem about the baron, which had had such dire consequences for the Pedant, was Jarno's work. Since Jarno had laughed in Wilhelm's presence about the whole incident, our friend concluded that this was the sign of a thoroughly corrupt sensibility; for what could be more cruel than to make fun of an innocent man one had caused suffering to, instead of making amends or somehow repairing the damage. Wilhelm would gladly have done this himself, for, by a strange coincidence, he had tracked down the perpetrators of the nocturnal attack.

Up till now he had been kept unaware of the fact that several of the young officers had been spending whole nights in jollification with some of the actors and actresses in a lower room in the old part of the castle. One morning, having got up early as usual, he happened to enter this room and found the young gentlemen engaged in an unusual form of toilet. They had crumbled chalk into a dish of water, and were brushing the paste on to their vests and trousers, without taking them off, in order to clean them up as quickly as possible. Astonished at such activities our friend remembered the white powder and the stains on the Pedant's coat, and his suspicions increased when he learned that several of the baron's relations were amongst the company.

In order to check out his suspicions further he made sure the young gentlemen were supplied with breakfast. They were very lively and told some amusing stories. One of them in particular, who had been a recruiting officer for a time, was full of praise for his captain's guile and skill in outwitting all kinds of persons and persuading them to enlist. He described in detail how young persons from good families who had been carefully educated, were fooled by promises of excellent treatment, and he laughed heartily at those simpletons who were at the beginning so delighted at earning praise and privileges from some highly regarded, gallant, shrewd and openhanded officer.

Wilhelm blessed his guiding spirit for so unexpectedly showing him the abyss which he had approached so unwittingly! He now saw Jarno simply as a recruiting officer; the embrace of the unknown officer was easily explained. He detested the sentiments of these two men and from that moment on, avoided everyone wearing a uniform; and he would have been delighted by the news he received that the army was moving on, were it not for his fear that this would separate him, maybe forever, from the lovely countess.

Chapter Twelve

The baroness had spent several anxious days, tormented by worries and unsatisfied curiosity. For the count's behavior since that adventurous episode was a complete mystery to her. His whole manner had changed; there was no more of his usual joking. He made no such demands on his friends and servants as previously. There was no longer that characteristic pedantry and officiousness about him; he was quiet, wrapped up in himself, and yet serene — altogether a different person. For the readings that he sometimes instigated he selected serious, often religious books, and the baroness was in a constant state of anxiety that behind this seemingly placid exterior there lurked some secret grudge, some tacit intention to avenge the outrage he had so accidentally discovered. She therefore decided to confide in Jarno, which was easy for her because her relationship with him was of the kind which does not normally involve concealing things from each other. Jarno had recently become her lover, but they were clever enough to keep the world unaware of their inclinations and their pleasures. The countess was the only one to see this new romantic attachment, and the baroness's determination to get the countess involved in something similar was most probably caused by her eagerness to avoid the reproaches that she often had to endure from that noble soul.

When the baroness told the whole story to Jarno, he burst out laughing and said: "The old fellow must surely think that he saw himself, and that this apparition foretells misfortune, perhaps even death, for him. And so he has become tame like all half-men when they think of that dissolution which no one has escaped or can ever escape. But let us quietly work on him so that he will no longer be a burden to his wife and his guests."

So they began, as soon as it was appropriate, to talk in the count's presence about presentiments, apparitions and the like. Jarno played the skeptic, and the baroness took the same line; they pushed this so far that the count took Jarno aside and reproved him for his free thinking, using his own experience to try to convince him of the possibility and reality of such phenomena. Jarno acted as though he were astonished, first expressing his doubts, but finally pretending to be convinced; and then had a good laugh with his friend in the peace of the night at this feeble man-of-the-world, suddenly cured of his incivility by a bogyman but still admired for the equanimity with which he awaited impending disaster, perhaps even death.

"He won't however be prepared for the most natural result of that apparition," exclaimed the baroness with the high spirits to which she always returned once some worrisome thought had been dispelled. Jarno was richly rewarded with her favors, and the two of them began plotting how to make the count even more tractable and to work on the countess's feelings for Wilhelm and intensify them.

With this purpose in mind, they told the countess the whole story. She was displeased at first, but then began to think more and more in her quiet moments about the scenario that was being organized for her, fleshing it out in detail.

The preparations undertaken on all sides soon made it clear that the army would indeed move on further and the prince change the location of his headquarters. It was even reported that the count would leave his estate and return to town. Our actors could therefore cast their own horoscope; but only Melina acted in accordance with it, the others sought to snatch every possible enjoyment from the moment.

Meanwhile Wilhelm was occupied with a very special task. The countess had asked for a copy of his plays, and he regarded such a request from so charming a lady as the highest possible reward.

Any young author who has not yet seen himself in print, will devote the utmost care to producing a clean and well-written copy of his works. For that is, so to speak, the golden age of authorship. One feels transported back to an era when the printing press had not yet deluged the world with so many useless writings, and only works of real quality were copied and preserved by the noblest of individuals; as a result, it is all too easy for one to arrive at the false conclusion that a carefully copied manuscript is a great work of art, worthy of being owned and displayed by a connoisseur and patron.

A banquet was arranged in honor of the prince, who was soon to depart. Many ladies from the neighborhood had been invited, and the countess had dressed in good time for the occasion. She was wearing a more sumptuous gown than usual, her hair and headdress were more elaborate, and she was wearing all her jewels. The baroness too had done her utmost to be dressed in splendor and with taste.

Philine, when she noticed that time was hanging heavy on the ladies as they waited for the guests to arrive, suggested they should send for Wilhelm, who was anxious to deliver his manuscript and read them some parts of it. He came, and was astonished to see how much the graceful appearance of the countess was enhanced by all this finery. At the bidding of the ladies he read aloud to them, but so inattentively and poorly that, if his listeners had not been so indulgent, they would quickly have sent him away.

As soon as he saw the countess, it seemed as if an electric spark had flashed before his eyes, and he hardly knew how to find breath for his recitation. That beautiful woman had always been a pleasure to look at, but now he thought he had never seen anything so perfect, and his mind was invaded by a multitude of reflections, the sum total of which was roughly this: "How foolish of so many poets and sensitive persons to inveigh against finery and splendor and to demand instead that women of all classes should dress in simple, natural clothes. They rail against finery without considering that it is not the poor old finery we dislike when we see an ugly, or not very pretty person decked out in such odd splendor. But I would ask all men of taste whether they would really prefer to have any of these pleats removed, these ribbons and lace, these puffed sleeves, these curls, these glistening gems. Wouldn't they be afraid of spoiling the pleasing effect that emerges so readily and naturally to meet their gaze? Of course they would! For if Minerva rose fully armed from the head of Jupiter, this goddess seems to have emerged light-footed from some flower in all her finery."

He kept looking at her as he was reading, as if to retain this impression forever, and made several mistakes; but he was not put out by this, though he would usually have been in despair if a wrong word had marred his reading.

A curious noise, as if announcing the arrival of the guests, brought the performance to a close. The baroness left, and the countess, before closing her dressing table, took a box of rings and put several of them on her fingers. "We will soon be parting," she said, fixing her eyes on the box. "Take this to remind you of a good friend who wishes nothing more than that all may go well for you." She then took out a ring with a coat of arms woven of hair and studded with gems, all covered with crystal. She handed this to Wilhelm, who was at a loss what to say or do, so transfixed was he to the spot. The countess closed up her dressing table and seated herself on the sofa.

"And am I to go empty-handed?" said Philine, kneeling before the right hand of the countess. "Just look at that man who has plenty to say at the wrong time but now can't even stammer out his meager thanks. Come along, sir! At least act as though you are grateful, or if no words occur to you, then at least follow my example." She took the countess's right hand and kissed it warmly. Wilhelm fell on his knees, seized her left hand, and pressed it to his lips. The countess seemed embarrassed, but not displeased.

"Oh dear!" said Philine. "I have seen so much finery in my time but never a lady so worthy of wearing it. What bracelets! And what a hand! What a necklace! And what a bosom!"

"Be quiet, you flatterer," said the countess.

"Is that a picture of the count?" asked Philine, pointing to a splendid medallion on a fine chain that the countess was wearing at her side.

"Yes, it was painted at the time of our wedding," the countess replied.

"Was he so young at the time?" asked Philine. "I know you have only been married for a few years."

"His youthful appearance was the work of the artist," the countess replied.

"He is a handsome man," said Philine. "But," she went on, putting her hand on the countess's heart, "did no other image ever creep into this secret compartment?"

"You are very impertinent, Philine!" she exclaimed. "I have spoilt you. Don't ever let me hear anything of that kind again!"

"When you are angry, you make me unhappy," said Philine as she jumped up and ran out of the room.

Wilhelm continued to hold the lovely hand of the countess. His eyes were fixed on the clasp of the bracelet, and, to his great astonishment, he saw that his initials were there in diamonds.

"Do I really have some of your hair in this precious ring?" he timidly asked.

"Yes, indeed," she said in an undertone. Then she regained her composure, and, grasping his hand, she said: "Do get up! Farewell!"

But he, pointing to the clasp, said: "Here by some strange chance, are my initials!"

"How so?" said the countess. "They are those of a lady who is a good friend of mine."

"They are my initials," he said. "Do not forget me. Your image remains graven in my heart. Farewell; now let me leave!"

He kissed her hand and was about to stand up. But as in dreams we are surprised by strange things bringing forth even stranger things, it suddenly happened, without knowing how, he found himself grasping the countess in his arms, her lips touching his, and their blissful exchange of passionate kisses was like the sparkling draft from the freshly filled goblet of a first love.

Her head was resting on his shoulder, and she was totally unconcerned about her disarranged curls and ribbons. She had put her arm around him. He embraced her eagerly and time and time again pressed her to his bosom. If only such a moment could last forever! If only harsh fate had not broken up these few precious moments! Wilhelm was frightened and stunned when this happy dream was shattered by a scream from the countess, who suddenly withdrew her hand and clutched her heart.

Stupefied he stood there. She covered her eyes with her other hand and, after a moment's pause, cried: "Now leave! Leave quickly!"

He still stood there.

"Leave me," she cried, taking her hand away from her eyes; and looking at him with an indescribable expression in her eyes, she added, in a voice full of love: "Leave me, if you love me!"

Wilhelm left her room and was back in his own before he knew where he was.

Unhappy creatures! What strange warning of chance, or fate, had driven them apart?

Book Four

Chapter One

His head propped on his arm, Laertes was gazing pensively out of the window into the open fields. Philine came creeping through the great hall, leaned on her friend and mocked at his serious expression. "Don't laugh!" he said to her. "It is horrible how quickly time passes, how everything changes and comes to an end! Just look—a little while ago there was a whole encampment out there, splendid to look at, the tents full of life and merriment, the whole area carefully patrolled. And now, suddenly, it is all gone. The only sign that remains will soon be the trampled straw and the holes where they cooked. Then it will all be ploughed up, and the presence of so many thousands of valiant men in these parts will be nothing more than a ghostly remembrance in the minds of a few old people."

Philine began to sing and dragged her friend into the great hall to dance. "Since we can't pursue time that is passed," she said, "let us at least celebrate it joyfully and gracefully while it is passing us by."

They had danced only a few steps when Madame Melina came through the hall. Philine was wicked enough to invite her to join the dance, reminding her of her misshapen appearance because of the pregnancy. "If only," said Philine behind her back, "I did not have to see more expectant mothers!" "Well, she is at least expecting something," Laertes replied. "But it doesn't suit her," said Philine. "Haven't you noticed that wobbling pleat in the front of her shortened skirt which always parades in front of her when she moves? She doesn't have either the sense or the ability to take herself in hand and to conceal her state."

"Never mind," said Laertes. "Time will take care of that."

"But it would be nicer," said Philine, "if children could be shaken off trees."

In came the baron with some kind words from the count and countess, who had left very early, and brought them some presents. He then went to see Wilhelm, who was occupied with Mignon in the adjoining room. The child was friendly and helpful. She had inquired about his parents, his siblings and his other relations, thereby reminding him of his obligation to give them some news.

The baron delivered parting greetings from the count and countess, and assured him of the count's great satisfaction with him, his acting, his poetic productions and his efforts on behalf of their little theater. As a tangible sign of this appreciation he pulled out a purse, through the fine mesh of which the glitter of new gold coins attracted the eye. Wilhelm stepped back, and refused to accept it. But the baron went on to say: "Just consider this gift as a recompense for the time you have expended and a recognition of your hard work, rather than as a reward for your talent. If such talent earns us reputation and the affection of others, it is only reasonable that we should by our efforts and application also acquire the means to supply our ordinary needs, for none of us is all spirit. If we were in a town where anything could be bought, this sum might have been used to buy a watch, a ring, or some such thing. But I am putting a magic wand into your hands for you to conjure up something precious that is to your liking, something you can use, and retain in remembrance of us. Do respect this purse. The ladies knitted it themselves, with the idea that the receptacle should endow the contents with the most pleasing form."

"Forgive my embarrassment and hesitation at accepting this present," said Wilhelm. "But it seems to annihilate the little I did and restrict the free play of such happy memories. Money is a fine way of settling something. I would not wish this house to settle with me in this fashion."

"That is not the case," the baron replied. "But since you are so sensitive, you will surely not demand that the count should remain entirely in your debt; he is a man who sets great store on being attentive and just. It has not escaped him that you have exerted every effort and devoted all your time to the fulfilment of his intentions; he also knows that in order to speed up certain necessary arrangements you spent some of your own money. How can I face him again if I cannot assure him that his recognition has given you pleasure?"

"If I were just to think of myself and could follow my own inclinations," Wilhelm responded, "I would, despite all your reasoning, steadfastly refuse to accept this handsome gift. But I cannot deny that, although it makes me uneasy, it comes at a time when it will relieve me of some embarrassment I have felt toward my family. For I must give them an account of how I have been spending my time and money, and I have not managed either well. Now, thanks to the generosity of his Excellency the count, I will be able to have the consolation of telling my parents about the good fortune that my strange detour has led me into. So I will let the sense of a higher obligation overcome my squeamishness and those slight pangs of conscience which warn us in such eventualities as this. And in order to be able to look my father straight in the eyes, I lower mine shamefacedly before yours."

"It is really odd," the baron replied, "what strange compunction one has in accepting money from friends and benefactors when one would be grateful and delighted at any other gift from them. Human nature has many such peculiar tendencies to create scruples and systematically nourish them."

"Isn't it the same with all matters of honor?" asked Wilhelm.

"True," said the baron, "and also with prejudices. We hestitate to weed them out, lest we should at the same time tear out healthy plants. But I am always happy when some people realize what they can and should disregard. I am pleasantly reminded of the anecdote of an intelligent poet who wrote several plays for a court theater which were greatly appreciated by the monarch. 'I must give him a suitable reward,' the generous prince declared. 'See if there is any particular jewel that would give him pleasure, or a sum of money, if he will accept it.' The poet jokingly responded to the courtier who brought the message: 'I am deeply grateful for such a gracious thought, and since the Emperor takes money from us every day, I do not see why I should be ashamed of taking money from him.'"

No sooner had the baron left the room, when Wilhelm eagerly counted the sum which had so unexpectedly and, as he thought, undeservedly, come to him. For the first time he seemed to have a sense of the value and worth of money (such as we usually acquire only later) as the gleaming pieces came rolling out of the delicately wrought purse. He made a tally and discovered that, mindful of the fact that Melina had promised to repay the advance forthwith, he had as much, or even more, than on the day he bought Philine that first bouquet. With secret satisfaction he thought of his talent, and with a certain pride he reflected on the good fortune that had directed and stayed with him. Confidently he now took up his pen to write to his family to relieve them of all anxiety by depicting his recent behavior in the best of lights. He avoided giving a factual account. Instead he merely hinted, in significant and mystical terms, at what it was that might have happened to him. The favorable state of his finances, the gains that his talents had brought him, the favor of persons of high station, the affections of women, his wide circle of acquaintances, the development of his bodily and mental powers, and his hopes for the future, all this built such a fantastic castle in the air, that not even a fata morgana could have produced a stranger combination.

Such was his mood of exaltation that, when he had finished his letter, he engaged in an extensive monologue, recapitulating the contents of the letter and picturing for himself an active and distinguished future. The example of so many noble warriors had excited him, Shakespeare's plays had opened up a whole new world, and from the lips of the beauteous countess he had drawn a fire that he found it hard to describe. This surely could not, should not, remain without some effect on him.

The stablemaster came in and asked if they were finished packing. "Unfortunately," said Melina, "nobody has thought about that yet." So now they had to get going quickly. The count had promised to provide transportation during the next few days for the whole company: the horses were all ready and could not be done without for long. Wilhelm asked where his trunk was, and discovered that Madame Melina had already taken it for herself; he asked where his money was, only to learn that Melina had carefully packed it at the very bottom of the trunk. Philine told him she still had space in hers, took possession of Wilhelm's clothes, and told Mignon to get everything else. Wilhelm, though somewhat unwilling, let this be done for him.

When everything was packed up and ready, Melina said: "It irritates me that we have to travel like circus folk and mountebanks. I wish that Mignon would put on women's clothes and the Harper have his beard cut." Mignon clung to Wilhelm and said passionately: "I am a boy, I don't want to be a girl." The old man remained silent, and Philine used the occasion to make some funny remarks about the quirks of their patron, the count. "If the Harper does cut his beard," she said, "he should sew it on to a ribbon and keep it, so that he could put it on if he were to meet the count somewhere; that beard was the sole reason for the count's generosity toward him." When they pressed her for an explanation of this strange remark, she told them the following: the count believed that it was a great aid to illusion if an actor continued to play his role and sustain his fictive character into real life, which was why he had so favored the Pedant, and thought it was very sensible of the Harper to wear his false beard not only on the stage but also during the day. He was pleased to see that the disguise looked so natural.

While all the others were making fun of the count's mistake and his strange opinions, the Harper drew Wilhelm aside, took leave of him, and implored him, with tears in his eyes, to let him go at once. Wilhelm assured him that he would protect him against anyone, that no one should be allowed to harm a hair of his head, let alone cut any of it off without his consent.

The old man was very moved by this, and there was a strange fiery glow in his eyes. "That is not what is driving me away," he cried. "I have long reproached myself for remaining with you. I must never stay anywhere, for misfortune pursues me and will harm those who associate with me. You have everything to fear if you do not let me go; but don't ask me why. I do not belong to myself. I cannot stay."

"To whom do you belong? Who can wield such power over you?"

"Sir, let me keep my horrible secret to myself. Give me leave to go! The vengeance that pursues me is not that of any earthly judge. I am caught up in inexorable fate. I cannot remain here, for I dare not."

"I will certainly not abandon you in this state of mind," said Wilhelm.

"It would be high treason against you, my benefactor, if I were to linger here. I feel safe with you, but you are in danger. You don't know whom you are harboring. I am guilty, and even more unhappy than guilty. My very presence dispels happiness, and when I appear every good deed is robbed of its force. I should always be in flight, never at rest, so that my evil genius may not catch up with me; for it is always after me and does not make its presence felt until I lay down my head to rest. I cannot better express my thanks to you than by leaving you."

"What a strange man you are! You can no more shake my trust in you than you can deprive me of the hope of seeing you happy. I do not want to pry into the mysteries of your superstitiousness, but if you believe that your life is entangled in strange associations and premonitions, then I would say to you, for your consolation and enlivenment: Associate yourself with my own good fortune, and let us see whose genius is the stronger, your dark spirit or my bright one."

Wilhelm took the opportunity to offer him more words of consolation; for he had believed for some time now that his strange companion was someone who had, through chance or fate, incurred some great guilt and was continually oppressed by the memory of it. Just a few days previously, Wilhelm had heard him singing, and noted these peculiar lines:

> For him the light of morning sun
> With flames the clear horizon paints,
> And round his guilty head there breaks
> The beauteous image of the whole wide world.

Whatever else the old man chose to say, Wilhelm always had a stronger counterargument. He knew how to give everything a positive turn, he knew how to speak honestly, sincerely and sympathetically, and as a result the old man seemed to brighten up again and abandon his melancholy thoughts.

Chapter Two

Melina hoped to find quarters for his company in some small but prosperous town. They had reached the place where the count's horses had brought them, and were looking around for carriages and horses to convey them further. Melina had taken charge of the transportation arrangements, and proved to be as niggardly as ever. Wilhelm, on the other hand, the lovely ducats from the countess still in his pocket, thought he had every right to spend them in a pleasant way, forgetting all too readily that he had proudly included them in the sum which he had so volubly told the baron he was sending to his parents.

His good friend Shakespeare, whom he very much liked to consider his godfather (after all, he too was named William) had acquainted him with a certain Prince Hal who had spent some time with base and dissolute companions and, despite his noble character, taken great pleasure in the rough, unseemly and foolish behavior of his earthy associates. He welcomed this as an ideal against which to measure his present state; this made it much easier for him to indulge in a self-deception that had an almost irresistible appeal.

He began to think about his clothes. A vest which could have a short cloak thrown over it, was a most appropriate garb for a traveler. Long knitted trousers and laced-up boots seemed to be just right for someone on foot. He acquired a splendid silk sash which he put on under the pretext of keeping his body warm, but he freed his neck from the restrictions of a tie, and had some pieces of muslin fastened to his shirt which became rather wide and gave the effect of an old-fashioned collar. The silk scarf, his one memento of Mariane, was loosely attached to the inside of his muslin ruff. A round hat with a brightly colored ribbon and a big feather completed the disguise.

The women assured him that the costume suited him perfectly. Philine seemed quite enchanted by it, and asked for some of his beautiful hair which he had lopped off to come closer to his Shakespearian ideal. She did this in a most agreeable way, and Wilhelm felt that, by acceding to her request, he was justified in behaving like Prince Hal. So he began to take delight in performing some merry pranks and encouraging the others to do likewise. They fenced and danced, thought up all sorts of pastimes, and washed down their high spirits with copious drafts of a tolerable wine they had discovered. In the midst of all this disorderly activity, Philine set her sights on our prim and proper hero. Let us hope that his guardian angel may look out for him.

One excellent form of entertainment which gave the company special pleasure, was the extemporization of a play in which they imitated and ridiculed their former patrons and benefactors. Some of them had well noted the characteristics of public politeness in persons of such high station, and their imitations were received with great acclaim by the rest of the group; when Philine produced from her secret archive some declarations of love that had been addressed to her, there was a general outburst of malicious laughter.

Wilhelm reproved them for their lack of gratitude. But they countered this by saying that they had worked hard for what they had received, and that the treatment of such worthy people as they believed themselves to be, had not been of the best. They complained about how little respect had been paid them, and how they had been put down. The mockery, teasing and mimicry started up again with everyone getting more bitter and more unjust.

Wilhelm reacted to this by replying: "I wish what you are saying were not so clearly the reflection of your own envy and egotism, and that you could judge the life of those people from the proper perspective. Being placed by birth and inheritance in a high position in society, is a matter of some consequence. If one's existence has been made easy by inherited wealth and one has been surrounded from one's youth by what I might call the appurtenances of humanity—and that in plenty—such a person is accustomed to consider these possessions as the ne plus ultra and is not so able to perceive the value of what nature has given to less fortunate beings. The behavior of persons of high station towards those of lesser station—but also amongst themselves—is determined by external signs of distinction: they will acknowledge anyone's title, rank, clothes and retinue but not so readily his natural merits."

The company strongly seconded his words. They thought it was horrible that a person of merit should be obliged to stand back, and that there was no sign of any spontaneous, sincere relationships in the world of the great. This last point they discussed in considerable detail.

"Don't blame them for that," said Wilhelm. "Rather be sorry for them. They rarely have a sense of the joys that are the reward of those inborn riches which we consider most important. We who are poor in material possessions are rich in the pleasures of friendship—and only we. We are not able to enrich our loved ones by gracious favors, or advance them by priviliged attention, or shower them with gifts. We have nothing but ourselves to give. We must give all of ourselves, and, if such a gift is to have value, we must assure our friends of its lasting nature. What a joy it is, and what happiness to provide for both the giver and the receiver! Devotion and loyalty impart a happy and lasting permanence to what might otherwise be merely passing. These are the richest possessions we have."

While he was saying all this, Mignon had crept up and put her slender arms around him, leaning her head against his breast. He placed his hand on her head, and went on to say: "How easy it is for a noble personage to win men's hearts and minds! A pleasant, relaxed, and only moderately humane behavior achieves miracles, and once a mind is captured, he has plenty of ways to maintain his hold over it. But for us, this is more difficult and not so easy to come by, which means that it is natural for us to put greater value on what we acquire and achieve. How touching is the devotion of some servants to their masters! How splendidly Shakespeare portrayed that! In such cases, loyalty and devotion are the expression of a noble soul striving to equal someone of higher station. By attachment and love, a servant becomes the equal of his master who is otherwise justified in considering him a paid slave. These virtues are only for those of lower station; they are germane to them, and become them well. If one can easily purchase one's freedom, one is easily tempted to cease recognizing what one owes to others. I believe it would be true to say that a person of station can *have* friends, but not *be* a friend."

Mignon pressed closer and closer to him.

"All right," said someone of the company. "We don't need their friendship, and we never asked for it. But they should have shown more understanding for the arts that they claimed to support. When we were playing at our best, no one listened. They were always taking sides; that's what really decided things. An actor, who was favored, always got the applause, and others did not receive the approbation they deserved, because they were not in someone's good graces. It was absurd how often mere stupidity and absurdity captured their attention and applause.

"When I think about all their malice and irony, I believe it's much the same with art as with love. How can a man of the world, with his manifold activities, preserve that concentration which the artist must have if he is to produce a perfect work of art, and which those must have who become involved in it in the way the artist himself would wish and hope for. Believe me, my friends, talents are like virtues; one must love them for their own sake, or give them up entirely. They are recognized and rewarded only if one exercises them in private, like some dread secret."

"Meanwhile, until some perceptive person discovers us, we can die of starvation," a man in the corner cried out.

"But not immediately," said Wilhelm. "So long as one can live and move, one always finds some nourishment, though it may not be of the best. But what have you got to complain about? Weren't we, just when things looked worst for us, unexpectedly taken care of and well provided for? And now, while we're still in good shape, why don't we think of some way of continuing to practice our skills and improve ourselves? We are doing all sorts of other things and, like schoolchildren, pushing everything aside that might remind us of the work we have to do."

"I agree," said Philine. "This is totally irresponsible. Let's choose a play and perform it on the spot. Everyone must do his very best, as if we were performing before a huge audience."

It did not take them long to decide on the play. It was one of those that were very popular in Germany at the time but are now quite forgotten. Some of the actors whistled an overture and each thought about his role in the play. They began, and continued to act out the play right through to the end and with great attention. Everything turned out surprisingly well. They applauded each other, and had an excellent time.

When they were finished, they were all uncommonly satisfied, their time had been well spent, and each of them was especially pleased with his own performance. Wilhelm was expansive in his praise and their own conversation was lively and cheerful.

"You should see," said Wilhelm, "how much we will improve by such exercises and not restricting ourselves to mere memorizing, rehearsing and mechanical repetition. Musicians are to be commended for practicing in groups, for thereby they acquire not only pleasure but also greater precision, attuning their instruments to each other, preserving the right tempo, and modulating the dynamics. No one thinks of gaining praise by too loud an accompaniment to another's solo; everyone tries to play in the composer's spirit, and to perform well what the composer has given him to play, be it much or little. Should we not work just as precisely and intelligently, after all, we are concerned with an art much more subtle than music: we are called on to represent pleasingly and with taste the most ordinary as well as extraordinary utterances of human beings? Can there be anything more abominable than being sloppy at rehearsals and relying on a lucky break in the performance? We should take great pains to concentrate our efforts on pleasing each other, and value the approval of the public only if we have already applauded ourselves for what we are doing. Why is the conductor of an orchestra more certain of himself than the director of a play? Because in an orchestra anyone who makes a mistake is so audible that he must needs be ashamed, but I have rarely encountered an actor whose mistakes, whether forgivable or unforgivable, so offend him that he acknowledges them and is ashamed of them! I only wish the theater were as narrow as a tightrope so that no one without the necessary skill would venture onto it; nowadays everyone thinks he can readily strut on the boards."

This speech was well received, for everyone was convinced that he was not its target, since he had just done as well as the others. They agreed to work together as a group, on this particular journey as well as in the future. Since this was a matter of the right mood and free choice, they resolved that no director should interfere in what must be their own decision. They considered it a foregone conclusion that a republican administration would be the most suitable for good people like themselves, and insisted that the office of director should rotate amongst them. The director should be elected by the whole company, and he should be assisted by a kind of small senate. They were so taken with this idea, that they wanted to put it into practice immediately.

"I have nothing against such an experiment on this journey," said Melina, "and I will gladly give up my directorship until we are again settled in some place." He hoped thereby to save money, and have the republic and its interim director take over some of the expenses. They deliberated how best to organize this new form of government.

"It's a migratory empire," said Laertes, "at least we won't have any border disputes."

They got down to business right away, and elected Wilhelm as their first director. The senate was established, the women had seats and votes, and laws were proposed, rejected and approved. Time passed by without their noticing it while they were engaged in this sport, and because it passed so pleasantly, they thought they had achieved something really useful which through this new form of government opened up new vistas for the national stage.

Chapter Three

Since the company was now in such a good mood, Wilhelm hoped to be able to talk to them about the poetic merits of the plays. "It is not enough," he said when they met again next day, "for an actor to look casually at a play, to judge it merely from first impressions and express approval or disapproval without due study. That may be appropriate for the spectator who merely wants to be moved or entertained but is not really concerned with passing judgment. An actor, on the other hand, must be able to account for his praise or disapproval of a play. And how is he to do that if he does not penetrate to the author's mind and intentions? I have observed in myself these last days the mistake of judging a play from one particular role without considering it in relationship to the others. I felt this so vividly that I would like to tell you about this particular example, if you would lend me willing ears.

"You are acquainted with Shakespeare's marvelous *Hamlet* from a reading of it that gave you such pleasure at the count's castle. We made the decision to perform it and, without knowing what I was doing, I agreed to play the part of the prince. I thought I was studying the role properly, and began by memorizing the most powerful passages—the soliloquies and those scenes which give free play to strength of soul, to elevation of spirit, and intensity, where Hamlet's troubled mind expresses itself with strong emotion. I also believed that I was really getting into the spirit of the part by somehow myself assuming the weight of his profound melancholy and, beneath this burden, following my model through the strange labyrinth of so many different moods and peculiar experiences. I learnt the part and tried it out, feeling that I was becoming more and more identified with my hero.

"But the further I progressed in this, the more difficult it became for me to perceive the structure of the whole, and finally I found it almost impossible to acquire an overview. So I went right through the play from beginning to end without skipping, and found that several things didn't fit together in my mind. At times the characters seemed to contradict each other, at times their speeches, and I well-nigh despaired of finding the right tone in which to act out the role as a whole with all its different nuances and deviations. I battled my way through this thicket for a long time without seeing a way out, until I finally found one particular path by which I thought I could reach my goal.

"I searched for any clues of Hamlet's character previous to the death of his father. I observed what this interesting young man had been like without reference to that sad event and its terrible consequences, and considered what he might have become without them.

"This sensitive, noble scion, this flower of kingship, grew up under the immediate influences of majesty; concepts of right and of princely dignity, the sense of what is good and what is seemly, developed in him simultaneously with an awareness of being born into high station. He was a prince, he was born a prince, and he was desirous of ruling so that good men should be unimpeded in the exercise of goodness. Winsome in appearance, courteous by nature, pleasing by temperament, he was fashioned to be a model for youth and a delight for everybody.

"Without being strikingly passionate, his love for Ophelia represented a gentle premonition of tender needs. His ardor for knightly activities was not entirely of his own making, for this desire had been sharpened and increased by the praise expended on another person. He had a clear sense of honesty in others and treasured the peace accorded to a sincere heart by the affection of a friend. To some extent he had learnt to respect and cherish what is good and beautiful in art and learning. He disliked anything that had no substance or taste, and when he developed real hatred it was only so that he could express his contempt for shifty, deceitful courtiers and have his mocking sport with them. He was by temperament detached, straightforward in behavior, and neither comfortable with idleness nor too desirous for activity. At court he continued his academic sauntering. His moods were more joyous than his heart, he was a good companion, forbearing, unassuming, and concerned. He could forgive and forget an insult, but he would never accept anyone who overstepped the bounds of what is good, right and proper.

"When we shall have read the play again, you will be able to judge if I am on the right track. At least I shall hope to be able to support my opinions by passages in the text."

His presentation received hearty approval; they all thought they could now understand how the actions of Hamlet might be explained. They were delighted to feel that they had really entered the mind of the author. Each of them decided to study some play or other in this way, and discover the author's meaning.

Chapter Four

They only stayed a few days in this place; nevertheless various members of the company became involved in adventures that were far from unpleasant. In particular Laertes, who was attracted by a lady with an estate in the neighborhood, but treated her so coldly and rudely that he had to suffer many a taunt from Philine. She took the occasion to tell Wilhelm about the unfortunate love affair that had turned this poor young man into an enemy of the whole female sex. "Who can blame him," she said, "for hating a sex which treated him so badly and made him imbibe in one concentrated draft all the evils that men have to fear from women? Just imagine: within the space of one day he was lover, fiancé, husband, cuckold, patient and widower! I don't know how he could have fared worse."

Laertes ran from the room, half laughing and half irritated. Then Philine began in her most endearing way to tell how, as a young man of eighteen, Laertes had just joined a company of actors when he met a beautiful girl of fourteen. She was about to leave with her father, who had had some disagreement with the director. Laertes instantly fell head over heels in love with her and used every persuasion to induce her father to stay. Finally he promised to marry the girl. After a few pleasant hours of courtship he was married, spent one happy night as a husband, but while he was at a rehearsal next day, was cuckolded in accordance with his station. Having rushed home much too early in an access of loving desire, he found to his dismay a previous lover in his place, set about him in a fit of uncontrolled rage, challenged both the lover and the girl's father, and received in the process a considerable wound. Father and daughter took themselves off during the night, and Laertes remained behind, doubly wounded. For his misfortune brought him into the hands of the worst surgeon in the world, and the poor chap emerged with black teeth and dripping eyes. He is to be pitied, for he is really the best fellow on earth. What grieves me most, is that the poor fool now hates all women: and how can you live if you hate women?"

Melina interrupted them to report that everything was ready to go, and that they could leave next morning. He produced a plan of how they should arrange themselves for the journey.

"If a good friend takes me on his lap," said Philine, "I am quite satisfied with our miserably cramped position and indifferent to everything else."

"I don't care," said Laertes who had come back and joined them.

"I find it tiresome," said Wilhelm and hurried off to secure, with his own money, another fairly comfortable carriage which Melina had refused to provide. A different seating arrangement was worked out, everybody was feeling happy at being able to travel in comfort, when the ominous news arrived that a gang of partisan soldiers had been spotted on the route they were about to take, and no good was to be expected from them.

In the town great attention was paid to this news, even though it was hazy and uncertain. Given the positions of the opposing armies, it seemed impossible that an enemy detachment could have crept through or that friendly troops stayed back so far. But the townsfolk vividly described the dangers attending the actors, and urged them to take another route. Most of the company became uneasy and fearful, and in accordance with their new republican constitution all of them were then assembled to discuss this extraordinary turn of events. They were almost unanimously of the opinion that they should avoid a calamity either by remaining where they were, or by taking another route. But Wilhelm, who did not share their fears, insisted that it would be disgraceful to abandon a plan they had arrived at after much consideration, simply because of a mere rumor. He urged them to take courage, and his reasoning was manly and convincing.

"This is still only a rumor," he said, "common enough in wartime. Sensible people say that this eventuality is highly unlikely and perhaps impossible. Should we therefore allow ourselves to be swayed in such an important matter by such vague talk? The route the count proposed is the one that our papers are made out for. It is the shortest route, and the best road. It leads us to the town where you have friends and acquaintances and can expect to be treated well. The detour would get us there too; but it will take us a long way out of our course and on sideroads in heaven knows what condition! How can we hope, at this late season, to find our way back on to the direct route—and just think of the time and money we will have wasted in the meantime!" He said a lot more, and pointed out so many advantages, that their fears were diminished and their courage increased. He was able to tell them so much about the discipline of the regular troops, and paint such a lamentable picture of the marauders and accrued rabble, even presenting the danger so amusingly and attractively that their spirits were all fired up.

Laertes was from the start on Wilhelm's side, and swore that he would not flinch or yield. The old Blusterer expressed similar sentiments in his own way, Philine laughed at the whole crew, and when Madame Melina, showing her usual spirit despite her advanced pregnancy, declared that the whole thing was heroic, her husband, hoping to save a packet by taking the shorter route, expressed no objections, and the proposal was heartily approved.

They then began to make preparations to defend themselves, should that prove to be necessary. They bought large bowie knives and slung them across their shoulders. Wilhelm supplemented these by two pistols which he stuck in his belt, and Laertes brought a good musket. So they set out in a state of high exaltation.

On the second day the drivers, who were well acquainted with the district, proposed that they should stop at midday on a wooded hilltop because the village was quite a way off and on such fine days this was what most people did. The weather was indeed beautiful, and everyone soon agreed to this. Wilhelm went ahead on foot through the hills, and everyone he encountered was amazed by his strange appearance. He surged ahead through the forest, happy and contented, with Laertes, whistling, behind him; only the women stayed in the carriages. Mignon ran alongside, proud of her bowie knife, which no one could refuse her when, after all, the whole company was arming itself. Around her hat she had put the beads which Wilhelm still kept as a memento of Mariane. The blond Friedrich carried Laertes's musket. The Harper displayed an expression of perfect peace. His long garment was hitched up into his belt so that he could walk more freely, and he was supporting himself on a knobby staff, his instrument having been left behind in the carriage.

With some difficulty they finally reached the top of the hill, recognized the place from the beautiful stand of beech trees that surrounded and shaded it. A large and inviting forest glade sloped down from it gently and made this a pleasant place to rest. A running brook would quench their thirst, and off to the other side they had a marvelous view across ravines and ridges of trees into a distance full of hope and expectancy. Villages and mills could be seen in the valleys, towns in the plain, and more hills in the far distance. This made the prospect all the more promising because those hills constituted only a minor obstacle in their path.

The first persons who arrived took possession of the area, lay down in the shade, started to build a fire, and waited for the others who came up one after the other and, with one voice, admired the lovely weather, this beautiful spot, and the splendid surroundings.

Chapter Five

Although they had spent many happy hours together indoors, they were all much more alive and alert when their minds were refreshed by the wide-open sky and the beauty of the landscape. Here they felt closer to each other and would have liked to spend their whole lives in such a delightful place. They envied the hunters, the charcoal burners and the woodsmen—all by their occupations tied to such agreeable locations. Most of all they envied the blissful indolence of gypsies reveling in the manifold delights of nature.

Indeed they were happy in the feeling that they had a certain kinship with such odd creatures.

By now the women were starting to boil potatoes, and to unpack and start cooking the food they had brought with them. Pots were put around the fire, and the whole company arranged itself beneath the trees and bushes. Their curious garments and their various weapons gave them an exotic appearance. The horses were led off to one side and fed, and if only the coaches could somehow have been concealed from view, our little group would have made a deceptively romantic impression.

Wilhelm was in a state of unusual delight, seeing himself as the leader of a nomadic tribe, and, with this in mind, talking to each and every one and building up this illusion of the moment into a thing of color and poetry. Feelings rose: they ate and drank, and joyfully declared again and again that they had never in their life experienced such a delightful time.

As the enjoyment increased, a desire for activity grew. Wilhelm and Laertes took up their rapiers and this time began to practice with a theatrical end in view. They wanted to perform the duel in which Hamlet and his opponent come to such a tragic end. Both of them were convinced that, in this important scene, one shouldn't just lunge back and forth clumsily, as happens in most theaters; they were hoping to provide a model of how one could make this scene into a spectacle that any knowledgeable fencer would respect. Everyone gathered round. They both fought with vigor and intelligence, and the interest of the spectators increased at every bout.

Suddenly a shot landed in a nearby bush, and before long there was another. The group dispersed in fright. Soon they noticed armed men advancing toward the place near the loaded coaches where the horses were being fed.

The women burst into a cry of alarm, and our two heroes threw down their foils, seized their pistols and rushed at the attackers, demanding an explanation of what was going on, and accompanying this by violent threats. When these were answered laconically by several musket shots, Wilhelm fired his pistol at a curlyhead who had climbed up on the carriage and was cutting the ropes around the luggage. It was a good shot and the fellow fell off immediately. Laertes had been similarly successful, and the two men, encouraged by this, were taking to their sidearms when part of the attacking force descended on them with curses and bellowings, fired a few shots, and came at them with glittering sabres. Our two heroes fought valiantly, and called on the others to prepare for a general defense. But soon after this Wilhelm lost all sight and consciousness of what was happening. Stunned by a shot that hit him between his chest and his left arm, and by a sabre-thrust that split his hat and almost penetrated his skull, he fell down and later had to learn the unfortunate end of this encounter from someone else.

When he came to, he found himself in the strangest position. The first thing he dimly perceived, was Philine's face bent over his. He felt weak, and when he tried to get up, he found he was lying in Philine's lap, and sank back again.

She was sitting on the grass, gently nestling the head of the prostrate youth, giving him in her arms as soft a bed as she could. Mignon was kneeling at his feet, fondling them and weeping over them, her hair tousled and soaked in blood.

When Wilhelm saw the blood on his own clothes he feebly asked where he was and what had happened to him and the others. Philine urged him not to exert himself: all the others were safe, she said, only he and Laertes were wounded. She did not want to say any more, and implored him to keep still because his wounds had been bandaged in great haste and not very well. He stretched out his hand to Mignon and inquired why there was blood on her hair: he feared that she too had been wounded.

To put his mind at rest, Philine told him that this good-hearted creature, on seeing her friend wounded, could not think of any other way, in the heat of the moment, to staunch the blood than by stopping the wound with her hair, though she soon realized the futility of this, and gave up. After that they bound up his wounds with sponges and moss; Philine had contributed her scarf.

Wilhelm noticed that she was leaning with her back against her trunk which appeared to be locked and quite undamaged. He asked whether the others had been as lucky in preserving their possessions. With a shrug of her shoulders, she pointed to the adjoining meadow, which was littered with broken boxes, smashed trunks, slashed knapsacks and every kind of small utensil. No one was to be seen. The strange little group was all alone.

Wilhelm soon found out more of what he wanted to know. The other men, who certainly could have offered some resistance, were soon so overwhelmed by fright, that they were easily overcome. Some of them had fled, others just looked in horror at what was happening. The drivers of the carriages, who, because of their horses, fought the most vigorously of all were nevertheless overpowered and tied up, and in a very short while everything was ransacked and the loot taken away. Our terrified travelers, once they no longer feared for their lives, began to lament their losses, and hastened as quickly as possible to the neighboring village, taking Laertes with them, who was only slightly wounded, as well as the slender remains of their possessions. The Harper had left his damaged instrument leaning against a tree, and gone with them to find a surgeon to care for his benefactor, who had been left there for dead.

Chapter Six

Our three unfortunate adventurers remained for a while in this strange situation, for no one came to their aid. Evening came and night was threatening to close in on them at any moment. Philine's calm began to change into agitation; Mignon kept running up and down, her impatience increasing with every moment. Finally their hopes were fulfilled and people were heard approaching. But they were assailed by new fears; they quite distinctly heard horses coming up the path they had arrived by, and were afraid that some new party of uninvited guests was about to return to the battlefield for extra pickings. But they were pleasantly surprised when out of the bushes came a lady mounted on a white horse, accompanied by an oldish man and several young gentlemen, with servants and attendants, and a troupe of hussars to follow.

Philine stared at this sight, and was about to call out to the lovely Amazon for help, when the lady herself turned her eyes in astonishment toward this strange group of three people, and rode up to them. She showed great concern for the wounded man, whose position in the lap of this light-hearted samaritan, seemed to her extremely peculiar.

"Is he your husband?" she asked Philine. "No, just a good friend," Philine replied in a tone of voice that was extremely distasteful to Wilhelm. His eyes were fixed on the gentle, distinguished, calm and compassionate features of the newcomer: he thought he had never seen anything more beautiful or noble. Her figure was concealed beneath a man's loose overcoat which she seemed to have borrowed from one of the attendants as a protection against the cool night air.

The horsemen had meantime also drawn nearer. Some of them dismounted, and so did the lady who inquired most compassionately about the circumstances of the accident, and more particularly about the wounds of the prostrate youth. She then turned quickly around, and went off to the side, back to the carriages that had slowly come up the hill and now arrived at the battleground.

She stood by the door of one of the coaches, talking for a while with those who had just reached the top; a rather thick-set man stepped out and was led by her to our wounded warrior. From the box that he held in his hand and a leather case with instruments that he was carrying, it was clear that he was a surgeon. His manner was brusque rather than ingratiating, but his hand was skilled and his assistance welcome. He examined Wilhelm carefully and declared that none of his wounds was serious, that he would dress them, and then they could take him to the next village.

The lady's anxiety seemed to be increasing. "Just look," she said, having walked up and down a few times, and fetched the old man again, "Look what they have done to him, and this all on our account!" Wilhelm listened to what she said, but without understanding it. She kept pacing up and down, as though she were unable to tear herself away from the sight of the wounded man, and yet afraid of offending against decorum by staying while they began to undress him. The surgeon had just cut open Wilhelm's left sleeve when the old man came up to her and, in a serious tone of voice, insisted that they continue their journey. Wilhelm had his eyes fixed on hers and was so taken with their expression that he hardly felt what was being done to him.

Philine rose to kiss the lady's hand. As the two of them stood side by side, Wilhelm thought he had never seen such a difference. Philine had never appeared to him in so unfavorable a light. She should not even approach such a noble creature—so it seemed to him—let alone touch her. The lady asked Philine various things, but in a low tone of voice. Then she turned to the old gentleman, who was still standing by unmoved, and said: "Dear Uncle, may I be generous on your account?" With that she took off the greatcoat, with the clear intention of covering the wounded and undressed man.

Wilhelm, captivated till then by the healing power of her glance, was now, once the greatcoat was off, amazed at the beauty of her figure. She came up and gently put the coat over him. When he opened his mouth to murmur some words of thanks, the vivid impression of her presence had the strangest effect on his impaired senses. Her head seemed to be surrounded by shafts of light and there was a glow spreading across her whole appearance. The surgeon was at that moment treating him rather less gently, he was about to extract the bullet that was still lodged in the wound. So the saint disappeared from his fainting sight: he lost all consciousness, and when he came to again, the horsemen and carriages, the beauteous lady and her attendants had all vanished into thin air.

Chapter Seven

When Wilhelm's wounds had been attended to and his clothes put back on, the surgeon left just as the Harper returned with several of the country-folk. They made a stretcher out of twigs and branches, carefully laid the wounded man on it, and carried him slowly down the hill under the direction of a cavalier on horseback whom the lady had left behind to be with them. The Harper, pensive and silent, carried his damaged instrument, others dragged down Philine's trunk, she herself sauntering after them with a bundle in her hands, Mignon running ahead or into the bushes, gazing back longingly at her sick protector.

He lay quiet on his bier, wrapped in the warm overcoat. Electric warmth seemed to be penetrating his body from the fine wool, and he felt transported into a state of extreme comfort. The beautiful owner of that garment had made a strong impression on him. He could still see the coat slipping from her shoulders, her noble form surrounded by shafts of light; and his spirit rushed through forests and crags in pursuit.

It was not until nightfall that the little procession reached the village and stopped in front of the inn where the rest of the company were staying, desperately lamenting their irreplaceable losses. The only parlor in the hostelry was jammed with people, some were lying on the straw, some spread over the benches, some squeezed behind the stove, and Madame Melina in a neighboring room awaiting her delivery, which had been brought on rather earlier than expected because of that frightening occurrence. As a result she was being assisted by the hostess of the inn, an inexperienced young woman from whom not much good was to be expected.

When the new arrivals demanded to be let in, there was general complaining. They said that it was solely on Wilhelm's advice and under his direction that they had chosen to take this dangerous route and exposed themselves to this misfortune, the consequences of which were entirely his fault. They prevented his being let in and told him to find accommodation elsewhere. Philine they treated still more shabbily; and even the Harper and Mignon had to suffer their part. But the cavalier assigned by the fine lady to look after these three unfortunate creatures soon lost all patience, cursed and swore at the whole lot of them, and ordered them to close up and make room for the new arrivals. At this they began to be more accommodating. He made a place for Wilhelm on one of the tables which he pushed into a corner. Philine had her trunk put down beside him, and firmly sat down on it. Everybody squeezed up as much as they could; and the cavalier went off to see if he could not find better quarters for the "married couple."

Anger and reproaches broke out again as soon as he left. Everyone reckoned up, and exaggerated, his losses. They objected to the foolhardiness which had cost them so dearly, and did not conceal their gleeful satisfaction at our friend's being wounded. They vented their scorn on Philine, claiming that the way she had prevented any damage being done to her trunk was absolutely criminal. From various gibes and personal remarks it was clear that, during the looting, she had worked her way into the good graces of the leader of the band of marauders and persuaded him by her craftiness or the bestowal of some favors, to let her have her trunk back. For a while she seemed to have been missing. She did not reply to these allegations, but sat clicking the heavy locks of her trunk to assure her enemies that it was still there and to make them even more furious at her good fortune.

Chapter Eight

Wilhelm, though weak from loss of so much blood and calm and peaceful since the appearance of his angel of mercy, could not fail to be irritated by the harsh and unjust words that these disgruntled people kept repeating while he maintained silence. Eventually, however, he felt strong enough to rise and reproach them for the ill-mannered way in which they were causing anxiety to their friend and leader. He lifted his bandaged head, and supporting himself by leaning against the wall, he said:

"I can forgive your insulting me, when you should be sorry for me, and opposing and rejecting me the first time that I might expect your assistance—I can forgive that as the painful result of the losses you have suffered. Up till now I have felt sufficiently rewarded for the service I have done you and the kindness I have shown you, by your friendly behavior toward me. Don't mislead me, don't force me to go back in my mind and add up all I have done for you, for any such reckoning could only cause me pain. Chance led me to you, circumstance and inclination have kept me with you. I have shared your work and shared your pleasures. What little knowledge I had, was placed at your service. If you now cast bitter reproaches on me as being responsible for the misfortune that has befallen us, you are forgetting that it was not one of us who first proposed we should take this route, and that you all discussed this and gave your approval, as I myself did. If our journey had turned out well, you would all have been proud at having proposed that we take this route in preference to any other, and remembered our discussion, and the vote we took. But now you put the whole blame, the entire responsibility, on me, and this I cannot accept because my conscience is clear and you were as much involved as I was. If you have anything to say, then speak out, and I will defend myself. If you have nothing to accuse me of, hold your peace, and stop tormenting me just when I need all the rest I can get."

The reaction of the girls to this was to start crying again and describing their losses in detail. Melina was quite beside himself, for he had suffered the heaviest losses—more than we can imagine. He was storming about and stumbling in the narrow room, hitting his head against the wall, cursing and swearing in a most unseemly manner, and when, just then, the hostess came out with the news that his wife had given birth to a stillborn child, he lapsed into outbursts of violence, and everyone howled, yelled, growled, and contributed to the general uproar.

· Wilhelm was consumed by sincere pity at their situation, but also by disgust at their pettiness; his mind was fully alert even though his body was still weak. "I almost despise you," he said, "pitiful as your situation may be. For no misfortune can justify heaping reproaches so unjustly on an innocent man. If I did have a part in the mistake we made, I too am paying for it. Here I lie, wounded, and if you all have had losses, I have lost the most. The costumes and sets that were looted, belonged to me; you, Melina, have still not paid me, but I release you forthwith from this obligation."

"What's the point of giving away what no one will ever see again?" said Melina. "Your money was in my wife's trunk, and it is your fault that you lost it. But if only that were all!" Then he began again to stamp and swear and shout. Everybody remembered the lovely clothes they had acquired from the count, the buckles, the snuff boxes, the watches and hats that Melina had wheedled out of the valet de chambre. Everyone remembered his own particular small articles of value, and they all looked in irritation at Philine's trunk, indicating to Wilhelm that he had not done so badly to associate with this beauty and through her good fortune save his own possessions.

"Do you really believe that I shall keep anything for myself, while you are in need?" Wilhelm cried. "Is this the first time that I have given you a fair share of what I had? Open the trunk, and let what is mine be used for general needs." "The trunk is *mine*," said Philine, "and I will not open it up until I decide I want to. The few gladrags which I've kept for you, won't bring in much even if you sell them to the most honest of Jews. Think of yourself, what it might cost to get you well again, and what might happen to you in some other part of the country."

"Philine," said Wilhelm, "you will not deprive me of anything that belongs to me, and such as it is, it will get us out of our first difficulties. But there are many ways of helping one's friends, and not all of them depend on the glitter of money. Everything in and of me shall be spent on these unfortunate people who will certainly regret their present behavior, once they come to their senses. Yes," he said, "I know what you all need, and I will do my best to help you. Give me once more your confidence, calm yourselves for the present, and accept what I can promise you. Who will take this from me in the name of all of you?"

He stretched out his hand, and said: "I promise not to desert or abandon you until every one of you has had his losses doubly or three times repaid, and until you have totally forgotten the state you are now in (no matter whose fault it is) and have exchanged it for a better one."

He kept his hand extended, but no one grasped it. "I repeat my promise," he said, falling back on his pillows. Everyone remained silent. They were ashamed but not consoled. And Philine sat on her trunk cracking nuts that she had found in her pocket.

Chapter Nine

The cavalier came back with some others, ready to make preparations to move the wounded man. The village pastor had been persuaded to take in the "married couple." Philine's trunk was carried out and she, quite naturally but in a seemly manner, followed after it. Mignon ran ahead, and when they reached the parsonage, Wilhelm was put into a good-sized double bed that had long been used for guests or persons of distinction. It was only then that they noticed that the wound had broken open. There had been a good deal of bleeding and a new bandage was needed. Wilhelm became feverish. Philine nursed him dutifully and when she was overcome by fatigue, her place was taken by the Harper. Mignon was determined to stay awake, but had fallen asleep in a corner.

In the morning, when Wilhelm had somewhat recovered, he learnt from the gentleman that the lady who had come to their assistance the preceding day, had recently left her estate in order to escape the turmoil of war and withdrawn to a quieter part till peace should return. He told Wilhelm that the elderly gentleman was her uncle, that they had gone first to a certain town, and that they had instructed him to take good care of Wilhelm and his companions.

At that moment the surgeon came in and cut short Wilhelm's expression of gratitude to the gentleman. He described the wounds in detail and assured Wilhelm that they would soon heal, if he would keep absolutely quiet and be patient.

When the cavalier had gone, Philine told Wilhelm he had left in her charge a purse with twenty gold pieces, had given the parson a sweetening in return for the accommodation and left money with him to pay for the surgeon's services. She herself was generally taken to be Wilhelm's wife, would always act as such in his presence, and would not allow anyone else to nurse him.

"Philine," said Wilhelm, "I am already indebted to you for what you have done in all the misfortune that has befallen us, but I would not wish to increase my obligations toward you. I am ill at ease when you are with me, for I do not know how to repay what you are doing for me. Give me back those things of mine that you rescued for me in your trunk, join up with the rest of the company, and look for some other place to stay. Accept my thanks and, as a small recognition, my gold watch. But leave me. Your presence disturbs me more than you know."

She laughed in his face when he stopped talking. "What a fool you are!" she said. "You'll never be sensible. I know better what's good for you. I'm going to stay right here. I won't move from the spot. I've never expected thanks from men, and not from you either. And if I love you, what's that to you?"

She did stay, and soon ingratiated herself with the pastor and his family; she was bright and cheerful, always giving little presents, knowing exactly what to say to everyone—and doing exactly what she pleased. Wilhelm did not feel too bad. The surgeon, not very knowledgeable but not unskillful, let nature take its course, and the patient was soon on his way to recovery. He was eager to be fully restored so that he could continue with what he had planned, and fulfill his ambitions.

Time and time again he recalled the incident which had left such an indelible impression on his mind. He saw the lovely Amazon riding out of the bushes, saw her come towards him, get off her horse, walk up and down, and occupy herself with his needs. He saw the coat falling from her shoulders, her face and figure disappearing in a blaze of light. All his youthful visions returned to his mind and associated themselves with this image. He now thought he had seen the heroic Clorinda with his own eyes; and he also remembered the sick prince with the beautiful loving princess approaching his bed. "Do not images of our future destiny appear before our unclouded eyes in the dreams of our youth as premonitions?" he kept saying to himself, "Is it not possible that Fate sows the seeds of what is later to befall us, a foretaste of the fruits we are later to enjoy?"

His sickbed allowed him ample time to relive the scene. A thousand times he recalled the sweet sound of her voice; and how he envied Philine at having been able to kiss her hand! At times the whole incident seemed a dream, and he would have considered it a fantasy if the coat were not still there to assure him of the reality of the apparition. The care he took of this garment he combined with a passionate desire to wear it; and whenever he got up from his bed, he hung it over his shoulder, fearing all day long that he might get a spot on it, or in some way damage it.

Chapter Ten

Laertes came to visit his friend. He had not witnessed that turbulent scene in the inn, he had been in an upstairs room. He was quite dispassionate about his losses, resorting to his usual reaction of: What does it matter? He recounted the ridiculous behavior of the other members of the company, chiding Madame Melina in particular and saying that the only reason she lamented the loss of her daughter, was that now she would not be able to christen her with the ancient teutonic name Mechtilde. As for her husband, it had become clear that he had plenty of money and did not need the advance which he had wheedled out of Wilhelm. He was intending to leave by the next postchaise, and would be asking Wilhelm for a letter of recommendation to his friend Serlo, the director of the theater, whose company he hoped to join, now that his own venture had collapsed.

Mignon had for several days been very quiet, and when asked why, she finally admitted that she had sprained her right arm. "That's the result of your foolhardiness," said Philine, and then related how the child had drawn her knife in the middle of the fight, and when she saw her friend in danger, had slashed at the assailants. Eventually she had been grabbed by the arm and hurled to the ground. They scolded her for not telling them sooner that she was hurt, but they had noticed that she was afraid of the surgeon who all this time had taken her for a boy. They tried to relieve the pain by putting her arm in a sling. But her discomfort increased, because she now had to leave the better part of nursing and caring for Wilhelm to Philine, and that engaging sinner was becoming daily more attentive, and more active.

One morning when Wilhelm awoke, he found himself in curious proximity to Philine. In the restlessness of his sleep he had moved way back in the big, wide bed and Philine was stretched out across the front of it. It seemed that she had been sitting reading, and had fallen asleep. A book had slipped from her hand, and her head was resting against his chest, her blond hair billowing loosely across it. The disorder created by sleep had increased her charms more than art or intention could have done, and a smiling, childlike peace was spread over her face. He looked at her for a while, reproaching himself, so it seemed, for the pleasure this gave him; and we cannot say whether he blessed or blamed the situation that imposed such immobility and moderation upon him. He had been looking at her closely for some time when she began to move. He closed his eyes quietly, but couldn't resist blinking. He peered at her as she tidied herself up and went off to inquire about breakfast.

All the actors had by now come to see Wilhelm, asking for recommendations and travel expenses with various degrees of rudeness and importunateness, all to Philine's disapproval. In vain did she inform Wilhelm that the gentleman had left the other actors quite a sum, and that Wilhelm was being cheated. They even got into a fierce argument about this, with Wilhelm insisting once again that she should go along with them and try her luck with Serlo.

Her even temper deserted her for a brief span, but then she recovered herself, and said: "If only I had my blond friend with me! Then I wouldn't have to bother about the whole lot of you!" She was referring to Friedrich, who had been missing since the encounter with the marauding soldiers and had not shown his face since.

The next morning Mignon brought the news to Wilhelm's bed that Philine had left during the night, having neatly arranged in the next room everything that belonged to him. He felt her absence: he had lost in her a faithful nurse and a lively companion, and he was no longer used to being alone. But Mignon was soon to fill the gap.

Since the time that frivolous beauty had begun to bestow on Wilhelm her friendly ministrations, the little girl had withdrawn more and more and kept quietly to herself. But now that the coast was clear again, she came forth with all her love and attentiveness, anxious to serve and eager to entertain.

Chapter Eleven

Wilhelm was making good progress toward recovery, and hoped in a few days to be able to proceed on his journey. He did not want to continue drifting through life without a plan; his path into the future was now to be measured with purposeful steps. The first thing he wanted to do, was to seek out that gracious lady who had come to his assistance, and thank her; then hasten to his friend the theater director and do what he could for the unfortunate actors, and at the same time call on those businessmen whose addresses he had been given, to carry out his instructions. He hoped that the same good fortune would attend him as previously, and that he would have an opportunity to compensate himself by some favorable speculation or other for his losses and repair his finances.

The desire to see again the lady who had rescued him grew stronger every day, and in order to decide on his route he sought advice from the pastor, who had excellent topographical and statistical knowledge and owned quite a collection of books and maps. Together they looked for the place where the lady's family had settled during the war and tried to get more information about her; but they couldn't find the place on any map or in any gazeteer, and the genealogical handbooks had nothing to say about the family.

Wilhelm became uneasy at this, and when he expressed his concern, the Harper said that he had cause to believe that the cavalier, for some reason or other, had concealed the lady's true name. Feeling that he was after all somewhere near her, and eager to have news of her, Wilhelm dispatched the Harper to see what he could find out. But his hopes were soon dashed. For despite all his inquiries, the Harper could not find any trace of her. In those days people moved about easily; no one had paid any particular attention to a group of travelers, and the Harper was obliged to return, in order not to be taken for a

Jewish spy because of his beard; but had no good news to report to his master. He gave a precise account of how he had tried to carry out his mission, being eager that no suspicion of negligence should be attached to him. He did all he could to alleviate Wilhelm's concern, reminding himself of everything that the cavalier had told him, and advancing various theories, until finally one particular matter came to light which enabled Wilhelm to understand some of her words which had puzzled him.

The robber band had not been lying in wait for the actors but for her, on whom they might well expect to find a considerable amount of money and jewels. They must have had prior knowledge of her movements. It was not known whether the attack was the work of volunteer soldiers, or of marauders or robbers. Be that as it may, it was fortunate for the rich entourage of the lady that what these men came upon first were these poor creatures who were suffering the fate that was intended for the others. This was what the lady had been referring to by her words, "all on our account," which Wilhelm well remembered. Delighted as he was that Fate in its foresight had designated him to be sacrificed for the sake of this peerless woman, he was close to despair at having, at least for the moment, lost all hope of ever seeing her again.

The commotion within him was aggravated by the curious fact that he had discovered a striking resemblance between the countess and his *belle inconnue.* They were as alike as two sisters, neither older than the other, but, seemingly, twins.

The memory of the delightful countess was one of extreme sweetness: he took constant pleasure in recalling her image. But now the person of the noble Amazon had interposed itself, and the two images became one, so that he was quite unable to keep hold of the one and let go of the other. And then their handwriting—how similar that was! He had kept a charming poem that the countess had written in her own hand, and in the overcoat he had found a slip of paper with a tender message of inquiry about the "uncle." Wilhelm was convinced that his rescuer had written this, sent it from one room to another in some inn on the way, and that the uncle had put it in his pocket. He compared the handwriting, and whereas the elegant pen strokes of the countess had especially pleased him beforehand, the similar but freer writing of the Unknown One now seemed inexpressibly fluid and harmonious. Her little note said next to nothing, but its very appearance, like previously that of the lady herself, seemed to set his spirits soaring.

He lapsed into a state of dreamy longing; and the passionate expressiveness of the free duet that Mignon and the Harper were singing, was like an echo of what he himself was feeling:

> Only they know my pain
>   Who know my yearning!
> Parted and lone again,
>   All joy unlearning,

I scan all heaven's demesne
  For any turning.
Ah, but my love and swain—
  Far he's sojourning.
Hot is my spinning brain,
  My insides burning.
Only they know my pain
  Who know my yearning!

Chapter Twelve

The gentle enticements of his kindly tutelary spirit did not move Wilhelm in any particular direction; they merely increased his former uneasiness. There was a certain warmth coursing secretly through his veins, definite and indefinite images floated before his mind and aroused desires that had no limit. He might wish for a horse, or wings, but although he felt he could not stay as he was, he was constantly trying to decide what he really wanted.

The thread of his destiny had become strangely entangled and he longed for the knots to be untied or cut. Many times, hearing a horse trot by or a carriage rumble on its way, he rushed to look out of the window, in the hope that it might be someone coming to visit him and, by pure chance, bringing him news that was certain, and happy. He regaled himself with thoughts of how Werner might surprise him by coming to these parts; or Mariane might turn up. He became excited every time he heard a post horn. Melina should be sending him news of how things were going with him, and above all the cavalier might return with an invitation to visit his idolized beauty.

Unfortunately none of this happened, and he was thrown back on his own company. As he thought over the past, one thing became ever more distasteful and intolerable, the more he pondered and reflected on it. This was his disastrous leadership in battle, the very remembrance of which filled him with dismay. For although, on the evening of that fateful day, he had made a pretty good show of talking himself out of any responsibility, he could not persuade himself that this was justified. He even had moments of depression in which he blamed himself for everything that had happened.

Self-love makes us exaggerate our faults as much as our virtues. He had inspired confidence in himself and manipulated the will of others; and he had forged ahead, driven by boldness and inexperience. But these were not sufficient to cope with the dangers that had befallen them. Openly and in the depths of his heart he blamed himself time and time again, and since he had promised not to desert the company he had so misled until he repaid with interest what they had lost, he now had a further indiscretion to reproach himself with, namely that of assuming responsibility for redressing the harm that had been done to all of them. There were times when he rebuked himself for giving such a promise in the excitement and pressure of the moment; at others he felt that his kindly extended helping hand, which no one was ready to accept, was a mere formal gesture compared with the vow he had made in his heart. He tried to think of ways to be useful and generous, and decided there was every reason for him to speed up his journy to Serlo. So he packed his things and, without being fully recovered or consulting either the pastor or the surgeon, hurried off in the company of Mignon and the Harper, eager to escape the inactivity that fate had imposed on him for so long.

Chapter Thirteen

Serlo received him with open arms, and said: "Is it really you? Are you still what you were? You don't seem to have changed much. Have you retained your passionate love for the noblest of all the arts? I am so glad you have come, and the mistrust I felt in your recent letters has completely vanished." Wilhelm was puzzled, and asked for an explanation. "You didn't treat me like an old friend when you wrote, but rather as an important person to whom one can, in good conscience, recommend people who are completely useless. Our whole future depends on the opinion of the public, and I'm afraid that Mr. Melina and his associates are hardly the sort of people we can integrate into our troupe."

Wilhelm was about to say something in their favor, but Serlo launched into such a harsh description of them, that Wilhelm was glad when a woman entered the room, whom Serlo introduced as his sister Aurelie. She received him very graciously, and their conversation was so pleasant that he did not really notice a certain sadness in her intelligent face which made it all the more interesting.

This was the first time for a long while that Wilhelm had really felt in his element. Whereas all he usually had were submissive listeners, he now found himself in the enviable position of talking to artists and connoisseurs who not only understood him perfectly but responded intelligently to what he said. With what speed they went through all the latest plays! What surety of judgment they displayed! How well they could estimate and appreciate how the public would react! How quickly they could explain things to each other!

Wilhelm's admiration for Shakespeare necessarily brought their conversation round to this author, and Wilhelm expressed his expectation that Shakespeare's marvelous plays would have a tremendous effect on the German public. He soon got on to *Hamlet*, which had so much occupied him of late.

Serlo assured him that he would have put on the play long ago if that had been possible, and he himself would have liked to play the part of Polonius. He added with a smile: "And we can find Ophelias, once we have the prince!" Wilhelm did not notice that Aurelie seemed displeased by her brother's jocular remark; instead he lapsed into his usual expansiveness, instructing them on how he would require the part of Hamlet to be played. He laid before them in detail the conclusions which we have seen him arrive at, and did all he could to make his opinions acceptable, despite the doubts that Serlo expressed regarding his hypothesis. "All right," said Serlo, "we'll grant you all that. But what else does it explain?"

"A great deal; in fact, everything," said Wilhelm. "Just imagine a prince as I have described him, whose father dies unexpectedly. Ambition and desire to rule are not his driving passions. He had acquiesced in the fact of being the son of a king, but now for the first time he is obliged to be more aware of the gulf that separates commoner from king. His right to the crown was not hereditary, but his father's long life had strengthened the claims of an only son and his hopes of assuming the crown. But now he sees himself, despite virtual promises, excluded, perhaps for ever, by his uncle, and feels so deprived of grace and possessions, so alienated amidst all that from the time of his youth he had considered his own. This is how his mind first takes on a melancholy cast. He feels that he is no more than all the other nobles — indeed not as much. He considers himself their servant, he is neither polite, nor condescending but feels degraded and destitute.

"His earlier state now seems to him like a vanished dream. In vain does his uncle try to cheer him up and make him take a different view of his situation; his feeling of insignificance never leaves him.

"The second blow that he suffers, is even more wounding and humbling — his mother's marriage. When his father died, this faithful, loving son still had a mother; and he hoped to honor with her the memory of the great man who had departed this life. But now he loses his mother as well, and in a fashion worse than if she had been snatched from him by death. The image of reliability, which every loving child likes to attach to his parents, is suddenly gone: no help from the dead, no support from the living. She is a women, and: 'Frailty, thy name is woman.'

"He now feels really dejected and isolated. No worldly joys can replace what he has lost. As he is not melancholy or pensive by nature, grief and contemplation are now a heavy burden. That's how he appears when we first see him. I do not believe I have read anything into the play that is not there, or overstressed any element in it."

Serlo looked at his sister, and said: "Was I wrong in the way I described our friend? He has just made a good beginning, and he will have much more to tell us about, and persuade us of." Wilhelm swore that his intentions were not to persuade, but to convince; and he asked for a few more moments of their time.

"Just to think clearly about this young man, this son of a prince," Wilhelm went on to say. "Visualize his position, and observe him when he learns that his father's spirit is abroad. Stand by him when, in that terrible night, the venerable ghost appears before his eyes. He is overcome by intense horror, speaks to the spirit, sees it beckon him, follows, and hears — the terrible accusation of his uncle continues to ring in his ears, with its challenge to seek revenge, and that repeated urgent cry: 'Remember me!'

"And when the ghost has vanished, what do we see standing before us? A young hero thirsting for revenge? A prince by birth, happy to be charged with unseating the usurper of his throne? Not at all! Amazement and sadness descend on this lonely spirit; he becomes bitter at the smiling villains, swears not to forget his departed father, and ends with a heavy sigh: 'The time is out of joint; O cursed spite! That ever I was born to set it right!'

"In these words, so I believe, lies the key to Hamlet's whole behavior; and it is clear to me what Shakespeare set out to portray: a heavy deed placed on a soul which is not adequate to cope with it. And it is in this sense that I find the whole play constructed. An oak tree planted in a precious pot which should only have held delicate flowers. The roots spread out, the vessel is shattered.

"A fine, pure, noble and highly moral person, but devoid of that emotional strength that characterizes a hero, goes to pieces beneath a burden that it can neither support nor cast off. Every obligation is sacred to him, but this one is too heavy. The impossible is demanded of him—not the impossible in any absolute sense, but what is impossible for him. How he twists and turns, trembles, advances and retreats, always being reminded, always reminding himself, and finally almost losing sight of his goal, yet without ever regaining happiness!"

Chapter Fourteen

Several persons came in and the conversation was interrupted. They were musicians accustomed to meet once every week at Serlo's for an informal concert. He liked music very much and said that an actor could never achieve a true conception of his art, or the right feeling for it, without a love of music. "You act much more easily and appropriately when your movements are accompanied and controlled by music; and every actor should, as it were, compose his part in his mind, although it's in prose, so that he doesn't drool it out monotonously to his own tune, but modulates its tempo and rhythm."

Aurelie appeared to be taking little interest in what was happening, and eventually led our friend into an adjoining room, where she walked up to the window, gazed at the starry sky, and said, "You still owe us more of your thoughts about *Hamlet*. I don't want to be precipitate, and would like my brother to hear what you have to say, but do tell me what you think about Ophelia."

"There is not much to say about her," said Wilhelm. "Her character is presented in a few strokes of the master's hand. Her whole being is pervaded by ripe, sweet sensuality. Her affection for the prince, whose hand she might justly feel she can claim, rises from the very wellsprings of her being, her heart abandons itself so completely to her desire that both her father and her brother are fearful for her and warn her openly. Her decorum, like the posy on her bosom, cannot conceal the perturbation of her heart—in fact it betrays it. Her imagination is infected, her tender modesty nevertheless breathes desire and love, and if the obliging goddess of fortune should shake the tree, the fruit would fall."

"But when she sees herself rejected, repulsed and reviled," said Aurelie, "when the best turns to the worst in her lover's madness, and he hands her not the sweet goblet of love but the bitter cup of sorrow . . ."

"Then her heart breaks," said Wilhelm. "The whole frame of her existence falls out of joint, her father's death bursts in upon her, and the whole structure of her lovely being collapses."

Wilhelm had not noticed the intensity of expression with which Aurelie was speaking. His attention had been entirely concentrated on the perfect structure of the work of art, and he had no idea of the totally different way Aurelie was reacting to the character, or that some deep grief of her own was being awakened by this shadow play.

Her head was still resting on her arms, and her eyes, filled with tears, were still gazing upward. Finally she could no longer suppress her hidden anguish, and seizing his hands she said to him as he stood there in astonishment: "Forgive, o forgive my troubled heart! The company of others restricts and oppresses me. I have to try to hide my feelings from my unfeeling brother. But your presence has released me from all these restraints. I've only just met you, but you're someone in whom I can confide." Words almost failed her, and she sank on to his shoulder. "Don't think the worse of me," she said, sobbing, "for opening up to you so quickly, for appearing so weak. Be my friend, remain my friend—I deserve it!" He spoke to her compassionately, but without effect. Her tears continued to flow, and stifled her words.

At that moment Serlo came into the room, a most unwelcome interruption, and, totally unexpected, with Philine, whom he held by the hand. "Here's your friend," he said to her. "He will be glad to see you."

"Well!" said Wilhelm in astonishment. "How is it that I find you here?" Philine walked up to him, calmly and unassumingly, bade him welcome, and praised Serlo's kindness in taking her into his excellent troupe, not because of merit but simply in the expectation that she would develop. She acted in a friendly manner toward Wilhelm, though with a certain distance.

But this pretense only lasted while the other two were in the room. For when Aurelie left to hide her agitation and Serlo was called away, Philine first looked to the doors to see that both of them were well and truly gone, then jumped around like a mad thing, sat on the ground and almost choked with tittering laughter. Then she leapt up, said nice things to Wilhelm, and seemed exceedingly pleased at having gone ahead to reconnoitre the terrain and build her own nest.

"There's plenty going on here," she said. "Just what I like. Aurelie has had an unhappy love affair with a nobleman, who must be a splendid fellow. I would like to see him some day. If I am not mistaken, he has left her a little memento; there is a three-year-old boy running around here, pretty as the sun.

Papa must have been extremely nice. Usually I can't stand children, but this one appeals to me. I've reckoned it out. Her husband dies, then this new admirer, then the age of the child—everything fits.

"Her friend has gone his own way, and hasn't seen her for a whole year: She is beside herself and utterly inconsolable. Silly fool!—As for her brother, he has a dancer in the company that he makes up to, a little actress that he is intimate with, and several women that he courts in the town; and now I too am on the list. Poor fool!—As for the rest, I'll tell you about them tomorrow. But now a word about your dear friend Philine: the silly fool is in love with you!" She swore that this was true and was a real lark. She implored him to fall in love with Aurelie. "Then there'll be a real chase. She runs after her faithless lover, you after her, I after you, and the brother after me. If that isn't enough to keep us amused for six months, I am ready to die after the first episode in the fourfold complications of this romance." She begged him not to spoil her game, and show her as much respect as she would seek to earn by her public behavior.

Chapter Fifteen

The next morning Wilhelm decided to call on Madame Melina, but found she was not at home. He inquired after the other members of the company and learnt that Philine had invited them all to breakfast. He went there out of curiosity and found them all quite consoled and in very good spirits. The clever little creature had gathered them together, regaled them with chocolate, and given them to understand that all avenues were not closed: she hoped by her influence to convince the director of the advantages of having such proficient people in his company. They listened attentively, drank one cup of chocolate after another, decided that this girl was not all that bad and that they would speak well of her in the future.

"Do you really think," said Wilhelm when he was alone with Philine, "that Serlo will keep our comrades?" "Not at all," replied Philine. "As for me I don't particularly want him to. The sooner they leave, the better. Laertes is the only I would wish to keep; the others we can get rid of gradually."

She made it clear to her friend that she was convinced he should no longer bury his talents but go on the stage under Serlo's direction. She was full of praise for the organization, the taste and intelligence that were in evidence here, and spoke so flatteringly to Wilhelm about his talents that his heart and imagination were as near to accepting this proposal as his mind and his reason withdrew from it. He did not admit to himself nor to Philine where his inclinations were leading him, and spent a restless day, unable to decide whether to go to his father's business associate and collect the letters that were probably waiting there for him. He realized how uneasy his family must have become by now, but shied away from receiving a detailed account of their concern and reproaches; he was looking forward to an evening of unsullied pleasure at the performance of a new play.

Serlo had refused to let him go to the rehearsal. "You must," he said, "get to know us at our very best before we allow you to see us in the planning stage."

Wilhelm was extremely satisfied with the performance which he attended next evening. It was the first time he had witnessed theater of such quality. One could see that all the actors had excellent talents, conducive dispositions and a clear and serious view of their art, and yet they were all different; they supported each other, inspired each other, and were exact and precise in every facet of their acting. One soon realized that Serlo was the soul of the enterprise and that he distinguished himself in it. The moment he stepped onto the stage and opened his mouth he revealed an admirably controlled mood, moderation in his actions, and a true sense of what was fitting, together with an exceptional mimetic talent. His inward composure radiated outward to the spectators, and the intelligent way in which he conveyed every nuance of the role delighted the audience because he was able to conceal the technique he had acquired by persistent practicing.

His sister Aurelie was just as good as he, and received even greater applause because she knew how to move hearts as well as to amuse and lighten them.

After Wilhelm had spent some days in this pleasant fashion, Aurelie one day asked to see him. He hastened to her room and found her lying on a couch. She seemed to be suffering from a headache, and could not hide the fact that she was in a state of feverish unrest. Her eyes brightened when she saw him. "Please forgive me!" she called out. "The confidence you have inspired in me, has made me weak. Up till now I have been able to occupy myself, when I was alone, with my sorrows. They provided me with strength and consolation. But now, I don't know how, you have loosened the bonds of my silence, and you will now unwittingly be a party to the battle I am fighting with myself."

Wilhelm responded with kindness and courtesy, assuring her that her person and her sorrow were constantly before his mind, and urging her to confide in him so that he might be able to become her friend.

While he was speaking, he noticed the little boy sitting on the floor and playing with all sorts of toys. He was, as Philine had said, probably about three years of age, and Wilhelm now well understood why the flippant girl, whose manner of expression was rarely so elevated, had compared him with the sun. For the loveliest golden curls hung over his big brown eyes and his round face, his gleaming white forehead arched over delicate dark eyebrows, and his cheeks glowed with health. "Sit down beside me," Aurelie said to Wilhelm. "I can see you are surprised as you observe this happy child. It's true that it gives me great joy to hold it in my arms, and I take good care of it. But I can measure my sorrows by this child, for they rarely let me appreciate the value of such a gift.

"Let me tell you about myself and my life, for I am very anxious that you should not misjudge me. I thought I would have a few peaceful moments, which is why I sent for you. Now you're here—and I've lost my thread.

"Just one more abandoned creature on this earth! you will say to yourself. You are a man and will think: Look how the fool reacts to a necessary evil, more certain to befall a woman than death itself, namely a man's infidelity! If my fate were ordinary, I would gladly bear ordinary sorrow. But my fate is so very extraordinary. Why can't I show it to you in a mirror, or have someone tell you about it! If it were just a matter of being seduced, surprised and then abandoned, there would be some consolation in despair. But my situation is far worse: I duped myself, deceived myself against my will—that is what I can never forgive myself for."

"But someone with sentiments as noble as yours cannot be completely unhappy," her friend replied.

"And do you know to what I owe these feelings?" asked Aurelie. "The worst possible education that a girl was ever ruined by, the worst example, one that misled my senses and my inclinations.

"After the untimely death of my mother I spent the best years of my growing up in the house of an aunt who made it a rule to disregard all principles of honesty. She abandoned herself blindly to every emotion, no matter whether she controlled its object or was enslaved by it, so long as she could forget herself in the whirl of enjoyment. What sort of view of the male sex could we innocent children form for ourselves from this? How obtuse, insistent, brazen and clumsy were all those whom she attracted to herself; how satiated, arrogant, empty-headed and ridiculous they became once they had satisfied their desires. I watched this woman degraded by base company for years on end. What encounters she had to put up with, what spirit she showed in accepting her fate, what shameful enslavements she had to learn to live with!

"That was my introduction to the male sex, my friend; and how utterly I despised them when quite decent men seemed, in their relations with our sex, to abandon every good feeling that nature otherwise might have made them capable of.

"Unfortunately I also on these occasions formed some negative opinions of my own sex. As a girl of sixteen I was more sensible than I am now, when I can hardly understand myself. Why are we so sensible when we are young, and why do we become ever more foolish!"

The boy was making a noise. Aurelie became impatient and rang the bell. An old woman came in to take him away. "Have you still got a toothache?" Aurelie said to the woman whose face was all bandaged up. "It's almost unbearable," said the woman in a hollow voice as she picked up the child, who seemed to go willingly, and took him away.

Aurelie began to weep bitterly when the child had gone. "I can't do anything but weep and moan," she said, "and I'm ashamed to behave like a baby before you. My concentration is gone and I can't go on talking to you." She broke off, and lapsed into silence. Her friend, since he had nothing of a general nature that he wanted to say and nothing particular that he could say, pressed her hand and sat looking at her. Not knowing what else to do he finally picked up a book from the table in front of him. It was the works of Shakespeare, opened up to *Hamlet*.

Serlo, who had just come into the room to inquire after his sister, looked at the book in Wilhelm's hand, and said: "So there you are again, you and your *Hamlet*! Good! Many doubts have occurred to me which would seem to reduce considerably the great admiration that you choose to have for it. Haven't the English themselves admitted that the main interest ceases with the third act, and the last two just barely hold the whole thing together? Isn't it true that, toward the end, the play doesn't move along at all?"

"It is quite possible," said Wilhelm, "that some members of the nation which has produced so many masterpieces should be misled by prejudices or limitations into making such false judgments. But that shouldn't stop us from looking at it with our own eyes, and being just. I am unwilling to criticize the plan of the play; in fact, I believe no greater plan could have been conceived. Indeed it isn't conceived at all, the play just is as it is."

"How can you explain that?" asked Serlo.

"I don't intend to explain anything," Wilhelm replied, "I just want to give you my thoughts."

Aurelie raised her head from the pillow, rested it on her hands and gazed at our friend who, absolutely convinced that he was right, continued: "It pleases and flatters us to see a hero who acts of his own accord, loves and hates according to the dictates of his heart, completing what he sets out to do by removing all obstacles that impede his progress toward some lofty goal. Historians and poets like to persuade us that such pride of purpose may be the lot of mankind. But in this case we are differently informed: the hero has no plan, but the play has. A villain is not punished according to some rigid concept of revenge narrowly applied: a monstrous deed is performed, extends its evil consequences, and drags innocent people into its orbit. The evildoer seems to be avoiding the fate that is in store for him, but then plunges into it where he thought he had found a safe way out. For cruel deeds bring evil to the innocent just as good deeds bring advantages to those who do not deserve them, often without the originator being punished or rewarded. How marvelously this is presented in the play before us! Purgatory sends a spirit to demand revenge, but in vain. Circumstances combine to hasten this, but in vain! Neither humans nor subterranean powers can achieve what is reserved for Fate alone. The time of reckoning arrives; and the good perish with the bad. A whole family is mowed down, and a new one emerges."

They looked at each other for a while, and then Serlo said: "You don't much compliment providence by thus elevating the poet. You seem to be assigning to the glory of the poet what others attribute to providence, namely a purpose and plan that he never thought of."

Chapter Sixteen

"Let me now ask you a question," said Aurelie. "I have once more looked over Ophelia's part, and am satisfied that I can play it under certain conditions. But tell me this: Shouldn't the poet have given her in her madness different songs to sing? Couldn't he have chosen parts of some sad ballads? What is such suggestive and indecent nonsense doing in the mouth of this pure young girl?"

"My dear friend," said Wilhelm, "I wouldn't change them one iota. There is deep meaning in what seems to be so strange and inappropriate about these songs. We know from the very beginning of the play what her mind is full of. The dear child lives quietly for herself, but she is hardly able to conceal her desires and wishes. Lustful tones resound throughout her mind and, like an imprudent nurse, she may well have tried more than once to sing her senses to sleep with ballads that merely keep them more awake. And when she has lost all control over herself and when her heart is on her tongue, this tongue betrays her and, in the innocence of her madness, she indulges herself before the king and queen by recalling those loose songs that she so much liked: the girl who was won, the girl who crept to her lover, and so forth. . . ."

He had not yet finished what he was saying, when he witnessed a curious scene which he was quite unable to account for.

Serlo had been pacing up and down, without any apparent purpose. But suddenly he went to Aurelie's dressing table, snatched up something that was lying there, and rushed toward the door with it. Aurelie had not really noticed what he was doing, but suddenly she threw herself in his path, violently grabbed hold of him, and succeeded in wresting from him the object he had picked up. They fought and struggled fiercely with each other, twisting and turning. He was laughing, she was furious, and when Wilhelm rushed up to tear them apart and quieten them down he saw Aurelie jump off to the side with a naked dagger in her hand while Serlo impetuously threw the sheath to the ground. Wilhelm drew back astonished, seeking in silent amazement for the possible cause of so strange a struggle about so unusual an object.

"You shall be the arbitrator between us," said Serlo. "What on earth is she doing with such a sharp weapon? Let her show it to you. This dagger is not suitable for any actress; it's as sharply pointed as a needle or a knife. Why this nonsense? She is such a violent person that some day or other she will do herself harm again. I have an intense hatred of such eccentricities: any serious thought of this kind is crazy, and to have such a dangerous plaything is ridiculous."

"I've got it back again," said Aurelie, lifting the shining blade. "In the future I will take better care of my trusty friend. Forgive me," she said, kissing the dagger, "for having been so careless."

Serlo now seemed to be becoming really angry. "Think what you will, brother," she went on; "how can you know whether I have not been granted a precious talisman to provide me in this form with help and advice in the worst of times? Must everything be harmful that looks dangerous?"

"Such crazy talk will drive me out of my mind!" said Serlo as he left the room in barely suppressed anger. Aurelie carefully returned the dagger to its sheath and put it into her pocket. "Let's continue the conversation which my unfortunate brother interrupted," she said, as Wilhelm started to ask her about their strange altercation.

"I have to agree that your interpretation of Ophelia is right," she said. "I wouldn't wish to misinterpret the poet's intentions, but I pity her more than I sympathize with her. Now let me tell you something which you have given me occasion to think about in the short time we have known each other. I admire your profound insights into literature, especially dramatic literature. You are able to penetrate to the very depths of what was in the poet's mind and to appreciate the subtlest nuances in its presentation. Without having ever seen things in reality you can recognize the truthfulness of their image. It seems as if some presentiment of the whole world lies within you, and this is brought to life and developed by your contact with poetry. For truly," she went on, "nothing comes into you from the outside world. I have rarely met anyone who knew so little of the people with whom he lives—indeed fundamentally misjudges them. Let me say this: when I hear you explaining Shakespeare, it seems as if you have just come from a council of the gods and heard them discussing how to make humans; but when you are associating with real people, you seem like some first child of creation growing up to gape at lions and monkeys, sheep and elephants in strange astonishment and good-natured devotion, treating them affably as your equals, simply because they live and move."

"My own maturity has often troubled me," said Wilhelm, "and I would be grateful to you, if you could help me gain a clearer understanding of the world around me. Earlier in my youth I turned my eyes inward rather than outward, and it is therefore quite natural that I have arrived at some general knowledge of the human race without in the least understanding particular human beings."

"That's true," said Aurelie. "At first I thought you were just playing a game with us when you said such positive things about the persons you sent my brother, and I compared your account of them with what they actually are."

This remark of Aurelie's, true as it might have been, and willing as Wilhelm was to admit his failings, had something about it that was oppressive, even offensive. Wilhelm said nothing. He collected his thoughts, trying to conceal his irritation and to ask himself whether her reproach was justified.

"You need not be embarrassed," said Aurelie. "One can always attain clarity of mind, but no one can give us fullness of heart. If your destiny is to be an artist, you cannot continue for much longer in a state of such imperception and ingenuousness. These are the outer coverings that protect a budding growth, and it is unfortunate if the tender plant is forced too soon. It is however a good thing if we do not always know the people for whom we work.

"I too was once in that blissful state, when I went on the stage with the highest opinion of myself and my nation. There was nothing that in my imagination the Germans didn't possess and nothing that they could not develop into. I spoke to my nation from my slightly elevated platform, edged by lights whose brightness and smoke obscured my view of what was in front of me. How glad I was at the sound of the applause that floated up from the crowd, how grateful for this tribute of acclaim from so many different hands. I went on like this for a long time, lulling myself, through the good relationship I had with a public that responded to everything I offered them, into a sense of complete harmony with the noblest and best of my nation, for I thought that this was what I saw before me.

"But unfortunately it was not just the personality and skill of the actress that appealed to the spectators; they also made claims on the lively young girl. I was given to understand in no uncertain terms that it was my duty to share with them privately the emotions I had aroused in them from the stage. Unfortunately, that was not what I wanted. All I desired was to raise their minds; I had no concern with what they called their hearts, and, no matter what type, age or class they belonged to, they all became burdensome to me and I was irritated at not being able to shut myself up in my room like any honest girl, and spare myself all this trouble.

"The men behaved in a manner familiar to me from my aunt's house, and they would have aroused the same loathing in me if I had not been amused by their idiosyncrasies and stupidities. Since I could hardly avoid seeing them either on the stage itself or in public places, or at home, I decided to be always on the lookout, and my brother gave me valuable assistance in this. And when you consider that slippery shop assistants, conceited merchants' sons, smooth men-of-the-world, brave soldiers and hasty princes, all came into my ken and tried to start a romance with me (each in his own way), you will surely forgive me for believing that I had become fairly well acquainted with my own nation. I saw them all get excited — the fantastically dolled-up students, the professors uneasy in their pride of humility, the tottering and self-satisfied prelates, the stiff and attentive officials, the coarse country squires, the ingratiating courtiers, the young priests off course, the nimble or actively speculating businessmen — but, my heavens, there were very few of them who could arouse the slightest interest in me. On the contrary: it was extremely distasteful to me to cash in on the approval of these fools and endure such wearisome boredom, though in general I was pleased by any approval I received.

"But when I expected some intelligent compliment on my acting, or hoped they would praise an author whom I respected, they would make one silly remark after another and mention some insipid play they would like to see me perform in. When I listened around in company to see if a particularly fine, ingenious or witty point had made its mark and would resurface at an appropriate moment, I rarely found any trace of this. A mistake — if an actor had said the wrong word or used a provincial pronunciation — that was what they fixed on as something so important that they couldn't get off the topic. Finally I no longer knew where I should turn; they seemed to think they were too bright to be entertained, and entertaining me by petting and pawing me. So I began to despise them all intensely, feeling as though the whole nation was purposely prostituting itself by the representatives it sent me. They seemed for the most part so clumsy, ill educated, badly informed, so lacking in graciousness of personality and taste. I often said to myself that a German can't even buckle a shoe without having learned how to do so from foreigners!

"You can see how blind and unjust my hypochondria made me, and it grew steadily worse. I might well have killed myself, but I chose another extreme: I married, or rather I got myself married. My brother, having taken over the direction of the theater, wanted very much to have an assistant. His choice fell on a young man, who was not unattractive, one who lacked everything my brother possessed—genius, vitality, intelligence and impulsiveness—but had everything that my brother lacked—concern for order, industriousness, organizational talent and the ability to manage money.

"This man became my husband, without my really knowing how; we lived together without my knowing why. Suffice it to say that things went well. Thanks to my brother's activities he took in a lot of money; and thanks to my husband's abilities we managed well. I didn't think any more about the world or my nation. I had nothing in common with the world, and I had lost any idea of the nation. When I appeared on stage, I did so in order to live, opening my mouth simply because I was required not to remain silent, having come there in order to speak.

"So that I should do this fairly well I had resigned myself to my brother's wishes. His concern was for applause, and money; for, let me tell you, he likes to be praised and he spends a lot. I no longer acted according to my feelings and convictions, but in the way he instructed me, and when I earned his thanks, I was satisfied. He was guided by the foibles of his public; money came in, he could live according to his desires, and we had good times with him.

"But I began to lapse into a mechanical kind of routine. I spent my days without much joy or interest, my marriage was childless, and lasted only a short while. My husband fell ill, his strength visibly diminished, and my concern for him broke up my state of indifference. During this time I made an acquaintance with whom a new life began for me, a new and shorter life, for it will soon be at an end."

She stopped, and after an interval of quiet continued: "My talkativeness has suddenly dried up, and I don't dare go on. Let me rest for a while. You must not go away until you have had a full account of my misery. Call Mignon and find out what she wants."

The girl had several times come into the room while Aurelie was talking. But since they had lowered their voices every time she appeared, she had settled herself outside in the hall, quietly waiting. When she was asked to come in again, she brought a book, which, from its binding and shape, they could see was an atlas. At the pastor's house she had for the first time seen maps, had put a lot of questions about these to him, and had informed herself as best she could. Her eagerness to learn had apparently been greatly increased by this new sort of information. She had implored Wilhelm to buy the book for her. She had deposited with the salesman her big silver buckles, and, since it was too late to do so today, she wanted to redeem them next morning. It was agreed that she should; whereupon she began to recite what she had learnt and in her own special way asked the strangest questions. Once again it became apparent that, for all her energy, her comprehension was slow and laborious. So too was her handwriting, though she took great pains over it. She still spoke a broken German; and only when she opened her mouth to sing, or played the zither, did she reveal the one organ she had to express her innermost self.

Since we are talking about Mignon, we must also mention the embarrassment that she had been causing our friend for some time. Whenever she came or went, bade him good morning or good night, she clasped him so firmly in her arms and kissed him so passionately, that the violence of her developing nature filled him with alarm. The twitching intensity of her movements increased daily, and her whole being seemed to suggest a suppressed state of unrest. She could not be anywhere without twisting string, crumpling cloth or chewing pieces of wood or paper. All these activities seemed only to deflect great inner commotion. The only thing that appeared to give her peace or serenity, was being with the boy Felix, and she played with him in the most delightful manner.

Aurelie, after a respite, determined to finish her account of what lay so heavily on her mind, became impatient at Mignon's importunity and indicated to her that she should leave. Since nothing else seemed to work, they had to send her away, very much against her will.

"It's now or never," said Aurelie, "if I am to finish telling you my story. If my tender beloved, my unjust friend, were but a few miles from here, I would say to you: get on your horse and try somehow to make his acquaintance, and when you returned, you would certainly have forgiven me and would pity me in your heart. But all I can do is tell you in words how lovable he was, and how very much I loved him.

"I came to know him just at that critical time when I was deeply concerned about my husband's life. My friend had just returned from America where he, in the company of several Frenchmen, had served with great distinction under the colors of the United States. When I met him, he behaved toward me with composure and civility, openness and generosity: he talked to me about myself, my situation, and my acting, like an old acquaintance, so full of understanding that for the first time I could enjoy seeing myself clearly in the mind of someone else. His judgments were apt without being negative, and just without being unsympathetic. There was nothing harsh about him, and when his tone became playful, it was never offensive. He seemed to be used to success with women, and that made me cautious; but he was never flattering or importunate, and so I was never worried.

"He did not cultivate many acquaintances in town. Most of his time was spent riding out to visit his many friends in the surrounding district and dealing with his business affairs. When he returned he would stop off at my house. He showed deep concern for my husband who was steadily failing and found a good doctor to alleviate his suffering. Since he had shown such interest in everything that concerned me, he allowed me in turn to share in his own experiences. He told me about his eagerness to be a soldier, about the campaign he had fought in, and about his family. He also spoke about his present occupations. In short, he had no secrets from me. He opened up his innermost self, letting me peer into the most hidden recesses of his soul, and revealing his capabilities and his passions. It was the first time in my life that I had enjoyed a relationship that appealed to my emotions as well as my mind. I was attracted by him, and enthralled before I could think about myself.

"I lost my husband almost in the same manner as I had found him; and the whole burden of the business affairs connected with the theater now fell upon me. My brother, incomparable on stage, was never much good at managing things. I had to take care of all that, and in addition studied my roles even more intently than before. I played them as I had in the past, but now with new strength and new life because of him, and for him, but not always with complete success if I knew he was in the audience. But there were times when, having seen me act, he surprised and delighted me by his unexpected approval.

"I am certainly a strange creature. No matter what part I was playing, I was really only concerned in praising him and honoring him by the lines I spoke; that was the state of my feelings, whatever the words might be. If I knew he was in the audience, I did not dare to speak out with full intensity; it was as though I did not wish to express my love and admiration for him to his face. If, however, he was not in the theater I had free range, and did my very best with a certain composure and extreme satisfaction. Applause began to please me once more, and if the public was pleased, I felt like saying to them down there: You owe that to him!

"Indeed my attitude to the public, and to the whole nation, had gone through a miraculous change. Suddenly my countrymen appeared to me once more in a very favorable light, and I was astonished at my former blindness.

"'How nonsensical it was for you to revile a nation just for being a nation,' I would say to myself time after time. 'How can individuals be so interesting? The question is whether in a mass of people there is a sufficient distribution of disposition, power and ability which, when developed by favorable circumstances, can be directed by outstanding people toward some common goal.' I was now pleased not to find much striking originality amongst my compatriots, I was glad to see that they did not scorn to take direction from elsewhere, I was glad to have found a leader.

"Lothario—let me call my friend by the name he liked best—had always presented the Germans to me in terms of their valor, and demonstrated to me that there was no more trusty nation in the world, so long as they were properly led; and I was ashamed at not having recognized this prime quality of my nation. He knew about their history, and he was acquainted with the most meritorious men of his age. Young as he was, he had an eye for the promise that was developing in the youth of his nation, and for the quiet achievements in so many fields of active older men. He gave me an overview of what Germany is and can become, and I was ashamed at having judged it from the motley throng in theater dressing rooms. He made it my duty to be truthful, intelligent and inspiring in my own sphere of activity, and I felt inspired every time I walked on to the stage. Mediocre passages turned to gold in my mouth, and if a poet had been there to assist me in what I was doing, I would have produced the most marvelous effects.

"That is how the young widow lived for months on end. Lothario couldn't do without me, and I was miserable when he wasn't there. He showed me letters from his relations, especially from his splendid sister. He took an interest in every detail of our circumstances. A closer and more perfect union could not be imagined. The word love was never mentioned. He went and came, came and went—and now, my friend, it is high time that you went."

Chapter Seventeen

Wilhelm could not put off any longer calling on his business friends. He went with some trepidation, for he knew he would find letters there from his family. He feared the reproaches they were bound to contain, for probably the firm had already been informed of the trouble he had caused. After all those chivalric adventures of his, he was not happy about appearing as a callow youth in their eyes, and so he decided to behave resolutely, and thereby conceal his uneasiness.

But to his great surprise and relief, everything went off fairly smoothly. In the bustle of these busy offices there had been little time for them to consult his letters, and only passing reference was made to his having stayed away so long. When he opened the letters from his father and from Werner, he found them all quite moderate in tone and content. His father, hoping for a detailed account such as on his departure he had urged his son to provide him with, even giving him a systematic plan of how to set it out, seemed in the beginning quite unperturbed by his silence, though he did complain about the mystifying nature of that first and only letter sent from the count's castle. Werner merely joked in his usual fashion, gave some amusing town gossip, and asked for news of friends and acquaintances whom Wilhelm would now be meeting in the city. Extremely glad to be relieved at such little cost, Wilhelm immediately sent back some lively letters, and promised his father a detailed journal with all the geographical, statistical and mercantile observations that he had asked for. He had seen a lot on his journey and hoped to put together an extensive report. He did not notice that he was in almost the same situation as when he had set up the lights and summoned the audience for a play that was not memorized, indeed not even written. When he there-fore started to apply himself to his composition, he came to realize that he could talk about his feelings and thoughts, his experiences of heart and mind, but not about external things which, as he now noticed, had not in any way attracted his attention.

He was helped by the knowledge of his friend Laertes. These two young men, for all their differences, had become close friends, and Laertes, with all his faults, was really an interesting person in his own peculiar way. Blessed as he was with radiant vitality, he could have grown old without worry-ing about his condition. But now misfortunes and sickness had robbed him of the unclouded delights of youth, though at the same time they had given him some insight into the mutability and fragmentation of life. From this had come his inclination toward moody, rhapsodic utterances in which he expressed his immediate reactions. He did not like to be alone, frequented coffeehouses and inns, and when he was at home, his preferred reading, indeed his only reading, was travel books. He could now indulge in this, for he had located a big lending library and his mind was soon buzzing with information about half the globe.

It was therefore easy for him to encourage his friend when Wilhelm told him about his complete lack of facts for the solemnly promised narration. "Let's make an incomparable work of art out of it," said Laertes. "Hasn't Germany been driven through, walked through, crept through, fled through from one end to the other? Hasn't every German traveler been reimbursed by the public for his smaller or larger expenses? Just tell me the route you took before you came to us; I'll know all the rest. I'll find you sources and information for what you are composing, and we will see to it that we get the right distances and the right size of populations, even if those have not been measured or counted. We can find out the revenues of the various districts from calendars and charts, for these are well known to be the most reliable sources. On this information we can base our political speculations—not forgetting some incidental observations on government. We'll describe a few of the princes as being true fathers of the fatherland, so that we will be more easily believed when we cast some blame on others and if we don't actually pass through the towns where some famous people live, we will at least run across them in inns where they will confide arrant nonsense to us. Let's not forget to include a delightful love affair with a simple country girl, and we'll have a work to delight not only fathers and mothers, but one that every bookseller will be glad to stock."

They went to work and both of them had a great deal of fun at it. In the evenings Wilhelm went to the theater and derived the greatest satisfaction from consorting with Serlo and Aurelie. And every day he was expanding the range of his ideas which had for so long been limited to a very narrow sphere.

Chapter Eighteen

It was with the greatest interest that Wilhelm learnt about the career of Serlo, even though piecemeal; for this strange man was not given to confiding in others, nor to coherent exposition. One could well say that he was born and raised in the theater. Even before he could talk he moved the hearts of the audience by his very presence on the stage, for authors of that time were well aware of the effectiveness of natural demonstrations of innocence, and when he first said "Father" and "Mother" in plays that everyone loved, he earned vigorous applause long before he had any idea what all the clapping was about. He descended in a flying machine as Cupid more than once, emerged from an egg as harlequin, and performed at an early age the sweetest tricks as a little chimney sweep.

Unfortunately, however, he had to pay heavily in between for the applause he received on his brilliant evenings. His father, convinced that a child's concentration was best aroused and maintained by beatings, thrashed him at regular intervals while he was learning a new part—not because he was lacking in skill, but rather that his achievement should be the more secure and lasting. In those days parents used to rain blows on children who stood around gawking when a marker was being erected, and old folks still remember the time and place where this happened. The boy grew up showing unusual mental and physical ability and great flexibility of acting powers, both in actions and gestures. While still a boy he could imitate persons so well that people believed they were seeing these very persons, despite the fact that they were quite different from the boy in figure, age and character, and different from each other. In addition he knew how to make his way in the world, and as soon as he was fairly sure of his own powers, he thought it perfectly natural to run away from his father who, as the boy's intelligence developed and his skill increased, thought it necessary to advance these still further by even harsher treatment.

The waggish boy was blissfully happy out there in the world because his merry pranks went down well everywhere. His lucky star led him first on Shrove Tuesday to a monastery, where the reverend father in charge of processionals, who had organized sacred performances for the delight of the Christian community, had just died. Here, suddenly, was a guardian angel to help them out! He took over the role of Gabriel in the Annunciation, and made a favorable impression on the pretty girl playing the Virgin Mary, who gracefully received his polite announcement with a display of humility and inner pride. He then acted in succession all the most important roles in the mystery plays, and formed quite a high opinion of himself when ultimately he was mocked, beaten and nailed to the cross as the Savior of the World.

On this last occasion some of the soldiers played their parts too realistically; and so, to take his revenge in the seemliest possible manner, he dressed them up in the sumptuous garments of kings and emperors at the Last Judgment, and then, at the very moment when they, delighted with what they represented, were about to enter Heaven ahead of all the others, he suddenly appeared before them in the shape of a devil, beating them vigorously with a pitchfork, to the extreme edification of all the spectators and beggars in the audience, and thrusting them mercilessly back into the pit where they were most uncivilly greeted by emerging fire.

He was astute enough to foresee that these crowned heads would take offense at his bold actions and not respect his high office as prosecutor-executioner; and so, before the Milennium arrived, he crept away quietly, and went to a nearby town where he was received with open arms by a group of people known at that time as the "Children of Joy." These lively people, intelligent and perceptive, well understood that the sum of our existence divided by reason never comes out exactly and that there is always a wondrous remainder. They set out at certain fixed times to get rid of this troublesome and, if it spreads through the whole mass, dangerous remainder, by indulging, one day a week, wholeheartedly in foolishness, and on that day punishing in allegorical presentations the follies they had observed in themselves and others during the other days of the week. If this way of doing things was cruder than some kind of coherent education in which the moral part of man accustoms itself daily to observing, warning and punishing, it was certainly more amusing and more reliable. For without their denying some pet folly, they treated it simply for what it was and nothing more, instead of its becoming through self-delusion a tyrant in the household and secretly enslaving man's reason, which thought it had long ago dispelled it. The fool's mask circulated within the group, and everyone was permitted to deck it out, on his own appointed day, according to the nature of his own, or another's, attributes. At carnival time they exercised the greatest freedom, and competed with the efforts of the clergy in attracting and entertaining the people. The solemn allegorical processions of virtues and vices, arts and sciences, continents and seasons presented in visible form a number of abstract concepts, and gave the people ideas of far-off things, and so these entertainments were not without their uses, whereas the ecclesiastical mummery merely intensified absurd superstitions.

Young Serlo was once again in his element. He was not endowed with real powers of invention, but he did possess extreme skill in making good use of what was available and arranging it so that it became plausible. His ideas, his powers of imitation, that biting wit which he was able to direct, at least one day a week, even against his benefactors, made him a valuable, even indispensable, member of the company.

There was, however, a restlessness in him that drove him out of this advantageous position into other parts of his native land, where he once more had to go through a different school. He went not only to Catholic areas but also to Protestant ones that avoided displaying images, where the good and the beautiful were worshipped with equal sincerity but less inventiveness. His masks were no longer of any use; he had to concentrate on appealing directly to heart and mind. In the short time that he spent with theatrical troupes, some small, some large, he took note of the special characteristics of all the plays and their actors. The monotony prevailing at that time on the German stage, the alexandrines with their ludicrous sound and rhythm, the dialogue that was either stilted or flat, the trivial and tedious moralizing—all this he observed; and soon noticed what really moved people and appealed to them.

He retained in his memory not just individual roles but whole plays that were playable, together with the particular tone an actor had used in performing his part and winning applause for it. On one of his journeys, when he was completely out of money, he lit on the idea of performing whole plays by himself, especially at manor houses or in villages, to cover his board and lodging. He would easily set up his "theater" in any inn, room or garden. With an impish display of seriousness and seeming enthusiasm he would capture the imagination of the spectators and deceive their senses by making before their very eyes a castle out of an old cupboard and a fan into a dagger. His youthful enthusiasm took the place of real deep feeling, his violence gave the appearance of strength, his flattery of tenderness. Those already accustomed to attending the theater were reminded of everything they had already seen and heard, and those who were not were given a foretaste of something marvelous that they wished to know more about. When something was successful in one place, he made sure to repeat it in another, and he experienced malicious glee when he could fool everybody right away, and in the same fashion as before.

His mind was so vigorous, open and uninhibited that he soon improved his performances by frequent repetition of individual parts and whole plays. He acquired the ability of reciting and acting in a manner closer to the spirit of the piece than that of the other actors he had taken as his models. He was gradually able to act in a way that appeared natural, but was, in fact, highly contrived. He seemed transported, but was carefully watching for effect, and his greatest pride was in gradually awakening the emotions of the spectators. This frantic activity soon necessitated a certain degree of moderation, and, partly by design and partly from instinct, he learnt to be economical with gestures and tone of voice, which is something that few actors seem to have any understanding of.

As a result he knew how to deal with rough, unfriendly people and win their favor. Since he was always satisfied with whatever board and lodging there was, gratefully accepted every gift, and even sometimes declined money if he thought he had already received enough, he was sent on to others with letters of recommendation, and for quite a while moved from one manor to another, giving a great deal of pleasure, enjoying himself in the process, and having various charming adventures.

He was, however, so cold-hearted that he could not really love anybody, and so clear-sighted that he did not respect anyone. All he saw were external characterizing signs and these he added to his actor's catalogue. He was, however, extremely offended in his self-assurance if he did not please everybody and win their applause. He had so sharpened his mind and attention toward how best to win such approval that he became ingratiating not only when he was on the stage but also in ordinary life. His temperament, talent and lifestyle combined to make him develop into a superb actor. For by what seemed an unusual, but in fact was a quite natural interplay of effect and reaction, by a combination of natural insight and studied technique, he lifted his powers of recitation and declamation, as well as his use of gestures, onto such a high plane that they took on a truthfulness and unconstrained openness that contrasted with the secretiveness, artificiality and anxious dissimulation of his life.

Perhaps we will say more about his life and adventures in some other place. For the present we simply observe that in later years, when he was already an established person with a respected name and a very good though not secure situation, he played the sophist in his conversation, which took on a subtly ironic and mocking tone and thereby prevented all serious communication. He displayed this especially in talking to Wilhelm whenever the latter chose to embark on a general theoretical discourse, as was so often the case. Nevertheless they enjoyed each other's company, and their different attitudes made for lively discussion. Wilhelm always wanted to deduce everything from the ideas he had already formed and to consider art in a general context. He wanted to establish definite, precise rules of what was good, right, beautiful and deserving of acclaim — in short, he treated everything with utmost seriousness. Serlo, on the other hand, took everything lightly: He never answered a question directly, but by some joke or anecdote would provide the most charming and agreeable explanation, which instructed and enlivened the company.

Chapter Nineteen

While Wilhelm was spending many a pleasant hour in this way, Melina and the others were in a much more disagreeable situation. At times they seemed to Wilhelm like a group of evil spirits whose very presence, not to speak of their sour faces and bitter reproaches, was utterly distasteful to him. Serlo had not even given them temporary positions, let alone hopes of a fixed engagement, despite the fact that he had become steadily more acquainted with their abilities. When the actors met socially at his house he would have them read; sometimes he read himself. He chose plays that were about to be performed, plays which had not been put on for a long time, usually only parts of these. After a first such run-through, he came back to sections which he had something to say about, and had these repeated, so that the actors' understanding was enhanced and the likelihood of making the right point increased. Lesser but meticulous minds can do more to put others at ease than confused and unpolished geniuses; and so Serlo, by the clear understanding that he imperceptibly imparted to them, could turn mediocre talent into remarkable ability.

One thing that helped greatly was that he had them read poems aloud, arousing in them a sense of the pleasure that well accented verse rhythms can produce, instead of, as usually happens in such gatherings, just having them read the sort of prose that came naturally to them.

By this means he had familiarized himself with all the actors who had recently arrived, made an assessment of what they were and what they might become, and secretly resolved to use what talents they had to his advantage, in view of a revolution that was threatening among the regular members of his company. He let matters rest for the moment, shrugged off all mediation by Wilhelm, deciding to bide his time, and, to Wilhelm's great surprise, made the proposal that he himself should become a member of the company. If he agreed to that, said Serlo, then he would also engage the others.

"So these people can't be quite so useless as you said they were," Wilhelm replied. "And if they are now to be taken on, their talents will be just as good without mine, I would think."

In strict confidence Serlo revealed to him the situation that he was in. His male lead was threatening to demand a higher salary as soon as his contract was due to be renewed. But Serlo was not inclined to agree to this, especially because this man's popularity with the public was declining. On the other hand, if he were to let him go, all his closer associates would leave with him, and a number of good, but also some mediocre actors, would be lost to the troupe. Then he explained to Wilhelm what he would gain in compensation from him and Laertes and the old Blusterer, and even Madame Melina. He even promised to get great success for the Pedant by giving him Jews, ministers and various villains to play.

Wilhelm hesitated for a moment, uneasy at the proposal. But feeling that he had to say something, he took a deep breath and replied: "Your kind words concern only the good that you see and hope for in us; how about the weaknesses, which have surely not escaped your keen judgment?"

"Those we will soon turn into strengths by hard work, careful thought and much practice. Your people may be artless or bunglers in their acting, but there is not one of them who does not show some degree of promise. As far as I can observe, there are no blockheads amongst them, and those are the only people impossible to train, no matter whether it is conceit, stupidity or hypochondria that makes them so clumsy and inflexible."

Serlo briefly outlined the conditions he was prepared to offer, asking Wilhelm for a quick decision and leaving him in some uncertainty.

While working on the fictitious travelogue which he together with Laertes had undertaken to write, partly for fun and partly because it was such a marvelous idea, he had become more observant than previously of conditions and everyday life in the real world. He now understood for the first time his father's purpose in so strongly urging him to keep a journal. More vividly than ever before he realized how valuable and satisfying it was to mediate between commercial interests and human needs, and help to extend vigorous activity in the farthermost mountain and forest regions of the country. When Laertes dragged him around this busy commercial town in which he found himself, he gained a clearer sense of one big center from which everything flowed and to which everything returned. This was the first time he had experienced real pleasure in the contemplation of such activity. In this state of mind he received Serlo's proposal; and all his desires and hopes, his belief that he had inborn talent for the theater, all his sense of obligation towards his helpless actor companions became alive again.

"Well," he said to himself, "here you are having to choose again between those two women who haunted your thoughts when you were young. The one does not look so paltry now, and the other not so splendid as she did. An inner voice impels you to follow one or the other, and there are valid external reasons for choosing either. But you can't decide. What you would prefer, would be for something from outside to tip the scales in one direction. And yet, if you are honest, you must admit that the urge towards a life of business proceeds entirely from external factors, whereas your inner desires are directed toward the development and perfection of your predisposition, both bodily and mental, toward what is good and beautiful. Must you not respect the power of Fate for having, without any cooperation on your part, brought you to the goal of all you wish? Are not all your previous thoughts and intentions being realized thanks to chance, without your doing anything about it? How very strange! The desires and hopes that a man cherishes in his heart would seem to be what he knows best; and yet, when they suddenly appear before him and are, as it were, pressing in upon him, he retreats from them, not recognizing them for what they are. All my dreams prior to that fateful night which separated me from Mariane, are now standing here before me, offering themselves to me. I came here in flight and yet have been led hither by some kindly hand. My intention was to seek refuge with Serlo; now he seeks me out and offers me conditions such as I could never have hoped for as a beginner. Was it simply my love for Mariane that made me so enthralled by the theater? Or was it love of art that made me so captivated by her? Was it the thought of future prospects, with the stage as the place to realize them, that attracted a restless, disorganized youth who wanted to live apart from the humdrum circumstances of middle-class life? Or was it something much purer, and nobler? What could possibly make you change your former opinions? Haven't you really followed your chosen path without being aware of doing so? Isn't the thing now to take the final step, since there are no other considerations involved; you can keep your solemn promise and relieve yourself honorably of your heavy responsibility toward the others."

Feelings and imaginings swept in on him in lively succession. He would be able to keep Mignon, he would not have to send the Harper away—these things weighed heavily with him. He was not yet quite decided, when he went to pay one of his customary visits to Aurelie.

Chapter Twenty

He found her lying on her sofa, and she seemed calm. "Do you think you will be able to go on stage tomorrow?" he asked. "Oh yes," she said with conviction. "You should know that nothing ever stops me from doing that. If only I could find some way of dissuading the spectators from giving me their applause. They mean well, but someday they will be the death of me. Just the day before yesterday I thought my heart would break. I used to be able to be satisfied with myself. If I had studied my part and was well prepared, I was pleased by the indications ringing out from all quarters that I had succeeded. But now I don't say what I want to say or how I want to say it. I get carried away, become confused, but my acting creates an even stronger impression. The applause is louder, and I think: if only you people knew what it is that delights you! My confused, impetuous, imprecise accents move you deeply, arouse your admiration, but you don't understand that these are the anguished cries of an unhappy woman, on whom you have bestowed your favor.

"I spent this morning learning my part, going over it, and trying it out. Now I am tired and worn out, and tomorrow it will begin all over again. Tomorrow evening is the performance. I drag myself around, bored at the prospect of getting out of bed and unwilling to go back to it. All I do is move in one continuous circle. Meager consolations sometimes occur, but the next moment I reject and revile them. I won't give in, won't give in to necessity—but why should what is destroying me, be necessary? Couldn't it be otherwise? I have to pay dearly for being a German, for Germans are temperamentally inclined to treat everything seriously, and being treated seriously by everything."

"My dear friend," Wilhelm interjected, "why don't you stop sharpening the dagger that you are constantly wounding yourself with? Have you no other thoughts? Are your youth, your figure, your health, your talents of no significance to you? If you have lost something of value through no fault of your own, is that any reason to jettison everything else? Is that really necessary?"

She was silent for a while, and then burst out: "I know it's a waste of time— love is a waste of time. What could I not have done, should have done! Now everything has turned to nothing! I am a miserable creature who's in love— nothing else! Have pity on me, for Heaven's sake, I am a poor wretched creature."

She collapsed into herself, and then after a short pause, violently cried out: "You are accustomed to everything coming your way without any effort. You cannot understand. No man can possibly appreciate a women who respects herself. By all the holy angels, by all the sacred images of bliss that a pure and generous heart may create for itself, I swear there is nothing more divine than a woman who gives herself to a man she loves! When we are worthy of the name of woman, we are cold, proud, superior, clever, clear-sighted;—but all these qualities we lay at your feet when we love, in the hope of gaining love in return. How consciously and willingly I threw away my whole existence! And now I am ready to despair,—I intend to despair! Not one drop of blood in me shall remain unpunished, not one fiber of my being stay untormented! Go on! Smile at me, laugh at my theatrical display of passion!"

Our friend was far from anything approaching laughter. The terrifying, half-natural and half-forced state of this woman tormented him too much for that. He shared the tortures that wracked her unhappy self; his mind was distraught, his feelings in a state of feverish excitement.

She stood up and paced up and down the room. "I keep recounting all the reasons why I should not love him," she said. "I know he isn't worth it. I turn my mind to something else, this way or that, wherever it chooses to go. I take up some new part in a play, even though it is not one that I am going to perform. I go over the old parts that I know so thoroughly, go over them again and again, every detail of them, rehearsing and rehearsing—o my friend, my trusted friend, what a terrible effort it is to separate oneself forcibly from oneself! My mind suffers, my brain is too tense; and so in order to avoid going mad, I return to the feeling that I love him.—Yes, I do love him, I do love him," she cried amidst constant tears, "I love him, and so—I want to die."

Wilhelm seized her by the hand and implored her not to get so worked up. "How strange it is," he said, "that we are denied not only what is impossible but so much that might be possible. You were not destined to find a faithful heart that would have given you every happiness. I was fated to have my whole salvation depend on an unfortunate girl whom I bent to the ground like a reed because of the strength of my devotion—I may even have broken her entirely."

He had already told Aurelie about his relationship with Mariane and could therefore speak of it again now. She stared fixedly into his eyes, and then asked him: "Can you truthfully say that you have never deceived a woman, never tried to elicit her favors by frivolous courtesies, wanton protestations and enticing oaths?"

"I can indeed," said Wilhelm, "and without boasting, for my life has been very simple and I have seldom been tempted to try any such thing. And what a warning it is for me, to see someone as lovely and noble as you reduced to such a pitiful condition! Let me, in your presence, swear a vow, one close to my heart, a vow whose shape and form has been decided on by the emotion that you have aroused in me and will be sanctified by this present moment: I swear to withstand all fleeting attractions and to preserve the serious ones close to my heart, for no woman to whom I will not devote my whole life shall ever hear from my lips a confession of love."

She looked at him with a fierce expression of indifference, and when he put out his hand moved away. "It's all of no consequence," she said. "A few woman's tears more or less, won't make the ocean any bigger. And yet," she continued, "if just one woman out of the thousands is saved, that is at least something—just one honest man discovered, that would be something to accept. Do you realize what you are promising?" "I do," said Wilhelm with a smile, and held out his hand. "I'll accept that," she said, and made a motion with her right hand so that he thought she was about to grasp his; but she plunged it into her pocket and in a flash pulled out the dagger and swept over his hand with its point. He withdrew his hand quickly but blood was already dripping from it.

"You men must be given a sharp cut if you are to take notice!" she cried in wild excitement, soon followed by an access of hasty busyness. She took her handkerchief and bound his hand to stop the bleeding. "Forgive a woman who is half crazy," she said, "but don't regret the loss of these few drops of blood. I am reconciled; I am myself again. On my knees I will beg your forgiveness; let me have the consolation of healing you."

She rushed to a closet, took out some linen and various implements, staunched the blood and looked carefully at the wound. It was in the ball of the hand just below the thumb and cut across the lifeline toward the little finger. She bandaged it quickly, pondering the matter seriously. He asked her several times: "How could you wound your friend?" "Quiet," she said, putting a finger to her lips, "be quiet!"

Book Five

Chapter One

Along with the two wounds that had not yet fully healed, Wilhelm had now acquired a third, which made him considerably uncomfortable. Aurelie would not allow him the services of a surgeon; instead, she bandaged him herself with all sorts of strange speeches, maxims and ceremonies, which made him extremely embarrassed. Not just he, but indeed everybody around her suffered from Aurelie's restlessness and peculiar behavior, and no one more than little Felix. The lively child became very impatient under such pressure, and more and more ill-behaved when she scolded or corrected him.

He began to take pleasure in certain things that are usually considered signs of ill-breeding, habits that she was in no wise prepared to condone. For example, he always preferred to drink out of the bottle rather than from a glass, and it seemed as if food from the dish tasted better than from his plate. Such impropriety was by no means ignored, and if he left the door open or slammed it shut, if when told to do something he remained rooted to the spot or rushed wildly out of the room, he was treated to a sharp lecture, yet without any noticeable effect. His attachment to Aurelie seemed to lessen from day to day, there was nothing affectionate in his tone of voice when he called her "Mother," and instead clung passionately to his old nurse, who did indeed let him do all he wanted.

But the nurse had been so sick for a while that she had been moved out of the house into quieter quarters, and Felix would have been left entirely on his own if Mignon had not become a loving companion and protective spirit to him as well as to others. Both children entertained each other in the most delightful way; she taught him little songs, and to the amazement of everyone he could recite them, for he had a good memory. She also tried to explain maps to him, for she was still much occupied with these; but she did not go about this in the best way. She was really only interested in whether various countries were cold or warm. She gave a vivid description of the poles and the terrible ice there, and how the warmth increased the further one got away from them. If someone was embarking on a journey, her only question was whether he was going north or south, and then she tried to trace his route on her little maps. When Wilhelm was speaking about his own journeys, she was especially attentive, and became quite sad when the conversation moved to another topic. Though she could never be persuaded to take a part in a play, and never went to a performance, she would learn odes and ballads by heart, and astonished everyone when, often quite unexpectedly and as if on the spur of the moment, she recited some such poem in her own serious and solemn way.

Serlo, always on the lookout for signs of a budding talent, tried to encourage her. What appealed to him most was the delightful variety of her singing which at times was full of life and gaiety; and because of this he came also to appreciate the Harper.

Although Serlo had no particular talent for music and did not play an instrument, he well knew the great value of this art, and did all he could to experience as often as possible a pleasure that he considered superior to any other. Every week he would have a concert, and now he had a marvelous little group of musicians, with Mignon, the Harper, and Laertes, who performed reasonably well on the violin.

Serlo used to say that we are so much inclined to busy ourselves with trivialities; our minds and senses are so easily made indifferent to the effects of beauty and perfection, that we should try to strengthen our faculty of appreciating these things. No one should entirely forego such pleasures, and it is only the fact of being unaccustomed to enjoying good things that makes so many people take pleasure in what is stupid and tasteless. One should, Serlo would say, listen to a little song, read a good poem, or look at a fine painting every single day, and if possible say something sensible about it. Given such sentiments—which were part of his nature—there was bound to be plenty of opportunity for agreeable entertainment by Serlo's associates.

In the midst of this pleasant state of affairs, a letter with a black seal was one day delivered to Wilhelm. Werner's seal indicated sad news, and Wilhelm was distressed at a brief notice of his father's death. He had died quite suddenly after a short illness, and had left his domestic affairs in very good order.

This unexpected news affected Wilhelm deeply. He was overcome by a profound sense of how insensitive and neglectful we are toward our friends and acquaintances while they are still with us, and only when our happy relationship with them is terminated, at least for a time, do we regret what we have failed to do. His distress at the untimely departure of this good man was mitigated only by the feeling that his father had been little loved, and the conviction that he had gained little pleasure from life.

Wilhelm's thoughts soon turned to his own circumstances, and here he felt extremely uneasy. No occasion is more dangerous for a man than when external circumstances produce a serious change in his situation without his thoughts or feelings being prepared for this. The result is change without change, and the tension is heightened all the more as we remain unaware of our being unprepared for the new situation.

Wilhelm suddenly found himself a free man, without as yet having achieved harmony within himself. His sentiments were noble, his intentions sincere, and his envisaged goal by no means contemptible. All this he could confidently assert; but he had often realized that he lacked experience, placed too much trust in the experience of others and attached too much value to what other people derived from their own convictions. Hence he was increasingly at a loss. He tried to acquire what he lacked by noting and assembling everything he heard or read that seemed to him worth considering. He wrote down ideas and opinions of his own and of others—sometimes even whole conversations—that interested him; but unfortunately he preserved much that was false alongside what was good, dwelt too long on one particular idea or one single maxim, and, as a result, abandoned his own natural way of thinking and acting by following the lead of others. Aurelie's bitterness and Laertes's cold contempt for humanity affected his judgment deeply. But no one was more dangerous to him than Jarno, a man whose keen intelligence delivered sharp, severe judgments on particular matters, but was wrong in giving these judgments an air of general applicability; judgments of the intellect are only relevant to a particular instance and false when extended to another.

Thus Wilhelm, in striving to achieve unity within himself, was in fact steadily depriving himself of the possibility of any such regenerative achievement; in this state of confusion his feelings were given free play, and thereby plunged him into even greater confusion about what he now had to do.

Serlo exploited the news of Wilhelm's father's death to his own advantage. Every day he had more cause to think about a different organization of the company. He must either renew the old contracts, which he did not much want to, because several members of the troupe who thought they were indispensable, were in fact becoming quite insufferable; but, on the other hand, he preferred to give the whole operation a new turn.

Without bringing pressure on Wilhelm, Serlo worked on Aurelie and Philine; and all the others who were longing for a fixed engagement did not give Wilhelm a moment's peace. So there he was, standing at the crossroads, and not knowing what to do. Curiously enough, it was a letter from Werner which, though arguing in the opposite direction, eventually brought him to a decision. We will leave out the beginning of the letter, but give the contents with little change.

Chapter Two

" . . . That's how it was; and it is probably right that in every eventuality a man should continue with his job and keep up the good work. The dear old man had only just departed this life when everything in the office took on a tone that was very different from his. Friends, relatives and acquaintances stormed in, but especially those who have something to gain from such occasions. There was fetching and carrying, counting, writing and reckoning; some brought cakes and wine, others just ate and drank; nobody seemed busier than the women selecting what they should wear as mourning.

"You will therefore forgive me, my friend, if I myself used the occasion to my own advantage by being as helpful and useful as I could to your sister, and, when the time was proper, I gave her to understand that it was now our business to accelerate the sealing of a union which both our fathers had delayed up to now out of an excessive sense of what was proper form.

"You must not think that what was in our minds was to take possession of that huge empty house. We are much too modest and sensible for that; so let me tell you what we intend to do. After we are married, your sister will move over into our house, and bring your mother with her.

"'How will that be possible,' you will say, 'for you will scarcely have room in that little place.' That's the art of the thing, my friend. Skillful arrangement makes everything possible, and you wouldn't believe how much room you can find when you don't need much. We will sell the big house, for which we already have a good offer. The money that we realize from the sale, we will invest at one hundred percent.

"I hope you are in agreement with this, and my fond expectation is that you will not wish to inherit any of the unproductive pastimes of your father and your grandfather. Your grandfather's major delight was in collecting a number of insignificant works of art which no one, that I can well say, enjoyed as much as he did; and your father lived in a household of expensive luxury that he never allowed anyone else to enjoy with him. We intend to do things differently, and I am hoping for your approval.

"It is true that in our whole house my only place is at my desk and I cannot yet see where we can some day put a cradle. But there is plenty of room outside the house: coffeehouses and clubs for the husband, walks and drives for the wife, and pleasant country excursions for us both. It is a very great advantage that our round table will be fully occupied, and my father will not be able to see friends who would only make frivolous remarks, when he has gone to such trouble to be a good host.

"Above all: There shall be nothing superfluous in our house! Not too much furniture, not too many utensils—no coach and no horses. Just money, which we will spend sensibly in doing what we want to. No extensive wardrobe, just what is newest and best; the husband can wear his coat till it is threadbare and the wife peddle her dress, when both have become somewhat out of fashion. There is nothing I dislike more than an accumulation of old possessions. If someone wants to give me a valuable ring on the condition that I wear it every day, I would not accept it. For what conceivable joy is there in dead capital? So here is my joyous credo: conduct your business, acquire money, enjoy yourself with your family, and don't bother about anybody else unless you can use them to your advantage.

"Perhaps you will say: 'Where do I figure in your neat little plan? Where am I to live if you sell my father's house and there is no room in yours?'

"That, brother, is indeed the crucial point, and I will help you on that score once I have expressed appreciation of your excellent report on how you have been spending your time.

"Tell me, how did you in so short a time manage to acquire such knowledge of so many useful and interesting things? I am aware of your many abilities, but I would not have believed that you were so attentive and zealous. Your travelogue has shown us how much you have profited from your journey. Your description of the iron and copper works is exemplary and reveals your comprehension of the subject. I went there once myself, but my account looks like shoddy work when compared with yours. Your whole account of linen production is extremely instructive, and your remark concerning competitiveness is very apposite. In some places you have made mistakes in addition, but those are easily excusable.

"What gave your father and myself most pleasure were your profound insights into the management and, above all, improvement of agricultural estates. We hope to be able to purchase a big estate, now in sequestration, which is situated in a very fertile area. We shall use the money from the sale of your father's house, transferring part and leaving the rest untouched. We are reckoning on your going there to supervise the improvements. In a few years the value of the land will increase by at least a third; we can sell it and look for a bigger buy, improve that, do another trade — and you are the man for that. Meanwhile we at home will not be idle with our correspondence, and will soon all be in an enviable position.

"Farewell for now! Enjoy your life while you continue your journey, and take yourself off to wherever seems pleasant and useful. We shall not need you for the first six months, so you can now look around in the world. The best education for a smart fellow like yourself in always through travel. Goodbye, I am happy to become more closely associated with you through marriage and to be united with you by the spirit of work."

Well written and full of good business sense as it was, this letter nevertheless displeased Wilhelm in several ways. Its praise of his fictitious statistical, technological and agricultural knowledge was a silent reproach to him; and the ideal of a burgher existence that his brother-in-law depicted, did not attract him in the least. On the contrary, he felt strongly drawn in exactly the opposite direction. He convinced himself that only in the theater would he be able to achieve the education he desired for himself, and he seemed all the more strengthened in this resolve by Werner's vigorous, though unwitting, opposition. He ran through all his arguments in favor of his intentions, confirmed in his belief that he had good reason to present them in a favorable light to a man as perceptive as Werner. He composed a reply, which we shall also communicate to our readers.

Chapter Three

"Your letter was so well written and so intelligently thought out, that there is nothing to be added. But you will forgive me if I say that one may have quite different opinions (and act accordingly), and yet also be in the right. Your way of thinking and your ideal of how to live aim at unlimited possessions and easy, light-hearted enjoyment; but I need hardly tell you that nothing of that kind holds any attraction for me.

"First, I must confess to you that my travelogue was put together from various books with the help of a friend, out of a sense of the need to give my father pleasure, and though I know about the things contained in it, and others as well, I do not understand them, and I have no desire to occupy myself with them. What help is it to me to make good iron if my soul is full of slag? What use is it to me to bring order into the management of an estate if there is disorder within myself?

"Let me put it quite succinctly: even as a youth I had the vague desire and intention to develop myself fully, myself as I am. I still have the same intention, but the means to fulfill it are now somewhat clearer. I have seen more of the world than you think, and made better use of it than you can imagine. Please devote some attention to what I am going to say, even though it may not correspond to your own notions.

"If I were a nobleman, our disagreement would soon be settled; but since I belong to the middle classes, I must stake out my own path, and I hope you will understand what I am doing. I don't know how it is in other countries, but it seems to me that in Germany general education of the self is possible only for the nobility. The middle class can acquire merit and, if driven to extremes, develop the mind; but in so doing it loses its personality, however it presents itself. A nobleman who consorts with distinguished persons is obliged to behave in a distinguished manner, which, since all doors are open to it, becomes a manner that is free and unconstrained, so that, whether at court or in the army, his currency is his person and the figure he cuts. As a result, he has good reason to regard the way he appears as a matter of importance, and to show that he does. A certain formal grace in ordinary affairs, coupled with a certain relaxed elegance in serious and important matters, becomes him well. He is a public person, and the more cultivated his movements, the richer his voice, and the more controlled and measured his whole personality, the more accomplished he becomes; if he always remains the same, whether talking to the highborn or the lowly, to friends or relations, no fault will be found in him and no one would wish him otherwise. He can be cold, but intelligent; dissembling, but prudent. If he is in control of himself at every moment of his life, no one has any further demands to make of him and everything else about him—ability, talent, wealth—seem only adjuncts or appendages.

"But then imagine a burgher who thinks he might make some claim to these qualities. He is bound to fail, and he will be all the more unhappy for having, as part of his nature, the ability and urge toward such a different way of life.

"Since a nobleman has no restrictions in his everyday life and may possibly be made into a king or the like, he has to appear before his fellowmen with an unspoken awareness of what he is. He can always move to the fore, whereas the burgher does best to respect quietly the limits imposed on him. The burgher should not ask: 'Who am I?' but 'What do I have? What insights, what knowledge, what ability, what capital?' The nobleman tells us everything through the person he presents, but the burgher does not, and should not. A nobleman can and must be someone who represents by his appearance, whereas the burgher simply is, and when he tries to put on an appearance, the effect is ludicrous or in bad taste. The nobleman should act and achieve, the burgher must labor and create, developing some of his capabilities in order to be useful, but without it ever being assumed that there is or ever can be a harmonious interplay of qualities in him, because in order to make himself useful in one direction, he has to disregard everything else.

"The differences are not due to any pretentiousness on the part of the aristocracy or the submissiveness of the bourgeoisie, but to the whole organization of society. Whether this will ever change, or what will change, does not really concern me. Given the present state of things, what I have to do is think about myself, maintain what I know to be the basic need of myself, and achieve its fulfillment.

"I have an irresistible desire to attain the harmonious development of my personality such as was denied me by my birth. Since I left home I have made successful efforts to improve my physical powers, and I have overcome much of my former diffidence in presenting myself as I really am. I have, for example, improved my voice and my speech and can truly say that in society I make a favorable impression. But every day my desire to be a public person becomes more and more irrepressible, with the result that I am always trying to please and be effective in wider circles. Add to that my fondness for poetry and everything connected with it, the need to develop my mind and my taste, so that, in the pleasures I cannot do without, I may gradually come to see good only in what is good, and beauty only in the truly beautiful. You can see that as far as I am concerned, all this is to be found only in the theater; only there can I really move and develop as I would wish to. On the stage a cultured human being can appear in the full splendor of his person, just as in the upper classes of society. There, mind and body keep step in all one does, and there I will be able simultaneously to *be* and to *appear* better than anywhere else. Should I seek other secondary ways of occupying myself, there will be enough routine chores to exercise my patience.

"Don't argue with me about this; for, before you have a chance to write, I will already have taken the decisive step. Because of prevailing prejudices I will change my name; anyhow I would be embarrassed to be known by the name of Meister, which implies mastery. Fare you well. Our finances are in such good hands that I do not need to bother about them; when I need money I will ask you for it. It won't be much, for I hope to support myself by my art."

Having sent off the letter, Wilhelm immediately did what he said he would, and, to the astonishment of Serlo and all the others, suddenly declared that he would become an actor and was ready to sign a contract so long as its conditions were reasonable. They soon agreed, for Serlo had talked about this earlier in terms that Wilhelm and the others found quite easy to accept. The whole pathetic company, with whom we have occupied ourselves for so long, were finally taken on, without anyone except Laertes expressing any gratitude to Wilhelm. They had made their demands without confiding in him, and likewise accepted their fulfillment without thanking him. Most of them preferred to credit their engagement to the influence of Philine, and it was to her that they expressed their thanks. The contracts were drawn up and signed, and by a strange connection of ideas there arose before Wilhelm's mind at the very moment that he was signing his fictitious name, the image of that place in the woods where he lay wounded in Philine's lap. The lovely Amazon came riding up on her white horse from out of the bushes, moved forward, and dismounted. Her generous concern made her pace to and fro, until finally she stood still in front of him. Her coat slipped from her shoulders, her face, indeed her whole body, shone, and then she disappeared. He wrote down his assumed name quite mechanically, without knowing what he was doing, and only after he had signed the contract did he notice that Mignon was standing beside him, holding his arm and gently trying to draw his hand away.

Chapter Four

One condition that Wilhelm made on joining the company was accepted by Serlo only with a certain proviso. Wilhelm had insisted that they should perform *Hamlet* in its entirety, and Serlo agreed to this interesting but extraordinary proposal only to the extent that it was feasible. They had been arguing about this for some time, the question being what was feasible and what was not, but so far they had not been able to agree on what could be cut without destroying the play.

Wilhelm was still at that happy stage in life when it seems inconceivable that there could be any blemish on a girl one loves or an author that one admires. Our feelings are so absolute and so all of a piece that we assert a similar perfection and harmony in the objects. Serlo, on the other hand, liked to analyze, maybe too much; his sharp intelligence tended to see a work of art as a more or less imperfect whole. He thought that there was no need to be so circumspect with plays as one found them; even Shakespeare, and especially *Hamlet*, would have to suffer somewhat.

Wilhelm was not prepared to listen to him talk in terms of wheat and chaff. "It's not a question of a mixture of wheat and chaff," he declared, "this is a tree with branches, twigs, leaves, buds, blossoms and fruit. Everything is related to everything else." Serlo replied that one shouldn't try to serve up a whole tree, but apples of gold in baskets of silver. They exhausted themselves in metaphor, and their opinions differed increasingly.

Wilhelm became nearly distraught when one day, after a long argument, Serlo suggested that the simplest way to settle things was to take a pen and strike out those things in the play that just would not get across, combine several characters into one, and, if Wilhelm did not himself have sufficient knowledge or courage to do this, he should leave it to him, Serlo, and the whole matter would soon be settled.

"That is not what we agreed on," said Wilhelm. "How can you be so reckless when you have such good taste?"

"My friend," said Serlo, "you will soon get that way yourself. I know all too well how despicable such a procedure is, and that it is perhaps something that has not happened in the best theaters. But our German theater is in such a sorry state. Our authors make such mutilations necessary, and the public accepts them. How many plays do we have that do not exceed our resources in personnel, scenery and theatrical machinery, that are too long, have too much dialogue or make demands exceeding the physical power of our actors? And yet we must go on playing, time after time, always offering something new. Shouldn't we use what we have to our advantage, since we achieve just as much by plays that are cut than by ones that aren't? It is the public that makes us do this, for there are few Germans and perhaps few spectators in any nation nowadays that have any sense of an aesthetic whole. They only praise or blame pieces, their pleasure is piecemeal, and whom does that please more than our actors, for theater remains just patchwork, a collection of bits and pieces."

"Not *remains*," said Wilhelm, "though that's what it *is*. But must everything remain as it is? Don't try to convince me that you are right. No power in the world would persuade me to abide by a contract signed in such gross error."

Serlo switched to a lighter touch and urged Wilhelm to think over their many conversations about *Hamlet* and work out by himself what would be a satisfactory version.

After spending a few days by himself, Wilhelm came back with an air of satisfaction. "I must be making a great mistake," he said, "if I don't think I've found a way of dealing with this whole matter. I even believe that Shakespeare himself would have done likewise if his mind had not been so fixed on the central idea and distracted by the novellas he was working from."

"Let me hear what you have to say," said Serlo, seating himself on the sofa somewhat pompously. "I will listen quietly and criticize sharply."

Wilhelm said: "I am not afraid of that. Just listen. After careful examination and reflection I can distinguish two aspects of the composition of the play. Very important is, first, the *internal* relationship between the personages and the events, the powerful effects that emerge from the characters and actions of the main personages—these are all excellently presented and the sequence in which they occur could not be bettered. No production of the play can destroy this, or in any way falsify it. This is what everyone demands to be shown and nobody would dare to interfere with something that makes such a deep impression on the minds of the observers. Almost all of this, I have been told, has been preserved on the German stage. But I believe a mistake has been made with regard to the second aspect of the play, namely the *external* circumstances affecting the characters, how they come to move from one place to another, how they are fortuitously brought into contact with each other; these have, in my opinion, been given insufficient importance, only referred to in passing, or even omitted. These threads are certainly rather loose and thin, but they do run through the whole play and tie up what would otherwise fall apart, and does indeed fall apart when they are left out, as if just leaving the ends were sufficient.

"To my mind these external circumstances include the troubles in Norway, the war with young Fortinbras, the ambassadorial mission to the old uncle, the settlement of the dispute, young Fortinbras's march into Poland, and his return at the end of the play. Likewise Horatio's return from Wittenberg, Hamlet's desire to go there, Laertes's visit to France and his subsequent return, the dispatching of Hamlet to England, his capture by pirates, and the death of the two courtiers because of the treacherous letter. All these things are circumstances and events which would give breadth to a romance, but they seriously disturb the unity of a play in which the hero himself has no plan, and are therefore defects."

"That's how I like to hear you talk!" said Serlo.

"Don't interrupt me," said Wilhelm. "You won't approve of everything I have to say. These faults are like temporary props for a structure and should not be removed unless they are replaced by some stronger support. My proposal would be not to tamper with the big situation at the beginning and, as far as possible, to leave it as it is both as regards its overall structure and the incidentals; and instead to replace all those desultory and distracting separate external motifs by one single motivation."

"And what would that be?" asked Serlo, rising from his comfortable position.

"I would make proper use of something that is already contained in the play," Wilhelm replied, "namely the troubles in Norway. Here is my proposal for you to consider.

"After the death of Hamlet senior, the recently conquered Norwegians become restless. The governor there sends his son Horatio, an old school friend of Hamlet's and superior in courage and shrewdness to all the others, to

Denmark, to press for the readying of the fleet, which is not proceeding space because of the easy living of the new king. Horatio knew the previous king, having fought under him in his last battles, and had always enjoyed his favor: the first scene with the Ghost will gain by this means. The new king then gives an audience to Horatio, and sends Laertes to Norway with the news that the fleet will soon be landing there, while Horatio is charged with speeding up its preparation. Hamlet's mother, however, will not agree to her son going to sea with Horatio, as Hamlet himself would have wished."

"Thank God for that!" exclaimed Serlo. "So then we can get rid of Wittenberg and the university, which were always a thorn in my flesh. I think your ideas are quite good, for, apart from the two offstage elements of Norway and the fleet, the audience does not need to supply anything in its thoughts. They can see all the rest, for that is going on before their eyes, and their imagination does not have to be chasing all over the place."

"You can easily see how I would link up all the rest. When Hamlet tells Horatio about his stepfather's crime, Horatio advises him to go with him to Norway, gain control of the army and return with it in force. When Hamlet becomes too dangerous for both the king and the queen, they have no easier means of getting rid of him than sending him to join the fleet and instructing Rosencrantz and Guildenstern to keep an eye on him; and when Laertes returns in the meantime, they send him after Hamlet, for Laertes is in a murderous temper. The fleet is delayed by unfavorable winds; Hamlet returns. His wandering through the churchyard could perhaps be better motivated. But his encounter with Laertes at the grave of Ophelia is a great moment and absolutely indispensable. The king can then decide that it would be better to rid himself of Hamlet at once. The celebration to mark his departure and his apparent reconciliation with Laertes is carried out with great ceremony, including chivalrous combats in which Hamlet and Laertes fence with each other. I cannot do without the four corpses at the end; no one should be left alive. And, since the people now have to elect a new king, Hamlet, as he dies, gives his vote to Horatio."

"Now you sit right down and work the whole thing out," said Serlo, "for your ideas have my complete approval, and let's not allow our satisfaction to dissipate."

Chapter Five

Wilhelm had been working for a long time on a translation of *Hamlet*. In doing so he had used the talented version by Wieland, which had been his first introduction to Shakespeare. Where he found something missing, he put it back, and so he had in his possession a complete text of the play when he talked with Serlo about an acting version, and had achieved relative agreement with him. He now set to work taking things out and putting things in, separating and combining, changing things and then putting them back as they were; for, pleased as he was with his own ideas, he felt that when he put them into practice, the original suffered in the process.

When he had finished, he read it aloud to Serlo and the others. They were extremely pleased with all he had done, and Serlo in particular expressed his approval on several points.

"You were quite right," he said, amongst other things, "in feeling that the external circumstances surrounding the action should be conveyed more simply than this great writer has presented them. Everything that happens off-stage and is therefore invisible to the spectators, should be the background against which the characters move and act. The one big vista entailing the fleet and Norway will add to the effectiveness of the play; if you leave that out, it becomes just a domestic tragedy and the whole stupendous idea that a regal household is destroyed by internal crimes and ineptness would not present itself in its full majesty. If, on the other hand, this background were to be portrayed as one of shifting complexity and confusion, this would detract from the effectiveness of the characters."

Wilhelm then proceeded to defend Shakespeare once more, pointing out that he was writing for an island people, for Englishmen with sea voyages and ships as their background, who are accustomed to seeing with their own eyes the coast of France and pirates, so that what would be confusing and distracting for us, was everyday experience for them.

Serlo had to admit this, but they both agreed that a simpler and more telling background was better suited for a performance on a German stage and the imaginations of German spectators.

The roles had already been assigned. Serlo took on Polonius, Aurelie was to play Ophelia, Laertes his namesake, and a young man, recently arrived and rather squat but nevertheless lively, was given the role of Horatio. They were in some doubt about who should play the king and who the Ghost. The only person available for either of these roles was the old Blusterer. Serlo suggested the Pedant for the king, but Wilhelm protested vigorously. They could not arrive at a decision on this matter. Wilhelm had also left intact the two characters of Rosencrantz and Guildenstern. "Why didn't you combine them into one?" Serlo asked. "That would be an easy saving."

"Heaven preserve me from shortcuts like that, which would work against both sense and effect!" Wilhelm replied. "What these two men are and what they do, cannot be embodied in one and the same person. It is in such details that Shakespeare reveals his greatness. The creepiness, the bowing and scraping, the approving, flattering and insinuating, their adroitness and strutting, wholeness and emptiness, their utter roguery, their ineptness—how could all this be portrayed by one person? There should be at least a dozen of them, if that were feasible. For they are not just something in society, they are society, and Shakespeare was very modest and wise to give us only two such representatives. Also I need them as a pair, so that in my version they will contrast with the one, good, honest Horatio."

"I understand what you mean," said Serlo, "and we can help ourselves out. We'll give one of them to Elmire" (that was the name of the Blusterer's oldest daughter). "It won't hurt so long as she looks good, and I will preen and train the doll so that she is a delight."

Philine was delighted that she was to be the duchess in the play within the play. "I'll make it seem so natural to marry a second husband quickly when one has loved the first so much. I shall hope to receive a huge burst of applause, and every man will wish he could be my third."

Aurelie made a sour face at these remarks; her dislike of Philine was increasing daily.

"It is really a pity that we have no ballet," said Serlo. "Otherwise you could perform a *pas de deux* with each of your husbands, and the old man could fall asleep in keeping with the rhythm and your feet and legs would look just fine on that cute little stage in the background."

"What do you know about my legs?" she said cheekily. "And as for my feet," she added, reaching quickly beneath the table for her slippers and placing them in front of Serlo. "These are my stilts and I defy you to find prettier ones."

"I was quite serious," he said; then, looking at the delicate footwear: "You're right. It would be hard to find anything prettier."

They had been made in Paris, and Philine had received them as a present from the countess, a lady whose beautiful feet were famous.

"What charming things!" said Serlo. "My heart leaps within me when I contemplate them."

"What words of rapture!" said Philine.

"Nothing transcends a pair of slippers of such delicate, beauteous workmanship," he exclaimed; "but their sound is even more charming than their appearance." He picked them up and let one after the other fall several times onto the table.

"What are you doing? Just give them back to me!" she cried.

"May I say," he added with simulated modesty and roguish seriousness, "that we bachelors, who are mostly alone at night and have fears like other men, pine for companionship in the dark and seek it in hostelries and other strange and unsuitable places; we find it very consoling if some goodhearted girl provides us with the support of her company. It's night, we are in bed, and hear a rustling. We are startled, the door opens, and we hear a sweet little piping voice, something creeps in, the curtains swish, click! clack! the slippers fall to the ground, and whoosh! we're no longer alone. Oh that sweet, unique sound of slippers falling on the floor. The smaller they are, the finer they sound. You may talk about nightingales, murmuring brooks, rustling winds, organs and pipes, I'll stick with my click! clack! – that is the best tune to dance to, over and over again."

Philine took the slippers out of his hands and said: "Just look how I have bent them! They're much too wide for me now." Then she played with them, rubbing one sole against the other. "How warm they get!" she said, putting one of

the soles flat against her cheek, then she went on rubbing and handed it to
Serlo. He was gracious enough to test the warmth, and "Click! Clack!" she
said, giving him such a sharp blow with the heel that he withdrew his hand
with a yelp. "I'll teach you to think otherwise about my slippers," said Philine
with a laugh.

"And I will teach you not to treat old people like children!" he shouted as he
jumped up, grabbed her and stole many a kiss, which she pretended to bestow
under pressure. In the struggle her long hair came loose, wound itself around
everybody, the chair fell to the ground, and Aurelie, disgusted by such goings-
on, stood up in anger.

Chapter Six

Although several parts had been left out in this new version of *Hamlet*, there
were still enough for the troupe to have difficulty in assigning them all.

"If things go on like this," said Serlo, "our prompter will have to leave his
box, become one of us, and take over a part."

"I've often admired the work he does," said Wilhelm.

"Yes, I don't believe we could have a better person to prod our memory.
None of the spectators will ever hear him, but on the stage we hear every word
he says. He has developed a special kind of voice, and as a sort of guiding spirit
whispers in our ears when we're in trouble. He knows instinctively which part
of his role an actor will remember correctly, and he senses well in advance
when memory will let him down. In some cases when I hardly had the time to
read through the part, he spoke each word ahead for me, and I was able to get
through it without mishap; but he does have certain peculiarities, which makes
him of little use to others. For example, he becomes so passionately involved
in the plays that he will give highly personal, emotional renderings of moving
passages that should just be declaimed. This unfortunate habit has more than
once put me off course."

"He has another odd habit which once let me down in a particularly tricky
passage," said Aurelie.

"But how is that possible when he is so attentive?" Wilhelm asked.

"He is so moved by some passages," said Aurelie, "that he weeps bitter tears
and for a time completely loses control of himself. And these are not what are
normally considered moving passages, but rather, if I may say so, those beautiful passages in which an author's power of feeling becomes evident, which
give most of us intense pleasure but cause others to look away."

"But if he has such a tender heart, why doesn't he become an actor?"

"Because his hoarse voice and stiff movements would not do well on the
stage, and his melancholy manners make him unsociable," Serlo replied.
"What trouble I have had trying to make him get along with me! But without
success. He reads excellently. I have never heard anyone read better. And

he really can respect the thin dividing line between declamation and emotionally charged recitation."

"That's it," said Wilhelm. "That's what we need. What a stroke of luck! We now have the actor who can recite the passage about the rugged Pyrrhus."

"Only someone as enthusiastic as you can bend everything to his ends," said Serlo.

"I would certainly have been very unhappy if that particular passage had been omitted; it would have crippled the play."

"I can't see why," said Aurelie.

"I hope you will agree with me when you have heard what I have to say," Wilhelm replied. "Shakespeare introduces this group of actors with a double purpose. First: The man who declaims the speech about the death of Priam with so much emotion, deeply moves Prince Hamlet. He pricks the conscience of the vacillating youth, and so this scene becomes the prelude to the play within the play, which makes such a deep impression on the king. Hamlet is put to shame by an actor who becomes so caught up in the sorrow of a fictitious personage, and conceives the idea of 'catching the conscience' of his stepfather the king by this means. What a marvelous monologue that is which concludes the second act! What joy it is to recite:

> O! what a rogue and peasant slave am I:
> Is it not monstrous that this player here,
> But in a fiction, in a dream of passion,
> Could force his soul so to his own conceit
> That from her working all his visage wann'd,
> Tears in his eyes, distraction in's aspect,
> A broken voice, and his whole function suiting
> With forms to his conceit? and all for nothing!
> For Hecuba!
> What's Hecuba to him, or he to Hecuba,
> That he should weep for her?"

"If only we can persuade our man to go on stage," said Aurelie.

"We will have to get him used to the idea gradually," Serlo suggested. "Let him read the speech at rehearsals, and let's say we're waiting for an actor to play the part. Then we'll see whether we can work on him."

Having agreed on this they went on to talk about the Ghost. Wilhelm could not bring himself to give the living king's part to the Pedant and the Ghost to the Blusterer, and thought that they should wait a while; there were several other actors coming their way and perhaps the right person might be found.

One can therefore well imagine how astonished Wilhelm was that same evening to find a letter addressed to him under his stage name, written in strange characters, sealed, and lying on his table, which said: "We know full well, o wondrous youth, that you are in a serious predicament. You can hardly find enough living persons for your *Hamlet*, let alone ghosts. Your zeal deserves to be rewarded by a miracle: We cannot perform miracles, but something miraculous shall happen. If you have confidence in us, the Ghost will appear at the appointed hour. Take courage, and be not afraid. A reply is not necessary, we will be informed of your decision."

He hurried back to Serlo with this curious message. Serlo read it several times, reflected, and then said that he thought this was a matter of importance, and they ought to consider whether they should take the risk. They talked back and forth. Aurelie was very quiet and smiled from time to time; and when some days later they returned to the subject, she made it quite clear that she thought this was one of Serlo's jokes. She urged Wilhelm not to worry and to wait patiently for the Ghost to appear.

Serlo was in the best of humor, for the actors who were leaving did all they could to perform well, so that they would be sorely missed, and he expected good takings from the public that would be anxious to see the new actors.

His association with Wilhelm also affected him. He began to talk more about art, for he was after all a German, and Germans like to be able to justify what they are doing. Wilhelm made a record of many of these conversations, and we will impart these to those of our readers who may be interested in dramaturgical questions, but sometime later, so as not constantly to interrupt the flow of the narrative.

Serlo was in an especially good mood one evening when talking about the role of Polonius and how he conceived it. "I promise you," he said, "this time to come up with a really worthy figure. I will convey his calm assurance, his insaneness and his thoughtfulness, agreeableness as well as tactlessness, free-spirited and yet eavesdropping, a rogue at heart who pretends to be truthful, each of these facets in its place. I will present a graybeard who is honest, long-suffering and timeserving, someone who is half a villain but also the perfect courtier; and for this I will make use of the few indications the author has given us. I will talk like a book when I am prepared, and like a fool when I am in a good mood. I will be insipid enough to parrot what others say, and yet refined enough not to show that I know when they are making a fool of me. I have rarely played a part with such anticipation and malicious enjoyment."

"If only I had as much to anticipate from my role," said Aurelie. "I have neither the youthfulness nor the gentleness to think myself into this character. But one thing I unfortunately do know: The feelings that turned Ophelia's head will always be with me."

"Let's not bother too much about all this," said Wilhelm. "For I can say that, despite my intense study of the play, my desire to act Hamlet has led me astray. The more I worked myself into the part, the more I have become aware that my physical appearance has absolutely none of the characteristics Shakespeare gave to Hamlet. And when I realize that everything in the role fits together into one piece, I have doubts whether I can do even a moderately good performance."

"You are reacting very conscientiously to your new profession," Serlo replied. "An actor fits himself as best he can to the role, and the role will necessarily have to adapt itself to him. But tell me, how did Shakespeare conceive Hamlet's physical appearance? Is it so different from yours?"

"First of all, he is blond," said Wilhelm.

"That seems to me far-fetched," said Aurelie. "Where did you get that idea?"

"As a Dane, a Norseman, he is bound to be blond, and have blue eyes."

"Do you think Shakespeare thought about such things as that?"

"I don't find it expressly stated, but I think it is undeniable if one considers certain passages in the play. The fencing is hard for him, sweat runs off his face, and the queen says: 'He's fat and scant of breath.' How can you imagine him, except as blond and portly? For people who are dark-haired are rarely like that when they are young. And do not his fits of melancholy, the tenderness of his grief, his acts of indecisiveness, better suit someone like that than a slim youth with curly brown hair from whom one would expect more alacrity and determination?"

"You are spoiling my whole image of him," said Aurelie. "Get rid of that fat Hamlet! Don't show us a portly prince. Give us instead some substitute to please us and engage our sympathies. We are not as much concerned with the author's intentions as we are with our own pleasure, and we therefore expect to be attracted by someone like ourselves."

Chapter Seven

One evening the company debated whether drama or novel should be ranked higher. Serlo asserted that this was a futile and ill-conceived argument, since each could be excellent in its own way, so long as it kept within the bounds of its genre.

"I am not quite clear about that," said Wilhelm.

"Who is?" said Serlo. "And yet it would be worth while going into the matter more closely."

They all talked back and forth, and the final result of their conversation was roughly this:

In the novel as well as in the drama we observe human nature and action. The difference between the two genres lies not merely in their external form—people talk in the one and are usually talked about in the other. Unfortunately many dramas are only novels in dialogue, and it should be perfectly possible to write drama in letters.

In the novel it is predominantly sentiments and events that are to be presented; in drama, characters and deeds. The novel must move slowly and the sentiments of the main personage must, in some way or another, hold up the progression of the whole toward its resolution. But drama must move quickly and the character of the main personage must press toward the end, not himself holding up this progression, but being held up in it. The hero of a novel must be passive, or at least not active to a high degree; from the hero of a play we demand effective action and deeds. Grandison, Clarissa, Pamela, the Vicar of Wakefield, even Tom Jones are, if not passive, yet "retarding" personages, and all events are to a certain extent fashioned after their sentiments. In drama, the hero fashions nothing according to himself, everything resists him, and he either clears obstacles or pushes them aside, or he succumbs to them.

They agreed that in the novel Chance might well be given free play, but that it must always be guided and controlled by the sentiments of the personages; whereas Fate, which, without any action by human beings on their part, drives them through circumstances unrelated to themselves toward an unforeseen catastrophe, can have its function only in drama. Chance may indeed produce pathetic, but never tragic situations; whereas Fate must always be terrible and becomes tragic in the highest sense if it brings guilty and innocent deeds that are not connected with each other into some dire connection.

These reflections led them back again to the peculiarities of *Hamlet* as a play. The hero, it was said, really only has sentiments, and it is only external events that work upon him, so that this play has something of the breadth of a novel. But since Fate determines its plan, since it begins with a terrible deed and the hero is driven ever further toward another terrible deed, it is tragic in the highest sense of the term and cannot but end tragically.

The next thing to do was to have a reading rehearsal. Wilhelm envisaged this as a sort of celebration. He had collated the parts in advance, so that there should be no objections raised about them. All the actors were fully acquainted with the play, and all he did before they began was to impress on them how important a reading rehearsal is. It is demanded of every musician that he should be able to play more or less at sight, and therefore every actor, indeed any well-bred person, should practice sightreading, extract the character of a drama, poem or story, and be able to reproduce this with some facility. Memorizing is of no use at all unless an actor has first thought his way into the spirit and intentions of the author; the letter is nothing without the spirit.

Serlo asserted that he would supervise all rehearsals, including the dress rehearsal, once they had agreed on the importance of having the reading rehearsal. "For," he said, "there is nothing more amusing than actors talking about studying. It is like freemasons talking about work."

The rehearsal went well, and the time was well spent, for it created a solid basis for the profit and repute they were to earn.

"You did well, my friend, to talk so seriously to our colleagues," said Serlo once they were alone together, "but I am afraid they will hardly come up to your expectations."

"Why not?" Wilhelm enquired.

"My experience has been that it is easy enough to set people's imaginations working, but, much as they like to be told tales, their minds are rarely productive. This is especially so with actors. An actor is quite content to take on a striking and worthy role, but rarely does more than put himself self-satisfiedly in the hero's place, without any concern as to whether other people will accept that. But having a vivid comprehension of what the author of the play had in mind, and knowing how much of one's own personality one must efface in order to do justice to the role, sensing that one is oneself quite different, and yet having the power to convince the audience that one is what one portrays, having the ability by the compelling truth of the presentation to turn planks into temples and cardboard into forests—that is given to few. The mind's power to create illusion in the spectators, fictitious truth producing solid effects by aiming solely at illusion, who amongst them can understand that?

"Let us therefore not insist too much on spirit and feeling. The safest way to proceed will be to explain quietly to our friends the meaning of the text and open up their minds. Those who have the right talent will quickly find their way into the sort of portrayal that is both intelligent and moving; and those who do not, will at least not act and speak all that badly. There is, according to my observation, nothing more presumptuous in actors (and indeed in everybody else) than claiming to understand the spirit without having a clear understanding of the letter."

Chapter Eight

Wilhelm arrived early for the first full rehearsal, and found himself alone on stage. He was surprised by what he saw and was beset with strange memories. There were sets for a forest and a village that were just like those in the theater of his home town on the day that Mariane had declared her love for him at a rehearsal and agreed to spend that first blissful night with him. The cottages on the stage were all alike, just as they are in the country; the morning sun shone actually through a half-open window on to a rather rickety stage bench near the door, but unfortunately not, as previously, on Mariane's bosom. He sat down, thought about this strange concatenation of circumstances, and even felt that he might see her again soon. But what he was looking at was only the set for an epilogue such as was at that time customarily given on German stages.

His thoughts were interrupted by the arrival of the other actors, together with two men who seemed interested in the theater and its equipment. These two greeted Wilhelm warmly. One of them was a sort of hanger-on of Madame Melina's, the other was a real devotee of the drama; any good company would be happy to have both as friends. It was hard to say whether they had more love of the theater or knowledge of it. They loved it too much to understand it properly, and they understood enough to approve of what was good and disapprove of what was not. They were not unmoved by what was mediocre, but their pleasure, both in anticipation and in retrospect, at what was really good, seemed to surpass their powers of expression. They delighted in the mechanics, were transported by what appealed to their mind, and their passion for the theater was so strong that even a piecemeal rehearsal would create some degree of illusion in them. The faults always receded into the distance, and the good things touched them deeply. They were the kind of admirers every artist wants. They liked to stroll from the wings down to the auditorium, and back again, they loved to linger in the dressing rooms. Their favorite occupation was to offer comments on the posture, costume, reciting and declamation of the actors, their liveliest conversation concerned the effects produced, and their efforts were constantly directed towards making sure that the actors were attractive, active and to the point, giving them their assistance and affection, and, though shunning extravagance, providing them with various little pleasures. They had secured the exclusive right of being present at every rehearsal and performance. They did not agree with Wilhelm on every point regarding the performance of *Hamlet*. Occasionally he yielded to their opinions, though on the whole he tended to stick to his own. All these conversations contributed to the development of his own taste. He let both men see how much he respected them, and they for their part were of the opinion that this united effort was the harbinger of a new era in the German theater.

The presence of these two men at the rehearsals was extremely useful. Above all they were able to persuade the actors that in a rehearsal positioning and movements should be coordinated with speaking just as in a finished performance, so that the combination would become completely automatic. Especially as regards the hands: there should be no ordinary, trivial actions during the rehearsal of a tragedy such as taking a pinch of snuff. If an actor does that, there is the risk that in the performance he might miss his snuffbox. They were also against actors rehearsing in high boots when the role called for shoes. And nothing distressed them more at rehearsals than actresses who put their hands in the pleats of their skirts.

Another good thing that emerged from the advice of these two men was that the actors learned how to drill and march. "Since nowadays there are so many military roles," they said, "there is nothing more pathetic than seeing men totally without training waddling about the stage in captain's and major's uniforms." Wilhelm and Laertes were the first to take instruction from a drill sergeant while at the same time vigorously continuing their fencing practice.

So these two friends of the theater spent a great deal of effort improving a company that had been brought together by such happy chance. They insured the future satisfaction of the public by talking to the actors about this their most passionate concern. It was difficult to overestimate the value of their efforts, because they concentrated particularly on what was of most importance, namely that it was the duty of the actors to speak loud and clear. On this they encountered more opposition than they had at first expected. Most of the actors wanted to be heard much as they usually spoke, not to speak so that they could be heard. Some blamed the building, others said one shouldn't shout if one was to speak naturally, intimately or tenderly.

Our two friends, patient beyond words, tried to clear up this misapprehension and to overcome such stubborn notions. They tried every argument and every form of flattery, and finally succeeded in their purpose by pointing to Wilhelm as a good example. He asked them to sit during rehearsals at the far end of the building, and to let him know when they could not hear what he was saying by knocking on the bench with a key. He articulated well, spoke in measured tones, raising his voice by stages, but never shouting even in the most violent passages. At each subsequent rehearsal there was less knocking of keys; gradually all the other actors accepted the procedure, and everyone now hoped that the play would be audible in all parts of the house.

One can see how human beings like to reach their ends only by their own means, how much trouble it takes to make them understand what is self-evident, and how difficult it is to implant in someone who has real ambitions the first conditions that will make his efforts likely to succeed.

Chapter Nine

Work proceeded on sets and costumes, and various other things. Wilhelm had some fancies about certain scenes and passages, and Serlo gave in to these, partly because of the contract and partly from being convinced by what he said, but also because he hoped, by obliging him in this respect, to win him over, and then, in the future, to influence him more and more toward his own ends and purposes.

For instance: Wilhelm wanted the king and the queen to be seated on their thrones in the first big scene with the courtiers off to the side and Hamlet placed unobtrusively amongst them. "Hamlet," he said, "must keep quiet, his black garments will sufficiently mark him out. He should conceal himself rather than be readily visible. Only when the audience is over and the king speaks to him as a son, should he step forward and the scene take its appointed course."

A major problem was presented by the two portraits, which Hamlet refers to so passionately in the scene with his mother. "I want them both to be life-size and placed on the back wall on either side of the main entrance, with that of the old king in full armor like the Ghost and on the side where it enters. He should be portrayed with his right hand raised in a gesture of command, slightly turned to one side and almost looking over his shoulder, so that he looks exactly like the Ghost when it goes out of the door. That will be very effective when Hamlet is looking at the Ghost and the queen at the portrait. The stepfather should be presented in full regalia but not make such an imposing impression as Hamlet's father."

There were various other points which we will perhaps have occasion to refer to later.

"Are you adamant about Hamlet dying at the end?" Serlo asked.

"How can I keep him alive," said Wilhelm, "when the whole play has crushed him to death? We've already talked about that at length."

"But the public will want him to remain alive."

"I will gladly grant you anything else, but that cannot be. We also wish that a fine man suffering from a mortal illness should live longer. His family weeps and beseeches the doctor, but he cannot save him; natural necessity cannot be withstood, but no more can a recognized artistic necessity. It would be making a false concession to the mob to arouse feelings that they desire rather than what they should have."

"The one who provides the money should have his choice of the goods."

"Yes, to a certain extent; but a large public deserves to be respected, and not treated like children from whom you take money. If, by showing them what is good, we develop in them a feeling or taste for what is good, they will be all the more willing to pay their money because they will have nothing to reproach themselves for. They can be flattered like a child you wish to improve and help toward greater intelligence, not like a rich grandee to perpetuate his failings from which one profits."

They also settled various matters related to the question of what should be changed and what could be left as it is. We will not go into that any further now, but perhaps we will sometime communicate this new version of *Hamlet* to those of our readers who may be interested.

Chapter Ten

The dress rehearsal was over. It had lasted an unconscionably long time. Serlo and Wilhelm found that there was still much to be concerned about; for, despite the length of time they had spent on preparation, there were certain matters that had been put off till the last moment. For example: The portraits of the two kings were not finished, and the scene between Hamlet and his mother, which they expected would have a terrific effect, was as a result still very thin because neither the Ghost nor its portrait were part of it. Serlo joked about this and said: "We would really be in a sorry situation if the Ghost were not to appear, the watch were to fence with thin air, and the prompter were to supply the Ghost's speech!"

"Let's not scare away our supernatural friend by our doubts," Wilhelm replied. "He will turn up at the right time, that's for sure, and surprise us as much as the spectators." "Yes," said Serlo. "But I'll be glad when tomorrow's over and the play has been performed. It has caused us much more trouble than I thought it would."

"No one will be more pleased than I," said Philine, "when the performance is over, even though I am not worried about my part. But having to listen over and over again to people talking about one and the same thing, whereas all they are really concerned about is a performance which, like hundreds of others, will soon be forgotten — that really tries my patience. For Heaven's sake, don't make so much fuss! When guests have finished a meal they always have some criticism of what they have been eating, and if one listens to them when they are back home, they talk as if they wonder how they managed to stick it out."

"Let's make good use of that comparison, my dear," said Wilhelm. "Just think how much must be contributed by nature and art, by marketing, salesmen and experts to produce a banquet, how long the stag must spend in the forest, the fish in the river or the sea, before it is ready to grace our table, all that to be achieved by the housewife and cook in the kitchen! Just think with what little thought we gulp down the efforts of some distant winegrower, shipper or merchant with our dessert, as if these were to be taken for granted. Do you really think that, on that account, all these people should not exert themselves in production and preparation, and our host should not assemble everything with the utmost care, just because the pleasure provided is not a lasting one? No pleasure is temporary, for it leaves a lasting effect; and our own work and effort conveys some sense of a hidden energy to the audience, and one never knows what effect that may have."

"I don't care about all that. But what I have noticed," said Philine, "is that men always contradict themselves. Despite all your conscientious efforts not to truncate this great author, you have left out the best remark in the play." "The best?" said Wilhelm. "Yes, the best, and one that Hamlet uses to his advantage." "And what might that be?" asked Serlo. "If you had a periwig on, I would snatch it off you," Philine replied; "something needs to be done to clear your head."

The two men thought hard, and conversation stopped. It was already late, so they got up to leave, but while they still stood there pondering, Philine sang a little song with a tune that was very engaging:

Do not sing in tones depressing
Of the loneliness of night;
No, O fair one, it's a blessing
Made for purposes of delight.

Just as man is given a wife to
Be his better half — agreed —
So is night the half of life too,
And the nicer half indeed.

How can day bring glad elation
Since it interrupts our joy?
It's just good for dissipation,
Worthless else for man or boy.

But when night comes to eclipse the
Gentle lamplight's dusky glow,
And from lips to nearby lips the
Mirth and love well up and flow —

When a wanton lad who's eager,
Full of fire, the hasty sort,
Often for a gift that's meager
Tarries for a bit of sport—

When the nightingale is singing
Songs of love to lovers' ears,
It's the sadder echoes ringing
That a wretched captive hears—

With a heart that beats the time then
You await the bell's reprise
Which with twelve slow bongs will chime then,
Pledging safety, rest and ease!

So, as through long days you hurry,
Mark this maxim to employ:
Every day is dark with worry,
And the night is bright with joy.

When she had finished she made a little bow, and Serlo shouted a loud bravo. She ran out of the room and rushed away laughing. They heard her clattering down the stairs with her heels, still singing.

Serlo went into the adjoining room, but Aurelie remained with Wilhelm who was waiting to bid her goodnight.

"How repulsive she is, repulsive to every one of my feelings," said Aurelie. "Even down to the smallest details. I can't bear those brown eyebrows with her blond hair, which my brother finds so attractive, and that scab on her forehead has something so loathsome, so vulgar about it that I always want to step back ten paces. She told me the other day—she thought it was funny—that, when she was a child, her father had thrown a plate at her head from which she still had this mark. She is certainly marked on her eyes and forehead, so much so that one should avoid her."

Wilhelm did not respond, and so Aurelie went on to express even more of her distaste: "It is almost impossible for me to say anything kind or polite to her, for I hate her so much, even though she is so endearing. I wish I were rid of her. You too, my friend, have a certain affection for this creature, a way of acting toward her that wounds my very heart, an attention that borders on respect which, by God, she does not deserve!"

"I am grateful to her for what she is," said Wilhelm. "Her manners leave much to be desired, but I must do justice to her character."

"Character!" Aurelie exclaimed. "Do you think such a creature has character? Oh, you men, that's just like you. And this is the sort of women you deserve!"

"If you harbor any suspicions on this score regarding me, I assure you that I can account for every minute I have spent with her."

"Well, well," said Aurelie. "It's getting late, so let's not quarrel. One and all, all and one! Good night, my friend; good night, my fine bird of paradise!"

Wilhelm asked her how he came to earn this honorific title.

"Some other time," said Aurelie. "Some other time. It is said they have no feet, only soar in the air, and nourish themselves from the ether. But that's only a fairy tale, just a poetic fiction. Good night, and pleasant dreams – if you are lucky."

She went to her room and he was left alone. Then he hurried off to his own room.

He paced up and down restlessly. The jocular but deliberate tone of Aurelie's words had offended him: He felt she was being profoundly unjust toward him. He could not act ungraciously or hostilely toward Philine. She had done him no wrong. And he felt so far from being in any way attracted to her, that he could proudly and steadfastly maintain that he had stood the test.

He was just about to undress and go to bed when, pulling back the curtains, he noticed to his great surprise a pair of women's slippers at the foot of the bed, one upright, the other turned over. He soon recognized them as Philine's. He also thought he observed that the bed curtains were displaced; it seemed they were moving. He stood and gazed with unaccustomed eyes, catching his breath in some emotion and irritation, then said sharply:

"Get up, Philine! What's the meaning of this?" he shouted. "Where's your common sense! What sort of behavior is this! Are we to be the talk of the household tommorow?"

But nothing stirred.

"I'm not joking," he said. "This foolishness is not to my taste."

Still no sound, still no movement!

Finally, determined and angry, he stepped up to the bed and tore the curtains aside. "Now get up," he said, "or I'll leave you here on your own."

But to his great astonishment he found his bed empty, the pillows and covers blissfully undisturbed. He looked around, but could not find a trace of the little minx. Nothing behind the bed, nothing behind the stove, nothing behind the closets. He searched and searched. Indeed a malicious observer might have thought that he was hoping to find something.

He could not sleep. He put the slippers on his table, walked around, stopping several times by the table, and if some imp of a spirit had been watching him, he would surely have reported that Wilhelm occupied himself for a good part of the night with the pretty little stilts, looking at them and fondling them, and it was nearly daybreak before he fell fully clothed into his bed and slept amidst a host of the strangest fantasies.

And he was still sleeping when Serlo came in, shouting: "Where on earth are you? Still in bed? How could you! I've been looking everywhere in the theater for you. There is still a lot to do."

Chapter Eleven

The morning and afternoon passed quickly, and the house was already full when Wilhelm hurried to dress. This time he did not don his costume with the same leisureliness as he had the first time; he was now anxious to be ready on time. When he joined the ladies in the greenroom, they all agreed that nothing was right: the plumes on his hat were off to one side, the clasp didn't fit, and they all began to take them apart, sew them together again, and put everything in order. The overture started with Philine's objecting to something about his ruff and Aurelie's about his cloak. "Let me be, dear girls," he said, "this untidiness will make me a real Hamlet." But the women would not let him be, and went on improving his appearance. The overture came to an end, and the play started. Wilhelm looked at himself in a mirror, pulled his hat further down over his face, and touched up his makeup.

At that moment someone came rushing in, crying: "The Ghost! The Ghost!"

Wilhelm had not had the time to remember his prime concern, whether the Ghost would arrive or not. Now all his fears were removed, and a most remarkable guest appearance was to be anticipated. The stage manager came to ask about various things, so that for the moment Wilhelm did not have time to look around for the Ghost. He had to hurry to take his place by the throne, where the king and queen, surrounded by all the courtiers, were established in all their glory. All he had time to hear were the last words of Horatio, who described the appearance of the Ghost, but with some confusion, as if he had forgotten his lines.

The drop curtain was raised, and Wilhelm saw that the theater was full. When Horatio had concluded his speech and been given his orders by the king (in accordance with the addition that Wilhelm had made to the play), he came up to Hamlet and, as if he were presenting arms before his prince, said: "There's a very devil behind that armor! He scared us all to death!"

In the meantime two men could be seen standing in the wings, tall, and dressed in white capes with hoods. Wilhelm had been so distracted, uneasy and nervous that he felt he had bungled the first monologue, though the audience applauded wildly when he left the stage, and now he was about to enter the gruesome winter night of the drama in a state of trepidation. He pulled himself together and delivered the timely speech about the drunken swinishness of the Danes with such fitting distaste that, like the spectators, he forgot about the Ghost, and was therefore quite terrified when Horatio said: "Look, my lord, it comes!" He turned around sharply, and the tall noble figure with its soft silent tread in the seeming heavy armor made such a strong effect on him that he stood there petrified and could only murmur the words: "Angels and ministers of grace defend us!" He stared at the figure, took a few deep breaths, and delivered his address to the Ghost in such a distraught, broken and compulsive manner that the greatest of artists could not have done better.

His translation of this passage was a great help to him, for he had kept very close to the original, conveying the surprise and fright, the horror that was seizing hold of Hamlet's mind as he said:

> Be thou a spirit of health or goblin damn'd,
> Bring with thee airs from heaven or blasts from hell,
> Be thy intents wicked or charitable.
> Thou com'st in such a questionable shape
> That I will speak to thee: I'll call thee Hamlet,
> King, father; royal Dane, O! answer me.

One could feel a strong reaction in the public. The Ghost beckoned, and to the sound of tumultuous applause the prince followed.

The scene changed, and when they reached the distant place the Ghost suddenly stopped and turned, so that Hamlet found himself too close to him. Wilhelm peered eagerly into the shut visor but all he could see were deepset eyes and a well-shaped nose. He stood before him, timid and observing; but when the first sounds emerged from beneath the helmet, uttered in a pleasing but somewhat rough voice, out came the words: "I am thy father's spirit," Wilhelm stepped back shuddering, and the whole audience shuddered. The voice seemed familiar to everyone, and Wilhelm thought it sounded like that of his own father. These mysterious feelings and memories, his eagerness to discover the stranger's identity without offending him, coupled with his own clumsiness in getting too close to him on the stage—all this tore Wilhelm in different directions. He changed position so often during the long narration of the Ghost, he seemed so uncertain of himself and ill at ease, so attentive but at the same time so distracted that his performance aroused the admiration of all and the Ghost heightened their terror. The Ghost spoke in a tone of vexation rather than of sorrow, but it was an anger of the mind, slow and inestimable. It was the malaise of a great soul that is deprived of all finiteness and consigned to infinite suffering. At last there came the moment when the Ghost descended, but he departed in a strange way, for a thin grey veil surrounded him and dragged him down, like a mist rising from the depths.

Then Hamlet's companions returned and swore upon his sword. The old mole worked in the earth so fast that, wherever they moved to, he was always beneath them, crying: "Swear!" They were constantly changing position as if the ground were burning their feet. The effect was heightened by little flames appearing wherever they stood. All this left a deep impression on the public.

The play continued without any mishap. Everything turned out as it should, the public showed its approval, and the actors' spirits rose from scene to scene.

Chapter Twelve

The curtain fell, and loud applause resounded from every corner of the house. The four noble corpses jumped up and embraced each other joyfully. Polonius and Ophelia came out of their graves and heard with keenest pleasure the vigorous applause that greeted Horatio when he stepped forward to tell the audience about the future program. But they would not let him announce any other play; they demanded that this one should be repeated.

"Well, we won the day!" said Serlo, "but let's not have any more intelligent talk tonight! First impressions are the most important. No actor should be blamed for being rather cautious or headstrong on a first night."

The cashier came up with a heavy till. "We've begun very well," he said, "and first opinions will work to our advantage. But where is the supper you promised? We have every right to feast tonight." They had agreed to remain in their costumes and have their own private celebration. Wilhelm had undertaken to find the place, and Madame Melina the food.

A room that was normally used for painting sets had been cleaned up and decked out with small bits of scenery to suggest a garden and a colonnade. As they entered they were dazzled by the bright light of lots of candles shining ceremoniously through plentiful clouds of sweet smelling incense on a richly laid table. There were shouts of joy at the décor and everyone took his seat. It seemed as if a band of regal spirits had assembled. Wilhelm sat between Aurelie and Madame Melina, Serlo between Philine and Elmire; everybody was delighted with the seating, and with themselves.

The two connoisseurs were also present and added to the delight of the company. They had, several times during the performance, stepped on stage and could not say often enough how satisfied they and the public had been. They went into details, praising each individual performance, the merits of this or that actor, the excellence of this or that section. The prompter, who was sitting quietly at the far end of the table, received great praise for his rugged Pyrrhus. The duel between Hamlet and Laertes could not have been better, Ophelia's lament had been inexpressibly sweet and noble, Polonius's acting so good that there was nothing to be said about it. Everyone who was present felt himself praised in and by the others.

Even the absent Ghost received his praise and admiration. He had spoken the part with the appropriate voice and in impressive fashion, they were truly amazed that he seemed to be well informed about what had been happening in the company. He had looked exactly like the portrait, as if he had sat for it himself; and the two men could not adequately express their admiration for the awesome effect produced when he first appeared close to his portrait and then walked right past it. So striking was the combination of truth and illusion that they had been quite convinced that the Queen had not seen the apparition. Madame Melina was praised for staring up at the portrait while Hamlet pointed down at the Ghost.

Everyone wondered how the Ghost could have got into the theater, and learned from the stage manager that the back door, which was usually blocked by sets, had been left free that evening because for the play they needed the feeling of a Gothic hall; and through this door two tall figures in white capes and hoods had come, each indistinguishable from the other, and both had left after the third act, probably through the same door.

What Serlo particularly liked about the Ghost was that he did not dither and moan like a workman about his sorry state, and then exhort his son in words suited to a great hero. Wilhelm remembered that particular speech and agreed to put it back into the stage copy.

They were all enjoying the party so much that they had not noticed that the Harper and the children were not present. But soon they turned up, bizarrely decked out, Felix with a triangle, Mignon with a tambourine, and the Harper with his heavy instrument hanging from his shoulders, holding it in front of him as he played it. They trooped round the table singing all sorts of songs. They were given something to eat, and received what the others thought was a service, by being given as much of the sweet wine as they could drink, for everybody had not stinted themselves in wine, whole baskets of which, and excellent wine at that, had been contributed by the two connoisseurs. The children jumped and danced, and Mignon was particularly uninhibited, more than she had ever been before. She played the tambourine as delicately and then as loudly as possible, sometimes lightly skimming her fingers over the skin, at other times beating on it with the back of her hand or her knuckles, even alternating between striking her knees or her head with the instrument, sometimes just making the bells ring, so that all sorts of sounds were enticed from this simplest of instruments. After the children had made quite a din, they fell into an unoccupied armchair across from where Wilhelm was seated.

"Keep away from that chair!" Serlo shouted. "It's probably reserved for the Ghost, and if he comes, you'll be in a bad way."

"I'm not afraid of him," said Mignon. "If he comes, we'll get up. He's my uncle; he won't hurt me." Nobody understood what she meant, except those who knew that she had called the man she thought was her father "the big devil." They all looked at each other, suspecting more strongly than ever that Serlo knew something about the apparition. They went on talking and drinking, and every now and again the girls would look anxiously in the direction of the door.

Sitting in the armchair like puppets hanging out of a box, the children started a little game of their own, with Mignon making a rasping noise as puppets do. They banged their heads together as if these were made of wood. Mignon was almost frenetically excited and, amusing as this had been in the beginning, it became such that it had to be curbed. But admonishing her seemed to have little effect, for she now began hysterically to rush around the table, tambourine in hand, hair flying, head thrown back and her body flung into the air like one of those maenads whose wild and well-nigh impossible postures still delight us on ancient monuments.

Encouraged by the talents and hubbub of the children, everyone tried to contribute something to the general entertainment. The women sang several canons, Laertes did an impersonation of a nightingale, and the Pedant treated them to a pianissimo concerto on the Jew's harp. All sorts of games were started, hands clasped and grasped beneath the table, sometimes with a definite indication of hope and affection. Madame Melina, so it seemed, did not attempt to conceal her strong liking for Wilhelm. It was already well into the night when Aurelie, who seemed to be the only person still in control of herself, rose and urged the others to break it up.

As everyone was leaving, Serlo gave a firework display, imitating the noise of rockets, squibs and firewheels; he did this with his mouth so skillfully that the illusion was complete if one closed one's eyes. After that everybody got up, the gentlemen gave their arms to the ladies and escorted them home. Wilhelm and Aurelie were the last to leave. On the stairs he was met by the stage manager, who said: "This is the veil in which the Ghost disappeared. It was caught in the trapdoor, and we have just discovered it." "A wondrous relic, indeed!" said Wilhelm, taking it from him. At that very moment he seemed to be grasped by his left arm, and at the same time felt a sharp pain. Mignon had been hiding, and seizing hold of him, she bit him in the arm, rushed past him on the stairs and disappeared.

When our friends emerged into the fresh air, they almost all felt that they had indulged themselves a little too much that evening, and they separated, without bidding each other good night.

Wilhelm threw off his clothes as soon as he got to his room, put out the light and dropped into bed. He fell asleep in no time, but was aroused by a noise which seemed to come from behind the stove. The image of the king in arms came before his heated imagination, and he sat up in order to address the spirit, only to find himself drawn back by a pair of tender arms, his mouth smothered by passionate kisses, and against his chest the breast of another that he did not dare to push aside.

Chapter Thirteen

Next day Wilhelm arose with an uncomfortable feeling, and found his bed empty. His head was still fuzzy from the not yet dispelled intoxication of the evening before, and the memory of the unknown nocturnal visit made him uneasy. His first guess was that it had been Philine, and yet the charming body he had clasped in his arms did not seem like hers. He had fallen asleep amidst eager caresses alongside his mysterious, silent visitor, but now there was no trace of who it was. He jumped up, dressed, and noticed that his door, which he usually kept locked, was ajar; he simply could not remember whether he had closed it the previous evening.

But the most mysterious thing of all was that he found the Ghost's veil lying on his bed. He had probably himself flung it down when he brought it home with him. It was of grey crepe, and there was a border with some words embroidered in black letters. He opened it out, and this is what he read: *For the first and last time, young man, flee*! He was astonished, not knowing what to make of this.

At that very moment Mignon entered, bringing him his breakfast. Wilhelm was surprised by the child's appearance, indeed he was frightened by it. She seemed to have grown taller during the night. She strode up to him with a certain dignity, and looked into his eyes with such a serious expression that he had to turn away. She did not touch him as she usually did—clasping his hand, kissing him on the mouth or cheek or arm or shoulder—but quickly left the room once she had put his things in order.

The time arrived for the reading rehearsal. The whole company assembled, all of them out of sorts because of the jollifications of the previous evening. Wilhelm controlled himself to the best of his ability, so that he should not be the first to offend against the principles which he had advocated so firmly. The extent of his experience assisted him in this; for technique and experience fill up those gaps in any art which temperament and mood so often create.

Actually it might be true to say that one should never begin anything that is intended to last—situation, profession, or lifestyle—by a celebration. Celebrations belong at the end, when something is successfully completed; initial ceremonies exhaust those desires and powers that should encourage aspiration and sustain us in the difficulties of achievement. Marriage is of all such occasions for a celebration the most unsuitable, none should be more marked by silence, humility and hope.

The day crept on and none had ever seemed so ordinary to Wilhelm. Instead of the usual entertainment in the evening, people began to yawn; the interest in *Hamlet* was flagging, and no one found it at all appropriate to repeat it the next day. Wilhelm showed the Ghost's veil, from which it was concluded that the Ghost would not return. Serlo in particular was of this opinion. He seemed well acquainted with the advice of this strange character, but the words: "Flee, young man, flee!" defied explanation. How could Serlo agree with someone who seemed to want to deprive him of the best actor in his company?

It now became necessary to give the part of the Ghost to the Blusterer and the King to the Pedant. They both declared they knew the roles, and no wonder, for the number of rehearsals and the detailed discussions they had had of the play, meant that they were all so well acquainted with it that they could easily switch roles. Some parts were given a quick run-through, and when the actors went their separate ways at quite a late hour, Philine whispered to Wilhelm: "I must have my slippers back. Don't bolt the door." By the time he was back in his room, he was in a state of confusion because of what she had said, feeling more and more certain that his visitor of the previous night had been Philine. We too must share this opinion, because we are not able to reveal the reasons which had made him doubt this and had aroused other suspicions. He walked restlessly to and fro in his room. And he did not bolt the door.

Suddenly Mignon rushed into the room, grabbed him and cried: "Master! Save the building! It's on fire!" Wilhelm jumped through the doorway and was met by a dense cloud of smoke pouring down from the stairs. From the street below the alarm was being sounded, and from above the Harper came rushing down the stairs breathless with his instrument in his hand. Aurelie came running from her room and deposited Felix in Wilhelm's arms. "Save the child!" she cried; "We'll look after the rest."

Wilhelm, who did not think the danger was all that great, decided he would first try to find the source of the fire and extinguish it before it could spread. He handed the child to the Harper and told him to hurry down the stone steps that led into a cellar and out into the garden, and to stay outside with the children. He also asked Aurelie to get their possessions out of the house by this route. He tried to go upstairs through the smoke, but there was no point in exposing himself to danger. For the flames seemed to be spreading from the neighboring house and had already engulfed the attic and one staircase; some who came to the rescue were, like him, overcome by smoke and flames. Nevertheless he urged them on and called for water, imploring them to retreat no more than step by step from the flames, and promising to remain with them. But at this moment Mignon rushed up crying: "Master! Save your Felix! The old man has gone mad! He's killing him!" Without a moment's hesitation Wilhelm tore down the stairs with Mignon close at his heels.

At the bottom of the staircase, just where it led into the cellar, he stopped in horror. Great bundles of straw and brushwood were stored there, and were now burning fiercely. Felix was lying on the ground and crying. The old man stood leaning against the wall, his head bowed. "What are you doing, you wretched man?" exclaimed Wilhelm. The old man said nothing. Mignon picked up Felix and dragged him with difficulty into the garden, while Wilhelm tried to separate the burning wood and smother the fire but only managed to increase the power and heat of the flames. Finally he too had to retreat to the garden, his eyelashes and hair singed as he dragged the old man through the flames, who followed him reluctantly, his beard scorched in the process.

Wilhelm hastened to join the children in the garden. He found them sitting on the steps of a pavilion, Mignon doing her best to calm down the child. Wilhelm took him on his lap, questioned him, stroked him, but could not get any coherent information out of either of the children.

By now the fire had taken hold of several houses and was lighting up the whole neighborhood. Wilhelm inspected the child by the red light of the flames, but could find no wound; there was no blood and there were no bruises. He felt the child all over, but there was no indication of pain. Gradually he settled down to a certain delight at the flames and the orderly progression in which the beams and rafters burned and provided such splendid illumination.

Wilhelm did not think about the clothes and what he might have lost. He thought only of these two human beings, so dear to him, who had escaped such danger. He pressed the little one with unaccustomed intensity to his breast, and would have embraced Mignon with equal affection and joy, had she not gently resisted, taking his hand and holding it firmly.

"Master," she said (she had never called him that before this evening, having addressed him first as "Sir" and then as "Father"), "Master! We have escaped great danger. Your Felix was near to death."

Much questioning finally elicited from her that when they reached the cellar, the Harper had taken the candle from her and set fire to the straw. He then put down Felix, laid his hands with strange gestures on the child's head and pulled out a knife, as if he were going to sacrifice him. She had rushed up and pulled the knife from his hand, screamed, and somebody from the house, who was bringing some things into the garden, came to her assistance, but must in the confusion have gone away again and left the old man with the child.

By now two or three buildings were burning fiercely. Nobody had been able to escape into the garden because of the fire in the adjoining cellar. Wilhelm was more concerned about his friends than his possessions. He did not dare to leave the children and feared still greater misfortune.

He spent several hours in trepidation. Felix was fast asleep in his lap, Mignon lay beside him, firmly clasping his hand. At last they had succeeded in containing the fire. The burnt-out buildings collapsed, daylight came, the children began to shiver, and he himself, lightly clad as he was, found the morning dew quite intolerable. He took the children up to the ruins of the buildings where there was still a pleasant amount of warmth from the ashes and smoldering wood.

The new day brought his friends and acquaintances together again. Everyone was safe; no one had lost much.

Wilhelm's trunk turned up, and around ten o'clock Serlo pressed for a rehearsal of *Hamlet*, or at least of those scenes where the casting had been changed. Then he had some altercation with the police. The clergy were demanding that after such a judgment from God the theater should remain closed, and Serlo was declaring that a performance of this interesting play was just what was needed to brighten up frightened minds—as well as being some sort of compensation for what he had lost during the night. Serlo had his way, and the theater was packed. The actors played their parts with extraordinary vigor and even more freedom and passion than the first time. The spectators, their feelings heightened by nocturnal terrors and their minds, after the boredom of a distracting and ill-spent day more than ever prepared for interesting entertainment showed more receptivity for the extraordinary nature of the play than the previous audience. They were mostly drawn there by what they had heard about the play, and so could not compare this performance with the earlier one. The Blusterer played the Ghost in the same spirit as the unknown stranger, the Pedant had carefully noted the performance by his predecessor, and his pitiful appearance worked very much to his advantage when, despite the purple and ermine, Hamlet truthfully called him a king of shreds and patches.

No one had ever inherited a throne in a stranger fashion. And although the others, especially Philine, made fun of his newly acquired dignity, he reminded them that so knowledgeable a man as the count had prophesied this for him, and much more, when he first set eyes on him. But Philine told him to be more modest and swore that she would put powder on his sleeves to remind him of the misfortune that had befallen him at the castle. He should wear his crown with humility.

Chapter Fourteen

They quickly looked around for new quarters and as a result the company became very scattered. Wilhelm had grown fond of the pavilion in the garden where he had spent the night; he soon got the keys and established himself there. Since, however, Aurelie was very cramped in her new quarters, he had to keep Felix with him, and Mignon would not leave the boy. The children had a nice room on the upper floor and he settled down in the lower part. They slept soundly, but he did not close an eye.

While the moon rose and illuminated the pleasant garden, the sad ruins from which smoke was still rising stood nearby. The air was mild and the night unusually beautiful. Philine had stroked his elbow as she left the theater and whispered something which he had not understood. He was confused and irritated, not knowing what to expect or do. She had been avoiding him for several days, and this was the first sign of recognition she had given him. Unfortunately the door he was to leave unlocked had been burnt, and the slippers with it. How she was to come into the garden, assuming that that was her intention, he did not know. He did not want to see her, though he would have liked to have it out with her.

What troubled him much more was the fate of the Harper, who had disappeared. Wilhelm was afraid that he might be found dead beneath the rubble. He had said nothing to anybody about his suspicion that the Harper had set the fire. For it was from the burning attic that he had first emerged, and his desperate state in the cellar adjoining the garden would seem to have been the result of some such unfortunate action. But during the police investigation it became apparent that the most likely source of the fire was to be found not in their building, but two houses away, and that the flames had spread along the adjoining roofs.

Wilhelm was pondering all this while seated in an arbor, when he heard someone approaching on a nearby walk. From the mournful strains he heard he recognized the Harper. The song, which he understood full well, was about the consolations of someone who feels he is near to madness. Unfortunately Wilhelm could only remember the last verse:

> Let me linger by the gate
> Unobtrusive, silently,
> Pious hand will give me food,
> I move on to other doors.
> Every one will show delight
> Just to see my face out there,
> Down their cheeks a tear will fall,
> Why they weep, I do not know.

At this point he reached the garden gate from which a path led to the main highway. Since he found it locked, he tried to climb over the fence, but Wilhelm held him back and talked to him in a kindly fashion. The old man asked him to open the gate because he wanted to, indeed had to escape. Wilhelm explained to him that he could get out of the garden but not leave the town without arousing suspicion. But to no purpose! The old man persisted, Wilhelm would not give way and dragged him almost forcibly into the pavilion, shut himself up with him, and had an extraordinary conversation with him, which, so as not to torment our readers with scattered thoughts and anxious feelings, we will rather say nothing about.

Chapter Fifteen

Wilhelm was really perplexed as to what to do about the unfortunate old man, who was showing definite signs of losing his mind. His reflections were interrupted by Laertes who, accustomed as always to be here, there, and everywhere, had met a man in a coffeehouse who had been suffering from acute attacks of melancholy. This man had been placed in the care of a country pastor, who made a special business of treating such people. The pastor had once again been successful. He was in town, and the family of the man, now restored to health, were expressing their profound respect and thanks to him.

Wilhelm went immediately in search of the pastor, told him about the case, and came to an agreement with him that on some pretext or other the Harper should be entrusted to his charge. Parting from the Harper was extremely painful for Wilhelm, and it was only the hope of seeing him restored to health that made him agree to such a step, so accustomed had he become to see the old man around and listen to his music that was so expressive of his mind and his feelings. The harp had perished in the fire, but a new one was found for him.

Also destroyed in the fire was Mignon's meager wardrobe, and when new things were to be bought for her, Aurelie proposed that she should now at last be dressed as a girl. "No, no!" said Mignon, and insisted on wearing something like her old outfit. So a new one of the same sort was provided for her.

There was not much time for reflection, for the performances were to start soon. Wilhelm often listened to the spectators, but rarely did he hear anything approaching what he would, in fact, have liked to hear, and more often things that depressed or annoyed him. One young man, for instance, described in glowing terms the splendid evening he had had at the first performance of *Hamlet*. But he went on to say, to Wilhelm's annoyance, that he had kept his hat on throughout the whole performance in order to irritate those behind him. He remembered this heroic deed with the utmost delight. Someone else said that Wilhelm had played the part of Laertes very well, but one couldn't be as satisfied with the actor who had played Hamlet. This confusion was quite natural, for Wilhelm and Laertes were somewhat alike, though it was a remote resemblance. Still another warmly praised his acting in the scene with his mother, regretting only that in this highly emotional sequence a white ribbon had popped out of his vest and spoilt the illusion entirely.

Several changes had to be made within the company. Since the evening after the fire Philine had made no sign of wishing to approach Wilhelm. She had taken quarters quite a way off—on purpose, so it would seem—spent most of her time with Elmire and only rarely came to see Serlo, which was indeed gratifying to Aurelie. Serlo, who had always been well disposed towards Philine, visited her sometimes, especially when he hoped to find Elmire with her, and one evening he took Wilhelm along. They were both amazed to find Philine in the inner room, in the arms of a young officer in a red uniform and white undergarments, whose face they could not see because it was turned away from them. Philine came to greet them, closing the door of the other room, and said, "You have caught me unawares, while I am having the most extraordinary adventure!"

"Not so extraordinary," said Serlo. "Let's have a look at your handsome and enviable young friend. You've whetted our curiosity so much already that we couldn't bear to be jealous."

"I must let you keep your suspicions for a while," said Philine jokingly. "But I can assure you that it's only a girl friend of mine who is staying for a few days with me incognito. You shall hear all about her later and you may well find her extremely interesting so that I shall have to exercise all my modesty and indulgence, for I fear you may forget your old friend for the new."

Wilhelm stood transfixed to the spot, for the red uniform had immediately reminded him of his beloved Mariane—the same figure, the same blond hair, though this officer seemed somewhat taller.

"For Heaven's sake," he cried, "do let us know more about your friend, let us see this dressed-up girl. We are now part of the secret, and we promise not to reveal it, but do let us see her!" "O how infatuated he is," said Philine. "Take it easy. Be patient. Not today!" "Then at least tell us her name!" said Wilhelm. "That would be keeping a fine secret!" Philine objected. "Well then at least her first name." "See if you can guess it," said Philine. "You can have three tries, but only three. Otherwise I would have to wait while you went through the whole church calendar." "All right," said Wilhelm. "How about Cecilie?" "Not Cecilie." "Henriette?" "Not a bit of it. Go easy. Your curiosity should take its time." Wilhelm hesitated. He trembled, wanting to speak but unable to do so. "How about Mariane?" he stammered out. "Bravo!" said Philine, twisting on her heel as usual, "You've got it." Wilhelm couldn't say another word, and Serlo, not noticing his perturbation, went on urging Philine to open the door.

They were both extremely surprised when Wilhelm hastily interrupted their jocular banter, threw himself at Philine's feet and passionately implored her to let him see the girl, saying: "She is mine, my Mariane, the one I have longed for every day of my life, the one who still exceeds all other women for me. Do at least go to her and tell her I am here, I, the one whose first love, whose youthful joys were fixed on her, and who now wishes to justify himself for having abandoned her so cruelly, to forgive her for all she may have done to him, and make no further claim on her, if only he may see her just this one more time, see that she is still alive and happy!"

Philine shook her head and said: "My dear friend, do lower your voice! Let's not deceive ourselves. If this is really your friend, then we must be considerate, for she will not be expecting to see you here. She has come here for quite different reasons, and you must know that there are certain moments when one would rather see a ghost than one's old lover. I'll ask her, I will prepare her, and we will together consider what would be best to do. I'll send you a message tomorrow telling you at what time you should come, or whether you should come at all. You must do exactly what I say, for I swear that no one shall see this lovely creature against my will or hers. I will keep my doors better locked, and don't try to use an axe to visit me!"

Wilhelm implored her and Serlo tried to persuade her; but all to no avail. They had to give way, and left.

One can well imagine what a restless night Wilhelm spent, and how slowly the daytime hours passed while he was waiting to hear from Philine. Unfortunately, he had to appear on stage that evening; he had never suffered such torment in his life. As soon as the performance was over, he rushed to Philine's quarters, without waiting for an invitation. He found her door locked. The people in the house said she had left early that morning with a young officer, saying she would be back in a few days, but they didn't believe that because she had paid what she owed and taken her things with her.

Wilhelm was beside himself at this news. He went straight to Laertes, suggesting they should follow her and, whatever the cost, find out definitely who her companion was. Laertes reproached his friend for his impulsiveness and credulity. "I bet," he said, "it is Friedrich. He comes from a good family, he's madly in love with the girl, and he has probably extracted enough cash from his relatives to be able to live with her again for a while."

These assertions did not convince Wilhelm, but they did make him pause. Laertes insisted that the whole yarn Philine had spun them was highly improbable, that the figure and hair could just as well be Friedrich's, that the two of them would already have twelve hours' start and not be easy to overtake, and, most important of all, Serlo could not dispense with either Wilhelm or Laertes for the performances.

Wilhelm was finally persuaded by these considerations to abandon any attempt at pursuing them himself. That same night Laertes found a trusty fellow to do it for them. He was a stolid man who had acted as courier and guide for several persons of quality but was at the time without employment. He was given money, informed of the whole matter, and given instructions to find the fugitives and catch up with them, never letting them out of his sight, and informing Wilhelm and Laertes when he discovered them. He mounted his horse that very same hour, and rode after the dubious pair, leaving Wilhelm somewhat more at ease.

Chapter Sixteen

Philine's departure did not create much of a sensation either in the theater or amongst the public. She had never been very serious about anything, was thoroughly hated by all the women, and the men preferred to see her off stage than on, so that her considerable talents as an actress passed unnoticed. The other members of the company worked even harder after she had left, especially Madame Melina, whose zeal and attention were remarkable. She took note of Wilhelm's principles, following him in theory and example, and acquired a certain something that made her more interesting. She achieved a correct style of acting, was able to reproduce the natural tone of conversation to perfection and even that of feeling to a certain degree. She learned how to adapt herself to Serlo's moods, worked at her singing to give him pleasure, and soon acquired sufficient skill in this for her to display her talents socially.

The company was enlarged by some newly engaged actors. Both Wilhelm and Serlo were influential in different ways, Wilhelm concentrating on the general meaning and tone of a play and Serlo conscientiously working away at all the details. The actors were fired by admirable enthusiasm and the public took an active interest in them.

"We're on the right path," said Serlo one day, "and if we stick to it, the public will get there too. It is quite easy to bedazzle people by presenting things in an outlandish and inappropriate fashion: but if one gives them an interesting production that is appropriate and sensible, then they will eagerly accept that. What our German theater lacks most is a sense of necessary limitations and restriction, everything is too higgledy-piggledy, too varied for us to have any standards of judgment—a fact that does not seem to bother either actors or spectators. My opinion is that it was not a good idea to extend the stage into a sort of endless panorama of nature; and now it is difficult for any director or actors to restrict themselves until acceptable limits have been established by public taste. Every valid society must exist within accepted boundaries; so too any theater, if it is to be good. Certain mannerisms and turns of phrase should be eradicated, certain subjects and certain forms of behavior should be excluded from the stage. One does not grow poorer by restricting one's household."

They partly agreed and partly disagreed about that. For Wilhelm and most of the others favored the English style of theater, whereas Serlo and some others preferred the French.

They agreed to work through the most celebrated examples of both styles of drama when they had a free hour (which, as with all actors, was unfortunately quite often), and select what was best and most worthy to serve as a model. They did make a start with some French plays, but Aurelie left the room every time the readings started. At first they thought she might be sick; and then one day Wilhelm, having observed this, asked her about it.

"I will never take part in such readings. How can I listen and exercise judgment when my heart is torn to shreds? I hate the French language from the bottom of my soul."

"How can one hate a language which has provided us with most of our culture and to which we must still be indebted if we are to give our substance any shape and form!"

"My judgment is not based on prejudice!" Aurelie declared. "It is rather an unfortunate impression, a distasteful memory of my faithless friend, which has deprived me of all affection for that beautiful, cultivated language. How I hate it now! During the time of our friendship he always wrote to me in German, and what sincere, true, strong German! But when he wanted to be rid of me, he began to write in French, whereas previously he had done that only as a joke. I recognized the significance of this. For what he was ashamed to say in his mother tongue, he could now set down in good conscience. It is an excellent language for reservations, half-truths and lies—a language that is *perfide*. Thank goodness that there is no German word I can think of to express the full meaning of *perfide*. Our poor word *treulos* is an innocent babe in comparison. *Perfide* is 'faithless,' mixed in with pleasure, arrogance and malice. What an enviable state of culture it is when so many nuances can be expressed in one single word! French is indeed the language of the civilized world and worthy of becoming the universal language so that people can all cheat and deceive each other. My friend's letters in French were always good to read. One could pretend, if one wanted to, that they sounded warm or even passionate; but on closer look they were nothing but phrases, cursed phrases! He robbed me of all pleasure in the language and its literature, even in those fine and precious works by noble poets in that tongue. I now shudder every time I hear a French word!"

She would go on like this for hours on end, venting her displeasure and totally disrupting everything. Sometimes Serlo would cut into these expressions of moodiness by some bitter remark; but usually the evening's conversation was wrecked.

Unfortunately, it is generally the case that something that is assembled by a variety of persons and circumstances rarely maintains its cohesion for long. Whether this be a theatrical company or an empire, a circle of friends or an army, a moment is usually reached when it is at its zenith, its best, its greatest unity, well-being and effectiveness. Then personalities change, new individuals arrive on the scene, and the persons no longer suit the circumstances and the circumstances the persons. Everything becomes different, and what had been unified begins to fall apart. One could well say that Serlo's troupe had for some time possessed a quality unmatched by any other German company. Most of the actors had their appointed place in it, with enough to do, and satisfaction at doing it. Their personal circumstances were tolerable, and every one of them seemed an artist of promise, for they had entered on their profession with enthusiasm and vigor. But it soon became clear that some of them were machines only able to achieve what could be done without feeling, and then those emotions began to make themselves felt, which usually tend to interfere with any well-organized undertaking and disrupt what sensible and thoughtful persons have striven to maintain.

Philine's departure was not quite so insignificant as had at first been thought. She had been very adept at keeping Serlo entertained, and had appealed, in varying degrees, to all the others. She had dealt very patiently with Aurelie's outbursts of violence, and her main concern had been to flatter Wilhelm. She had therefore been a sort of liaison between all of them, and her loss soon made itself felt.

Serlo could not exist without some little love affair. Elmire, who had grown up quickly and, one could almost say, become quite beautiful, had been attracting his attentions for some time, and Philine was smart enough to encourage what she saw to be a budding relationship. "One must," she would say, "at times take to matchmaking; there is nothing else left when we grow old." As a result Serlo and Elmire were already sufficiently acquainted for them to join forces when Philine departed, and their little romance had an even greater appeal for them because they had every reason to keep it secret from her father, who would not have been at all amused by such irregularity. Elmire's sister was in the know, and so Serlo had to be attentive to both girls. One of their worst faults was a passion for sweetmeats, which one could almost call gluttonous. In this respect they were considered to be quite unlike Philine, who now began to take on in retrospect a new air of graciousness because she had seemed to live on air, eat very little and sip only the bubbles from champagne, and that with the utmost delicacy.

But Serlo, in order to please his beloved, had to combine breakfast with lunch and then supper with dinner. He also had a plan that he was anxious to carry out. Having noticed a certain affection growing between Wilhelm and Aurelie, he was eager that this should develop into something serious. What he had in mind was to transfer all the more routine aspects of managing the theater to Wilhelm and so acquire a reliable and active assistant such as his previous brother-in-law had been. He had tacitly been transferring a good deal of this to Wilhelm and, with Aurelie looking after the finances, he was resuming the lifestyle he preferred. But there was one thing that deeply concerned both him and his sister.

The public has an odd way of reacting to persons of acknowledged merit by becoming less and less interested in them and favoring instead much lesser, but newly arrived, talents, making excessive demands on the former and delighting in everything about the latter.

Serlo and Aurelie had plenty of occasions to reflect on this matter. The new members of the company, especially those who were young and handsome, received all the attention and applause, whereas Serlo and Aurelie, despite all their efforts, left the stage without the welcome sound of clapping. There were certainly legitimate reasons for this. Aurelie's pride was very evident and her scorn for the public was well known, and Serlo favored individuals, but his sharp remarks about the ensemble were common knowledge and constantly bandied about. The new actors were either from other parts of the country and unfamiliar, or young, pleasant and needing help, so they easily gained their supporters.

Very soon there developed a certain amount of friction and dissatisfaction amongst the members of the company. For when it was observed that Wilhelm was taking over the duties of a producer, most of the actors became increasingly uncooperative as he tried to bring more order and precision into what they were doing and insisted that the mechanics of the production should proceed smoothly and with regularity.

In a short time the whole operation, which for a time had been running almost perfectly, became as undistinguished as that of any company of strolling players. Unfortunately it was just when Wilhelm, by unrelenting effort, had succeeded in mastering what the job demanded and had trained himself to meet these demands, that he came to the melancholy conclusion that this occupation did not merit the expenditure of time and effort that it required. The work was burdensome and the recompense inadequate. He would rather have done something which, when it was over, would have allowed him some peace of mind such as this work did not permit him. For once all the mechanical difficulties had been overcome, his thoughts and feelings were still totally occupied with reaching the goal which the mechanics were designed to achieve. He had to put up with Aurelie's complaints about her brother's extravagance, had to disregard Serlo's hints encouraging him in the direction of marrying Aurelie, and had to conceal his distress at what troubled him most, for the messenger he had sent after the dubious "officer" had not returned. Nothing had been heard from him, and our friend was afraid that he might have lost his Mariane for a second time.

Just at that time the theater had to be closed for a few weeks because of a period of state mourning. So Wilhelm used this opportunity to visit the pastor in whose care he had left the Harper. He discovered that the place where this man was living was peaceful and pleasant, and the first thing he saw on his arrival was the old man giving lessons on his instrument to a young boy. The Harper was delighted to see Wilhelm again, stood up and shook his hand, and said: "You see, I am still of some use in this world. Please allow me to go on with what I am doing, for my time is carefully organized."

The pastor received Wilhelm warmly and told him that the old man was doing quite well and there was hope of a complete recovery. Their conversation quite naturally turned to methods of curing madness.

"Apart from the physical aspect, which often creates insuperable difficulties and requires the advice of a thoughtful doctor, I find the treatment quite simple," said the pastor. "Basically it is the same as one uses to prevent healthy people from going mad. One has to encourage them to occupy themselves, accustom them to the idea of order, give them the sense of having a common form of life and destiny with many others, and show them that unusual talent, extreme good fortune and excessive misfortune are merely minor deviations from what is normal. Then no madness will ensue, or if it is already there, it will gradually disappear. I have organized the old man's day so that he gives lessons on the harp, and helps in the garden. As a result he is much brighter in spirits. He wants to taste the cabbage he has planted, and he wants to give careful instruction to my son so that he will be able to play the old man's harp, for he wants the boy to have it when he dies. As a pastor I have not said much to him about his strange fears, but an active life brings with it so much occupation that he will soon feel that his doubts can only be overcome by activity. I don't want to rush things, but if I can get rid of his beard and his cowl, I will have achieved a lot; for nothing brings us closer to madness than distinguishing ourselves from others, and nothing maintains common sense more than living in a normal way with many people. Unfortunately there is much in our educational system and everyday life that preconditions us and our children to madness."

Wilhelm stayed for a few days with this intelligent man and heard lots of interesting stories, not just about mad folk, but also about some considered bright or even wise, whose oddities bordered on madness.

The conversation became even more interesting when the doctor made one of his frequent visits to his friend in order to assist and support him in his humane efforts. He was an oldish man who, despite his delicate health, had spent many years in the exercise of such noble duties. He was a great lover of the country, and could hardly exist anywhere but in the open air. On the other hand he was very sociable and for several years now had cultivated friendship with all the country pastors in the neighborhood. He tried to encourage everyone who had some useful occupation, and to suggest ways of spending one's time to those who had not. Since he was in constant contact with nobles, magistrates and judges, he had over the past twenty years quietly contributed to the advancement of agriculture and actively promoted crops, animals and human beings, helping to bring about what one may truly call enlightened attitudes. "There is really only one misfortune that can happen to us," he would say, "and that is when some fixed idea takes hold of us which does not affect our active life and may detract from it. I have such a case at the moment. The persons concerned are a rich married couple of high station, but so far all my efforts have been fruitless, and I believe this case belongs in your territory, my dear pastor. If I tell you about it I am sure this young man will keep it to himself.

"One day when a nobleman was absent from his residence, someone had the not very laudable idea of dressing up a young man in the nobleman's clothes. His wife was to be deceived by this, and although this was presented to me as having been intended as a joke, I am very much afraid that there was the intention of leading the worthy lady astray. The husband returns unexpectedly, goes to his room, thinks he sees himself, and thereupon falls into a state of melancholy, convinced that he is soon to die. He consorts with persons who cajole him with religious ideas, and I don't see how he is to be prevented from joining the Moravians with his wife, and depriving his relatives (he has no children) of the greater part of his fortune."

"With his wife?" said Wilhelm, much alarmed by what he had just heard.

"Yes," said the doctor who simply interpreted Wilhelm's outburst as an expression of human sympathy, "and unfortunately this lady is burdened with an even greater sorrow which makes separation from the world by no means distasteful to her. When the young man was taking his leave of her, she was incautious enough not to conceal a growing affection for him. He boldly clasped her in his arms and pressed hard against her breast a diamond medallion of her husband that she was wearing. She felt a sharp pain, which gradually went away, leaving at first a small red patch, but then no trace. As a man I am convinced she has nothing to reproach herself with; as a doctor I am sure that the pressure on her breast will have no bad effects, but she is convinced that there is a lump there and when by feeling the place I try to dispel this illusion, she says that only then does the pain go away, for she has firmly persuaded herself that this will end in cancer, and with it all her youth and loveliness."

"Heaven help me!" said Wilhelm, striking his brow and rushing out of the house. He had never been in such a state of alarm.

The doctor and the pastor, surprised by this strange reaction, had to devote their full attention to him that evening when he returned and poured out reproaches on himself in an account of what had happened. Both men showed great concern for him, especially when he described his general situation in the darkest of colors.

The next day the doctor agreed to accompany Wilhelm back to town and do what he could for Aurelie, whom our friend had left in a disturbing condition. They found her worse than they had expected. She had a kind of intermittent fever; nothing much could be done about that because she herself induced and encouraged the attacks. Wilhelm's companion was not presented to her as a doctor. He behaved pleasantly and cautiously. There was talk about the condition of her body and the state of her mind, and the newcomer recounted various stories of people who, despite a certain sickliness, lived to a great age; although nothing is more detrimental to the health of such people than intentional revival of passionate feelings. He also admitted that he had found it most beneficial for sickly people, whose health could not be completely restored, to cultivate religious sentiments. He said this quite discreetly, as if he were referring to past experiences of his, but he promised to bring his new friends a manuscript which they would find interesting to read. It had come from a lady now dead, who had been a friend of his and earned his great respect. "This manuscript," he said, "is something that I value greatly, and I am entrusting the original to you. The title, which I have myself supplied, is: *Confessions of a Beautiful Soul.*"

The physician gave Wilhelm the best advice he could regarding diet and medication for the unhappy and wrought-up Aurelie. He promised to write, and if at all possible, to come and see her again.

During Wilhelm's absence, a change had begun to occur, which he could not have expected. Since he took over control of the routine side of the operation he had spent quite liberally, having his eye on the production in hand and getting what best suited in the way of costumes, sets and properties. He also told actors how indispensable they were, since there was no better way of getting the best out of them. Wilhelm felt justified in this because Serlo never claimed to indulge in precise reckoning and was satisfied with hearing his theater praised, and pleased when Aurelie, who managed all the accounts, told him they had no outstanding debts, and provided him with enough money to cover his expenses incurred extravagantly on behalf of his new loves and on himself.

Melina, who was in charge of the costumes, had been observing all this, and, with Wilhelm away and Aurelie increasingly sick, he coldly and maliciously suggested to Serlo that they should take in more and spend less, and either put some money aside or go on living it up even more than before. Serlo listened attentively as Melina came forward with a plan.

"I wouldn't like to suggest," he said, "that there is any one of the actors who is being paid too much. They are all worthy people and would be welcome anywhere. But for what they bring in, they are paid too much. My proposal would be that we should go in for opera; and as for straight plays, you could take on any of these yourself, all by yourself. Don't you feel nowadays that your talents are not properly recognized? Your colleagues are not first rate, they are just good, and so justice is not given to your talents which are truly outstanding. So why don't you feature yourself, as has been done before, surround yourself with mediocre or even bad actors for meager wages, work on the public through stage effects, as only you know how, and use all the rest to perform operas. You will see how with the same effort and expenditure you will create more satisfaction and take in infinitely more money."

Serlo was so flattered by all this, that no objections he might have offered would have carried any weight. He hastened to assure Melina that, with his love of music, he had long wanted to do something of this kind; but he realized that public taste would be sidetracked even more, and this hybrid of a theater —half play and half opera—would simply eradicate what little taste there was left amongst the public for a major work of art.

Melina referred rather crudely to Wilhelm's "pedantic" ideals, his presumptuous claims of educating the public, instead of being educated by them; and both he and Serlo vehemently asserted that all they wanted was to make money, get rich and enjoy life, and to rid themselves of anyone who stood in the way of such plans. Melina regretted that Aurelie's feeble health did not augur a long life, but rather the opposite. Serlo seemed to regret that Wilhelm wasn't a singer, and thus indicated that he did not consider him indispensable. Melina came up with a whole list of savings that could be made, and Serlo saw in him a threefold replacement for his late brother-in-law. They both thought they should keep quiet about this conversation, and as a result felt more closely bound to each other. They took every occasion to discuss in secret everything that turned up, disapprove of everything that Aurelie and Wilhelm did, and in their thoughts promote their new plan.

But although they kept silent about the project, not betraying anything by word of mouth, they were not diplomatic enough to conceal by their behavior what was in their minds. Melina frequently opposed Wilhelm on matters that lay within Wilhelm's jurisdiction, and Serlo, who had never been indulgent toward his sister, became more and more bitter as her sickness increased and she deserved every consideration because of the passionate vicissitudes of her moods.

At this time they were preparing a performance of Lessing's *Emilia Galotti*. It was very well cast and they could all display the full range of their talents within the restricted compass of this tragedy. Serlo was just right as the sinister Marinelli. Odoardo, Emilia's father, was well played, Madame Melina played the mother with considerable insight, and Elmire carried off the role of Emilia to her great advantage. Laertes played Emilia's short-lived fiancé Appiani with great style, and Wilhelm had spent several months studying the part of the Prince. He often reflected on a certain matter and discussed it with Serlo and Aurelie, namely: What is the difference between noble and aristocratic behavior, and to what extent the one is, or is not, part of the other.

Serlo, who played Marinelli straight, as courtier, without any caricature, had various good things to say on this subject. "Aristocratic behavior is difficult to imitate," he said, "because it is fundamentally negative and presupposes a long period of continuous experience. Such behavior should not present a display of dignity, for that would be liable to appear as formality and pride; it should rather avoid all that is undignified or vulgar. One should never forget oneself, always consider oneself as well as others, never allow oneself any lapses, do neither too much nor too little for others, appear not to be affected or disturbed by anything, never be hurried, always be in control of oneself and externally maintain an equilibrium however tormented one may be inside. A noble man can relax for a moment, a nobleman never. The nobleman is like a well-dressed man: he will never lean up against anything and everyone will avoid brushing against him. He is marked off from others, but cannot stand alone. For as in every form of art what is most difficult has to be achieved effortlessly: the nobleman, despite his distinct status, has to appear in combination with others, never stiff, always pliant—always as the first but never putting himself forward. To appear aristocratic one really has to be an aristocrat. And perhaps that is why, on the average, women can more often give themselves this appearance than men, and why amongst men it is courtiers and soldiers who achieve it most readily."

After this Wilhelm despaired of ever playing the Prince, but Serlo gave him encouragement, making some subtle observations about details and giving him a costume that would turn him into a really fine prince, at least in the eyes of the public.

Serlo promised to comment on Wilhelm's presentation of the part when the performance of the play was over. But an unpleasant argument between him and Aurelie prevented any critical assessment. Aurelie had played the part of the Countess Orsina, the Prince's cast-off mistress, in a way such as one is hardly likely ever to see again. She knew the part very well and had played it rather coolly in the rehearsals; but in the performance she opened up all the floodgates of her personal sorrow, and the result was a performance such as no poet could have imagined in the first heat of his invention. Tumultuous applause rewarded her anguished efforts, but after the performance she lay half lifeless in a chair.

Serlo, having already expressed his disapproval of what he called her exaggerated acting and the way she had bared her soul before the public (which was more or less acquainted with her unfortunate story), had ground his teeth and stamped his feet, as he often did when he was angry. "Just let her be," he said, when he found the others grouped around her in the chair. "One of these days she will appear stark naked on the stage, and then they will really applaud."

"Ungrateful wretch!" she cried. "I'll soon be carried naked to where there is no applause anymore!" With this she jumped up and rushed to the door. Her maid had forgotten to bring her coat, the sedan chair was not waiting for her, it had been raining and a bitter wind was blowing through the streets. She was overheated, but they could not stop her from deliberately walking slowly and eagerly drinking in the cool fresh air. But by the time she reached home she was so hoarse that she could hardly speak, and she did not tell anyone that she was completely stiff from the neck down. Soon afterwards a sort of paralysis of the tongue set in and she began to mix up her words. She was put to bed; some things improved, but others did not. She was running a high fever and her condition became dangerous.

Next morning she was peaceful for a time, and sent for Wilhelm. She handed him a letter. "This," she said, "has long been waiting for the appropriate moment, which has now come. I feel that my life is approaching its end. Promise me that you will deliver this letter personally, and add a few words of your own to avenge my sorrows on this faithless man. He is not without feeling; my death shall at least cause him a few painful moments."

Wilhelm took the letter and consoled her, trying to remove the expectation of death from her mind. "No, no!" she said. "Don't deprive me of my only hope. I've been waiting for it for a long time and will embrace it gladly."

Soon after this the manuscript arrived from the doctor. She asked Wilhelm to read to her from it, and the effect that it had on her can best be judged by the reader from his own perusal of it in the next book. The poor woman's violence and pity suddenly all calmed down. She took back the letter she had handed to Wilhelm, and wrote another one, apparently in a much quieter frame of mind. And she instructed Wilhelm to console her friend for any grief that he might feel at her death, and to assure him that she had forgiven him and wished him every happiness.

From this time on she was very quiet and her mind seemed to be totally occupied with certain thoughts aroused in her by Wilhelm's reading of the manuscript. The decline of her strength was not all that visible, and Wilhelm was therefore shocked one morning when he came to visit her to find her dead.

He had respected her so much and had spent so much time with her that he felt her loss very acutely. She was the only person who was really well disposed toward him, for in these past days he had become only too conscious of Serlo's indifference. He therefore decided to deliver Aurelie's message immediately, and requested leave for a period of time. His absence was welcomed by Melina, who had been engaged in extensive correspondence to secure a male and a female singer, who were to provide attractive intermissions and prepare the public for the forthcoming productions of operas. The loss of Aurelie and the absence of Wilhelm would be compensated for in this way, and Wilhelm himself expressed his approval of such a scheme because it would permit him an extended absence.

He now conceived his mission as one of unusual importance. Aurelie's death had affected him deeply, and since he was losing her so early, he was bound to feel anger towards the man who had shortened her life and made her existence such a painful one.

Despite the last gentle words of the dying woman, he was determined to issue a severe judgment on the faithless friend when he delivered the letter. Since he could not leave this to the mood of the moment, he thought up a speech which became more and more emotional as he elaborated it. Once he was satisfied that his disquisition was well composed, he committed it to memory, and set out on his journey. Mignon was with him as he packed, and she asked whether he was going south or north? When he told her it would be the latter, she said: "Then I will wait for you here." She asked him for Mariane's string of beads, which he could not deny the dear creature; she already had the scarf. But she put the Ghost's veil in his knapsack, although he told her he had no use for it.

Melina took over the management, and his wife promised to keep a motherly eye on the two children, whom Wilhelm was not happy to leave behind. Felix was cheerful as he left, and when asked what he wanted Wilhelm to bring him, he said: "Bring me a father." Mignon took Wilhelm's hand, stood on tiptoe, and gave him a big, trusting kiss, but without any tenderness, saying: "Master, don't forget us, and come back soon."

And so, with many a thought and many a feeling, we leave our friend as he sets out on his journey and record at this point in our story a poem which Mignon had recited several times with great feeling and which we have neglected to offer before because of the pressure of telling about so many unusual incidents.

Bid me not speak, let me be silent,
My secret I am bound to keep,
My inmost heart to thee I'd open,
But fate decrees I may not so.

There comes a time when sun's advancing
Dispels the dark and brings the light;
The stony cliff unfolds its bosom
And hidden streams bestows on earth.

All men find peace in friend's embrace
Each breast unloads its pain in words.
My lips by solemn oath are closed,
Only a god may unseal them new.

Book Six
Confessions of a Beautiful Soul

Up to my eighth year I was a healthy child; but I have as little memory of those years as I have of my birth. Then, when I had just turned eight, I had a hemorrhage, and from that moment on I was all feeling and memory. Every little detail of what happened then is as present to me now as if it had occurred only yesterday.

During the nine months of convalescence which I bore patiently, the foundations of my present way of thinking were laid—or so it seems to me now. For during that time my mind received various impulses that helped in the shaping of a specific character.

I suffered and I loved—that was the rhythm of my heart. During my sharp spells of coughing and debilitating fever I kept very quiet, like a snail withdrawn into its shell; but as soon as I could breathe again I wanted to feel something pleasant, and since all other pleasures were denied me I entertained myself through eyes and ears. I was brought dolls and picture books, and anyone who came and sat on my bed had to tell me a story.

From my mother I liked to hear biblical stories, and my father entertained me with objects of nature. He had quite a nice collection, and would show me one drawer after another, explaining everything carefully. All sorts of dried plants and insects, anatomical specimens, human skin, bones and mummified objects found their way on to my bed, and birds and animals that he had shot were shown me before they were taken to the kitchen. And so that the Prince of this World should not go neglected in this company, my aunt told me love tales and fairy stories. I absorbed everything, and it all took root. I had moments when I intimately communed with the Invisible Being, and I can still remember some verses which I dictated to my mother at that time.

I often recounted to my father what I had learnt from him. I never took medication without asking where the ingredients came from, what they were called, and what they looked like. Nor had my aunt's stories fallen on barren soil. I imagined myself dressed in beautiful clothes and meeting the most charming princes who could not rest till they found out who this unknown beauty was. Then there was a similar adventure with a delightful little angel, in white garments and with golden wings, who was much drawn to me; and this I kept developing in my mind till I almost reached the point that he actually appeared.

After a year I was more or less recovered, but nothing wild remained with me from my childhood. I couldn't play with dolls any longer, I wanted objects that would return my love. Dogs, cats and the many kinds of birds that my father fed—all these delighted me; but I would have given anything to possess a creature that had played a very important part in one of my aunt's stories. This was a lamb that a peasant girl had found in the forest and succoured, but there was a prince spellbound in that little animal, and he finally emerged as a handsome youth and rewarded his benefactress with his hand in marriage. I would so much have liked to have such a lamb!

But there was none to be found, and since everything around me was taking its natural course, I almost had to abandon all hope of having something so precious for my own. Meanwhile I consoled myself by reading accounts of miraculous adventures. Amongst these I liked best the one called the *Christian German Hercules*, the pious love story which was completely to my liking. For whenever anything happened to his Valiska—and terrible things did happen— the hero would pray before he rushed to her assistance, and the text of the prayers was included in the book, which pleased me greatly. My inclination toward the Invisible, which I had always felt in some obscure way, became strengthened by this reading. For God was to become my closest friend—that was certain.

While I was growing older, I read all sorts of things and not in any particular order. But I do remember that the book I then liked best was the *Roman Octavia*. The persecution of those early Christians, put here into a novel, totally captivated my attention.

But then my mother began to complain about my incessant reading; and to humor her my father would take the books away from me one day—and give them back to me the next. She was smart enough to realize that nothing was to be achieved in this direction, but she did succeed in insisting that I should pay equal attention to the Bible. I did not need to be compelled to do that, for I read the sacred books with the liveliest of interest. My mother was much concerned that no seductive books should come into my hands, and I myself would immediately have rejected anything of the baser sort. For my princes and princesses were all very virtuous, and I knew more about the natural history of the human race than I let appear, for I had learnt it mostly from the Bible. Puzzling passages I associated with particular words and objects that I encountered, and got to the truth in my thirst for knowledge and ability to put things together. If I had heard about witches, I would have had to become acquainted with witchcraft too.

I have to thank my mother, and my own curiosity, for learning to cook as well as reading books. There was always something worth looking at in the kitchen, and cutting up a chicken or a suckling pig was a real occasion for me. I would bring my father the innards, and he would talk to me about them as if I were a young student. He often took pleasure in calling me his errant son.

I passed the age of twelve, learnt French, dancing and drawing, and had the usual religious instruction. During the latter, many feelings and thoughts were aroused, but none that affected my state of mind. I was glad to hear God talked about, and I was proud to be able to talk about Him better than most of my peers. I eagerly read a number of books at this time that would enable me to blabber about religion, but it never occurred to me to ask myself what my situation was, whether my soul was a mirror that would reflect the bright sun of eternity. I had taken that for granted.

French I learnt with great enthusiasm. My teacher was a fine man. He was neither a superficial empiricist nor a dry grammarian; he was acquainted with various branches of knowledge, and had seen much of the world. He satisfied my desire for knowledge with many things besides language instruction. I loved him so dearly that I always awaited his arrival with heartthrobs. I did not have much difficulty with drawing and would have made more progress in that area, if my teacher had had more brains and more knowledge. But all he had were his hands and practice in using them.

Dancing was at first what I enjoyed least. My body was too fragile, and I only learnt to dance with the help of my sister. But pleasure in this activity increased greatly when our dancing master had the idea of arranging a ball for all his pupils.

Amongst the various boys and girls there were two who stood out from the others, two of the Chamberlain's sons, one the same age as myself, the other two years older, but both of them so handsome that their appearance surpassed what was generally considered to be beauty in children. Once I had seen them, I was quite unaware of anyone else in the group. From that moment on I paid more attention to my dancing and wished to dance as well as possible. How did it happen that these two boys singled me out, I wondered. Anyway, within an hour we were the best of friends and before the little celebration had come to an end, we had decided where we would meet again. What a joy that was for me! And I was simply delighted when next morning I received a bouquet from each of them with a polite little note inquiring how I was. Never again have I felt as I felt then. Pleasantries were exchanged, messages went back and forth, rendezvous were arranged at church or on walks, they invited me and my sister at the same time, and we were sufficiently cautious in disguising all this, so that our parents never learnt any more than we thought was advisable.

So now I had acquired two admirers at once. I could not decide between them, for I liked them both and we were all good friends. Suddenly the elder one fell seriously ill, and since I had often been very sick myself, I knew what to send him in the way of kind words and tasty morsels. His parents were so grateful for my attentions that they granted their dear son's wishes and invited me and my sisters to visit him as soon as he was up and about. The affectionate way he received me was not like that of a child, and from that day on my preference was for him. He warned me to keep this concealed from his brother, but his emotion could not remain hidden, and the younger brother's jealousy made this into a full-scale romance. He played one trick after another

on us, delighted in spoiling our pleasures, and increased the passion that he
was determined to destroy.

So now I had found the little lamb I yearned for, and this passion of mine
affected me like all other sickness: it made me withdraw from the busy throng,
and silent. I felt alone and deeply affected, and the thought of God came back
into my mind. He was my intimate companion, and I prayed and prayed for
my ailing friend, shedding many a tear.

Childish as this whole train of events was, it nevertheless contributed
greatly to the development of my emotional life. In our French lessons we
were required by our teacher to write, not the usual translations, but letters
of our own composition. I delivered my own love story using the names of
Phyllis and Damon. The old man soon saw through this and, to encourage
frankness on my part, he praised my effort highly. As a result I became even
bolder, opened up my heart, and kept faithfully to every detail of the truth. I
cannot remember at what point it was that he had occasion to remark: "How
charming, how natural this is! But your dear Phyllis should take care, for this
could soon become quite serious."

I was disturbed by the fact that he did not consider it serious already and,
somewhat piqued by this, I asked him what he meant by "serious." He
answered without any hesitation, explaining himself so clearly that I could
hardly conceal my alarm. But then my irritation returned and since I disliked
the idea of his harboring such thoughts, I summoned up my courage, defended
my heroine and said, with flaming cheeks: "But, sir, Phyllis is an honest girl!"

Then he was malicious enough to tease me about my heroine and, since we
were speaking in French, played on the various meanings of the word *honnête*
to expatiate on the "honesty" of Phyllis. I felt how absurd it all was, and was
completely bewildered. Not wishing to make me fearful, he terminated the
conversation for the moment, but returned to it on other occasions. The plays
and stories that I read and translated for him gave him ample opportunity to
demonstrate that so-called virtue is a feeble protection against the claims of
passion. I did not disagree anymore, but maintained my inner irritation, and
found his various remarks troublesome.

I gradually lost all contact with my dear Damon, thanks to the chicanery of
his brother. Soon after this, both these promising youths died. I grieved: but
they were soon forgotten.

Phyllis grew up fast, quite restored to health and ready to make her way in
the world. The crown prince married and took over the reins of government
on his father's death. Town and court entered on a flurry of activity, and my
curiosity found much to occupy itself with. There were plays and balls, and
everything else associated with these, and although our parents restricted
us as much as possible, we had to appear at court, where I was presented.
Foreigners poured in, every house saw important people, several noblemen
arrived with letters of recommendation to my family and still more were
introduced to us. My uncle's house became a meeting place for people from
all nations.

My worthy mentor continued to warn me, gently and yet pointedly, and in my heart I disliked him for this. I was in no wise convinced of the truth of his allegations, and perhaps I was right at the time, and he was wrong to think women so weak in every situation, but he spoke so persuasively that there was one occasion when I thought he might be right; this was when I said to him that since the danger was so great and the human heart so weak I would ask God to protect me.

This straightforward answer seemed to please him and he praised my intentions. But I had not meant this seriously, these were just empty words, for my feelings toward the Invisible One were well-nigh completely extinguished. The busy crowd of people surrounding me had so distracted me and borne me along, that these had become the emptiest years of my life. For days on end I had nothing to talk about, nothing salutary to think about, nothing to do but go along with the crowd. Even my beloved books remained untouched. The people I associated with had no inkling of serious study: they were German courtiers, and that class of people had at the time no trace of culture.

One would think that such a life had brought me to the edge of ruin. I lived in a continual whirl of gaiety, never had a reflective moment, never prayed, never thought about God or myself. But I consider it providential that none of the many rich, handsome, well-dressed men appealed to me. They had a certain lewdness that they did not trouble to conceal, and that scared me away. They laced their talk with ambiguities that offended me, and I maintained cold aloofness toward them. Their rudeness was sometimes quite beyond belief, and I did not mince my words on that score. My teacher had also told me in confidence that most of these disreputable customers constituted a danger not only to a girl's virtue but also to her health. So I cringed at the thought of them and became really concerned if one of them somehow got too close to me. I avoided cups and glasses, and even chairs they had been sitting on. As a result I became completely isolated, both morally and physically, and all the nice things they said to me I proudly took for incense that was scattered out of a sense of guilt.

Among the strangers was one young man who stood out: we jocularly called him Narcissus. He had acquired a good reputation in the diplomatic service, and hoped, with the various changes taking place at court, to get a good position there. He soon became acquainted with my father, and both his knowledge and his behavior gave him the entrée into the close circle of the most distinguished men. My father said much in his praise, and his handsome figure would have made even more of an impression if his whole manner had not shown a certain degree of self-satisfaction. I saw him, thought well of him, but we did not speak to each other.

He appeared at a big ball, and we danced a minuet together; but even that did not lead to a closer acquaintance. Then came more vigorous dances which, for the sake of my father, who was concerned about my health, I always avoided. I retired to a neighboring room and joined some older women at the card tables whom I was friendly with. Narcissus, having danced for a while, came into the room where I was; when he had recovered from a nosebleed that had afflicted him while dancing, he began to talk to me about various things. Within a short while the conversation became so interesting, though without any trace of tenderness, that we lost all desire to resume dancing. For this we were teased by the others, but that did not trouble us. Next evening we continued our conversation – and preserved our health.

This is how our acquaintance came about. Narcissus called on me and my sisters, and now I began to realize how much I knew, what I thought and felt, and what I could express in conversation. My new friend, having always moved in the best circles, had not only a complete mastery of historical and political events, but also extensive acquaintance with literary matters, and every new publication, especially those in France, was known to him. He brought or sent me many agreeable and useful books, but this had to be kept even quieter than an illicit love affair. Learned women had been ridiculed, and even educated women were unwillingly tolerated, probably because it was considered impolite to put so many ignorant men to shame. Even my father, though he welcomed this new opportunity for me to improve my mind, insisted that this literary exchange should remain a secret.

Our relations with each other continued like this for almost a year, and I cannot say that Narcissus ever expressed any love or affection for me. He remained courteous and obliging, but showed no strong emotion; in actual fact it seemed to be the charms of my youngest sister, who at that time was extraordinarily beautiful, that appealed to him most. He bestowed on her all sorts of pleasant names from various foreign languages, several of which he spoke very well, delighting in introducing their individual idiom into his own German speech. She did not respond particularly to his pleasantries, for she was cut from a different cloth. She was impulsive and he was touchy, so they rarely agreed on details. But he won the good graces of my mother and my aunts, and so gradually became a member of the family.

I do not know how long we would have continued in this fashion, were it not for a strange episode that changed our whole relationship. I was invited with my sisters to a certain house where I did not enjoy going. The company was too mixed and some of the people there were, if not coarse, at least extremely vulgar. On this occasion Narcissus was invited too, so for his sake I was prepared to go, because I knew there would be someone there to whom I could talk as I would wish. We had a lot to put up with already at table, for some of the men had been drinking heavily; and afterwards we had to play a game of forfeits. There was a lot of noisy activity. Narcissus had to pay a forfeit, and he was told to whisper something pleasant in everybody's ear. He stayed too long with the lady next to me, who was the wife of a captain. Suddenly the captain boxed his ears so soundly that the powder from his wig flew into my eyes, for I was sitting right next to him. Once I had wiped my eyes and recovered somewhat from my fright, I saw the two men with naked swords. Narcissus was bleeding, and the other man, inflamed with wine, anger and jealousy, could hardly be restrained by the rest of the company. I took Narcissus's arm and led him through the door and up into another room, and since I did not think he was safe from his crazy opponent, I bolted the door.

Neither of us thought that the wound was serious. All we saw was a slight cut on the hand. But then a stream of blood began to pour down his back, and we saw that he had a large wound in the head. Now I was really frightened. I rushed on to the landing to get help, but there was nobody there because everybody was still downstairs trying to tame the raging man. Finally up came a daughter of the house, in such gay spirits that I was really alarmed by her excessive mirth over what she considered an infernal hubbub and ridiculous performance. I urged her to send for a doctor, and she, in her own wild way, jumped downstairs to fetch one herself.

I returned to my wounded man, bound up his hand with my handkerchief and his head with a towel that was hanging on the door. He was still bleeding profusely; he was pale and seemed about to faint. There was no one nearby to help me, so, quite spontaneously, I put my arm around him and tried to cheer him up by coaxing and stroking. This seemed to restore his spirits; he retained consciousness but was deathly pale.

Finally our busy hostess arrived and was shocked to find my friend in this condition in my arms and both of us spattered with blood. For nobody had imagined that Narcissus was wounded; they all thought I had managed to get him out unharmed.

Suddenly wine, sweet-smelling waters and restoratives in abundance appeared from nowhere, a doctor turned up, I could well have left. But Narcissus held me firmly by the hand, I would have stayed there even if I had not been held fast. While he was being bandaged I continued to moisten his lips with wine, paying little attention to the fact that the whole company was now assembled around us. The doctor finished what he was doing, and the wounded man took a silent but grateful leave of me, and was carried to his house.

Our hostess then took me into her bedroom. She had to undress me completely, and I cannot fail to admit that when I first happened to see myself in the mirror while they were washing his blood off me, I thought I could consider myself beautiful, even without my clothes. I could not put any of these back on, and since everyone else was smaller or bigger than I, I arrived back at my parents' house much to their astonishment in an odd assortment of garments. They were much angered by the fright I had had, the wounding of our friend, the stupidity of the captain, in fact by the whole affair. My father was almost prepared to avenge his friend on the spot and challenge the captain. He chastized those present for not immediately taking action against such a murderous onslaught, for it was all too clear that the captain, after striking Narcissus, had drawn his sword and wounded him from behind; the cut on the hand had only happened when Narcissus tried to draw his own sword. I was extremely upset and affected by all this: but how can I express myself? The emotion that had been lurking in the depths of my heart, had suddenly burst forth like a flame ignited by air. And if joy and pleasure are conducive to the arousing and secret nourishing of love, it is sudden fright that most readily causes love to declare itself decisively. My parents gave their young daughter medication, and put her to bed. And, early next day, my father went immediately to see his wounded friend, who lay quite ill with a high fever.

My father told me very little of what they said to each other, and tried to set my mind at rest regarding the possible consequences of the incident. There was talk as to whether an apology should be considered sufficient, whether the matter should be taken to court, or what else should be done. I knew my father too well for me to believe that he would consider the whole thing settled without a duel. But I kept quiet, for I had long since learnt from my father that women should not interfere in such matters. Furthermore, it did not appear that anything had occurred between the two friends that affected me. But then my father told me about a conversation he had had with my mother. Narcissus, he told me, had been greatly moved by the assistance I had given him, had embraced my father, declared he would be eternally in my debt and desired no joy in life if he could not share it with me. He had requested permission to regard him as a father. Mama repeated all this faithfully to me, adding the salutary reminder that one should not attach too much importance to what is said in the first heat of the moment. "Indeed no," I replied with affected coolness, and heaven knows what or how much I was feeling when I said that.

Narcissus was ill for two months, could not write because of the injury to his hand, but showed by various obliging signs of attentiveness that he was mindful of me. This unusual degree of courtesy became linked in my mind with what I had learnt from my mother, and my head was continually beset by fancies. The whole town was discussing what had happened. People talked to me about it in a particular tone of voice, and drew conclusions that concerned me greatly, much as I tried to dispel them. What had previously been normal flirtation, now became serious affection, and the more I tried to conceal my unsettled state of mind from others, the more intense it became. The thought of losing him terrified me, and the prospect of a closer relationship made me tremble. The thought of marriage inevitably has something frightening about it for a moderately discerning young girl.

These violent perturbations made me think once more about myself. The many images of a distracting life, which had been pursuing me day and night, were suddenly dispelled. My soul came to life again, but the communion with the Invisible Friend, so long interrupted, was not so easily restored. We remained somewhat distant from each other for a while; there was something there, but nothing comparable to what had been.

A duel took place in which the captain was seriously wounded, but I knew nothing about it until it was already over. Public opinion was all on the side of my beloved, who finally reappeared on the scene. With bandaged head and hand he was brought to our house. How my heart leapt at his visit! The whole family was present, and there was a general polite exchange of thanks on both sides, but he did find the opportunity to give me a few secret signs of his affection, which only increased my agitation. When he was completely recovered he came to see us throughout the whole winter, on the same footing as before, and for all his signs of affection, nothing was openly said.

I continued to maintain myself in this fashion. There was no person I could confide in and from God I was too estranged. I had completely forgotten Him during those four wild years, and although I began to think of Him again now and then, my acquaintance had cooled off. It was only ceremonial visits that I now paid Him, and since I always wore fine clothes when I appeared before Him and gladly displayed my virtue, honesty, and the advantages I believed I had over others, He seemed to disregard me in all my finery.

A courtier would have been very disturbed if his prince, from whom he expected good fortune, had behaved like this toward him. But I was not discouraged by this, for I had all I needed — good health and comfortable circumstances. If God were pleased that I thought of Him, that was good; but if He were not, I still considered I had done my duty toward Him.

At that time I did not think about myself in this way, but this is a true picture of what my soul was like. Yet circumstances were to contribute to a change and purification of my feelings.

Spring came and Narcissus began to visit me unannounced when I was home alone. He came now as a lover, and asked me if I would give him my heart and, when he had secured an honorable and well-paid position, in due course my hand in marriage. He had already been given a post in our social circle, but since people were somewhat fearful of his ambitious nature, he was at first more kept back than speedily advanced in station; and since he had money of his own he was accorded only a meager emolument.

Strong as my inclinations toward him were, I knew that he was not the sort of man that one could deal quite openly with. I therefore constrained myself and referred him to my father, whose approval he seemed to have no doubts about, while wishing to be assured of mine without further delay. Eventually I did say yes, but insisted on the approval of my parents as a necessary precondition. He then made a formal approach to both of them, they expressed their agreement, and he was given their approval on the understanding that, as was soon to be expected, he should be advanced in position. My sisters and aunts were informed of this and sworn to secrecy.

So now my beloved had become my fiancé, and the difference between the two was very obvious. If only the lovers of all well-intentioned girls could be turned into prospective bridegrooms, our sex would be well served, even if no marriage resulted from such relationships. The love between two persons is not thereby diminished; it becomes more reasonable. Countless petty sillinesses, all the flirtatiousness and moodiness suddenly disappear. If our betrothed tells us we look better in our mob cap than in our best headdress, then any sensible girl amongst us will no longer care about how she does her hair, for it is perfectly natural that he should think like a solid citizen and prefer a housewife to a society doll. And that applies to everything.

And if such a girl is fortunate enough for her man to be intelligent and knowledgeable, she will learn more than all the universities or all her travels abroad could teach her. She will not only absorb all the culture he gives her, but take pains to advance herself by this means. Love makes possible much that is impossible, and ultimately there emerges that submissiveness which is so proper and necessary to the female sex. A fiancé does not lord it like a husband: he asks and his beloved tries to sense what he wishes and to fulfill his desires before he expresses them. Experience taught me what I would not have missed for anything. I was happy, as happy as one can be in this world – that is to say, for a short while.

A whole summer passed in these tranquil joys. Narcissus never gave me the slightest cause for complaint. My fondness for him increased, my whole being was bound up with him; he knew this, and delighted in it. But in the meantime something of apparently little consequence developed, which gradually imperilled our relationship.

Narcissus acted toward me like a fiancé but never dared to of ask me what was as yet forbidden us. Yet our opinions differed sharply on the limits of what was virtuous and moral. I wanted to tread warily and would not allow any liberties that the world should not know of. He, used as he was to snacking, found this diet rather severe. This led to constant disagreements; he appreciated my standpoint but tried to undermine it.

I remembered what my old language teacher had said to me about things getting "serious," and the arguments I had used at that time to counter his allegations.

In the meantime I had become somewhat better acquainted with God. He had given me such a beloved bridegroom, and I knew how to thank Him for that. My earthly love absorbed my whole mind and activated it to a point that my relationship with God did not conflict with it. It was quite natural that I should express my anxiety to Him, but I did not realize that what made me so anxious was something that I ardently desired. I thought I was endowed with great strength of mind and did not, for example, pray to be delivered from temptation, for in my thoughts I had moved far beyond temptation. In this tawdry garb of self-righteousness I made bold to appear before my God. He did not reject me; my slightest approach to Him left a pleasant impression in my mind, and this impression encouraged me to seek Him out more frequently.

Except for Narcissus everything else in the world was dead to me, nothing else had any attraction. Even my passion for dressing up took on the sole purpose of pleasing him, and if I knew he would not be there to see me, I did not devote much time or trouble to this. I liked to dance, but when he wasn't there, I felt that I couldn't abide all this moving about. Once at a brilliant soirée where he was not to be present, I could not find anything new to wear, or adapt what I had to what was fashionable. I was quite indifferent to both; or rather, both were equally tiresome to me. My evening seemed to me well spent in playing some card game with elderly persons—something I normally had no desire whatsoever to do—and if it so happened that some old friend of mine teased me about this, I would smile for the first time in the whole evening. The same thing happened on walks and other social diversions:

> Him alone have I selected,
> Born was I for him alone,
> Nothing but his favor craving . . .

I was therefore often lonely in society, and complete isolation would have pleased me best. But my busy mind could neither sleep nor dream: I went on thinking and feeling and gradually achieved a facility for expressing my thoughts and sentiments to God. Then different feelings began to arise within me though they did not conflict with the others. For my love for Narcissus was quite in accord with the plan of the whole of creation, and never conflicted with my basic duties. There was no opposition here despite the immense differences. Narcissus was the only person whose image hovered before my mind and claimed all my love; the other feeling was not connected with any image and was inexpressibly pleasant. I don't have it anymore and cannot give it to myself again.

My beloved, who knew all my other secrets, knew nothing about this. I soon noticed that he thought differently. He would often bring me books that attacked with light or heavy artillery what one could call communion with the Invisible. I read these books, because he had brought them to me, and finally could not recall a single word of them.

We also disagreed about studies and the acquisition of knowledge. His attitude was that of men in general. He made fun of learned women and yet kept trying to educate me all the time. He talked to me about everything except jurisprudence and, while constantly bringing me books of various kinds, repeatedly expressed the dubious precept that a woman should keep her learning more secret than a Calvinist his religion in a Catholic country. Although I found it natural not to present myself to the world as more intelligent and better informed than previously, he was at times the first not to be able to resist showing his vanity by praising the qualities of my mind.

One well-known man of the world, highly regarded for his influence, talents and intelligence, who was receiving great acclaim at our court, singled out Narcissus and associated with him continually. They argued about the virtuousness of women. Narcissus imparted to me the general drift of their conversation. I did not hesitate to add my comments, and my friend asked me to set these down in writing. I could write French fairly fluently, having laid a good foundation for this with my old teacher. My correspondence with my friend had been in French, and at that time one could acquire refinement and culture only by reading French books. My little essay pleased the count, and I also had to give him some short poems that I had recently written. Narcissus seemed quite unconstrained in his desire to benefit his beloved, and the whole episode ended to his delight with the count sending him an elegant rhymed epistle in French just as he was about to leave us, which referred back to their friendly arguments and praised Narcissus for being about to acquire, after so many doubts and errors, a true sense of what virtue is, and that in the arms of a charming and virtuous wife.

The poem was shown first to me, and then to all and sundry, and everyone had his own opinions about it. There were various episodes of this kind, and as a result every newcomer whom Narcissus thought well of, was introduced into our household.

Another count and his family spent some time in our town because of the excellent doctor that we had there. Narcissus was treated like a son by this family, and he took me along to see them. The conversation between these distinguished persons was a real delight for heart and mind, and even the usual social diversions did not seem here so empty as elsewhere. Everyone knew how we stood in relation to each other. They treated us as circumstances demanded, and never broached the essential. I mention this particular family because my acquaintance with them was to have a considerable influence on the further course of my life.

We had now been betrothed for almost a year, and our springtime was past. Summer arrived, and everything became hotter and more serious.

Through several unexpected deaths, certain positions at court had become open for which Narcissus was eligible and qualified. The moment was approaching when my whole future destiny was to be decided. While Narcissus and his friends at court were doing all they possibly could to remove whatever disadvantageous impressions he might have created, so that they might help him to secure the desired position, I myself addressed my suit to the Invisible Friend. I was received in such friendly fashion that I took pleasure in returning to Him. I expressed quite openly my desire that Narcissus should obtain the position, but my entreaties were not insistent, nor did I demand that this should come about because of my own prayers.

The position was filled by a very inferior competitor. I was appalled at the news, rushed to my room, and closed the door firmly. My first bitter reaction was to burst into tears; my next thought was that this could not have happened just by chance, and so I decided to accept it in the belief that this apparent misfortune would rebound to my advantage. And then my tenderest feelings came to the fore, dispelling the clouds of my grief. I felt that, with the help I had, anything could be endured. And I went to dinner in a tranquil frame of mind, much to the amazement of the other members of the household.

Narcissus did not have my strength of mind, and I had to console him. He had to suffer unpleasantness even from his own family and this disturbed him, but our relationship was based so much on trust that he confided in me about everything. His negotiations to find a position elsewhere were equally unsuccessful; I suffered on his account and my own, but took everything to the place where my concerns had been so well received. My experiences in this quarter were so soothing that I returned there ever more often, always seeking the consolation that I had found before. But I did not find it always. I felt like someone wishing to warm himself in the sun when the shadow obstructs him. What was causing this? I asked myself, seeking the reason and coming to the conclusion that it all depended on the state of my own soul: if it were not entirely directed straight toward God, I remained unwarmed, felt no reciprocity, could not make out His answer. Then came the second question: What was obstructing my relationship? Here there was a whole realm of possibilities and I spent almost the whole second year of my friendship with Narcissus involved in this investigation. I could have concluded this earlier, for I soon found the answer; but I was not willing to admit it and tried in various ways to avoid doing so.

What I soon discovered was that foolish pastimes and trivial occupations were obstructing the directness of my soul's approach to God. The why and wherefore was now quite clear to me; but how was I to exist in a world where everything was folly and emptiness? Gladly would I have let the matter rest, and lived without thinking about it, like other people whom I saw prospering. But I could not do that. My inmost self constantly opposed it. If I thought of changing my situation by withdrawing from society, I found this impossible to do. I was now confined within a narrow circle, unable to give up certain relationships, and disaster after disaster poured increasingly in upon me. I would often go to bed weeping, and get up next morning after a sleepless night with nothing changed. I needed strong support and this was not to be vouchsafed me by God when I was running around in a fool's cap.

I then began to think about all my activities. First I considered dancing and card playing. Nothing had ever been thought, said, or written for or against these which I did not consult, ponder, discuss, elaborate on, or reject, tormenting myself in the process. If I were to give up such pastimes I would be sure to offend Narcissus, because he was mortally afraid of our being ridiculed for appearing so anxiously moralistic in the eyes of society. Since I did not engage in these things, which I considered foolish, dangerously foolish, out of a sense of pleasure to me, but simply in order to please him, all this became terribly difficult for me.

It would be hard for me to describe without tiresome repetition and undue wordiness the efforts I made to pursue these activities which diverted me but disturbed my inner peace, without closing my heart to the influence of the Invisible Being, and how painful it was to realize that the conflict was not to be resolved in this way. For as soon as I donned the robe of folly, this did not remain a mask but enveloped my whole being.

May I interrupt my narration at this point and offer some observations on what was going on inside me? What could have affected my taste and my whole temperament at the age of twenty-two, nay, even earlier, so that I felt no pleasure in things which provide most people of my age with harmless entertainment? Why weren't they harmless to me? My answer had to be that these things were not harmless to me because I was not, like others of my age, unaware of my own soul. Indeed I knew from experiences which had come to me unsought, that there are higher emotions which guarantee us a pleasure not to be gained in idle entertainments, and that these higher pleasures provide a source of strength when misfortune overtakes us.

But the social pleasures and diversions of youth must have had a strong attraction for me, because I had not been able to engage in them as if I were not involved. But now I could, if I so desired, show great indifference to many things which were then bewildering to me and threatened to assume mastery over me. There was no middle course; I had to give up either these pleasant pastimes or the enlivening feelings within me.

But the conflict in my soul was soon settled without my being conscious of this happening. Despite the fact that I still had a certain hankering after the pleasures of the senses, they no longer provided me with satisfaction. Much as one may enjoy drinking wine, the pleasure dissipates when one finds one-self in a fully stocked wine cellar where the bad air is almost suffocating. Good clean air is better than wine—that I felt quite strongly—and it would not have taken much reflection on my part to see that what is good is preferable to what is attractive, had I not been held back by the fear of losing Narcissus's good graces. But when finally, after much debate and constant consideration, I took a sharp look at the nature of the bond that held me to him, I became aware that it was not all that strong and could easily be broken. I realized that it was a glass cover enclosing me in an airless space, and if only I could summon up enough strength to shatter it, then I would be free.

No sooner thought, than done. I removed my mask and began to act always according to the dictates of my heart. My fondness for Narcissus remained, but the thermometer that had been standing in hot water was now in the open air, unable to rise any higher than the temperature outside. Unfortunately, it sank considerably. Narcissus began to withdraw and act like a stranger. He had every right to do so, but my thermometer went down when he was no longer near. My family noticed the change, was surprised, and questioned me about it. I declared with almost manly defiance that I had made enough sacrifices, that I was prepared to suffer every adversity together with him until the end of my days, but demanded complete freedom to determine my actions accord-ing to my own convictions. I would never stubbornly insist on what I thought was right without listening to the opinions of others, but I myself must decide on my own happiness and I would not accept pressure from elsewhere. The reasoning of the greatest physician in the world would never persuade me to eat or drink something that was normally considered healthy and was enjoyed by many, if I myself knew it would be harmful to me, such as coffee, for instance, and I would never consider any action that bewildered me as morally suited to me.

Since I had been quietly working toward this conclusion for a long time, arguments about it were welcome rather than irritating to me. I aired my feelings and sensed the importance of the decision I had made. I did not yield an inch, and those to whom I did not owe a childlike respect were sharply dealt with. I soon won over my own family. My mother had entertained similar sentiments ever since she was a young girl, but they had never fully matured, for she had never been pressured by necessity, never had to pluck up courage to defend her convictions. She was pleased to see her latent desires fulfilled in me. My younger sister seemed to take my part; my other sister remained quiet and attentive. My aunt was the one who raised most objections. The reasons she gave seemed to her incontrovertible, and they were so because they were ordinary reasons. I was finally forced to tell her that she had no voice in this matter, and she, for her part, only rarely indicated that she still thought she was right. She was the only one, I should add, who really considered the matter closely, and quite dispassionately. I am not doing her an injustice by saying that she had no soul and very limited opinions.

My father reacted in accordance with his character. He expressed himself in few words, but did speak to me quite often about the matter. His reasoning was sensible and as such, irrefutable; and it was only my strong sense of being in the right that gave me the power to argue against him. But soon there came a change in the scenario: I had to appeal to his heart. Oppressed by his intelligence, I lapsed into emotional outbursts. I gave free rein to my tongue and my tears. I revealed to him the strength of my love for Narcissus, the compulsion I had been obliged to exercise over myself these past two years, and the certainty I now felt that I was doing right by being prepared to suffer the loss of my beloved and the likelihood of happiness, ever, if needs be, to sacrifice wealth and possessions for the sake of what I knew to be right; that I would rather leave my country, my parents and my friends and earn my bread elsewhere, than abandon my convictions. My father concealed his emotion, said nothing for a while, and then openly declared his agreement.

From that time on, Narcissus ceased to come to our house, and my father to attend the weekly gatherings where Narcissus would be present. The whole affair created quite a stir at court and in the town. People spoke about it in the way that such things are usually discussed when the public feels heavily involved, because it had been pampered into thinking it can exert some influence on the decision-making of weak minds. I was sufficiently acquainted with the world to know that one is often reproved for doing something by the very same persons who persuaded one to do it, and, quite apart from that, my state of mind was such that all these fleeting expressions of opinion were of no significance.

On the other hand, I did not deny myself the indulgence of my affection for Narcissus. He had become invisible to me, and my feelings had not changed toward him. I loved him dearly—in a new way, and somehow more firmly than before. If only he would not disturb my convictions, I would be his; but without this condition I would have refused to share a kingdom with him. For several months I kept these feelings and thoughts to myself, and then, when I felt sufficiently calm and composed, I wrote him a polite, but not affectionate letter asking why he no longer came to see me.

Since I knew that as a person he was not given to expressing his opinion on minor matters, but instead did what he thought was right without saying anything about it, I now presented my proposal as a matter of immediate importance. I got back a long letter which seemed to me rather tasteless, couched in a wordy style and empty phrases, saying that without a better position he could not offer me his hand, that I knew better than anybody how difficult things had been for him, that he believed a protracted and fruitless engagement might harm my reputation, and that I should permit him to maintain his present distance. As soon as he were in the position to make me happy, the promise he had given me would be sanctified.

I answered him immediately, saying that since our relationship was now public knowledge it might well be too late to patch up my reputation, of which my conscience and my innocence were the strongest safeguards. I relieved him of his obligation toward me without further hesitation, expressing the wish that he would thereby find happiness for himself. Within the hour I received a brief reply saying basically the same as his previous letter, namely that once he had secured a position, he would ask me if I were willing to share his joy with him.

This seemed to me saying as good as nothing. I told my relations and friends that the whole affair was over and done with, and indeed it really was. For when nine months later he did receive a most desirable advancement, he asked again for my hand in marriage, but this time with the condition that, as the wife of a man who would have to establish a suitable household, I should change my way of thinking. I thanked him politely, and tore my heart and mind away from the whole affair, with the same eagerness as one leaves a theater after the final curtain has been lowered. Shortly afterwards he found himself a rich and socially respected wife (which was now quite easy for him), and since I knew he would now be happy in the way he desired, I felt completely at ease.

I should not fail to mention that several times, both before and after he obtained his appointment, I received offers of marriage, all of which I declined without further consideration, though my father and mother wished I had been more accommodating.

After my stormy March and April, fine May weather seemed to be bestowed on me. I enjoyed good health and an indescribable peace of mind. Wherever I turned my thoughts, I knew I had gained by my loss. Young as I was, and full of feeling, I found God's creation much more beautiful than when I had to have parties and card playing to while away my hours in His lovely garden. No longer ashamed of my piety, I did not need to conceal my love of art and study.

I drew, painted and read, and found enough people to encourage me in this. In place of the society I had withdrawn from, or rather that had withdrawn from me, I gathered a small circle around me that provided much richer entertainment. I did have a leaning toward social life, and I cannot deny that when I had abandoned my former friends, I had shuddered at the thought of loneliness. But now I was sufficiently, perhaps even too well, compensated for my loss. My acquaintance grew not only with persons nearby, who shared my sentiments, but also with several from farther places. My story had become common knowledge, and there were many persons curious to meet a girl who valued God more than her betrothed. In Germany at that time a particular religious trend was noticeable. Several ducal and princely houses became concerned about the salvation of their souls. There were also members of the lesser nobility who shared the same concern, and it was even widespread amongst the other social classes.

The family of the count whom I mentioned earlier began to cultivate closer relations with me. Its size had increased by the addition of relatives coming to live in our town. These admirable people sought out my company, and I theirs. The family circle was a large one and in that household I became acquainted with many princes, dukes and lords of the Empire. My sentiments were no longer a secret to anybody, and whether they were respected or just tolerated, I attained my goal and was not assailed for this.

There was another way in which I was brought back into society. A stepbrother of my father's, who had visited us only very occasionally, came and spent a considerable time with us. He had given up a respected and influential position at another court because things had not gone as he wished. He was a man of keen intelligence and sober character, and therefore very like my father; but my father had a certain gentleness, which made it easier for him than for my uncle to yield on certain matters, and, when something was against his convictions, not doing it himself but being prepared to let it happen, keeping his disapproval to himself or venting it only in the intimate circle of the family. My uncle was much younger, and his self-assurance was bolstered by his external circumstances. His mother had been very rich, and in addition he now had expectations of a sizeable inheritance from her close and distant relatives. He needed no financial support from anywhere, whereas my father had to eke out his modest means by what he earned from his position.

Domestic misfortunes had made my uncle even sterner. He had suffered the early loss of a loving wife and a promising son, and from that time on he seemed to want to keep aloof from everything that did not depend on his own will.

Occasionally one heard it said in our family, with some satisfaction, that he would probably not marry again, and so we children could consider ourselves heirs to his large fortune. I paid little attention to this, but the behavior of my siblings was affected by it. He was strong-willed but never contradicted anyone, preferring to listen attentively to the opinions of others and trying to support them by arguments and examples of his own. If you did not know him you might think he shared your opinions, for he had such outstanding intelligence that he could transport himself with ease into the minds and thinking of everyone else. This did not happen so readily in my case, for I had feelings of which he had no comprehension. Although he was considerate, sympathetic and understanding in speaking to me about my sentiments, it was abundantly clear that he had no conception of the true reasons for my actions.

Secretive as he normally was, the purpose of his unaccustomed visit was eventually revealed. He had selected my youngest sister as the one he had decided on to get married and be given happiness in the fashion he desired. It is true that with her physical and intellectual gifts, especially when supplemented by a sizeable fortune, she could claim the very best of suitors. His feelings about me were demonstrated by his securing for me the position of a canoness, from which I soon began to receive emoluments.

My sister was not particularly pleased with his efforts on her behalf, and not as grateful as I was. She confided in me a matter of the heart that she had so far very wisely concealed, for she was afraid of what in fact did actually happen, namely that I would advise her in the strongest possible terms against a union with a man who should not have been attractive to her. I did my utmost, and was successful in persuading her. My uncle's intentions were too serious and too plain, and the prospect for my sister, worldly-minded as she was, too attractive, for her not to muster sufficient strength to reject an involvement that her own mind disapproved of. She began to cease evading the gentle hints of our uncle, and a basis was soon established for him to pursue his intentions. She became a lady-in-waiting at a neighboring court, where he was able to entrust her to the surveillance and nurture of a friend of his who, as chief governess, stood in excellent repute. I went with her to her new habitation. We were both well satisfied with the reception we received, and I was often obliged to smile at my new social role as a young, pious canoness.

Previously I would have been perplexed by this situation, maybe to the point of losing my head; but now I remained quite calm. I spent several hours having my hair dressed and decking myself out, with no other thought than that this was the fancy dress I was required to put on. I talked to everybody in the crowded halls without being affected by the cast of mind or appearance of any person that I met. When I returned home, the only sense I had was that of dragging my tired feet behind me. My mind profited from mingling with the many people that I encountered, amongst them several women who were models of all the virtues and of proper, dignified behavior, especially the governess to whom my sister had the good fortune to be entrusted for her education.

But on my return home I became aware of certain unpleasant physical results from my stay at court. Despite my extreme abstemiousness and strict diet I was no longer in complete control of my time and my powers. Meals, exercise, getting up and going to bed, dressing and going out for rides — none of this had been dependent on my own will and inclination as it was back home. One cannot stand still in the midst of the social whirl without being impolite, and so I did everything that was required of me, and willingly, because I considered it part of my duties and knew it would not last long, but also because I felt in better health than ever before. Nevertheless the unaccustomed restlessness of my life must have taken a heavier toll on me than I had realized. For no sooner had I arrived home and given my parents a satisfying account of my doings than I suffered a hemorrhage which, although not serious and of short duration, left me noticeably weaker for a long time.

I now had to recite a new lesson to myself, and did so gladly. There was nothing binding me to the world of society, and I was convinced that I would never find there what was right for me. And so I entered on a state of peace and calm, and in renouncing one sort of life, I was sustained in life.

I had to suffer new afflictions when my mother was stricken with a serious illness, which lasted five full years till nature took its course. During that time there was much to test me. Often, when her anxiety became too acute for her to manage, she would call us at night to come and stand round her bed so that she might be at least distracted, if not made better, by our presence. Even more difficult, in fact almost impossible to bear, was the pressure on me when my father too began to feel wretched. He had suffered from violent headaches since the time of his youth; while frequent, they did not last more than thirty-six hours. But now they were continuous, and when they got really severe, my heart was torn with pity for him. In these troublesome times I was more aware than ever of my own physical frailty, which hindered me in the fulfillment of my most sacred, my tenderest duties, or made them extremely burdensome to me.

I was now able to examine myself to see whether the path I had chosen was one of truth or of fancy, whether I had only been imitating others, whether the object of my faith was a reality or not; to my great consolation I always found that it was. My heart was directed straight to God, I had sought and found communion with the "beloved ones," and this it was that lightened my burden. Like a traveller in search of shade, my soul sped to this place of refuge when all else oppressed me from without, and I never returned unsolaced.

In recent times many champions of religion, more from zeal than from true religious feeling, it would seem, have urged their brethren in the spirit to publicize instances of prayer being answered, probably in order to have chapter and verse with which to outwit their opponents by proof and argument. How little they know what true feeling is, how few real experiences they themselves will have had!

I can vouch that I never returned empty-handed when I went to God in distress and anxiety. That is claiming a lot, but I cannot, I dare not try to be more explicit. Important as all these experiences were for me at the crucial moments, any attempt to try to list them individually would be flat and make them sound insignificant, maybe improbable. I was merely happy that so many different occasions had proved that I was not without God in this life, just as every breath I drew proved I was alive. God was near to me, I was constantly in His presence. That is what I can declare as the ultimate truth, and can do so without resorting to the language of theological systems.

How I wished that I could have lived without recourse to such systems. But who can so early reach a state of complete blissful absorption in his own self without reference to external forms and systems? I was seriously concerned about my eternal salvation, and humbly placed my trust in the experience and repute of others. I applied myself thoroughly to the system of achieving conversion advocated by the pietist theologians at Halle, but I could not adapt myself to it at all.

According to the stages of this system, a change of heart must begin with a deep sense of alarm at one's sinfulness. In this state of extremity the heart must recognize the punishment one has deserved, and have a foretaste of hell which will sour the sweetness of sin. Then one should experience a noticeable assurance of grace, but this will not often come readily in the process but must be sought after.

None of this was in any way applicable to me. For when I sought out God in all sincerity, He was always to be found and never reproached me with my past actions. I did see afterwards where I had acted unworthily, and I knew in what ways I was still unworthy, but the recognition of my failings did not cause me any alarm. Not for a moment was I overcome by the fear of hell, indeed the whole idea of evil spirits and a place of punishment and torment after death was entirely alien to my thinking. The people I knew whose hearts were closed to love and trust in the Invisible One, who lived without God, seemed to me extremely unhappy already, so that hell and external punishment would, I thought, constitute a lesser rather than a severer punishment. When I thought about those people whose hearts were full of hatred and closed to all that was good, loading evil onto themselves and others, closing their eyes by day in order to assert that there is no light from the sun, then they seemed to me wretched and miserable beyond degree. What sort of hell could one think of to make their situation worse?

For ten full years this was my mental attitude. It sustained me through many trials, including my beloved mother's suffering and death. I was honest enough not to conceal my serenity of spirit during these afflictions when I was talking to persons conventionally trained in piety. I had to suffer many a friendly reproof from them to the effect that it was high time I seriously understood the importance of laying a firm religious foundation in times of good health.

But there was no lack of seriousness in me. I allowed myself to be momentarily convinced by what they said, and would willingly enough have felt sad and terrified. But to my astonishment I found that I could not. When I thought about God, I was happy and content. Even during my dear mother's painful last days on earth, I was not afraid of death. But in these momentous hours I learned much more than my uncalled-for instructors believed, and different things.

As time went on I became skeptical about the opinions of some well-known people, but I kept these feelings to myself. There was one particular woman friend, in whom I had confided too much, who was always trying to meddle in my affairs. I was obliged to break loose from her too, and finally told her firmly that she should not expend such efforts on me, for I did not need her advice: I knew my God and He alone should be my guide. She was very offended and I believe she has never quite forgiven me.

My decision to extricate myself in spiritual matters from the influence and advice of my friends resulted in my acquiring the courage to pursue my own course in external relationships. But without the help of my faithful Invisible Guide things would not have turned out so well for me, and I still marvel at the wise and propitious guidance that I received. Nobody really knew what I was about—not even I myself.

The thing, that evil thing that has never been explained, which separates us from the Being we owe our life to, the eternal Being by whom all that we call Life is sustained, the thing that is called Sin—this I did not yet know.

In my communion with the Invisible Friend I had the feeling of deep pleasure at the involvement of all my powers. The longing to enjoy this continuously was so intense that I would gladly forgo anything that impeded it; and here experience was my best teacher. But I was like a sick person without medication who resorts to dieting. It helped me somewhat, but not enough.

I could not remain all the time in isolation, although I found that was the best means of avoiding my natural tendency towards dispersing my thoughts. But when I returned to the hurly-burly, this affected me more strongly. My greatest advantage was that more than anything I loved to be quiet, and so ultimately I always withdrew to my solitude. In a kind of twilight state I recognized that I was weak and miserable, and tried to spare rather than expose myself.

For seven long years I persisted in this careful diet. I did not see anything wrong in myself, and I thought my state was enviable. Had it not been for some unusual circumstances I would have remained at this stage, and I departed from it in the strangest manner. Against the advice of all my friends I entered on a new human relationship. Their arguments made me hesitate at first, so I addressed myself to my Invisible Friend without delay, and since He expressed approval, I continued on my path without further concern.

A man of intelligence, feeling and talents had bought a house in the neighborhood. He and his family were amongst those newcomers whose acquaintance I had made. We were very much alike in customs, habits and domestic arrangements, and soon became close friends.

Philo, as I shall call him, was a man in middle life, who was extremely helpful to my father, whose powers were beginning to fail, in certain business matters. He soon became a close friend of the family, and since, as he said, he saw in me someone who had neither the extravagance and vanity of high society nor the bloodless timidity of the conventiclers, we two became intimate friends. He was both agreeable and useful to me.

Although I did not have the slightest inclination to engage in worldly affairs or have any influence in them, I did like to hear people talk about them and discover what was going on around me. I sought dispassionate, clear information: feeling, affection and intensity I reserved for my God, my family and my friends. I may say that my family and friends were jealous of my attachment to Philo, and they were right in more than one respect to warn me about it. I suffered much in the stillness of my heart, for I could not dismiss their objections as entirely empty or selfish. I had long been accustomed to give less weight to my own opinions, but this time I could not stifle my convictions. I beseeched my God to warn, hinder, or guide me in this matter too, and since my heart did not gainsay me afterwards, I felt relieved, and continued along my chosen path.

There was a vague general resemblance between Philo and Narcissus, but Philo's religious education had given his emotional life greater unity and strength. He had less vanity and more character. Narcissus had been shrewd, meticulous, persistent and tireless in worldly matters; Philo was clear, sharp, quick and incredibly expeditious. From him I learned all about the private circumstances of those distinguished persons I knew by sight, and I enjoyed surveying the busy throng from my lookout. Philo did not withhold anything from me, and gradually told me all about his own public and private relationships. I was afraid on his behalf, because I foresaw certain situations and complications developing, and bad things came sooner than I had anticipated. For there were certain matters that he had always avoided telling me about, but he finally revealed sufficient of these to make me assume the worst. The effect of this on me was devastating, for I encountered experiences which were quite new to me. With infinite sadness of heart I saw in Philo some sort of counterpart to the hero of Wieland's novel *Agathon*, who had to repay the cost of his education in the sacred grove of Delphi with heavy overdue interest—and this second Agathon was the man I was so closely associated with! I was filled with ardent concern for him, I suffered with him, and we both found ourselves in a very strange state of mind.

Having occupied myself for a long time with the state of his soul, I turned my attention to my own. The thought that I was no better than he came over me and descended like a cloud which darkened my mind. I didn't just think this, I felt it, felt that I was no better than he, and felt it so strongly that I would not wish to have any such feeling again. The transition was not sudden. For more than a year I had been feeling that if some invisible hand had not prevented me, I could have become the foulest of evildoers, for I sensed the tendency in my heart. What a discovery this was!

Up to then I had not experienced the reality of sinfulness in the least, but now the possibility of sin had become terrifyingly clear and conceivable to me.

I was not yet acquainted with evil, but I feared it; I felt that I could be guilty, but I could not reproach myself. Convinced as I was that a disposition such as I now recognized mine to be, would not make for a union with the Supreme Being after death such as I hoped for, I did not have any fears of incurring such separation at present. Despite the evil that I discovered in myself, I loved Him, hated my own feelings, wished to hate them even more intensely, my only desire being to be freed of this sickness and this whole disposition toward sickness. I was sure that the Great Physician would not refuse me help in this.

The only question was: How was this defect to be overcome? By virtuous actions? This I did not even contemplate, for during the past ten years my exercise of virtue had been far more than outward actions, and yet the horrors I now recognized had been deeply ingrained in my soul all the while. Couldn't they have broken loose as they did when David saw Bathsheba? Was David not also a friend of God, and was I not deeply convinced that God was my friend?

Was this perhaps an inescapable weakness in all mankind? Are we to accept the fact that we sometimes sense the sovereign power of inclination and, with the best will in the world, can do nothing more than deplore what we have done and then fall into the same situation on a similar occasion?

I found no solace in treatises on morals. Neither the severity of their efforts to make us subdue our instincts, nor their accommodating attempts to make virtues out of instincts, were in any way satisfying to me. The basic ideas that my communion with the Invisible Friend had instilled in me, had a much more decisive importance for me.

Once when I was studying the songs written by David after that ugly catastrophe, I was struck by his assertion that the evil within him was already in the material from which he was made; but he wished to be freed from sin and prayed earnestly for purity of heart.

But how was I to attain this? The answer, I knew, was given me in symbolic form in the Bible, where it was written that the blood of Christ shall wash away all sin. I now perceived for the first time that I had not really understood these words I had so often repeated, and such questions as: What does that mean? or, How is that to take place? tormented me day and night. Finally I seemed to catch the glimmer of an answer: What I was seeking was to be found in the mystery of the Incarnation through which the Word, in which we and all things are made, becomes flesh. It was revealed to me in darkling distance that our ultimate maker once descended to the depths in which we travail, penetrating and absorbing them, passed through every stage of our human condition from conception and birth to the grave, and, emerging from this strange detour, rose once again to those clear bright heights where we too must dwell in order to gain happiness.

Why must we always resort to images of external conditions in order to speak of such innermost things? What are heights and depths, darkness and light to Him? Only we have an above and below, a day and night. And He became like us so that we might be part of Him.

But how are we to share in such immeasurable beneficence? By Faith, the scripture tells us. But what is Faith? Merely accepting the report of an event as truth, how can that help me, I asked myself. I need to experience its effects and results. It must require an unusual state of mind for human beings, to be able to make such Faith part of themselves.

"Grant me such Faith, oh almighty God!" was the prayer of my heavy heart. I leaned over the little table at which I was sitting, hiding my tear-stained face in my hands. I was in the state that we must be in if God is to hear our prayer; and how rarely are we in that state!

How can I find the proper words to describe what I felt at that moment? A strong impulse lifted my soul to the cross on which Jesus died. I cannot call it other than an impulse, like that which carries one toward an absent friend, someone one loves dearly, making a connection that is more intense, more real than one would have imagined. My soul drew nigh to the incarnate, the cruci-fied One, and at that moment I knew what Faith was.

This is Faith! I cried, and leapt up half in fright. I examined myself in order to make quite sure what I did feel, what I did perceive, and I was soon persuaded that my spirit had acquired the facility to rise aloft—a faculty that was quite new to it.

Words fail us when we have such feelings. I could clearly distinguish what I felt from any fancies of the mind—there were no imaginings, no images, and yet what I felt had the certainty of being attached to something definite, just as one's imagination conjures up the features of a distant loved one.

When my first rapture had abated, I recognized that what I was experienc-ing was something I had felt before, but never with such intensity. I had never been able to prolong such a state of mind for myself. I do believe that every human being has had some such feelings at one time or another; for it is undoubtedly this sort of experience that teaches us all that there is a God. From time to time I had been content to feel such an access of strength, and would probably have remained satisfied with this, had it not been for the mis-fortunes which had constantly and unexpectedly been my lot and the conse-quent diminution of my powers and abilities. But now, since that one great moment, I had taken on wings. I could now rise above all that had threatened me before, like a bird effortlessly soaring with joyful song above a raging tor-rent, beside which a dog remains standing, barking anxiously.

My joy was beyond description and although I revealed none of this to any-body, my family noticed a new radiance about me, without knowing the cause. If only I had maintained silence and striven to preserve in my soul the purity of the mood! If only I had not allowed myself to be misled by circumstances into revealing my secret, I could have spared myself a huge detour.

During the past ten years of my Christian experience I had not myself pos-sessed the strength I needed, and so I had done what other serious-minded persons in my condition had, namely supported myself by filling my imagina-tion with images related to God, which is definitely useful, for by this means the evil effects of injurious images are prevented. Our soul grasps at one or the other of these spiritual images and by so doing it soars upward like a young bird flitting from branch to branch. So long as one has nothing better, this exercise is not to be discounted.

We are provided with images and impressions directing us toward God by the activities of the church, by bells, organs and hymns, and especially by the homilies of preachers. My desire to profit from all this was so intense that neither bad weather nor poor health would prevent me from going to church, and church bells of a Sunday were the only thing that would make me impatient when I was lying on my bed of sickness. I listened with great attention to our chief Court Preacher, who was an excellent man. His colleagues were also of value to me, and I knew how to pick out the golden apples of the divine Word from the ordinary fruit in such earthly vessels. I supplemented these public religious exercises with all sorts of private "devotional practices," as they are called, but all this did was to feed my imaginative powers and refine the activity of my senses. I had grown so accustomed to this course of action, and set such a high value on it, that I did not have the sense of anything higher. My soul had feelers, but no eyes; it felt, but didn't see. If only it would acquire eyes so that it could really see!

I still continued to go and listen eagerly to the sermons. But what an experience I had! I no longer found what I had previously valued. These preachers were gnawing away at shells, whereas I was enjoying the kernels. I soon grew tired of them, but I was too spoilt to limit myself to what I had discovered for myself. I had to have images for my feelings, impressions from outside, and I believed this to be a truly spiritual need.

Philo's parents had connections with the pietistic community at Herrnhut, and in his own library there were many writings by its founder, Count Zinzendorf. On several different occasions he spoke to me in clear and reasonable terms about these works, and urged me to look at some of them, if only in order to acquaint myself with a particular psychological phenomenon. I myself considered Count Zinzendorf as a thorough heretic; so I did not look at the Moravian hymnal either, which Philo had pressed upon me. But one day, lacking all other external stimulation, I chanced to pick it up, and, to my astonishment, found hymns in it which, in their own very different and strange form, seemed to point in the direction of my own feelings. There was no rigid, commonplace, school terminology in them. I became convinced that these people felt what I felt, and I took great pleasure in committing this or that verse to memory and sustaining myself for several days by this means.

Almost three months had passed since that moment when I had been granted insight into the truth. So finally I reached the decision to tell my friend Philo everything and ask him to let me have those books from his library which I was now extremely curious to see. I did this, despite the fact that there was something in my heart that strongly urged me not to.

I told Philo my whole story in every detail. Since he was one of the main characters in it, and since my account contained a homily that was a call for him to repent, he was deeply affected by it. He burst into tears; and

I was happy at the thought that a complete change of heart was taking place in him too.

He provided me with all the works I asked for, and I soon had more than ample food for my imagination. I made great progress in the Zinzendorf way of thinking and speaking. Let it not be thought that I do not continue to respect Count Zinzendorf's way of doing things. One must have just regard for what he does. He is no empty enthusiast: he speaks about great truths mostly in bold, imaginative flights, and those who have disparaged him, do not recognize or appreciate his qualities.

I became extremely attached to him; and if I had been my own master I would certainly have left my home and friends, and gone to join him. We would undoubtedly have understood each other well, but we would not have found it easy to get along with each other for a length of time.

Thanks be to my presiding genius, which kept me confined at that time to my domestic sphere! It was quite a big trip for me to go into the garden. The care of my ailing old father gave me plenty to do, and I spent my leisure hours in cultivating the noblest flights of my imagination. The only person I saw was Philo, whom my father loved dearly; but his frankness toward me had been somewhat curtailed by what I had recently said to him. The effect of my words had not been deep: he tried several times to adapt himself to my terms, but without success, and so avoided all further discussion of this subject, which was not difficult for him because, with his broad range of knowledge, he could always introduce new topics into the conversation.

So I became a Herrnhut sister of my own accord, and had to conceal this change of mind and inclination from the Court Preacher whom I had good reason to respect and had as my confessor, and his many excellent qualities were not diminished in my eyes by his strong opposition to the Herrnhut community. Unfortunately, this fine man would suffer great distress on my account and that of many others!

Several years previous to this he had elsewhere become acquainted with a certain pious, honest gentlemen, with whom he still maintained an active correspondence, for this man was an earnest seeker after God. As his spiritual mentor he was therefore deeply distressed when this nobleman embraced the Herrnhut persuasion and dwelt for a long time in their community. He was equally pleased when this same man fell out with the brethren and came to live in his own vicinity, placing himself once again completely, so it appeared, under his guidance.

The newcomer was displayed in triumph to the most beloved lambs of the pastor's flock, though he was not brought to our house, because my father was no longer seeing anybody. He was well approved of: The outward polish of the courtier combined with the inner sincerity of one of the brethren, and, in addition to that, many fine natural qualities that soon made him into a major saint for all those who came to know him, much to his spiritual patron's delight. Unfortunately his quarrel with the Herrnhut community was only superficial in nature and concerned with external circumstances; in spirit he still belonged to them completely. He believed in the basic validity of the cause, but also did not reject the frills and flounces that Count Zinzendorf had added. He was by now quite accustomed to their ways of thinking and speaking, and although he endeavored to conceal this fact from his old friend, he necessarily came out with their hymns, litanies and metaphorical language when he saw he was in the company of like-minded persons, and thereby gained their approval. I myself knew nothing about all this, drifted along in my own way, and it was quite a while before he and I met each other.

One day I went to visit a woman friend who was sick, and when I got there I found several of my acquaintances deep in a conversation, which was broken off at my arrival. I pretended not to notice this, but did observe to my great astonishment several pictures of persons and events connected with Herrnhut hanging in fine frames on the wall. I quickly grasped what must have happened since I had last been in this house, and celebrated the change by reciting some appropriate verses. My friends were naturally amazed by this. We opened our hearts to each other and from that moment on were of one mind and intimate associates.

I now took opportunities to go out as often as I could, but unfortunately this was only possible once every three or four weeks. I became acquainted with the nobleman apostle and gradually with the whole clandestine community. I attended their meetings whenever I could and, because of my social sense, I took great pleasure in hearing testimony from others, and myself testifying to others about the things I had up till then worked out for myself and within myself.

I was not so completely absorbed by all this as not to notice how few of them understood the real meaning of delicate words and phrases, and even then were no more helped than they had been by the old symbolic language of church ritual. But I continued to use these words and expressions, not allowing myself to be led astray into thinking I was called upon to judge their hearts and minds, for, in my own case, many a harmless religious exercise had prepared me for higher things. I made my particular contribution by insisting, when my turn came to speak, on that meaning which is more concealed than expressed in words that deal with delicate and intimate matters; and, for the rest, tacitly agreeing that everyone should be allowed to express himself in his own way.

These quiet times of secret sociability were followed by a stormy period of open disagreements and hostilities, which produced factions at court and in the town and led to a real uproar. Our Court Preacher, that fierce opponent of the Herrnhut community, had come to the humiliating discovery that his best and most devoted parishioners were all siding with the brethren. He was deeply offended, and, having expressed himself quite intemperately in the first moment of shock, he could not later retract, even if he had wished to. There were violent debates, in which, thank goodness, my name was not mentioned, since I was only an occasional participant in what he considered their horrible meetings, and because our zealot of a leader could not dispense with the support of my father and my friend Philo in his dealings with the townspeople. I maintained my neutrality in silent satisfaction, for to engage in discussion of such feelings and topics, even with well-meaning persons, had become distasteful to me when they could not grasp the essentials and only occupied themselves with superficial matters; and to argue about these things with adversaries when one could hardly make one's own friends understand, seemed to me useless and even disadvantageous. For I soon noticed that kind and noble persons, unable to keep their minds free of aversion and hatred, soon lapsed into injustice and, while striving to preserve some external set of forms, almost destroyed what was best in their own inner convictions.

However wrong this worthy man may have been in such matters and however much people tried to incite me to take sides against him, I could not deny him my heartfelt respect. I knew him well and I could easily adapt myself to his way of seeing things. I never knew a person completely without faults, but these are more conspicuous in superior persons. We earnestly desire that those who are especially privileged should not have to pay tribute or tithes. I respected him for the excellent man that he was, and hoped that the influence of my silent neutrality might help bring about peace, or at least an armistice. I do not know what effect I might have had on him; for God dealt with the matter quickly by taking him unto Himself. Over his bier all those wept who had but recently exchanged words with him. His righteousness, his God-fearing nature, was never doubted by anyone.

I too had to put away childish things at this time, for these took on a different aspect for me during this period of troublesome conflict. My uncle had quietly continued with his plans for my sister's future. He presented her with a young man of wealth and station as her future bridegroom, and produced a dowry as rich as could be expected from him. My father gladly signified his agreement, and my sister was free and quite ready and willing to assume the married station. The wedding was arranged to take place at my uncle's castle, family and friends were invited, and we all arrived in high spirits.

This was the first time in my life that entering a house aroused my admiration. I had often heard people speak of my uncle's taste, his Italian architect, his fine collections and library; but I had measured this against what I already knew, and had a very mixed image in my mind of what it would be like. How astonished I was at the impression of gravity and harmoniousness that came to me as I entered the house, and this increased with every new room that I walked into. Splendor and magnificence had usually led me away from myself, but here I felt led back into myself. The grandeur and dignity of the arrangements for all the festive celebrations aroused in me a sense of calm and composure, and it was just as incomprehensible to me that one man could have thought all this out and arranged for it to be done, as that many different persons could have combined their efforts to achieve such a unified, grand result. And with all this, our host and his helpers seemed quite at ease, totally without stiffness or empty ceremoniousness.

The marriage ceremony began quite unexpectedly in a heart-warming way, excellent vocal music came to us as a surprise, and the priest gave to the ceremony the solemn feeling of truth. I was standing next to Philo, and instead of wishing me happiness, he said with a deep sigh: "When I saw your sister extend her hand, it was as though I had been showered with boiling water." "How so?" I asked. "I always have that feeling at weddings," he said. I laughed, but have had good occasion to remember his words since.

The joyous state of the company, which included many young people, seemed even more striking because of the distinguished quality of everything that surrounded them. The household utensils, table linen, dishes and center-pieces were as fine as everything else. I had already thought that the architects seemed to belong to the same school as those who arranged the decorations, but now it seemed as if those responsible for setting the tables had been instructed by the architect too.

Since we were to be together for several days, our thoughtful and consider-ate host had provided various sorts of entertainment. I did not have the unpleasant experience I have often had in a large, mixed company, when peo-ple are left to themselves and tend to turn to the most trivial of pastimes so that neither the best nor the worst of them shall feel deprived of entertainment. My uncle arranged things quite differently. He had appointed two or three masters of ceremonies, if I may call them such. One of these was in charge of amuse-ments for the young people—dances, excursions, and various pastimes which he thought up and himself directed; and since young people like to be outdoors and are not afraid of fresh air, the garden and the conservatory were turned over to them, with all the adjoining galleries and pavilions which, although only made of clapboard and canvas, suggested in these magnificent surround-ings real stone and marble. How rare it it is that the person who invites his guests to a festivity feels such a real obligation to take care of their needs and comfort! Hunting expeditions, card parties, short strolls, and occasions for intimate conversations were provided for the older guests, and those accustomed to go to bed earliest were given lodgings farthest removed from all the noise.

All these excellent arrangements made the space in which we were living seem like a world of its own, and yet, if one examined it closely, the castle was not all that big, and it would have been hardly possible to accommodate so many people, and attend to all their different individual needs, without a pre-cise knowledge of its layout and a mind such as that of our host.

Equally pleasing as the appearance of a well-built person is the experience of a well-organized household that reveals the presence of an understanding and intelligent host. Just to come into a clean house is a pleasure in itself, even though it be lacking in taste and overornate, for it does at least show the presence of one aspect of a cultured owner. But how much more satisfying it is to feel the presence of high culture, even though this be only culture of the senses. This was visible to a high degree in my uncle's home. I had heard and read a great deal about art. Philo was himself a great connoisseur of paintings and had a fine collection of his own. I myself had done a good deal of sketching; but on the one hand I was far too much occupied with my own feelings and expressing what I had to, and on the other hand everything I saw seemed to disperse my concentration. Now for the first time, external things brought me back to myself, and I learnt the difference between the natural beauty of the song of the nightingale and a four-part alleluia from human throats. I did not conceal my joy at this discovery from my uncle who, when everything else had been taken care of, spent much time conversing with me. He spoke very modestly about his possessions and achievements, but with great conviction about the principles that had governed his collections and their arrangement, and I could easily see that he was sparing my feelings by subordinating all the good that he was lord and master of to what I considered to be right and best.

"If we can imagine," he said to me one day, "that the Creator of the world should take on the form of His creature and inhabit the world for a time in this guise, then this human creation must seem perfect indeed if the Creator Himself could ally Himself so closely with it. In the concept of humanity there cannot be a contradiction with the idea of godhead, and if we often feel remoteness and difference from the godhead, then it is our urgent responsibility not to dwell on our weaknesses and faults like the devil's advocate but to seek out our finest qualities by which we can legitimately confirm our godlikeness."

At this I smiled, and replied: "Don't embarrass me so by your kind attempts to speak my language. What you have to tell me, is so important for me that I would prefer to hear it in your very own language, and then I will translate what I cannot quite accept of it, into mine."

"I will go on," he said, "in my own language without changing my tone. Man's greatest achievement is to be able to control circumstances as much as possible, and allow himself to be controlled by them as little as possible. The whole world is spread out before us like a stone quarry before a builder, and no one deserves to be called a builder unless he can transform these raw materials into something corresponding to the image in his mind, with the utmost economy, purposefulness and sureness. Everything outside us is just material, and I can well say the same about everything about us: but within us there lies the formative power which creates what is to be, and never lets us rest until we have accomplished this in one way or another in or outside ourselves. You, my dear niece, have perhaps chosen the best way; you have striven to unite your moral self, your profoundly loving nature, within itself and with the Supreme Being, and we others are not to be blamed either if we strive to know the full extent of our sensual being and actively promote its unification."

Through such conversations we became ever more closely acquainted with each other and I succeeded in making him speak to me without adapting to my way of thinking, just as he would with himself. "Don't believe I am flattering you," he said, "if I praise your manner of thinking and acting. I respect a person who knows quite clearly what he wants and steadfastly proceeds in that direction, with a true sense of direction and purpose. Whether the purpose is noble or not, and deserves praise or blame—that is only a subsequent consideration. Believe me, my dear, the greater part of misfortune, and what is considered evil in the world, comes about because people fail to recognize their true goals, or, if they do, to work steadily toward them. They are like those who have the sense that a tower should be built, but whose materials and efforts only suffice for a cottage. If you, my friend, whose highest aspiration was to come to terms with your moral nature, had adapted yourself to your family, a fiancé, or perhaps a husband, instead of making the great and bold sacrifices that you have, you would have been in continual conflict with yourself and never known a single moment of peace."

"You have used the word 'sacrifices,'" I said, "and I have often thought that we do sacrifice lesser things to higher aspirations, as if to a god, even though those lesser things are dear to our heart; as when a cherished lamb is brought to the altar lovingly and willingly for the sake of a beloved father's health."

"Whether it be reason or feeling that makes us abandon one thing for another, or choose this over that, it is my belief that steadfastness and persistence are the qualities most to be respected in any human being. One can't have the goods and the money one pays for them at the same time, and a man who craves for the goods without the heart to pay for them, is in just as bad a state as one who regrets a purchase when he has already made it. But I am far from censuring such persons: they are not really responsible, but rather the complicated conditions of their existence that make it difficult for them to control themselves. For instance, you will find fewer bad innkeepers in the country than in towns, and fewer in small towns than in large ones. Why is that? Man is born into a limited situation, he can comprehend aspirations that are simple, readily accessible and precise, and he accustoms himself to using means that are close at hand; but as soon as he branches out from his restricted sphere, he knows neither what he would like to do nor what he is obliged to do, and it is a matter of complete indifference whether he is confused by a multitude of objectives or disconcerted by their loftiness and importance. Either way he will be unhappy at having to strive after something that he cannot combine with ordinary regular activity.

"Nothing can be achieved in the world," he continued, "without serious-mindedness, and there is little of this to be found amongst those we deem cultured. They approach work and business affairs, art, and pleasures with a sort of self-defensiveness. They live their lives in the way one reads a pile of newspapers, just to be finished, and I well remember a young Englishman in Rome who once said at a party that he had polished off six churches and two galleries that day. People want to learn a lot, and know a lot, especially regarding those things which are not really important to them, and they don't notice that hunger is not stilled by snatching at air. When I get to know somebody, I always ask at once what is he occupying himself with, and how and in what order. And my interest in him will always depend on the answers he gives."

"Perhaps, uncle, you are rather too strict and deprive yourself of acquaintances that you could be useful to and really help."

"Is one to be blamed for losing interest in them, seeing that one has labored for so long with them and for them, and all in vain? How one suffers in one's youth from those who think they are inviting us to a pleasant excursion by promising us the company of Sisyphus or the Danaids! Thank goodness I have been able to keep free of such persons, and if one of them should chance to stray into my purview, I usher him out as politely as possible. For from such people one hears the bitterest complaints about the confusion of worldly events, the shallowness of learning, the frivolity of artists, the hollowness of poets, and the like. They never understand that neither they nor all those like them would ever read a book written according to their demands, that they are ignorant of what real poetry is, and that even a fine work of art will only earn their approval if it has already been accredited with excellence by someone else. But let's stop talking about all this. Now is not the time to complain or censure."

He directed my attention to the various paintings hanging on the wall. My eyes fixed on those which looked pleasant or had a notable subject. He let this happen for a while, and then said: "Now pay some attention to the spirit that produced these works. Noble souls like to see God's hand in His creation; but why shouldn't we give some consideration to the hands of His imitators?" He then drew my attention to some pictures that had not struck me particularly, and tried to make me understand that only study of the history of art can give us a proper sense of the value and distinction of a work of art. One must first appreciate the burdensome aspects of technical labor that gifted artists have perfected over the centuries, in order for one to comprehend how it is possible for a creative genius to move freely and joyfully on a plane so high that it makes us dizzy.

With this in mind he brought together a number of pictures, and when he explained them to me, I could not avoid seeing in them images and symbols of moral perfection. When I told him this, he said: "You are absolutely right, and one should not pursue the cultivation of one's moral life in isolation and seclusion. We are more likely to find that a person intent on moral advancement will have every cause to cultivate his senses as well as his mind, so as not to run the risk of losing his foothold on those moral heights, slipping into the seductive allurements of uncontrolled fancy and debasing his nobler nature by indulging in idle frivolities, if not worse."

I never suspected that this was aimed at me, but I did feel affected when I thought back to certain rather insipid things in those hymns which had contributed to my edification. I also realized that the images which had attached themselves to my spiritual concepts would hardly have found favor in my uncle's eyes.

Philo had been spending a good deal of time in the library and now he took me there. Together we admired the selection and number of books it contained. They had been assembled, in every sense of the word; for they consisted almost entirely of works that would help us toward true enlightenment and the achievement of proper perspective, either by providing us with the right materials or by giving us a sense of the unity of our mental powers.

I had read a great deal in the course of my life, and in some areas there was hardly a book that was not known to me. It was therefore particularly pleasant for me now to think in terms of a whole and observe where I had gaps, whereas previously I had always thought in terms of the confusion caused by limitation and the vast extent of what there was to learn.

We made the acquaintance of an unassuming, but very interesting man. He was a physician and a naturalist, and seemed to belong more to the presiding deities of the house than to its actual, present inhabitants. He showed us the collection of specimens which, like the books in the library, were arranged in glass cases along the walls of the rooms, enlarging rather than narrowing the space between them. This reminded me of the joys of my youth, and I showed my father several things that he had brought to the sickbed of his child before she had any real sense of the world around her. This doctor did not conceal the fact, either then or in our later discussions, that it was his interest in religious sentiments that made him seek me out. But he never failed to praise my uncle's tolerance and respect for everything that demonstrated and advanced the unity and worth of human nature, demanding this from everybody else, and consistently opposing and condemning every kind of mere self-satisfaction and exclusive narrowness.

My uncle was extremely happy at my sister's marriage, and he spoke to me several times about what he intended to do for her and her children. He had splendid estates, which he managed himself and hoped to bequeath to his nephews in excellent condition. He seemed to have special thoughts regarding the small estate where we were at the moment: "This I will only give to the person who knows, appreciates and can enjoy what it contains, who understands the responsibility of those who are rich and belong to the nobility, especially in Germany, to establish something that shall serve as a model."

Very soon the majority of the guests had departed, and we ourselves were getting ready to leave. To conclude the celebrations, my uncle most considerately provided us once again with an entertainment of the highest quality. We had openly expressed our delight at the unaccompanied choral music at my sister's wedding, and we had urged him to let us hear this again. But he had not seemed to take any notice. We were therefore extremely surprised when he said one evening: "The dance music has gone, our young, flighty friends have deserted us, even the married couple looks more serious than it did a few days ago. And so, since the time to leave has come, and we may never see each other again, or at least as we are now, this calls for a festive atmosphere that I cannot better induce than by having that music repeated which you asked for earlier."

He then had four- and eight-part motets performed by the same choir, now increased in size and profiting from further practice, and this, I may well say, gave us all a foretaste of heaven. So far I had only been acquainted with hymn-singing, in which pious souls, often with hoarse throats, believe they are birds of the forest singing praises to God, because of the pleasant feeling it gives them, or with the vanity of concert music that provokes admiration for the talents of the performer, but rarely provides even passing pleasure. But now I heard music issuing from the richest depths of noble, human hearts, through practiced organs and in perfect harmony, speaking to the very best in us and making us fully aware of our godlikeness. The motets were sacred, with texts in Latin; they were like jewels in the golden ring of this cultured, secular society. By them I was spiritually uplifted and made happy, without laying any claim to so-called spiritual enlightenment.

On our departure we were all given handsome presents. I received the cross of my order, more artistically and delicately wrought and more richly enamelled than is usual. It was suspended from a large diamond, by which it was fastened to the ribbon, and this stone he considered one of the finest from his collection of gems.

My sister left with her husband for his estates, and we all went back to our homes, returning, as regards external circumstances, to what seemed a very ordinary life. We had returned to earth from a fairy palace and had to accommodate ourselves to this, each of us adjusting in his own way.

The unusual experiences that I had undergone in the new environment of my uncle's house left me with pleasing impressions, but these did not continue to be so vivid in my mind, although he did all he could to sustain and revive them by sending me from time to time some of his finest and most agreeable works of art, and then exchanging these for others when I had had sufficient time to enjoy them.

I was too accustomed to occupying myself with the affairs of my own heart and soul and talking about these with like-minded persons to pay much attention to a work of art without soon withdrawing again into myself. It was my custom to view a painting or an engraving as letters in a book. Good printing gives pleasure: but who reads a book for the quality of the printing? A pictorial presentation had to say something to me — teach me, move me, improve me; and no matter how much my uncle had to say about works of art in his letters, I continued to react as I always had.

Not only my own nature but also external events, changes in my family, distracted me from such consideration, even sometimes from my own self, for I had to tolerate and perform duties which exceeded my feeble physical powers.

My unmarried sister had always been my right hand. She was healthy, strong and infinitely kind, and it was she who had taken over the responsibility of running the household while I was occupied with the care of our aged father. But she was struck with a catarrh that turned into pneumonia; and in three weeks she was dead. Her death afflicted me so deeply that even today I hardly dare to think about it.

I was sick in bed myself before she was laid in her grave. The old trouble in my chest seemed to be flaring up again, I was racked by coughing and so hoarse that I could hardly speak.

My married sister had a miscarriage because of fear and anxiety. My poor old father was afraid of losing at one and the same time his children and all hopes of grandchildren. His justified tears increased my sorrow, and I prayed to God for the restoration of some degree of health in myself, asking merely that my life should be prolonged until after my father's death. I recovered, and was as well as I could ever be, assuming once more my obligations and fulfilling them as best I could.

My sister became pregnant again. Various concerns, which in such cases are usually borne by mothers, were loaded on me. She was not entirely happy in her marital life, but this was not something my father should be made aware of. I myself had to be the judge of such matters. Things were made easier by the confidence which my brother-in-law always placed in me. Both he and my sister were good people, but instead of being considerate of each other, they were always arguing; and in their desire to live in complete harmony with each other they never achieved unity in anything. I was now learning to deal seriously with worldly matters, and practice what I had been singing hymns about.

My sister gave birth to a son, and my father's indisposition did not prevent him from traveling to see her. When he saw the child, he was overcome with joy and satisfaction, and at the christening he seemed to me inspired, quite different from his usual self, almost like a spirit with two faces, one of which looked forward joyfully to the region he would soon be entering, while the other contemplated, full of hope, this new earthly life awakened in the boy who was descended from him. All the way home he never ceased talking to me about the child and its healthy appearance, and he expressed his eagerness that the qualities of this new citizen of the world should be well nurtured and developed. He continued to speculate on this after we arrived home, and it was not until a few days later that we noticed he had a kind of fever, which came on after meals in the form of an enervating temperature, though without any chills. But he would not lie down, and every morning he would leave the house to attend punctiliously to his business affairs, until finally some more lasting and more serious symptoms prevented him from this. I will never forget the orderliness and tranquility with which he attended to the affairs of the household and the arrangements for his own burial, as if it were the affair of someone else.

With a composure of mind unusual in him, which almost approached joy, he said to me one day: "Where has that fear of death gone which I used to feel so strongly? Why should I fear to die? God is merciful, the grave holds no terrors for me, I shall have eternal life." One of the most pleasant occupations in my solitary life is to recall the circumstances of his dying, and nobody will argue me out of the sense I had then of the workings of some higher force.

My father's death changed my whole mode of living. From a life of strictest obedience and extreme restrictions I passed into one of greatest freedom, which I enjoyed like food I had long had to do without. Whereas I had usually not been able to spend more than a couple of hours each day away from the house, there was now hardly a day that I remained in my own room. The friends with whom I had only been able to snatch fleeting visits, now wanted to see me all the time, and I them. I was often invited to meals, walks and excursions, and never declined. But once I had run the gamut I came to see that the greatest value of freedom is not to do everything one wants to when this is favored by circumstances but rather to be able to achieve what is good and right by the most direct way, without let or hindrance. And I was old enough by now to arrive at this conviction myself without instruction from others.

What I could not deny myself, however, was to continue to strengthen as quickly as possible my contacts with the members of the Herrnhut community, and I eagerly participated in one of their very next functions. But here too I did not find what I had hoped for. I was honest enough to tell them this, and they tried to persuade me that their little group was nothing compared to a regularly organized community. I was prepared to accept that; but my belief was that the true spirit should be able to emerge from a small group just as well as from a large assembly.

One of their bishops, a pupil of Count Zinzendorf himself, devoted much attention to me. He spoke perfect English, and because I knew some too, he decided this was an indication that we belonged together. But I didn't think so at all, for his whole manner was very distasteful to me. He was a knife grinder from Moravia, and his whole way of thinking was that of an artisan. I got on much better with a certain Mr. von L . . . , who had been a major in the French army; though I could not display the same subservience as he showed towards his superiors—indeed it felt as though someone had slapped me when I saw his wife and other respected ladies kissing the bishop's hand. Meanwhile a journey to Holland was agreed upon, which, however, never came about—and that certainly turned out to my advantage.

My sister gave birth to a daughter, and now it was the turn of us women to be pleased, and think about how the little girl could be brought up as we had been. My brother-in-law, on the other hand, was very disappointed when, in the following year, another daughter arrived, for, with his vast estates, he wanted to have boys around to help him manage them.

Because of my feeble health I kept myself to myself, and achieved a certain equilibrium in my life of calm repose. I had no fear of death, I even wished to die, but at quiet moments I felt that God was granting me time to examine my soul and bring myself ever closer to Him. In my many sleepless nights I had a feeling which I find hard to describe. It was as if my soul were thinking without my body, looking on the body as something apart from itself, like some garment or other. My soul vividly recalled past times and events and sensed what was to come. These times were all gone by, and what was to come would also pass; the body will be rent like a garment, but I, the well-known I, I am.

I was persuaded by a noble friend who became ever more closely acquainted with me, not to yield too much to the consolation afforded by this lofty thought. This was the physician whom I had met at my uncle's house. He had informed himself about the state of my mind and body, and he explained to me that such feelings, if nurtured without reference to external things, will drain us dry and undermine our existence. "Man's first task," he said, "is to be active, and one should use those intervals when one is obliged to rest, to acquire a clear knowledge of external things, for that will assist us in all our further activity."

Since he was aware of my tendency to consider my body as a thing apart, and because he knew that my constitution, its failings and the medical means of treating these were fairly well known to me, so much so that I had almost become a doctor myself in attending to my own ills and those of others, he directed my attention away from the human body and various salves to the other objects of creation around me, so that I wandered around as if in paradise and, if I may continue the metaphor, only after this was I allowed to sense from afar the presence of the creator walking of an evening in the cool of the garden. With gladness I now perceived God in Nature as clearly as I felt Him in my heart; and I gave thanks that He should have deigned to give me life by the breath of His mouth.

My sister and all the rest of us were hoping for the birth of another boy, which my brother-in-law dearly desired. But, sad to say, he did not live to see it happen. This fine man died from the results of an unfortunate fall from his horse, and my sister, after having given birth to a lovely boy, followed him soon afterwards. It pained me to look at the four children she left behind. So many healthy people had died before me, sick as I was; and was I not destined to see some of these promising fruits wither and die? I was sufficiently acquainted with the world to know how many dangers there are for a child — especially one belonging to the upper classes of society—when it is growing up, and it seemed to me that these perils had increased since the time of my youth. I felt that, with my infirmity, I was not in a position to do much for these children, if indeed anything. I was therefore very glad when our uncle decided to devote his whole attention to the upbringing of these dear little creatures. This, of course, was quite natural for someone of his frame of mind, and the children deserved it in every way, for they were comely and, despite their differences from each other, they all gave promise of becoming kind and intelligent human beings.

Once my physician friend had made me aware of family resemblances in children and relatives, I began to take special pleasure in following this up. My father had carefully preserved the portraits of his ancestors, and had himself and his children painted by reasonably good artists, along with my mother and her relatives. We knew therefore the characteristics of the whole family, and, having pondered and compared these, we looked for similar traits of mind and body in the children. My sister's eldest son seemed to resemble his paternal grandfather, of whom there was a good portrait as a young man in my uncle's collection. This grandfather had liked to present himself as a fine officer, and the boy preferred nothing more than handling a gun when he came to see me. My father had bequeathed us a fine assortment of guns, and the little boy would not rest until I had given him a brace of pistols and a hunting piece, and he had figured out for himself how to manipulate a flintlock. He was not at all clumsy or hasty in his movements, but rather gentle and thoughtful.

The eldest daughter claimed the greater part of my affection, probably because she looked like me and, of all the four, it was she who clung to me most. But I must say that the more I observed her growing up, the more she put me to shame. I could not fail to be amazed at her; I might almost say that I developed respect for her. One could not imagine a more noble presence, a more peaceful disposition, a greater evenness of attention to every kind of goal or object. Never for a moment was she idle, and everything she turned her hands to became a worthy object. Nothing troubled her so long as she could do what was demanded of her by circumstances, and she could be quite content when she did not find anything that needed doing at the moment. This ability to remain active without feeling the need for some particular occupation, was something that I never again encountered. Her behavior toward the needy and suffering was always exemplary. I must confess that I myself had never had the ability to make an occupation out of works of charity. I was not parsimonious in my gifts to the poor, and often gave more than I should have in my circumstances, but in a way I was buying myself off, and if someone were to receive my full care and attention, this would have to be someone of my own flesh and blood. But with my niece it was just the opposite, and I admired her for this. I never saw her giving money to a pauper; what she received from me for this purpose, she would use to fulfill practical needs. She was never more attractive in my eyes than when she rummaged around in my clothes and linens, always finding something I was no longer wearing or using, then cutting it up and making a garment for some ragged urchin. This was her greatest delight.

Her sister soon revealed quite a different disposition. She had inherited many of her mother's qualities, showed promise quite early on of becoming very charming and attractive, and she seems to be fulfilling that expectation still, being very much concerned about her appearance and knowing how to dress and carry herself in a striking way. I can still remember the delight she showed as a little girl at looking at herself in a mirror when I put around her neck the lovely pearls my mother had bequeathed me, which she happened to find in my room.

As I observed these various characteristics in the children, I took pleasure in the thought that, after my death, my possessions would be divided amongst them and preserved by them. I could envision my father's guns passing through the fields on my nephew's back, and game hanging out of his hunting bag. I could see all my garments on the backs of little girls as they left church after their Easter confirmation, and my finest clothes on some modest burgher girl on her wedding day. For my niece Natalie took especial delight in decking out children and poor honest girls, though she herself showed no sign of love for, or need for attachment to, any visible or invisible being such as I had felt so strongly in my youth. When I thought that the youngest of the girls would be wearing my jewels and pearls at court, I was quite content to see my possessions, like my body, returned to the elements.

The children grew apace and to my delight they have become healthy, handsome human beings. I have borne with patience the fact that my uncle has kept them apart from me, and I do not see them very often when they are nearby or in town. A wonderful man, whom people take for a French abbé (though no one knows really where he comes from), has been entrusted with the supervision of all four children, who are being educated and provided for in different places. At first I could not perceive any plan or purpose in this education. But then the doctor informed me that the Abbé had convinced my uncle that, in order to promote a child's education, one must first find out where its desires and inclinations lie, and then enable it to satisfy those desires and further those inclinations as quickly as possible. If someone has chosen a wrong path, he can correct this before it is too late, and once he has found what suits him, stick to this firmly and develop more vigorously. I hope this strange experiment will succeed. Perhaps it may, with such good material.

But one thing I cannot condone about these educators, that they deprive children of anything that might lead to their communing with themselves and with their Invisible, and only true Friend. And I am often irritated with my uncle that for this reason he thinks I would be detrimental to the children. Nobody is really tolerant in practice, for however much someone may assure us that he is leaving a person to his own desires and inclinations, in effect he does all he can to exclude them from activities not acceptable to himself.

The manner in which these children are being kept away from me, is all the more distressing as my conviction increases of the reality of my faith. Why shouldn't this have a supernatural origin and a real, natural goal, seeing that it proves to be so effective in practice? Only through our practical activity do we become fully aware of our own individual existence; and why shouldn't we by this means demonstrate also to ourselves that there is a Being who gives us this power to do good?

Since I am always moving forward and never backward, since my actions are always drawing nearer and nearer to the idea of perfection which I have worked out for myself, and I find it easier every day to do what I think is right, despite my bodily infirmity that restricts me so much—is this accountable solely to human nature, whose corruption I have become so profoundly aware of? Not for me, at least.

I cannot recall having followed any commandment that loomed before me as a law imposed from without: I was always led and guided by impulse, freely following my own persuasion, and experiencing neither restriction nor regrets. Thanks be to God that I am fully aware to whom I owe my happiness, and can accept my good fortune in humility. For I will never be tempted to pride myself on my own ability and powers, having so clearly recognized the monster that grows and feeds in every human breast, if some higher power does not preserve us.

Book Seven

Chapter One

The spring had arrived in all its glory. An early thunderstorm, which had been threatening to break all day, rolled down the mountains, the rain moved into the valley, the sun burst forth again in splendor and a marvelous rainbow appeared against the dark grey background. Wilhelm rode up toward it and gazed at it with a feeling of sadness. "Why is it," he said, "that the brightest colors in life always appear against a dark background? Must raindrops, or tears, fall if we are to experience true joy? A bright day is no different from a gray one if we observe it unmoved. And what is it that moves us but the silent hope that the native desires of our hearts may not remain without objects to focus on? We are moved by the account of good deeds, the contemplation of harmonious objects, and as a result we feel that we are not completely adrift in this world, but are drawing nearer to some sort of destination toward which all that is deepest and best in us has long been impatiently tending."

Meanwhile a traveler had caught up with him, walking briskly up to his horse; and, after a few innocuous remarks, said to Wilhelm: "If I am not mistaken, I have met you somewhere before."

"I think so too," said Wilhelm. "Didn't we take part in an amusing river trip together?"

"That's right!" said the other.

Wilhelm looked at him more closely, and, after a few moments of silence, said: "I don't know how it is that you have changed. At the time I thought you were a Lutheran pastor, but now you look more like a Catholic priest."

"This time, at any rate, you are not mistaken," said the man, taking off his hat and revealing the tonsure. "But where has your theatrical company gone to? Did you stay with them for a long while?"

"Longer than I should have. Unfortunately, when I think back on the time I spent with them, I seem to be peering into an unending void. Nothing about it means anything to me anymore."

"You're wrong about that. Everything that happens to us leaves its traces, everything contributes imperceptibly to our development. But it is dangerous to try to draw up a balance sheet, for in doing so we become either proud and carefree, or depressed and discouraged, and the one is as bad as the other in its results. The safest thing remains to concentrate on what lies immediately ahead; and that, for the moment," he added with a smile, "is to make sure we find quarters for the night."

Wilhelm asked him how far it was to Lothario's estate, and he said it was just over the hill. "Then perhaps I'll see you there," he said. "I still have a few errands to do in the neighborhood. So goodbye for now!" With these words he hastened up a steep path, which seemed the shortest way over the hill.

"He's certainly right," said Wilhelm as he rode along. "One should think of the first thing one has to do, and for me nothing is more pressing than to deliver the sad message I am charged with. Let's just see if I can still remember my speech to put this cruel man to shame!"

He began to recite to himself his work of art. He could recall every word of it, and the more his memory was activated, the more his boldness and passion increased. Aurelie's sufferings and death were still very much in his mind.

"Spirit of my beloved friend!" he cried. "Draw nigh and give me a sign, if you can, that you are pacified and reconciled!"

With such words and thoughts he reached the top of the hill and observed on the other side a strange looking building which he immediately decided must be Lothario's residence. Originally it had been an irregular building with turrets and gables; but even more irregular were the later additions, some close by and others at a distance, connected with the main building by galleries and covered walks. All external symmetry and architectural distinction seemed to have been sacrificed to considerations of domestic comfort. There was no sign of ramparts or moats, nor of formal gardens or broad allées. An orchard and kitchen garden ran right up to the buildings, and there were other small domestic gardens set in between. A cheerful looking village was to be seen nearby; all gardens and fields seemed to be in very good condition.

Wilhelm rode on, immersed in his own impassioned reflections and hence not thinking much about what he saw around him, stabled his horse at an inn, and proceeded without further ado to the castle.

An old retainer received him at the door and informed him very politely that he would hardly be able to see the master of the household that day, because he had lots of letters to write and had already sent away several tradesmen. Wilhelm pressed him further and finally the old man gave in, and reported Wilhelm's arrival to his master. He came back and conducted Wilhelm into a large, ancient hall, asking him to be patient for a while because it might be some time before his master would be able to see him. Wilhelm walked restlessly up and down, casting a few glances at the lords and ladies whose pictures were hanging on the walls. He repeated to himself the beginning of his speech, and it seemed to him more appropriate than ever in the presence of all these people in armor and high-standing collars. Whenever he heard a noise he took up position so as to be ready to receive his adversary

with suitable dignity, hand him the letter and then assail him with a whole
battery of reproaches.

After several false alarms he was beginning to get cross and dispirited, when
in through a side door came a good-looking man in topboots and an unostenta-
tious surtout. "What good news do you bring me?" he said in a kindly tone of
voice to Wilhelm. "I'm sorry to have kept you waiting so long."

As he said this he was folding a letter that he held in his hand. Wilhelm,
somewhat nonplussed, handed him Aurelie's communication, saying: "I bring
you the last words of a lady friend of yours which will not leave you unmoved."

Lothario took the letter and went back to his room where, as Wilhelm could
see through the open door, he first addressed and sealed a few more letters,
then opened Aurelie's and read it. He apparently read it through several times,
and Wilhelm, though he felt that the pathos of his speech hardly suited the
unpretentiousness of his reception, nevertheless got ready to deliver his oration and was walking up to the dividing door when in from a door in the wall
came the priest.

"I have just received the strangest message," said Lothario to the Abbé, and
then, turning to Wilhelm, he said: "Excuse me if I am at the moment not in the
mood to talk further with you. Do stay the night here with us! And would you
please, Abbé, look after our guest and see that he has all he needs." With this
he bowed to Wilhelm, and the priest took Wilhelm by the hand, who readily
followed him.

Silently they walked along strange looking passageways and finally arrived
in a very pleasant room. The priest ushered him in, and left without further
explanation. Soon after this a bright young boy appeared, announced that he
was to wait on Wilhelm, and brought him his supper; and while he was serving
this he told him a good deal about the arrangements of the household, how one
took breakfast and the other meals, the division between work and recreation,
and much else that redounded to the praise of Lothario.

Pleasant as the boy was, Wilhelm was anxious to get rid of him. He wanted
to be alone, for he felt stifled and oppressed by his present situation; he
reproached himself for having carried out his intentions so inefficiently and
only delivering half his message. One moment he was determined to communicate the rest on the very next day, but then he realized that Lothario had
aroused quite unexpected feelings in him. The house in which he found himself was so very strange, that he could not adapt himself to these conditions.
He decided to undress, opened his rucksack and, taking out his nightclothes,
found the Ghost's veil, which Mignon had packed along with the other things.
The sight of this aggravated the melancholy of the mood he was in. "Flee,
young man, flee!" He repeated the words to himself, then thought: "What are
these mysterious words supposed to mean? What should I flee? Where to? It
would have been better if the Ghost had said: 'Return to yourself!'" He looked
at the engravings on the wall, finding them mostly not worthy of his attention;
but one of them depicted a shipwreck with a father and two beautiful daughters

awaiting death from the encroaching waves. One of the daughters bore a certain resemblance to the Amazon. Wilhelm was overwhelmed by a sense of pity, he felt an irrepressible need to open up his heart, tears burst from his eyes, and he could not contain himself until sleep overcame him.

Strange dream visions overcame him toward morning. He found himself in a garden where he had often been as a child, and joyfully recognized the familiar hedgerows, walks, and flowerbeds. Mariane came up to him, he spoke tenderly to her, without any reference to the past disturbance of their relationship. Then his father appeared, in his housecoat, and, with more than customary friendliness, asked his son to bring up two garden chairs, took Mariane's hand and led her to an arbor. Wilhelm went to the conservatory to fetch the chairs, but found it empty. He did, however, see Aurelie standing at a nearby window. He went up to speak to her, but her back was turned, and although he went and stood next to her, he could not see her face. He looked out of the window, and, in another garden, he saw a group of people, some of whom he immediately recognized: Madame Melina was sitting beneath a tree, toying with a rose that she held in her hand, Laertes stood beside her counting out money from one hand into the other. Mignon and Felix were lying in the grass, she stretched out on her back, he lying face downward. Philine came up and clapped her hands above the children's heads. Mignon did not move, but Felix jumped up and ran away from Philine. At first he was laughing as he ran and Philine chased him, but suddenly he cried out in fear as the Harper pursued him with long, slow strides. He ran straight up to a pond, Wilhelm rushed after him, but too late to reach him before he had fallen into the water. Wilhelm stood rooted to the spot. Then he saw the beauteous Amazon on the other side of the pond. She stretched out her right hand toward the child and went to the bank. The child moved through the water in the direction of her extended finger, and followed her as she went, until she reached and pulled him out of the pond. Meanwhile, Wilhelm had drawn nearer, the child was burning all over, and drops of fire were falling off him. Wilhelm became more and more alarmed, but the Amazon quickly took a white veil from off her head and covered the child. The fire was soon quenched, and when she lifted up the veil, two boys jumped up and played mischievously with each other while Wilhelm and the Amazon walked hand in hand through the garden. He could see his father strolling with Mariane way off, in an allée with tall trees which seemed to encircle the whole garden. He directed his path in their direction, was walking right across the garden with his lovely companion, when suddenly the blond Friedrich stood in their path and blocked their progress, with raucous laughter and all sorts of foolery. Despite this, they insisted on continuing on their path, so he hurried away toward the other, more distant couple. But his father and Mariane seemed to be running away from him, he ran faster and faster after them, and they seemed to Wilhelm to be soaring through the trees in flight. Impulse and desire impelled him to go to their assistance, but the Amazon's hand held him back — and how gladly he let himself be held! And so, with this mixed feeling, he woke up and found his room brightly lit by the morning sun.

Chapter Two

The boy summoned Wilhelm to breakfast. The Abbé was already there, and said he had heard that Lothario had gone out for a ride. The Abbé himself was pensive and not very talkative, but he did ask after the circumstances of Aurelie's death, and listened with interest and compassion to Wilhelm's account. "Alas!" he said, "for someone who is deeply concerned about how infinitely complicated the operations of nature and art must be to produce a cultured human being, and himself has done all he can to educate his fellowmen, it is enough to make one despair, when one sees how wantonly a person can destroy herself, or be destroyed with or without being responsible. When I reflect on that, then life seems to me such a casual gift that I would approve of anyone who does not value it too highly."

He had just finished speaking, when the door burst open and a young woman came rushing in, pushing aside the old manservant who had tried to stop her. She tore up to the Abbé and, grasping him by the arm, was hardly able to speak for weeping and sobbing, but did manage to blurt out: "Where is he? Where have you put him? This is outrageous treachery! Admit it! I know what you're up to! But I'm determined to get him, and I want to know where he is."

"Calm yourself, my child," said the Abbé, with affected composure. "Go to your room. You shall be told everything in due course. But you must be in a position to listen when I do tell you." He offered her his hand, intending to escort her out of the room. "I won't go to my room," she cried. "I hate these walls within which you have kept me a prisoner so long. But I've found out everything. The colonel has challenged him to a duel and he has ridden out to meet him, and perhaps at this very moment . . . Several times I thought I could hear the sound of shooting. Harness the horses, and ride out with me, or I'll fill the whole house and the whole village with my cries." Weeping bitterly, she rushed up to the window. The Abbé restrained her and tried to calm her.

A carriage was heard arriving. She opened the window and cried: "He's dead! They're bringing him back." "He's getting out of the carriage," said the Abbé. "He's alive, you see." "He's wounded," she replied anxiously, "otherwise he would have come on horseback. They're bringing him in. He is gravely wounded!" She ran out of the door and down the steps, the Abbé rushing after her and Wilhelm following behind. He saw the lovely girl greet the arrival of her lover.

Lothario, leaning on a companion whom Wilhelm recognized as his old acquaintance Jarno, spoke kindly and lovingly to the disconsolate girl; then, supporting himself on her, he walked slowly up the steps, greeted Wilhelm, and was then led to his room.

Soon after this Jarno came out and walked up to Wilhelm. "It seems," he said, "that you are predestined to encounter actors and theater everywhere you go. We are in the midst of a drama that is not precisely amusing."

"I am glad," replied Wilhelm, "to see you again in these peculiar circumstances. I am puzzled and frightened, and your presence will bring me calm and composure. Tell me, is there any danger? Is the baron seriously wounded?" "I don't think so," Jarno replied.

After a short while a young surgeon came out of the room. "Well, what do you think?" Jarno asked him. "It is very serious," he said, replacing his instruments in a leather case. Wilhelm noticed a ribbon hanging out of the case, which seemed familiar to him. Bright contrasting colors, a strange pattern of gold and silver in curious shapes, this distinguished the ribbon from all others he had ever seen. Wilhelm was convinced that these instruments were those of the old surgeon who had tended his wounds in the forest, and the hope of finally discovering some trace of the Amazon brought new life to his whole being.

"Where did you get that case?" he cried. "Who owned it before you? Please tell me." "I bought it at an auction," the man said. "What does it matter to whom it belonged?" He moved away as he spoke, and Jarno said: "If only that young fellow would speak the truth!" "Then he didn't buy the case at an auction?" said Wilhelm. "Right!" said Jarno. "That's as far from the truth as Lothario's being in danger."

Wilhelm was still immersed in a host of thoughts, when Jarno asked him how things had been going with him. He told him in general terms, and when he got to Aurelie's death and the message he was bearing, Jarno exclaimed: "But that is very strange!"

The Abbé emerged from the room, signalled to Jarno to take his place, and then said to Wilhelm: "The baron requests that you stay here for a few days more to enrich the company and enliven him in his present circumstances. If you need to send any message to your relatives, your letter will be immediately dispatched, and so that you may understand the strange occurrence which you have been witness to, I have to tell you something that is not really a secret. The baron has had a little adventure with a lady, which has attracted more attention than it should have, because she was too eager to relish the triumph of having snatched him from a rival. Unfortunately, after some time he did not find her as amusing as he had, and he avoided her, but she with her passionate temperament was not able to reconcile herself to what had happened. There was a violent and public disagreement at a ball, she considered herself gravely insulted and wanted revenge, but no knight was there to defend her, until her husband, from whom she had long been separated, heard about the affair, took her part, challenged the baron to a duel, and has wounded him today. But the colonel, as I have heard, fared even worse."

From this time on our hero was treated like a member of the family.

Chapter Three

The invalid was read to several times, and Wilhelm was happy to do him this small service. The young woman, whose name was Lydie, would not leave his bedside, her care of the wounded man engaging all her attention. Lothario seemed distracted too and asked not to be read to any longer.

"Today," he said, "I feel so strongly how stupidly people let time pass. There are so many things I have been intending to do, so many plans I have thought about, and yet one procrastinates, even regarding one's very best intentions! I have read the proposals for the changes I wish to introduce on my estates, and I can truly say that I am glad that the bullet did not take a more dangerous route."

Lydie looked at him affectionately, even with tears in her eyes, as if she wanted to know whether she and his friends could not assist in increasing his pleasure in living. But Jarno answered: "Changes such as you have in mind are best first considered from every angle before one makes a decision."

"Lengthy consideration usually indicates that one has not clearly visualized the point at issue, and hasty actions that one does not even know what it is," said Lothario. "It is quite apparent to me that, in many matters concerning the management of my estates, I cannot do without the services of my farmhands, and also that I must rigidly insist on certain rights; but it is also clear to me that certain dispositions, though advantageous to me, are not absolutely essential, and some of them could be changed for the benefit of my workers. One doesn't always lose by giving up something. Am I making better use of my estates than my father? Will I be able to increase my revenues? And should I alone derive all the extra profit from this? Should I not grant advantages to those who work with me and for me, from the greater knowledge that our progressive era has provided us with?"

"That's how we human beings are!" said Jarno, "and I do not reproach myself for observing the same characteristic in myself. We want to acquire all we can, in order to be able to dispose of it as we wish, and money that we do not expend ourselves, always seems ill spent."

"Yes, indeed," replied Lothario. "We could do without much of our capital, if we did not so arbitrarily dispose of the interest."

"There is one thing I have to remind you of," said Jarno, "and that is why I would advise you not to proceed with the alterations right now. These would result in temporary losses. You still have debts, and repaying these will restrict you. I would therefore advise you to postpone your plans until you are completely in the clear."

"And meanwhile leave it to a bullet or a rooftile to destroy the results of my life and activity for ever? My dear fellow, that is one of the major mistakes of all educated persons: they refer everything to an idea, very rarely to a specific object. Why did I run up debts? Why did I break with my uncle and leave my siblings to look after themselves, except to follow an idea? In America I thought I could achieve something, I felt I was needed overseas, and could be useful there — if action was not accompanied by danger, it seemed to me unimportant, not worth doing. But now I see things differently: What is nearest at hand, seems to me now most important and most desirable."

"I well remember the letter you sent me from overseas," said Jarno. "You wrote: 'I will return, and in my own house, my own orchard, in the midst of my own people, I will say: *Here, or nowhere, is America!*'"

"Yes, my friend, and I still say the same," Lothario responded. "But at the same time I reproach myself for not being as active here as I was over there. To achieve some sort of steady existence, all we need is reasonableness, and we become the embodiment of reasonableness and nothing else, when we do not perceive the abnormal demands that every normal day exacts from us, or even if we do, we make a thousand excuses not to meet these demands. Reasonableness is fine for one's self, but not of much value for the community."

"Let's not discredit reasonableness too much, for we should recognize that when something extraordinary occurs, it is usually foolish."

"Yes, but that is because men do extraordinary things without respecting orderliness. Take, for instance, my brother-in-law, who has given all the money he could realize to the Herrnhut brethren, in the belief of thereby furthering his salvation. By disposing of just a small part of his income, he could have made many people happy and secured for himself and them a heaven on earth. Our sacrifices rarely represent a personal impulse, for by renouncing what is ours and giving it to others, we are acting out of despair, not from conscious determination: all we are doing is relieving ourselves of the weight of our possessions. I must confess that, during these last few days, I have constantly had the count in my mind, and I have firmly decided to do out of conviction what he is doing from fear and delusion. I shall not wait until I am well again. The papers are here, all we need is fair copies. Let the magistrate help you. Our guest will help you too. You know as well as I do what the issue is; and I will lie here, recovering or dying, and proclaim: *Here, or nowhere, is Herrnhut!*"

When Lydie heard her friend mention dying, she flung herself down beside his bed, hung over him, and wept bitterly. The surgeon came back; Jarno gave Wilhelm the papers, and persuaded Lydie to leave.

"For Heaven's sake," said Wilhelm when he and Jarno were alone in the hall, "what is all this about the count? What count is it who is joining Herrnhut?"

"The one you know full well," Jarno replied. "You yourself are the ghost that drove him into the arms of religion. You are the villain who reduced his nice wife to a state where she finds it tolerable to follow her husband."

"Is she then Lothario's sister?" Wilhelm asked.

"Yes, she is."

"And does Lothario know . . . ?"

"Everything."

"Let me get out of here!" Wilhelm cried; "how can I possibly face him? What can he possibly say?"

"That no one should cast stones and no one should compose long speeches to put others to shame, unless he delivers them before a mirror."

"You know that too?"

"And a good deal more," said Jarno with a smile. "But this time I won't let go of you so easily, and you need have no more fear of my trying to make you enlist. I'm not a soldier anymore, and even when I was, I should not have aroused such suspicions in you. Since I last saw you, a lot has changed. After the death of my friend and benefactor, the prince, I withdrew from society and all worldly relationships. I took pleasure in furthering what was reasonable, and did not keep silent when I thought something was absurd. As a result I gained the reputation of having a restless mind and a malicious tongue. There is nothing more feared by the general mass of human beings than shrewdness; they should fear stupidity, if only they knew how fearful that is. But shrewdness is uncomfortable and to be avoided, whereas stupidity is simply destructive, and one can wait out its results. But let that pass. I have what it takes, and I'll tell you more about what I am planning. You shall participate in this, if you wish. But tell me, how have things been with you? I can see; indeed I can sense that you too have changed. How is it now with that old fancy of yours of achieving something good and beautiful in the company of gypsies?"

"I've suffered enough for that!" Wilhelm exclaimed. "Don't remind me where I came from and where I am tending. People talk a lot about the theater, but unless one has been on the stage oneself, one cannot conceive what it is like. How ignorant actors are of themselves, how utterly thoughtless they are in the conduct of their work, how exorbitant their demands are—no one has any idea. Every one of them wants to be first and foremost and exclude all the others. None of them understands that by this means he and the others cannot hope to achieve much. They all think they are absolutely unique, but in fact they are totally unable to do anything that is not mere routine, though they are always restless and clamoring for something new. They work strenuously against each other, and yet a modicum of self-interest and self-love would suffice to bring them together again. One cannot speak of any mutual behavior toward each other, for constant mistrust is kept up by hidden malice and slanderous talk. Those who don't live a loose life, live foolishly. They all make claim to the utmost respect and are sensitive to the slightest blame. The one knew better than the other what was right: why then did he do the opposite? They are always lacking something, have no confidence in anyone or anything, and it seems as though what they most retreat from is reasonableness and good taste, and what they most strive after is the unlimited exercise of their own arbitrary desires."

Wilhelm paused before continuing his oration, and Jarno broke in with riotous laughter. "Those poor actors," he cried, throwing himself on to a chair,
and still laughing, "those poor, dear actors! Don't you realize," he went on,
once he had recovered, "don't you realize that you have been describing the
whole world, not just the theater? I could provide you with characters and
actions from all classes of society for your savage brushstrokes. Forgive me,
but I must continue to laugh at your belief that these fine qualities are limited
to the stage."

Wilhelm composed himself, for Jarno's uncontrolled, ill-timed laughter had
quite disconcerted him. "You can't conceal your dislike of the human race if
you assert that these faults are to be found everywhere." "And you," Jarno
countered, "show your ignorance of the world if you place such heavy responsibility for them on the theater. I would gladly excuse an actor for any fault
that arose from self-deception and a desire to please, for if he does not appear
as something to himself and others, he is nothing at all. His job is to provide
appearances, and he must needs set high store on instantaneous approval, for
he gets none other. He must try to delude and dazzle, for that's what he's
there for."

"Please allow me now to smile," Wilhelm replied. "I would never have
thought that you could be so reasonable and considerate."

"In all seriousness, that is my opinion," said Jarno. "I can readily forgive an
actor all the human failings, but not humans for an actor's failings. But don't
let me start intoning my lamentations about that: my objections would be
much more vehement than yours."

At this point the surgeon came out of Lothario's room and, on being asked
how he was, he said: "Pretty well. I hope to have him fully recovered soon."
He then rushed out without Wilhelm being able to ask him once more and this
time more eagerly about the bag in which he carried his instruments. The
desire to find out more about the Amazon gave Wilhelm more confidence in
talking to Jarno, to whom he explained what he wanted to know and asked for
his assistance. "You already know so much," he said to Jarno, "couldn't you
find that out for me?"

Jarno thought for a moment and then said: "Be patient and don't trouble
yourself any more. We'll get on her trail. But for the moment it is Lothario's
situation that concerns me. His condition is serious—I gather that from
the politeness and encouragement of the surgeon. I would like to get Lydie
out of the way, for she is not doing any good, but I don't know how to set
about that. Our old physician is coming tonight, I hope. Then we can discuss
what next to do."

Chapter Four

The old physician arrived. He was the good little doctor we already know, the
one who delivered to us that interesting manuscript. He came primarily to

examine Lothario, and he seemed not at all satisfied with his condition. He had a long talk with Jarno, but neither of them made any reference to this when they appeared at dinner.

Wilhelm welcomed him most cordially and inquired after the Harper. "We still have some hope," said the doctor, "of effecting a recovery for that poor, unhappy creature." "That man was a sorrowful addition to your strange and restricted existence," said Jarno. "What happened to him later? Do tell me."

After Jarno's curiosity had been satisfied, the doctor continued: "I have never witnessed a mind in such a peculiar state. For many years now he has not taken the slightest interest in anything outside of himself, even to the point of not noticing much at all. Completely shut up in himself, all he looked at was his own hollow and empty self, which was a bottomless pit for him. How touching it was when he spoke of his sorry state! 'I see nothing before me, and nothing behind me,' he would say, 'nothing but the endless night of loneliness in which I find myself. I have no feeling left, except that of my guilt, but even that is only a distant, shapeless ghost that lurks behind my back. There is no height or depth, no forwards or backwards, nothing to describe this continual sameness. Sometimes I cry out: "forever, forever!" in the face of this terrifying indifference, and that strange, meaningless word is a beacon of light in the darkness of my condition. No gleam of any godhead comes to me in this continual blackness, my tears are shed all for myself and because of myself. There is nothing more horrifying to me than friendship and love: for these evoke in me the wish that the phantoms surrounding me might be real. But even these two specters from the abyss have only risen to torment me and rob me finally of my own precious consciousness of my monstrous existence.'

"You should hear how he unburdens his heart like this in his moments of confidentiality," the doctor continued. "Several times I have been deeply moved in listening to him. When something happens that compels him for a moment to realize that time has passed, he seems astonished at this, but then rejects whatever change has occurred as simply one more phantom. One evening he sang a song about his grey hair; and we all sat there and wept."

"Oh, do get the song for me!" Wilhelm cried.

"But," said Jarno, "have you not been able to find out something about what he calls his 'crime,' the reasons for his strange garb, his behavior during the fire and his frenzied rage at the child?"

"We have only been able to make surmises about his life story: direct questioning would be against our principles. Since we have observed that he had a Catholic upbringing, we thought we might gain some relief for him by suggesting he go to confession. But every time we try to get him to go to a priest, he avoids this in the strangest manner. Since, however, I do not wish to leave your request for more information about him completely unanswered, I will tell you what we surmise. He spent his early years in the priesthood, which is why he still wears his long gown and will not shave his beard. The joys of love were foreign to him for most of his life, but later it may be that some episode with a woman closely related to him, and possibly her death at the birth of some unfortunate creature, completely destroyed his mind.

"His strongest delusion is that he brings misfortune wherever he goes and that he will die at the hands of an innocent boy. At first he was afraid of Mignon, until he found out that she was a girl; then he became terrified of Felix, and since, despite all his misery, he passionately loves life, his dislike of the boy seems to have come from this delusion."

"What hope, then, do you have of his recovery?" Wilhelm asked.

"Things are developing slowly, but not backwards," the doctor replied. "He continues in his specific occupations, and we have accustomed him to reading newspapers, which he now looks forward to with great eagerness."

"I would be curious to see his songs," said Jarno.

"I will bring you some of them," said the doctor. "The pastor's eldest son, who always makes transcripts of his father's sermons, has written down several verses and put them together into songs without the old man noticing."

The next morning Jarno came to see Wilhelm and said: "You must do us a favor. Lydie must be removed from here for a while. Her violent and, I may say, inconvenient passion is impeding the baron's recovery. His wound is such that he needs peace and quiet, even though, with his good health, it is not dangerous. You have observed how Lydie torments him with her vigorous ministrations, uncontrollable anxiety and unceasing tears and—well, the doctor expressly demands that she leave the house for a while," he added with a smile. "We have pretended that a certain woman, with whom she is very friendly, is staying in the neighborhood, wants to see her, and is expecting her visit any day. Lydie has been persuaded to go the magistrate, who lives only two hours' drive from here. He is informed of the situation and will express his regrets that Miss Therese has just left. He will probably pretend that one might still be able to catch up with her, and Lydie will hurry off and, if luck is with us, she will be directed on from one place to another. When she finally insists on returning here, she should not be thwarted. Darkness will aid our purposes, and the coachman is a smart fellow with whom one can come to an agreement. What you have to do, is seat yourself beside her in the carriage, entertain her, and manage the whole adventure."

"You are giving me a strange and highly dubious assignment," Wilhelm replied. "Frustrated true love is a troublesome thing. And should I be the instrument to prolong its anguish? Never in my whole life have I deceived anyone in this way. For my view has always been that to engage in deceit, even for good or useful purposes, can lead us too far."

"But how can we educate children except by this means?" said Jarno.

"That may be all right with children," said Wilhelm, "if we love them dearly and watch over them carefully. But with people of our own age, especially when they do not always appeal so loudly for forbearance, it may often turn out to be dangerous. But," he continued after a moment's reflection, "don't conclude from this that I decline this obligation. The respect that I have for your intelligence, my affection for your friend and my desire to hasten his recovery by whatever means, will encourage me to forget myself. It is not enough to risk one's life for a friend; one must, if needs be, disclaim one's convictions for his sake. We are obliged to abandon our deepest feelings and desires on his account. I will accept this commission, though I foresee the anguish I will have to suffer from Lydie's tears and desperation."

"On the other hand," said Jarno, "you will experience no small recompense by getting to know Therese, a woman with few like her. She would put a hundred men to shame, and I would call her a real Amazon, whereas others who go around like her in ambiguous clothing are nothing but dainty hermaphrodites."

Wilhelm was struck by this remark. He now hoped to find his Amazon in Therese, especially since Jarno, from whom he tried to find out more, broke off what he was saying, and hurried away.

This new, impending expectation of seeing once more the person he so much loved and adored, aroused within him the strangest perturbations. He now interpreted the assignment given him as an express indication of providential guidance, and the fact that he was perfidiously about to separate a poor girl from the object of her devoted, impassioned love became just a fleeting consideration, like the shadow of a bird passing over the brightness of the earth.

The carriage stood ready. Lydie hesitated for a moment before getting into it, and said to the old retainer: "Give my greetings once more to your master, and tell him I will be back before evening." There were tears in her eyes as she once again looked back while they were leaving. Then she composed herself, and turning to Wilhelm, she said: "You will find Therese a very interesting person. I am surprised that she is here in this area, for you must know that she and the baron were deeply in love with each other. Despite the distance, Lothario used to go to see her frequently. I was with her at the time, and it seemed that they could not live without each other. Then things suddenly went wrong, without anyone knowing why. Lothario had got to know me, and I cannot deny that I was really jealous of Therese, did not conceal my affection for him, and did not discourage him when he seemed suddenly to prefer me to her. She behaved toward me in a manner that I could not have wished better, despite the fact that it seemed almost as if I was robbing her of a worthy lover. This love of mine has cost me so many tears and so much suffering! At first we met only occasionally and furtively in some neutral place, but I could not put up with that sort of life for long: I was only happy, only truly happy, when I was with him. When I was separated from him, my eyes filled with tears and my pulse raced. Once he was absent for several days, and I was frantic, started out after him, and surprised him here. He received me affectionately, and if that wretched business had not intervened, I would have had a glorious life. But what I've suffered since he has been in danger, I cannot describe; and even at this very moment I am thoroughly reproachful of myself for having left him for just a day."

Wilhelm was about to ask her more about Therese when they arrived at the magistrate's house. The magistrate came out and expressed deep regret that Therese had already left. He offered the travelers some breakfast, and added that they should be able to catch up with her carriage in the next village. It was decided therefore to go straight on, and the coachman did not waste any time. But they passed through several villages without seeing a sign of her. Lydie then insisted they should turn back. But the coachman went on, as though he had not understood. Finally she demanded, this time with great firmness, that they must go back. Wilhelm called to the coachman, giving him the sign they had agreed on. He replied: "We don't need to take the same road back, I know a shortcut which will be much more convenient." He then drove off to the side through a forest over long tracts of meadowland. At length, since no familiar place came into view, he confessed that he had unfortunately lost his way, but said he would soon know where he was, once they reached the next village. Night began to fall, and the coachman managed things well by constantly asking directions but never waiting for the answers. So they rode the whole night long, and Lydie never closed an eyelid. She kept seeing familiar things in the moonlight, but they immediately disappeared. In the morning things seemed more familiar, and all the more unexpectedly so. The carriage stopped before a small, nicely built house. A woman came out and opened the carriage door. Lydie stared at her, looked around, stared at the woman again, then fell senseless in Wilhelm's arms.

Chapter Five

Wilhelm was shown into an upstairs room. The house was new, quite small, and extremely tidy and clean. It was Therese who had welcomed him and Lydie as they got out of the carriage, but she turned out not to be his Amazon: she was a totally different person. She was well built, though not tall, moved about very briskly, and her bright, blue eyes seemed to take in everything that was happening.

She came into Wilhelm's room and asked if there was anything he needed. "Forgive me for putting you in a room that still smells of paint," she said, "but my little house is only just finished, and you are inaugurating this room, which is intended for my guests. If only there were a more agreeable reason for your being here! Poor Lydie will not give us a very easy time, and in addition I must crave your indulgence because my cook has just left my service at this very inconvenient time, and one of my menservants has crushed his hand. This means that I shall have to do everything myself, but so long as you all accept this, it should be all right. There is no greater plague than servants. They never want to do what they are employed for, not even for themselves." She said a good deal more about other matters. She seemed altogether to enjoy talking. Wilhelm asked after Lydie, and whether he could see her and make his excuses.

"That won't have any effect on her at the moment," said Therese. "Time will make the excuses, and bring her consolation. Words are of little value in such cases. Lydie does not wish to see you. 'Don't let him come anywhere near me,' she was saying when I left her. 'I almost despair of humanity—such an honest face, such openness and sincerity of behavior but secretly so full of guile!' Lothario is totally exculpated: he said in a letter that it was his friends who persuaded him, forced him, to do this. And Lydie counts you amongst these 'friends,' and condemns you with the rest."

"She does me far too great an honor by placing the blame on me," said Wilhelm. "I cannot yet claim to enjoy the friendship of that excellent man: at the moment I am just an innocent tool. I don't approve of what I did, but still I was able to do it. We were all concerned about the health, even whether he would remain alive, of this man whom I respect more highly than anyone I have ever met. What a man he is, and what persons he has gathered around him! Believe me: In this company I have, for the first time, had a real conversation, and for the first time in my life I find my own words returned to me, enriched from the mouth of another—richer, fuller and endowed with greater import. What I had dimly sensed, suddenly became clear to me, and I learned how to see what I had thought. Unfortunately this pleasurable state was interrupted by concern and moodiness, and finally cut short by this disagreeable assignment. I took it upon myself in complete seriousness, for I thought it was my duty, even against my own feelings, to discharge my obligation to this admirable group of people."

Therese had been observing her guest in a sympathetic manner as he spoke. "Oh, how sweet it is," she declared, "to hear one's own convictions voiced by another. We only really become ourselves when someone else thoroughly agrees with us. I have exactly the same feeling about Lothario as you do. People do not always do him justice, but all those who are closely acquainted with him, are infatuated with him; and even in my case, where painful feelings are associated with his memory, I cannot resist thinking about him every day of my life." A deep sigh and a becoming tear accompanied her words. "Don't think I am so easily moved to softness!" she said. "It's only my eye that sheds the tear. There is a little wart on the lower lid, it has been treated, but the eye is somewhat weakened by this, and tears appear at the slightest provocation. This is where the wart was. You can't see any trace of it now."

Indeed he could not; but he did look straight into her eye which was clear as crystal. He felt he was looking into the very depths of her soul.

"Well," she said, "we've both found the password for a relationship. Let's deepen it as soon as possible. The history of every human being lies in his character. Let me tell you my life story; and please grant me the same favor, so that we may remain in contact with each other even when we are apart. The world is so empty if we think of it just as a collection of mountains, rivers and cities; but to find someone somewhere who sees eye to eye with us, someone with whom we can continue to commune in silence, makes the whole world into a populated garden."

She tore herself away, promising to fetch him soon for a walk. Her presence had affected Wilhelm very favorably, and he longed to know more about her relationship with Lothario. Eventually he received a summons from her, and she came out of her room to meet him.

They went down the steep, narrow steps, and then she said: "These steps could be wider and bigger if I had listened to your generous friend's proposal, but to remain worthy of him I had to preserve that part of myself which he so valued in me. Where is the steward?" she asked, when she had reached the bottom of the steps. "You must not think I am so rich that I need a steward. I can myself well look after the few fields that my little estate contains. The steward belongs to my new neighbor who has bought a fine estate, which I know inside out. The dear old man is afflicted with gout, and all his helpers are new to this area. So I am happy to help them get things organized."

They took a walk through fields, pastures and orchards. Therese instructed the steward on everything, explaining every detail, and Wilhelm had good cause to marvel at her knowledge, precision, and ability to suggest ways of dealing with every problem that came up. She never wasted time in getting to the essential point, and each problem was soon settled. "Give your master my best wishes," she said, as the man was leaving. "I will come and see him as soon as I can, and I hope he will soon be fully recovered." When the steward had left, she turned to Wilhelm with a smile, and said: "As a matter of fact, I could get rich quickly, if I so desired; for my dear neighbor would not be disinclined to marry me."

"An old man with gout?" said Wilhelm. "I cannot imagine how you at your age could embrace such a counsel of despair?" "I am not tempted in that direction!" Therese replied. "One is rich if one knows how to manage what one has. Being wealthy is a burdensome affair, if one does not understand what it entails."

Wilhelm expressed his amazement at her managerial abilities. "Definite inclination, early opportunities, external impetus and continuous occupation in useful pursuits make all sorts of things possible in this world of ours," said Therese, " and once you have learnt what instigated me in these matters, you will not be so surprised at this seemingly unusual talent of mine."

When they returned to the house, she let him into her garden, which was so tiny that he could hardly turn around in it, so narrow were the walks and so thickly planted the beds. He had to smile when they walked back through the courtyard, for there was the firewood all neatly cut, split and stacked crosswise, as if it were part of the building. All the receptacles were clean and in place, the little house was painted red and white and amusing to look at. Everything that handiwork could produce, all with good proportions but made to serve the purpose, to last and to delight, seemed to be assembled here. His dinner was brought to his room, and he had ample time to collect his impressions. He was especially struck by the fact that here, once again, he had met a very interesting person who was closely associated with Lothario. "It is understandable," he said to himself, "that a man of the quality of Lothario should attract such admirable women! Manly dignity has far-reaching effects! It's a pity, however, that there are those who get short shrift in the process. Go ahead, say what it is that you are afraid of: should you one day discover your Amazon, that being above all beings, she will, despite all your hopes and dreams, probably turn out, to your shame and humiliation, to be—his bride."

Chapter Six

Wilhelm had been spending a restless afternoon, and was somewhat bored, when, toward evening, his door was opened and in came a comely young huntsman who saluted and said: "Well, shall we go for a walk?" Wilhelm instantly recognized Therese by her lovely eyes.

"Excuse this costume, which, unfortunately, is at the moment only a costume. But since I intend to tell you about the days when I preferred to see myself in this garb, I want to recall that time as visibly as I possibly can. Come along! Let's go to the place where we used to rest from all our hunting and walks, and that will add to the picture."

They walked off, and, as they went, Therese said: "It's not right that you should just let me talk. You know enough about me already, but I know nothing about you. Tell me something about yourself, while I am gathering strength to tell you about my life and my situation." "Unfortunately," said Wilhelm, "I have nothing to relate except one mistake after another, one false step after the other, and I cannot think of anybody I would rather not tell about the constant confusion I was and still am in, than you. Your appearance, your whole nature, and everything around you, show that you have reason to be satisfied with the life you have led, its clear and steady progress, with no time wasted, and no regrets to labor over."

Therese smiled, and said: "We must wait and see if you still think the same when you have heard my story." They walked on, and after some general remarks had passed between them, she asked him: "Are you unattached?" "I believe so," said Wilhelm, "but I wish I wasn't." "Fine!" she said. "That suggests a complicated romance, and shows me that you do have something to relate."

During this exchange they climbed up to the top of the hill and sat down beneath a large oak tree that cast its shade all around. "Here beneath this German tree," said Therese, "I will tell you the tale of a German maiden. Listen carefully.

"My father was a wealthy nobleman of this province, a clear-sighted, industrious, upright man, loving father, reliable friend, and generous host, whose only fault in my eyes was that he was too easy on his wife, who did not properly appreciate him. I regret having to say that about my own mother. Her personality was the very opposite of his. She was impulsive, erratic, with no concern for her household nor love for me, her only child. She was extravagant, but beautiful, witty, full of all sorts of talents, the delight of the circle she gathered around herself. Her circle was certainly never large, or did not remain so for long, and it consisted mainly of men, for no woman felt comfortable in her presence, and she could not tolerate merit in any others of her sex. I resembled my father in appearance and personality. Just as a duckling soon finds water, so my element from my earliest years was the kitchen, the store room, barns and attics. Even during my years of play, my natural instinct and my sole concern were to preserve order and cleanliness in the house. My father was delighted at this and gradually provided my childish desires with appropriate opportunities for fullfillment. But my mother did not love me, and never concealed this fact for a moment.

"I grew up, my activities increased, and with them my father's love for me. When we were alone together, when we walked across the fields or when I helped him check his accounts, I could feel how happy he was. When I looked into his eyes, it was as though I was peering into my own self. For it was in the eyes that I resembled him most. But his spirits flagged and his expression changed when he was with my mother. He made gentle excuses for me when she attacked me savagely and unjustly. He took my part, not in order to protect me, but because my good qualities merited that I be excused. He never opposed any of her wishes. She developed a great passion for acting, a theater was built, and there was no lack of men of all shapes and ages, to appear on stage alongside her, but few women. Lydie, a nice girl who had been educated with me and from early on had shown every prospect of becoming quite charming, took over the supporting female roles, an old chambermaid played aunts and mothers, whereas the female leads, both heroic and pastoral, were always reserved for my mother. I cannot tell you how ridiculous it seemed to me that people I knew very well dressed up and stood on the stage, demanding to be taken for something other than what they really were. What I saw, was always just my mother, Lydie, and this or that baron or secretary, whether they presented themselves as princes, counts, or peasants, and I did not understand how they could presume I would believe they were sick or well, in love or not, miserly or generous, when I usually knew they were the very opposite. So I was not often to be found amongst the spectators. I trimmed the lights, in order to have something to do, got their suppers, and next morning while they were still asleep, I would create some order in their costumes, which they had usually flung down all over the place the previous evening.

"My mother seemed to approve of what I did, but I never gained her love. In fact she despised me, and I remember very well that more than once she said bitterly: 'If mothers could be as unsure as fathers, one would never take this scullion for my daughter.' I will not deny that her behavior gradually set me apart from her completely, her actions seemed like those of a stranger to me, and since I was accustomed to watch servants like a hawk (for, between you and me, that is the basis of all good housekeeping), I became struck by the relationships between my mother and the members of her entourage. It was easy to observe that she did not look on all these men with the same eyes. I watched more carefully, and soon noticed that Lydie was her confidante and was becoming steadily more acquainted with emotions she had been imagining to herself since her early years. I knew about all my mother's rendezvous, but I kept quiet, not telling my father anything that might distress him. Finally I had to, for there were certain things she could not engage in without bribing the servants, who began to defy me, ignoring my father's instructions and my own commands. The complete disorder that ensued as a result was unbearable to me, and I complained to my father, telling him everything.

"He listened to me quietly, and finally said, smiling: 'My dear child, I know all about that. Keep calm, and be patient; it is only for your sake that I put up with this.'

"But I wasn't calm, and I wasn't patient. I reproved my father in my own heart, for I did not think he needed to put up with so much, for whatever reason. I insisted on maintaining order, and was determined to bring matters to a climax.

"My mother had wealth in her own right, but she spent more than she should, and that, as I could see, led to altercations between my parents. Nothing happened to change matters until my mother's emotions led to a certain development.

"Her first lover became ostentatiously unfaithful—and our house, the neighborhood, and all the circumstances of her life became distasteful to her. She wanted to move to another estate, but then that would be too isolated for her. So she wanted to go to town, but there she would not cut a sufficient figure. I don't know what passed between her and my father. All I know is that he finally agreed, under conditions which I never ascertained, that she should take the trip to the south of France that she desired.

"He and I were now free and lived in seventh heaven. I really believe that my father suffered no loss by the considerable sum that he paid out to be rid of her presence. All the servants we no longer needed were dismissed, and fortune smiled on the order we established. We enjoyed several good years, with everything going according to our wishes. But unfortunately this happy state of affairs did not last long. My father quite unexpectedly suffered a stroke, which paralyzed his right side and deprived him of the power of clear speech. You had to guess at what he was asking for, for he never produced the word he had in his mind. I suffered many anxious moments when he insisted on being alone with me, and, after having sharply dismissed with a gesture all the others, was not able to produce the word he wanted. He would grow extremely impatient, and his condition caused me great unhappiness. I was quite sure that he was trying to communicate something of special concern to me, and I greatly desired to know what it was. Normally I could tell everything from his eyes, but now his eyes no longer spoke to me. One thing was clear: he did not want or require anything except to tell me something which, alas, I never found out. A second stroke followed, and he became totally inactive and incapacitated. And very soon he was dead.

"I don't know how I got the idea that somewhere he had deposited money that, on his death, he wanted to come to me rather than to my mother. I searched for it while he was still alive, but without success. Then after his death everything was sealed. I wrote to my mother and offered to remain at the house to be in charge of things, but she rejected this and I had to leave. A reciprocal will came to light according to which she acquired ownership and use of everthing, and I at least for the term of her life, remained her dependent. It was now that I believed I could understand the hints my father was giving me. I regretted that he had been such a weak character and so unjust to me after his death. Some of my friends even said that it would have almost been better if he had disinherited me, and urged me to contest the will, but I could not bring myself to do that. I revered my father's memory too much and put my trust in fate, and in myself.

"There was a lady in the neighborhood who owned large estates, with whom I had always been on good terms. She was pleased to take me into her household, and I was soon to become the head of it. She lived a regular life, and liked to have order in everything, and I gave her valiant help in her battles with stewards and retainers. I am not miserly, nor am I spiteful, but we women are more seriously concerned than any man to see that nothing is wasted. All fraudulent action arouses our displeasure; we want people to have only what they deserve.

"I was now once again in my element, lamenting in my quieter moments the loss of my father. My patroness was satisfied with me, and there was only one small thing that disrupted the peace of my existence. Lydie came back; my mother had been cruel enough to reject the poor girl now that she was thoroughly corrupted. She had learnt from my mother to consider passion as a way of life, and had accustomed herself never to display moderation in anything. When she unexpectedly reappeared, my benefactress took her in too. Lydie was eager to assist me, but she was of no use at anything.

"About this time my lady's relatives, and future heirs, would frequently come to the house and occupy themselves by arranging hunts. Lothario was sometimes among them, and I decided in no time that he was far superior to the rest, though he did not pay any particular attention to me. He was polite to everybody, but it soon became clear that it was Lydie he was attracted to. I always had plenty to do and was therefore socially rarely much in evidence. Lively conversation has always been the spice of life for me, but I must confess that in Lothario's presence I said less than usual. I had enjoyed taking with my father about everything that came up. If you don't talk about things, you don't really think about them adequately. There was no one I enjoyed listening to more than Lothario, when he was telling about his journeys and his military campaigns. The whole world lay as open and clear before him as the small sphere of my own activity. What I heard from him was not outlandish adventures, exaggerated half-truths of a traveler with limited perceptions always putting himself ahead of the country he was describing. He didn't tell us about places, he took us there. I have rarely experienced such unadulterated pleasure.

"One evening I had the inexpressible satisfaction of hearing him talk about women. The topic came up quite naturally. Several ladies from the surrounding area were visiting us and were saying all the usual things about the education of women. Our sex was treated unfairly, they were saying: Men want to restrict all higher culture to themselves, we are not allowed to study, we are only to be playthings or housekeepers. Lothario said little to all this, but when the company had diminished in size, he did speak his mind openly. 'It is strange,' he said, 'that a man is thought ill of for wishing to place a woman in the highest position she is capable of occupying; and what is that but governing a household? Whereas the man labors away at external matters, acquiring possessions and protecting them, even maybe participating in the government of a state, he is always dependent on circumstances, and, I may say, controls nothing that he thinks he is controlling. He always has to be politic when he wants to be reasonable, covert when he wants to be open, deceitful when he wants to be honest, and for the sake of some goal that he never attains, he must every moment abandon that highest of all goals: harmony within himself. But the sensible housewife really governs, rules over all that is in the home and makes possible every kind of satisfying activity for the whole family. What is the greatest joy of mankind but pursuing what we perceive to be good and right, really mastering the means to our ends? And where should these ends be if not inside the home? Where should we expect to encounter the constantly recurring, indispensable needs, except where we get up in the morning and lay ourselves to rest at night, where kitchen and wine cellar and storerooms are always there for us and our families? And what a round of regular activity is required to maintain this constantly recurring order of things in undisturbed, never failing sequence! How few men are able to reappear like a star, regularly presiding over the day as well as the night, making household implements, sowing and reaping, preserving and expending, and treading the circle with calm, love and efficiency! Once a woman has assumed this internal governance, she makes thereby the man she loves into the sole master. Her attentiveness acquires all skills, and her activity uses them all. She is dependent on nobody and assures for her husband true independence—domestic independence, inner independence. What he owns, he now sees secured; what he acquires, he sees well used, and then he can turn his mind to bigger things, and if fortune favors him, be to the state what his wife is so admirably at home.'

"He followed this up with a description of the wife he desired. I blushed, for what he described was myself, just as I was. I secretly revelled in my triumph, and all the more so because everything indicated that it was not me he was referring to, for he did not really know me. I cannot remember a more pleasing experience in my whole life than to see a man I respected giving preference to my character over my appearance. I felt rewarded, and encouraged.

"When the others had left, the lady who had become my friend said with a smile: 'What a pity that men do so much thinking and talking about things they never put into practice, otherwise an excellent match for my dear Therese would have been just discovered.' I laughed at her statement, adding that men's minds look around for housekeepers, but their hearts and their imagination long for other qualities; and we housekeepers can't compete with charming young girls. I said this so that Lydie should hear it; for she made no secret of the big impression that Lothario had made on her, and he for his part seemed to pay more and more attention to her every time he visited us. She was poor, not a person of quality, and could not contemplate marriage to him; but she could not withstand the delights of being charming and being charmed. I had never been in love, and was not then, but although it pleased me greatly to see how my character was rated by a man I so highly respected, I cannot deny that I was not entirely satisfied. I wanted him to get to know me and take a personal interest in me. I had no thought of what this might lead to.

"The greatest service I could perform for my benefactress was to bring some order into the beautiful woodlands on her estates. These valuable tracts of land, which were increasing steadily in value owing to various circumstances and the passage of time, were being treated without any imagination, plan or order, and there was no end of stealing and trickery. Whole hillsides were bare, and only the oldest stands of trees had equal size of growth. I went through every such area with an experienced forester, had measurements made, trees cut down, others started, and soon everything was progressing favorably. So as not to be encumbered, whether on foot or on horseback, I had men's clothes made for me. I moved around a lot, and everyone was scared of me.

"I heard that the company of young people, including Lothario, were organizing another hunt, and for the first time in my life I decided to appear in my true colors, or perhaps I had better say, as I wanted to appear in Lothario's eyes. I put on my men's clothes, slung my gun over my back, and went out accompanied by our own huntsman, to await the others at the edge of the estate. They arrived, but Lothario did not recognize me right away. One of my lady's nephews introduced me to him as an accomplished forester, joked about my youthfulness, and continued the game, praising me all the while, until Lothario finally recognized me. This nephew backed me up in all this, as though we had planned it ahead. He described at length and with gratitude all that I was doing for his aunt's estates, and consequently also for him.

"Lothario listened attentively, then inquired about all sorts of things connected with the estates and the neighborhood, and I was glad to be able to display my knowledge. I passed my examination with flying colors, then asked his opinion about various improvements, which he approved, mentioning similar cases, and strengthened my arguments by giving them an appropriate context. My satisfaction steadily increased. But fortunately I only wanted to be understood, not to be loved, for when we returned to the house I noticed more clearly than ever that his attentions to Lydie indicated a growing affection. I had achieved my aim, but I was not at ease. From that day on he displayed real respect and close confidence in me, began to talk to me when others were present, asked me for my opinion and seemed to trust my views on household matters as though I knew everything. His interest encouraged me greatly, and even when the talk was about agricultural or financial matters, he drew me into the conversation, and when he was not present I did all I could to acquire more knowledge of the area, even of the whole district. This was not difficult for me, because it represented on a bigger scale what I already knew in a smaller sphere.

"He began to visit us more frequently from then on. The conversation turned on a variety of subjects, but ultimately it always came down to questions of economics in the broader sense, and there was much talk of the vast results that can be achieved by efficient use of time, money and ability, even by means that may seem quite small in themselves.

"I did not resist the affection that was drawing me toward him, and unfortunately I soon became aware how strong, how sincere and pure my love for him was, when I observed ever more clearly that his repeated visits were in order to see Lydie, not me. At least that was her passionate conviction. She confided in me, and that was consoling to some extent. What she interpreted in her own favor, seemed to me of little significance. There was no sign of any intention of a lasting union, but I could easily see the emotional girl's craving to belong to him at any price.

"That's how matters stood when my lady surprised me one day with an unexpected communication. 'Lothario,' she said, 'offers you his hand in marriage; he wants to have you at his side for his whole life.' She then described at length my qualities, and told me something that I was very glad to hear: that Lothario was quite sure he had found in me the person he was looking for.

"I had now achieved my greatest joy: a man wanted me, whom I greatly respected, and at his side, and in his company I could envision the free and full expansion of my natural inclinations and practiced talents for the benefit of many people: my whole existence seemed at once to be extended into infinity. I gave my consent. He came and talked to me, gave me his hand, looked in my eyes, embraced me, and pressed a kiss on my lips—the first, and the last, he ever gave me. He confided to me his whole situation, told me what his American campaign had cost him, the debts he had incurred on his estates, the friction this had caused with his great-uncle, and the latter's way of caring for him, namely to find a rich wife for him, since an intelligent man needs someone to take over the domestic side of his affairs. Lothario hoped through his sister to persuade the old man to agree to his union with me. He outlined his financial resources, his plans and prospects and solicited my cooperation. But until his uncle gave his agreement, everything should remain secret.

"Just after he left, Lydie asked me whether he had said anything about her. I said that he hadn't, and bored her with an account of some economic matters. She was restless, ill-humored, and Lothario's behavior when he returned, did nothing to improve her state of mind.

"But I see that the sun is going down, my friend. That's fortunate for you, for otherwise you would have had to listen to my whole story, which I enjoy recounting to myself, in every detail. So let me speed things up! We are now reaching a period that it is not good to dwell on.

"Lothario introduced me to his wonderful sister who, in turn, introduced me to his uncle. I won the old man over, he agreed to what we wanted, and I returned to my lady with the joyful news. The whole matter was no longer a secret in the household. Lydie found out about it, and couldn't believe what she heard. When finally she could doubt it no longer, she immediately disappeared from sight, and nobody knew where she had taken herself off to.

"The wedding day was approaching. I had asked him several times for a picture and reminded him of his promise one day when he was about to leave. 'You have forgotten to give me the frame you wanted to have it mounted in,' he said. He was referring to the fact that I had received from a woman friend a gift that I greatly prized. The outer glass covering had a monogram fastened by strands of her hair, and inside there was a piece of ivory on which her portrait was to have been painted—but to my great sorrow she died. Lothario's affection brought me joy while her loss was giving me pain, and so I wanted to fill the gap left in her gift to me by the portrait of my friend.

"I went quickly to my room, fetched my jewel case, and opened it in his presence. Inside he saw a medallion with a woman's picture on it. He took it into his hands, examined it carefully, and quickly asked: 'Who is this a picture of?' 'My mother,' I replied. 'I could have sworn that this was a certain Mme. de Saint Alban whom I met several years ago in Switzerland,' he said. 'That's who it is,' I replied with a smile. 'So you met your mother-in-law without knowing it. Saint Alban is the romantic name that my mother uses when she's travelling: she's still using it, in France.' 'I am the most unfortunate of men!' he cried, putting the medallion back in the jewel case. He covered his eyes, left the room immediately, and threw himself into the saddle. I called after him from the terrace. He looked around, waved, then rushed away—and I have never seen him since."

The sun went down, and Therese gazed straight at the evening glow, her eyes brimming with tears. Silently she laid her hand on that of her new friend. He kissed it lovingly, she dried her tears, and stood up. "Let's go back," she said, "and pay some attention to the others."

Their conversation as they walked back was not animated. They arrived at the garden gate and saw Lydie sitting on a bench. She got up, but avoided them, and went back into the house. She was holding a paper in her hands, and there were two little girls with her. "I see," said Therese, "that she still keeps with her what is her only consolation—Lothario's letter, in which he assures her that, as soon as he is better, she shall return to him, but for the time being she should stay quietly with me. She hangs on his words and consoles herself with them, but she has a poor opinion of his friends."

The two children came up, welcomed Therese, and gave her an account of all that had happened while she was out. "Here you see another branch of my activity," she said. "I have entered into an arrangement with Lothario's sister. Together we are educating a group of children—I take care of the vigorous, eager, domestic types and she takes charge of those who reveal quieter and more refined talents. For it is reasonable to provide in every way possible for the happiness of menfolk and the smooth running of the household. When you have met my good friend, his sister, your life will be different: her beauty and her goodness make her the object of everyone's adoration." Wilhelm did not venture to tell her that unfortunately he had already met the countess and his fleeting acquaintance with her would always remain painful for him. He was very glad that Therese did not continue this particular conversation, her household duties requiring her immediate attention. When she had left, he was overcome by a sense of distress at this last piece of news regarding the countess: that she was obliged to substitute for her own happiness the hope of providing happiness for others. He admired Therese for not feeling any need to change her way of life despite the unexpected sad change in her expectations. "How happy those are," he said to himself, "who do not have to reject the whole of their past life in order to accommodate themselves to fate!"

Therese came to his room, and asked to be forgiven for disturbing him. "Here in that wall cabinet is my whole library," she said. "It consists of books that I don't throw away, rather than those I wish to keep. When Lydie wants a religious book, she'll be able to find something of the kind. People who are worldly most of the time, get the idea they must be religious when they're in trouble. Things that are good and moral are like medicine they force down when they feel bad, and any priest or moral teacher is regarded as a physician one dispenses with as soon as possible. I must however confess that morality for me is a kind of diet, but only becomes a diet if practiced as a rule of life the whole year through."

She rummaged amongst the books and found a few so-called devotional works. "Recourse to such books is something that Lydie learnt from my mother," said Therese. "My mother lived on novels and plays so long as her lover remained faithful. But when he left, these other books came into their own. I simply cannot understand how anyone could believe that God speaks to us through books. If the world itself does not reveal to someone its relationship to him, if his heart does not tell him what his duties are, he is unlikely to learn that from books which provide us with little more than names for our mistakes."

She left Wilhelm to himself, and he spent the evening examining this little collection of books. It did seem to have been quite arbitrarily assembled.

Therese remained just the same for the few days that Wilhelm stayed with her. She told him in great detail, and at various intervals, about the results of what she had already related. Dates and places were all vividly present in her mind, and we will summarize that part which our readers need to know.

Unfortunately, the reason for Lothario's rapid departure soon became all too obvious. He had encountered Therese's mother during her journey, and succumbed to her charms, which she readily bestowed. This unfortunate interlude now prevented him from joining a woman, who seemed destined by nature to be his. Therese continued in her clearly defined sphere of activity and duties. As for Lydie, it became known that she was secretly dwelling in the neighborhood, happy that the marriage, for some unknown reason, had not taken place. She tried to draw closer to Lothario, and it seemed that he, more out of desperation than desire, more from surprise than due reflection, more from boredom than intention, responded to her wishes.

Therese was not upset by this. She made no further claims on him and, even if he had become her husband, she might have had strength enough to put up with his relationship with Lydie, so long as it did not disturb her domestic order. At least she often expressed the opinion that a woman who kept her household duties in good order could tolerate any flight of fancy on her husband's part, and still be certain that he would come back to her.

Therese's mother soon reduced her capital to a state of shambles, for which the daughter had to suffer, since nothing much remained for her. The old lady who had so befriended Therese, died and left her this small freehold estate and a sizeable amount of capital. Therese adapted herself immediately to her restricted circumstances. Lothario offered her a better piece of property and Jarno was the go-between. But this Therese declined, saying: "I want to show Lothario in something small, that I was worthy of sharing with him something that was bigger. But if some circumstance or other should put me in a situation of embarrassment for myself or others, I claim the right to address myself without further ado to my dear friend."

Nothing remains less concealed or less exploited than purposeful activity. As soon as she had established herself on her small estate, the neighbors came to make her acquaintance and seek her advice, and the new owner of the adjoining estates made it quite clear to her that it was entirely up to her whether she would accept his hand in marriage and become heir to the greater part of his fortune, or not. She had already mentioned this to Wilhelm and joked about marriage and mismarriage.

"There is nothing people enjoy talking about more than when a marriage takes place which they consider a mismarriage, or *mésalliance*. And yet 'mismarriages' are commoner than marriages, for most unions turn out soon enough to be misfits. Mixture of social classes through marriage only merits the name of 'mismarriage' when the one party cannot share in the established, accustomed and therefore necessitated existence of the other party. Different strata of society have different lifestyles that they cannot share or exchange with each other, and that is why marriages of this kind are better not concluded. But exceptions, and very happy exceptions, are possible. For instance the marriage of a young girl to an old man is always a misfit, but I've known such a marriage to turn out quite well. For me there could only be one kind of mismarriage — if I had to spend my time in shows and ceremonies. I would much rather marry an honest farmer's son from the neighborhood."

Wilhelm thought it was now time for him to return to Lothario's residence, and he asked Therese to create an opportunity for him to take his leave of Lydie. The hot-tempered girl was persuaded to see him and he was able to say a few kind words to her, to which she replied: "I have overcome my earlier distress. Lothario will always remain dear to me, but I regret that he is surrounded by friends whose real natures are now known to me. The Abbé is quite capable of leaving a person in a state of distress, or plunging him into it, on account of some mood that comes over him. The doctor always wants to clear things up. Jarno has no soul, and you, my friend, have at least no character! Continue what you are doing, allow yourself to be used as a tool by these three men, and they will certainly give you plenty of assignments. I realize that for a long time my presence has been distasteful to them. I have never discovered their secret, but I know that they have one. Why all these locked rooms? These mysterious corridors? Why can't anyone get to the big tower? Why did they confine me to my own room? I must confess that it was jealousy that first made me discover this; I feared that some favored rival was hidden away somewhere. I don't believe that any longer. I am convinced that Lothario loves me and means well, but I am equally convinced that he is misled by his pretentious, false friends. If you want to do him a service, if you are to be forgiven for the trouble you have caused me, then get him out of the hands of these men. But what can I hope for! Give him this letter, and repeat what it says: that I will always love him and rely on him. Oh!" she cried, standing up and sobbing on Therese's neck, "he is surrounded by my enemies, they will try to persuade him that I have made no sacrifices for him. The best of men like to hear they deserve every sacrifice without having to show their gratitude."

Wilhelm's leave-taking from Therese was a happier one. She expressed the desire to see him again soon. "You know all about me!" she said. "You let me do all the talking. Next time it will be your duty to respond equally confidentially."

While he was on his way back, he had ample time to reflect on this new, radiant personality. What confidences she had bestowed on him! He thought how happy Mignon and Felix would be in her care, and then he thought about himself and what a delight it would be to dwell in the presence of such a clear-minded human being. As he drew near to Lothario's castle, he was struck by the tower with the numerous corridors and side buildings. And he decided to ask the Abbé or Jarno about them.

Chapter Seven

When Wilhelm entered the castle he found that Lothario was well on the way to recovery. Neither the doctor nor the Abbé was there, but Jarno was. Lothario was soon well enough to ride, alone or with his friends. His talk was both serious and pleasant, his conversation with others instructive and stimulating. There were often signs of a quite delicate sensitivity, though he did what he could to conceal this; and if it showed itself against his will, he seemed almost to disapprove.

One evening he was very quiet at dinner, though he looked quite cheerful. "You must have had some adventure or other today, but apparently a pleasant one," said Jarno. "What a sound judge you are of people!" Lothario replied. "Yes indeed, I have had the most delightful adventure. Perhaps I would not have thought it so charming at any other time, but today·it caught me in a very receptive mood. Toward evening I was riding through the various villages on the other side of the water, a route I had often taken in earlier years. My bodily sickness must have mellowed me more than I thought; I felt soft but, as my strength revived, I felt born anew. Every object around me appeared in the same light as they had in former years, so pleasant, so delightful, so charming—such as they had not seemed to me for a long time. I realized this was a form of weakness, but accepted it willingly, and rode gently on, understanding exactly how some people get to like illnesses that induce pleasant feelings. You know perhaps the reason why I used to take this particular path in the past?"

"If I remember correctly," said Jarno, "it was some little love affair involving a farmer's daughter."

"One might call it a big love affair," Lothario said in reply, "for we were both very much in love with each other, seriously in love and for quite a long time. Chance would have it that today everything combined to bring back to me those first days of our love. Boys were once again shaking june bugs out of trees, and the ash trees were no further in leaf than they were the first day that I saw them. It was a long time since I last saw Margarete, for she married and moved far away, though I had happened to hear that she had come with her children a few weeks earlier to stay with her father."

"So this particular route of yours was not accidentally chosen?" said Jarno.

"I cannot deny that I did hope to encounter her," said Lothario. "When I was drawing near to the house I saw her father sitting outside the door, with a child, about a year old, standing by his side; and as I came closer, a woman appeared briefly at an upstairs window. And when I got to the gate, I heard someone rushing down the steps. I thought this was certainly she, and flattered myself that she had recognized me and was running to meet me. But I was quite disconcerted when she rushed out of the door, picked up the child whom the horses were coming up to, and carried it back into the house. This gave me an unpleasant feeling, and my vanity was only slightly appeased when I noticed that her neck and one ear were reddened as she hurried away.

"I remained standing where I was, spoke to her father, and peered up at all the windows in search of some sign of her. But found none, and since I did not want to ask after her, I rode on. My irritation was somewhat tempered by the strange observation that, although I had scarcely been able to see her face, she seemed totally unchanged; and ten years is a long time! She seemed as young as ever: just as slim and just as quick on her feet, her neck almost lovelier than before, her cheek just as capable of that loving blush as ever—and yet the mother of six children, perhaps more. This vision was so appropriate to the world of magic surrounding me, that, feeling totally rejuvenated, I rode on further and did not turn back until the sun was going down over the next patch of woodland. And though the evening dew reminded me of my doctor's instructions and I knew it would be advisable for me now to go straight home, I did not, but instead went back by way of the farmhouse. I noticed that a woman was walking to and fro in the garden, which is surrounded by a low hedge. I rode up to the hedge on the outside path, and soon found myself near the person I was seeking.

"Although the evening sun was in my eyes, I could see that she was working near the hedge, which only partly obscured her. I believed this was my old love. As I came up to her, I stood still, not without some heartthrobs. Tall branches of wild roses, swayed by a gentle breeze, were concealing her somewhat. I spoke to her, and asked how she was. She answered me, rather softly: 'Quite well.' Then I noticed that there was a child behind the hedgerow picking flowers and I took the occasion to ask her where the other children were. 'This is not my child,' she said. 'That would be too early!' and at that moment it so happened that I caught sight of her face through the branches, and did not know what I should say to what I saw. For it was, and was not, my loved one. She was almost younger, almost lovelier than when I had known her ten years ago. 'Aren't you the farmer's daughter?' I asked, in some confusion. 'No,' she said. 'I'm her cousin.' 'But you are so extraordinarily alike.' 'That's what everyone says who knew her ten years ago,' said the girl.

"I proceeded to ask her about various other things. Although I had soon realized my mistake, I was quite pleased with it and could not tear myself away from the living image of former happiness that stood before me. The child had gone off in the direction of the pond looking for flowers. She took leave of me and ran after the child.

"Meanwhile I had discovered that my former beloved was indeed in her father's house, and as I rode back I was busy guessing whether it was she or her cousin who had protected the child from the horses. I went over the whole train of events in my mind and would find it hard to think of anything that could have delighted me more. But I do feel that I am still not well; so let's ask the doctor to relieve us all from further indulgence in this mood."

When love stories are being narrated, what usually happens is that one leads to the other, just like ghost stories. So our little group of people found much to retail in the way of recollection of times past. Lothario had most to relate. Jarno's stories all had their own individual stamp. And we know what Wilhelm had to contribute. He was afraid that someone would remind him of his experience with the countess; but nobody thought about that.

"It is true," said Lothario, "that there is no pleasanter sensation than when one's heart, after a period of non-involvement, opens up in love to some new object; but I would gladly have done without that for the whole rest of my life, if fate had permitted me to join myself to Therese. Youth doesn't last forever, and childhood shouldn't either. What can be more desirable for a man who knows the world and what he has to do in it and hope from it, than to find a wife to work alongside him, taking care of everything that he cannot, operating in a broad sphere whereas he must follow a strait course? What a blessed life I dreamt of with her: not the blessings of ecstatic bliss, but the joys of a secure earthly life: order in joy, courage in misfortune, concern for every little detail, and a soul able to cope with larger matters and, in due course, dismiss them. I saw in her those qualities we admire when history shows us women far superior to any men: a clear perception of circumstances, ability to deal with all eventualities, that confidence in dealing with detail which works to the advantage of the whole without their thinking about it. You will surely forgive me," he said, turning to Wilhelm with a smile, "for being seduced away from Aurelie by Therese. With Therese I could hope for lifelong happiness, whereas with Aurelie I could not hope for one happy hour."

"I cannot deny that I came here with great bitterness," said Wilhelm, "and had made up my mind to upbraid you for your behavior toward Aurelie."

"I certainly deserve blame for that," said Lothario. "I should not have confused friendship with love. I should not have allowed affection to invade the respect she deserved, affection that she could neither arouse in me nor receive from me in return. She was not lovable when she loved, and that is the worst misfortune that can befall a woman."

"That may be," said Wilhelm in reply. "But we cannot always avoid the reproach that our actions and sentiments have been diverted in some strange way from their natural course. There are responsibilities we must never lose sight of. May she rest in peace; and let us, without blaming her or ourselves, scatter blossoms of pity upon her grave. But let me ask you this: faced with the grave of this unhappy mother, why do you not take charge of the child, a boy that everyone would delight in but you seem entirely to neglect? How can you, with all your good-heartedness and delicate feelings, completely deny those of a father? You have not said one word the whole time about the precious child whose grace and charm beggar description?"

"Whom are you referring to? I don't understand," said Lothario.

"Why, your son, of course: Aurelie's son, that lovely child who only lacks the care of a loving father to make him happy."

"You're making a big mistake," said Lothario. "Aurelie never had a son. At least, not by me. I know nothing about a child. If I did, I would of course have taken charge of it. As for the present situation: I will consider this little creature as a bequest from her, and gladly take charge of its education. Did she ever give any indication that the child belonged to her or to me?"

"I do not recall any express statement to that effect," said Wilhelm. "But it was generally assumed to be so, and I myself never doubted it for a moment."

"I can offer some clarification," said Jarno, breaking into their conversation. "An old woman, whom you must have seen often, brought the child to Aurelie, who was delighted to take it over, hoping that its presence would mitigate her sufferings. And it did indeed provide her with many happy moments."

Wilhelm was greatly disturbed by this report. He had a clear mental picture of the good-hearted Mignon standing beside the handsome Felix, and this made him wish to remove them both from their present environment.

"Let's deal with that right away," said Lothario. "We'll place the strange girl in the charge of Therese, where she couldn't be in better hands. And, as for the boy, I would suggest that you, Wilhelm, should take care of him. For what women leave unfinished in our education, children complete by our association with them."

"I think," said Jarno, "that you should abandon your association with the theater, for you have no talent for it."

Wilhelm was thunderstruck. He had to compose himself, for Jarno's harsh words had deeply offended his self-esteem. "If you can convince me of that," he said with a forced smile, "you will be doing me a great service, though it is always sad to be shaken out of a pleasant dream."

"Let's not discuss that any further at the moment," Jarno replied. "I would urge you to go and fetch the children. The rest will take care of itself."

"I am prepared to do that," said Wilhelm. "I am uneasy, both eager to find out more about the boy and anxious to see the girl again who has attached herself to me so peculiarly."

It was agreed that he should leave as soon as possible. He was ready to go the next day, his horse was saddled, but he first wanted to take his leave of Lothario. When dinner time came around, they all seated themselves at table, but without their host. He arrived rather late, but did not join them. "I bet you have been testing out your tender feelings again today, and have not withstood the urge to see your former beloved once more." "Correct!" said Lothario. "Tell us how it went. I'm very curious," said Jarno.

"I won't deny that this whole adventure was unduly obsessing my mind, and so I decided to ride out there once more and really see the person whose rejuvenated appearance had caused me such a pleasant illusion. I dismounted at some distance from the house, had the horses led off to the side so as not to disturb the children playing by the gate. I went into the house, and it so happened that she came walking toward me, for it was she, and I recognized her despite the fact that she had greatly changed. She was heavier, and seemed to be taller. Her grace of manner shone through a certain setness, and her gaiety had been transformed into a quiet reflectiveness. Her head, which she had formerly held aloft so freely and easily, hung a little, and there were slight wrinkles in her forehead.

"She lowered her eyes when she saw me, but there was no blushing to indicate that her feelings were engaged. I gave her my hand; she gave me hers. I asked after her husband: he wasn't at home. I inquired after the children: she stepped up to the door and called them in. They gathered around her. There is no more charming sight than that of a mother with a child in her arms, and none more dignified than that of one surrounded by a group of children. I asked what their names were—just in order to have something to say. She invited me to step inside and wait for their father. I did this, was led into the parlor, where I found that almost everything was still as it had been, and, strange to say, her attractive cousin, her living image, was sitting on the same stool behind the distaff where I had so often seen my loved one, and looking exactly like her. A little girl, the living image of her mother, had followed us, and I found myself presently situated between past and future, strangely like being in an orange grove where in one small area blossoms and fruits are ranged side by side. Her cousin left the room to get some refreshments. I pressed the hand of the woman I had once loved so dearly, and said: 'It is a great joy for me to see you again.' 'You are very kind to say that,' she replied. 'I can assure you that I too am extremely pleased to see you. Many has been the time that I have wished to see you once more during my life, sometimes at moments that I thought might be my last.' She said this in a firm voice, without pathos, quite naturally, in the tone that had always delighted me. Her cousin came back, then her husband arrived—and I will leave you to imagine my feelings as I stayed, and when I left."

Chapter Eight

On his way to the town Wilhelm thought about all the fine women he knew or had heard about, their strange lives, so deprived of happiness, painfully present to his mind. "Oh, poor Mariane," he cried, "what more do I have to learn about you? And you, glorious Amazon, noble guiding spirit, to whom I am so greatly indebted, whom I am always trying to find again and never can, in what sad circumstances shall I find you when we meet again!"

None of his acquaintances were at home. So he ran to the theater, expecting to find them rehearsing. Everything was quiet, the whole house seemed empty, but he saw that one shutter was open. When he walked on to the stage he found Aurelie's old servant-woman stitching together some pieces of canvas for a new piece of scenery, and the only light coming in was what was needed for her to see what she was doing. Felix and Mignon were sitting on the floor beside her, holding a book. Mignon was reading aloud and Felix repeating the words after her as if he already knew his letters and could really read.

Both children jumped up to welcome him. He embraced them fondly and then led them back to where the old woman was. "Are you the one who brought this child to Aurelie?" he asked her in a solemn tone of voice. The old woman looked up from her work and turned her face toward him. He looked at her in the light, shuddered, and stepped back a few paces: it was old Barbara. "Where is Mariane?" he cried. "Far away," said the old woman. "And Felix . . .?" "Is the son of that unhappy girl who loved too ardently. May you never realize the pain you have caused us! May the treasure that I hand over to you make you as happy as he has made us unhappy!"

She stood up with the intention of leaving. But Wilhelm held her fast. "I'm not trying to run away from you," she said. "Just let me fetch a document that will give you both pleasure and pain." She left, and Wilhelm gazed at the boy in timorous joy, for he could not yet acknowledge the child as his own. "He is yours," said Mignon, "he is yours," and she pressed the child against his knees.

The old woman returned, and handed him a letter. "Here are Mariane's last words," she said. "She is dead, then?" he cried. "Yes, dead!" said Barbara. "I wish I could spare you all my reproaches."

Surprised and bewildered, Wilhelm broke open the letter. He had only read the first words of it when bitter sorrow overcame him. He dropped the letter, fell down on a mossy bank, and lay there for some time. Mignon busied herself with him, Felix picked up the letter and tugged her until she responded by kneeling down beside him and reading it aloud to him. Felix repeated the words after her, and Wilhelm was therefore obliged to hear them twice over. "If this letter should ever reach you, then have pity on the unhappy girl who loved you. Your love has killed her. This boy, whose birth I shall outlive but a few days, is yours. I die faithful to you, however much appearances may speak against me. In losing you, I lost all that bound me to life. I die content, because they assure me that the child is healthy and will live. Listen to what Barbara has to say, forgive her, farewell, and do not forget me!"

What a painful and yet, thank goodness, unclear and mysterious letter, the contents of which he only really understood as the children, stumbling and stammering, read it aloud and repeated it.

"There you have it!" said the old woman, not waiting until he had recovered himself. "Give your thanks to Heaven that, after the loss of such a good young woman, you are left with such a marvelous child. When you learn how true she was to you, right up to the end, how unhappy she was, and what sacrifices she made for your sake, you will be utterly distressed."

"Let me drink to the dregs the cup of sorrow and joy!" he exclaimed. "Convince me, indeed persuade me by what you have to say, that she was a good girl who deserved my respect as well as my love; then leave me to my sorrow at her irreplaceable loss."

"Now is not the time," she replied. "I have work to do, and I don't want anyone to find us together. Let it remain a secret that Felix is yours, otherwise I will have to put up with too many reproaches from the company for my previous pretenses. Mignon won't give us away: she is a good girl and keeps her mouth shut."

"I've known it for a long time, but I haven't said anything," Mignon answered. "How is that possible?" the old woman said. "How did you find it out?" Wilhelm asked. "The Ghost told me." "How? When?" "In the cellar when the old man drew the knife. I heard someone say: 'Go and get his father.' Then I knew it was you." "But who said this to you?" "I don't know. In my heart, in my head, I was so terrified, I was trembling, I prayed, then I heard it, and I understood."

Wilhelm pressed her to his heart, told her to look after Felix, and left. Only then did he notice that she had become much thinner and paler since he went away. The first of his acquaintances that he ran across was Madame Melina, who welcomed him warmly. "I hope," she said, "that you will find everything as you would wish it." "I doubt that," said Wilhelm, "and I'm not expecting to. Why don't you admit that all the arrangements have been made to dispense with my services?" "But why did you go away?" she said. "It's never too early to realize that no one is indispensable in this world," said Wilhelm. "How important we think we are! We imagine that we are the only real driving force in our sphere of activity and that when we are no longer there, everything will come to a standstill and wither away. But the space, at first hardly noticed, is filled up quite quickly, and even becomes the seed-ground of more pleasant, if not better things."

"And no allowance is made for the sorrow of our friends?" she asked in return.

"Our friends," Wilhelm replied, "will do well to reconcile themselves immediately to the change and say to themselves: Wherever you are, wherever you settle, be active and gracious, and let your life be untroubled."

On further inquiry Wilhelm discovered that what he had expected, had indeed happened: opera had been introduced, and was captivating the public. His former roles had now been divided up between Laertes and Horatio, both of whom were receiving much greater acclaim than he himself had ever done.

At that moment in came Laertes, and Madame Melina exclaimed: "Just look at this fortunate young man who will soon be a capitalist and heaven knows what else!" Wilhelm embraced him and felt the fine texture of his coat. The rest of his clothing was simple, but all of the highest quality. "Explain the mystery!" Wilhelm said to him. "It is high time you knew that my restlessness is at last paying off," said Laertes. "The head of a big business house is profiting from my unsettledness, as well as from my knowledge and acquaintanceships, and allows me a good cut for myself. I would give a great deal if I could also negotiate trust from the women, for there is a pretty niece in the office and I can see that, if I so desired, I could soon become a made man."

"You probably don't know," said Madame Melina, "that there's been a wedding here. Serlo is married to the lovely Elmire, her father having refused to approve of the continuation of their private intimacy."

They told him about many things that had occurred in his absence, from which he perceived that he had long since become estranged from the general tone and spirit of the company.

He waited anxiously for Barbara, who had announced that she would come to see him at the strange hour of dead of night, when everyone was asleep, as if she were a young girl creeping to her lover. While he was waiting, he read through Mariane's letter time and time again, read the word "faithful" from her beloved hand with inexpressible delight, and then, with horror, the announcement of her impending death, which she seemed not to fear.

It was past midnight when there was a noise at the half-open door and Barbara came in with a basket. "I am here," she said, "to give you an account of all our sufferings, but I expect that you will remain quite unmoved. Your eagerness to see me is simply in order to satisfy your curiosity and I expect that you will envelop yourself in your own cold selfish interests, as you always did while our hearts were breaking. But look here! This is how I brought out the champagne on that happy evening, put three glasses on the table, and you began to beguile us and make us drowsy with happy childhood tales, whereas tonight I will enlighten you and keep you alert with sad truths."

Wilhelm did not know what to say when the old woman removed the cork and filled three glasses. "Drink up," she said, quickly emptying her own glass, "drink up before the mood passes. I will let this third glass lose its sparkling bubbles, in memory of that unhappy girl. How red her lips were when she spoke of your then, and how pale and rigid they have become for evermore!"

"You old witch, you monstrous fury!" Wilhelm cried, jumping up and banging his fist on the table. "What sort of evil spirit can it be that possesses and impels you? Who do you think I am, if you imagine that even the simplest account of Mariane's sorrow and death would not distress me greatly, and why do you need to have recourse to such devilish tricks to increase my torment? If your incessant tippling won't refrain from indulging itself at a funeral feast, then go ahead, and drink as you talk! I have always loathed you, and I cannot contemplate the idea of Mariane's being innocent, when I look at her companion."

"Take it easy, sir," she said in reply. "You won't rattle me. You still owe us a great debt, and one doesn't allow oneself to be insulted by debtors. But you're right: just the simplest account will be punishment enough for you. Listen then to Mariane's struggles, and her victory in the battle to remain yours."

"Mine?" said Wilhelm. "What sort of fairy tale is this to be?"

"Don't interrupt me, just listen to what I have to say. Then believe what you will—it makes no difference any longer. On that last evening with us did you not find a note and take it away with you?"

"I did not find it at the time, but afterwards. It was tucked in the scarf, which I grabbed in the heat of my emotions and put in my pocket."

"What did the note contain?"

"The expectations of a discontented lover to be better received the following night than he had the previous one. And I saw with my own eyes that his hopes were fulfilled, for it was daybreak when he came creeping out of your house."

"You may well have seen him then, but only now shall you learn how sadly Mariane spent that night and how vexed I was. I will be quite honest and not deny or gloss over the fact that I did encourage Mariane to give herself to this man named Norberg. She followed my advice, but, I can truly say, with distaste. He was rich, appeared to be in love with her, and I hoped he would remain constant. Soon after this he had to go on a journey, and it was then that Mariane came to know you. What I had to put up with as a result of that! The things I had to prevent, or to tolerate! 'Oh!' she would cry, 'if only you had spared my youth and my innocence for four more weeks, then I would have found a worthy object for my love. I would have been worthy of him, and love would have given me with a clear conscience what I have now sold against my will.' She abandoned herself entirely to her affection, and I dare not ask if you for your part were happy. I had unlimited power over her mind, for I was acquainted with every means of satisfying her smallest desires; but I had no power over her heart, for she never approved anything I did for her or tried to persuade her to do, if it was againsts the dictates of her heart. She only yielded to inescapable need, and need soon become oppressive to her. In her early youth she had been provided with everything, but her family lost its fortune through a series of complicated circumstances. The poor girl had grown accustomed to various needs, and some good principles had been implanted into her young mind, which made her uneasy but did not help much. She had absolutely no adroitness in worldly affairs, she was innocent in the true sense of the word, she had no idea that one could buy something without paying for it. What she feared most was being in debt, she would always rather give than take, and it was this sort of situation that forced her to give herself in order to clear up a number of minor debts."

"And couldn't you have saved her from that?" Wilhelm exclaimed angrily.

"Of course," the old woman replied, "with hunger and want, sorrow and privation, but I was never prepared for that."

"You hideous, despicable procuress! So you sacrificed this unhappy creature for the sake of your own swilling and gluttony?"

"You would do better to control yourself and stop using such insulting expressions," said the old woman. "If you want to curse and swear, why not go into one of your fine houses—you will find mothers there who are anxiously concerned to find the most loathsome men for their lovely, radiant daughters, so long as they are very rich. And you will see the poor young creatures trembling at the fate in store for them, and utterly distressed, until some more experienced woman friend points out to them that by marrying they will acquire the right to dispose of their hearts and persons as they wish."

"Hold your tongue!" Wilhelm shouted at her. "Do you really think one crime can be excused by another? Get on with your story without further asides!"

"Then listen, and stop reproaching me! Mariane became yours against my will. I have nothing to blame myself for in the whole adventure. Norberg came back and rushed to see Mariane. She received him coldly and petulantly and did not even allow him one kiss. I needed all my skill to excuse her behavior. I told him that a father-confessor had pricked her conscience, and that when conscience speaks, one must respect it. I finally got him to leave and promised to do my best for him. He was rich and coarse, but he was basically good-natured, and loved Mariane intensely. He promised me to be patient, and I worked all the harder to see he was not too much tested. I had a hard time with Mariane: I persuaded her – in fact I forced her finally, by threat of leaving her, to write to her lover and invite him for that night. Then you came and acciden-tally picked up his reply in her scarf. Your unexpected arrival wrecked my plans. No sooner had you left than all her torment returned. She swore she would not be unfaithful to you. She was so full of passion, so completely beside herself, that she aroused my heartfelt pity. I finally promised her that I would pacify Norberg that night and try to get him to leave on some pretext or other. I urged her to go to bed, but she seemed not to trust me. She remained fully dressed, but finally fell asleep in her clothes, overwrought and drained by tears as she was.

"Norberg came. I tried to ward him off, presenting to him in darkest colors her anguish of conscience and remorse. He asked only to see her, and I went into her room to prepare her for this. But he followed me in and we both approached her bed at the same moment. She awoke, jumped up angrily and tore herself away from us, imploring, beseeching, threatening and finally declaring she would not give way. She was unwise enough to let drop a few hints as to where her real affections lay, which poor Norberg interpreted in a spiritual sense. At length he left her, and she locked herself in. I kept him for a long time, talking to him about the condition she was in, telling him she was pregnant and should therefore be treated with consideration. He was so proud at the thought of becoming a father, so looking forward to having a son, that he agreed to everything she demanded of him, promising to go away for a while rather than cause her anxiety and harm. With such thoughts in his mind he crept off in the early morning, and you, sir, standing sentry as you were, would have needed only to look into your rival's heart, which you thought was so privileged and happy, for your own assurance, though his appearing at that moment had persuaded you to despair."

"Are you telling the truth?" Wilhelm asked. "Truth, such as I hope will cause you once more to despair," she replied.

"You would certainly be driven to despair if I could describe to you in true colors the morning that followed. How happy she was when she woke up! Her voice was so cheerful when she called me in, she thanked me eagerly, pressing me affectionately to her bosom. 'Now,' she said, looking at herself smilingly in the mirror, 'now I can be pleased with myself and my appearance, now that I belong to myself and my beloved friend once again. How sweet it is to have overcome! What a glorious feeling it is to follow one's own heart! How thank-ful I am to you for taking my part and using your shrewdness and wits to my advantage! Help me to attain my greatest happiness.'

"I went along with what she was saying, not wishing to upset her. I encouraged her in her expectations, and she caressed me fondly. When she left the window for a moment I had to stand guard, for sometime you were bound to walk past and we were anxious at least to see you. And so the whole day passed, and we were restless. We were sure you would come that night at the usual hour. I was watching on the stairway, time hung heavy on me, and so I went back up to her room. To my surprise I found her in her officer's costume, looking charming and radiant. 'Don't I deserve to appear in men's clothing today? Haven't I been bold? I want my lover to see me as he did that first evening, and I will hug him as warmly and with even more abandon than I did then. For now I am much more his than I was when I had not yet broken loose in a noble decision. But,' she added somewhat pensively, 'I have not yet completely won out. I must still take the great risk of telling him everything about my situation, in order to be worthy and certain of him—then it will be up to him whether he keeps me or rejects me. This is a scene which I am arranging for us both; and if he finds himself able in his heart to reject me, then I will once more belong only to myself, find consolation in that punishment, and bear whatever fate has in store for me.'

"It was with such feelings and hopes, sir, that the lovely girl waited for you; but you never came. How shall I describe that state of waiting and hoping? I can still see her, speaking in such passionate, loving terms of the man whose cruelty she was still to experience!"

"Dear, old Barbara," Wilhelm cried, jumping up and grabbing her by the hand. "That's enough pretense and preparation. Your calm sober tone has given you away. Mariane is still alive, living somewhere in the neighborhood. Give her back to me. It was not by chance that you chose this late, lonely hour to visit me, and prepared me by recounting that excellent tale. Where have you hidden her? I'll believe everything you say, I give you my word on that, when you show me where she is and restore her to my arms. I saw her shadow passing over us. Let me now clasp her firmly in my arms. Then I will kneel before her, asking for forgiveness, congratulating her on her success in her battle with herself and you—and then I will bring my Felix to her. Tell me: Where have you hidden her? Don't leave me any longer in this state of uncertainty! You've achieved your purpose. Now, where is she? Let's use this light to find out, to see her lovely face once more!"

He dragged the old woman up from the chair; she looked blankly into his face, tears streamed from her eyes and she was seized by a sudden access of grief. "What unfortunate confusion is it that gives you any such hope? I have indeed hidden her—beneath the earth, and neither the open light of the sun nor the intimate gleam of a candle will ever shine upon her sweet face. Take little Felix to her grave, and tell him that there lies his mother whom his father unjustly condemned. Her loving heart no longer throbs impatiently to see you. She is not waiting in some nearby room for me to finish my story. The dark chamber has received her where no bridegroom may follow, from where no one can walk toward his beloved."

She threw herself down beside a chair and wept bitterly. For the first time Wilhelm was completely convinced that Mariane was dead, and he was overcome with grief. Barbara rose to her feet, declared that she had nothing more to say to him, and threw a wallet on to the table. "These letters," she said, "will make you ashamed that you were so cruel. Read them through with dry eyes, if you can." She crept quietly away, and Wilhelm did not have the heart that night to open the wallet, which was the same one as he had given Mariane, for he knew that in it she had carefully kept all the messages he sent her. Next morning he felt able to take this upon himself, he opened the seal, and little pencilled notes in his own hand fell out, reminding him of every occasion from the first day of their relationship to that last ghastly moment of parting. In bitter distress he read through a whole series of notes she had written to him which, he could see from their content, had been returned by Werner.

"None of my letters has got through to you, none of my pleas and appeals has reached you. Was it you yourself who gave those cruel orders? Am I really never to see you again? I will try once more; I implore you to come! I shall not insist on keeping you here, but if only I could press you one more time to my heart."

"When I was sitting beside you, holding your hands, gazing up into your eyes, and from the depths of my heart would say, lovingly and trustingly: 'you dear, good man,' you used to like to hear that, and I had to say it over and over again. So now I say once more: 'dear, dear, good man,' be as good as you were, come, and don't let me perish in misery."

"You think I'm to blame, and I am, but not in the way you think. Come, so that I may have the consolation of your knowing all about me, no matter what may happen to me afterwards."

"It is not for my sake alone, but also for yours that I am asking you to come to me. I can feel your unbearable suffering in fleeing me. Please come, so that our parting may be less cruel! Never perhaps was I more worthy of you than when you thrust me into utter misery!"

"I implore you by all that is sacred, by everything that can move a human heart, to consider that a soul is at stake, a life, two lives, one of which must always remain dear to you. Your mistrustful nature will not believe this, but I will maintain it even in the hour of my death: the child that I carry is yours. Since I fell in love with you, nobody else has even clasped my hands. If only your love and your goodness had been the companions of my youth!"

"You will not listen to me? Then I must keep silent, but these letters will not disappear. Perhaps they will speak to you when my lips are covered by a shroud, and the sound of your regrets shall no longer reach my ear. My only comfort throughout the whole sad course of my life shall be to know that I was not guilty, though I cannot call myself innocent."

Wilhelm could not read any further. He gave way entirely to grief, but was even more oppressed when Laertes came in and he tried to conceal his feelings from him. Laertes pulled out a purse full of ducats, counted them and firmly declared there was nothing more splendid than being about to be rich, for then nothing can disturb or impede us. Wilhelm remembered his dream, and smiled; but at the same time he recalled with a shock that in that same dream Mariane had left him and followed his dead father, and that both of them had floated over the garden like spirits.

Laertes distracted him from his reverie by taking him to a coffeehouse, where he found himself surrounded by several persons who had enjoyed seeing him on the stage, and were glad to see him again; but they regretted that, as they had heard, he was intending to give up acting. They spoke so perceptively and positively about him and his acting, the quality of his talent, and their hopes for him—so much so that Wilhelm finally exclaimed: "If only you had shown such appreciation several months ago! How I would have valued that! How encouraging that would have been! I would then never have so totally turned away from the theater in my mind, and no longer despaired of my public."

"You should never have felt like that about your audience," said an elderly man in the group. "The public is large, and keen understanding and sincere appreciation are not as rare as you think. But no artist should demand unlimited approbation of what he does; for unlimited approval is not worth much, though you gentlemen of the stage do not care for limited approval. I know full well that, in life as in art, we must seek our own opinion before doing or producing something, and only after we have done or produced it, should we pay attention to the opinions of others; and, once one has had some experience in this, one will know how to deduce a total judgment from a variety of opinions, for those persons whose opinion could spare us this labor, usually keep silent."

"But they shouldn't," said Wilhelm. "I have often heard that persons who themselves express no opinion on even good plays, complain when no opinions are expressed."

"Well, let's be vocal today, anyhow," said one young man. "You must dine with us, and then we will be able to catch up on what we should have said to you, and sometimes to dear Aurelie."

Wilhelm declined the invitation and went to visit Madame Melina. He wanted to talk to her about the children, since he was intending to take them away from her.

The secret that Barbara had entrusted to him he was not well able to keep to himself. Every time he looked at Felix he gave himself away. "Oh, my child, my dear child," he cried, picking him up and pressing him to his chest. "What did you bring me, father?" the child asked. Mignon looked at both of them, as if to warn them not to give themselves away. "What's all this about?" said Madame Melina. The children were taken aside, and Wilhelm, feeling he did not have to maintain secrecy on what the old woman had told him, revealed the whole story to Madame Melina. She looked at him with a smile. "O, men are such credulous creatures! It's easy to sell them a bill of goods if their thoughts were tending in that direction anyway; and there are times when they blindly assert the value of what they previously had termed a passing infatuation." But she could not suppress a sigh, and if Wilhelm had not been completely blind, he would have noticed that her behavior revealed a fondness for him that she had never entirely overcome.

He then spoke to her about the children, telling her that he was intending himself to keep Felix, but send Mignon to the country. Although Madame Melina was unwilling to be parted from both children at once, she thought his proposal was a good one, indeed a necessary one. Felix was becoming rather wild, and Mignon seemed to need fresh air and a different environment, for the poor child was sickly, and was not getting any better.

"Make no mistake about it," said Madame Melina. "I was not being frivolous when I expressed some doubts whether the boy is really yours. That old woman is not all that much to be trusted; and yet someone who can use untruth to her advantage, can also speak the truth if that seems useful to her. She pretended to Aurelie that Felix was the son of Lothario, and we women have this peculiarity that we love the children of our lovers, even if we do not know, or profoundly hate, their mothers." Felix came running into the room, and she clasped him to her breast with affection unusual in her.

Wilhelm went straight home and asked Barbara to come to see him, which she agreed to do but not before dusk. He received her angrily, and said: "There is nothing more disgraceful than depending on lies and idle fictions. You've already done enough harm with such things, and now, when what you have said may determine my whole life's happiness, I'm full of doubts and don't dare to embrace this child, whose undisturbed possession could make me blissfully happy. The very sight of you fills me with hatred and contempt."

"If I'm to be honest, I must say that your behavior seems to me insufferable," she replied to this outburst. "And even if this were not your own son, it is such a beautiful, such a delightful child, that anyone would buy it for any price, just to have it around. Doesn't he deserve your taking charge of him? Don't I deserve for all the pain and trouble I have taken on this child's account, don't I deserve some little support for the rest of my life? Oh you fine gentlemen, you who have everything, you do well to talk about truth and honesty; but there would be much to say on how a poor creature whose meager needs were never answered, who in all her troubles was entirely without friends, help or advice and had to make her way amidst selfish people and finally succumb — there would be much to say about that, if you would only listen. Have you read Mariane's letters? She wrote them at the time of her greatest unhappiness. In vain did I try to reach you and give you those letters, but your brutal brother-in-law had so hedged you around that all my guile and skill did not suffice, and when at length he threatened me and Mariane with imprisonment, I had to abandon all hope. Doesn't everything in those letters confirm what I have told you? Doesn't Norberg's own letter remove all your doubts?"

"What letter from Norberg?" Wilhelm asked.

"Didn't you find it in the wallet?" she replied.

"I haven't yet read all it contains."

"Then hand me the wallet! Here, this is the document I mean. It was Nor-berg's unfortunate letter that caused the confusion, but this other one will clear things up, if indeed there is anything to clear up." She took a sheet of paper out of the wallet, Wilhelm recognized the hateful hand, pulled himself together, and read these words: "Tell me, girl, how can you treat me like this? I would not have believed that a goddess could change me into a sighing swain. Instead of greeting me with open arms, you draw back as though in distaste. Is it right that I should spend the night sitting on a trunk with old Barbara in her room, with my beloved girl behind two closed doors? That is absolutely absurd. I promised to allow you some time for reflection and not to rush you, but I am maddened by every hour we lose. Haven't I done all I could to give you all the presents I could think of? If you still doubt my love, what else would you like to have? Just tell me, and you shall have it. I wish that priest who put such stuff in your head would go deaf and blind! Why did you have to land one like him; there are plenty of others more indulgent toward young people. All I can say is that things must change. I shall expect an answer these next few days, for I have to go away again soon, and if you are not kind and friendly again, then I will not come to see you anymore. . . ."

The letter went on at length in this fashion, always returning to the same point (to Wilhelm's painful satisfaction), and thereby vouching for the truth of Barbara's account. Another letter proved quite clearly that Mariane had not yielded, and several others sadly revealed to Wilhelm the whole story of this unfortunate girl right up to the time of her death.

Barbara had succeeded in calming the vulgar fellow down by degrees. She told him when Mariane died, leaving him to believe that Felix was his son. He sent her money from time to time, but she kept this for herself, having talked Aurelie into taking over the responsibility for Felix's upbringing. Unfortunately this secret source of funds soon dried up. Norberg had gone through most of his fortune in riotous living, and constant love affairs hardened his heart against the child he imagined to be his firstborn son.

Probable as this all sounded, and admirably as it all fitted together, Wilhelm could still not confidently give way to joy; he seemed to be afraid of a gift bestowed on him by some evil fate.

The old woman sensed his state of mind and said: "Only time will heal your uncertainty. Regard the child as not your own, pay careful attention to it, observe his talents, personality and abilities, and if you don't gradually come to see yourself in him, then you must have bad eyesight. For I can assure you that if I were a man, nobody would plant a child on me, but it is fortunate for us women that in such matters men are not as clear-sighted as we are."

After this Wilhelm came to an agreement with Barbara that he should take Felix with him and she would take Mignon to Therese. He would give Barbara a small allowance to spend however she wished.

He then summoned Mignon, to prepare her for the change. "Master!" she said. "Keep me with you, it will do me both good and ill." He explained to her that she was now fully grown and something should be done for her further education. "I am educated enough to love and to sorrow," she replied. He said she should pay attention to her health, that she needed constant care and the services of a competent doctor. "Why should they care for me, when there are so many to care for," she answered.

Having tried very hard to persuade her that he could not take her with him, he told her that he would take her to the house of friends, where he would often come to see her. But she seemed not to have heard anything he said. "You don't want me with you?" she asked. "Then perhaps it would be better to send me to the old Harper. The poor old man is so much alone." Wilhelm tried to assure her that the Harper was well taken care of. "I long for him every hour of the day," she said. "I did not notice that you were so attached to him while he was still living with us," said Wilhelm. "I was afraid of him when he was awake, I could not bear to look into his eyes," she said, "but when he was asleep, I would sit by his bedside, warding off the flies, and could never see enough of him. He gave me support in moments of terror. No one will ever know how much I owe him. If I had only known the way, I would have run to him before now."

Wilhelm gave her an account of the situation, and told her she was such a reasonable child, that this time too she should follow his wishes. "Reason is cruel," she said, "the heart is better. I will go wherever you wish, but let me have your Felix."

After much talk to and fro she stuck to her position, and so Wilhelm had to resign himself ultimately to entrusting both children to Barbara, who would take them to Therese. This was all the easier for him, because he was still afraid of acknowledging the handsome Felix as his son. He picked him up and carried him around. Felix liked to be lifted up to a mirror, and Wilhelm, without admitting it, searched out resemblances to himself. When these seemed apparent he would press the child to his bosom, but then, suddenly frightened by the thought that he might be deceiving himself, he would set the child down and let it run off. "Oh," he would cry, "if I were to claim this precious creature as my own and then it was taken away from me, I would be the unhappiest man on earth!"

The children left, and Wilhelm now decided to take his formal departure from the theater, feeling that he was already divorced from it, and only needed to make the break final. Mariane was no more, his two guardian spirits had left, and he followed them eagerly in his thoughts. The handsome boy was constantly in his mind's eyes, a vague vision of beauty, and he pictured him walking hand in hand with Therese through the fields and woods, growing up in the open air and alongside this open-minded, serene companion. Therese herself seemed to him even more estimable when he thought of Felix in her company. He thought about her, with a smile, when he was in the audience at the theater, for like her he found that these performances hardly created any illusion for him.

Serlo and Melina were very polite as soon as they found out that he made no further claims to his previous position. Some members of the public wanted to see him appear again on stage, and, of the actors, no one more than Madame Melina.

It was with some feeling that he took his leave of her, saying: "If only people would not venture promises for the future! One is unable to keep the smallest of them, let alone realize those ambitions which are substantial. How ashamed I am when I remember what I promised you all on that unfortunate night when we were huddled together—despoiled, sick, injured and wounded—in that wretched inn. Misfortune had bolstered up my courage, and what value I placed on my own good intentions! But nothing has come of all that, absolutely nothing! I leave as your debtor, and I am lucky that no one respects my promise for more than it was worth, and no one has ever pressed me to make it good."

"Don't be unjust toward yourself," Madame Melina replied. "If no one else recognizes what you have done for us, I at least will acknowledge it. Our whole situation would have been totally different if we had not had you with us. Our intentions, like our desires, look quite different when they are accomplished and fulfilled, and we think we have not done or achieved anything."

"You will not calm my conscience by your friendly interpretation," Wilhelm replied. "And I will always think of myself as your debtor."

"It is quite possible that you are that, but not in the way that you think," she said. "We think it scandalous not to fulfill a promise given by word of mouth. But, my friend, a good person always makes too many promises, just by being himself! The confidence that he inspires, the affection he awakens, the hopes he arouses, are limitless; he will always remain a debtor, without being aware of that. Farewell. Our external conditions have turned out well under your guidance, but with you leaving, a gap will open up in my heart that will not be so easily filled."

Before he left, Wilhelm wrote a long letter to Werner. They had exchanged a few letters, but because they could never agree on anything, they had stopped writing to each other. Now that Wilhelm was about to do what the other had so ardently advocated, contact was possible again. He was in a position to say: I am leaving the theater and I am associating myself with men whose company is bound to lead me into a life of firm, honest activity. He inquired after his money and was surprised at himself for not having done so earlier. He did not know that people much concerned with their own inner life are apt to neglect external circumstances. This was the state in which he found himself: he seemed, for the first time now, to be aware that he needed external means to promote effective activity. He ventured forth in quite a different frame of mind than on his first journey. The prospects before him were appealing, and he hoped to achieve happiness along the way.

Chapter Nine

When Wilhelm arrived back at Lothario's estate, he found that much had changed. Jarno greeted him with the news that Lothario's uncle had died, and Lothario had gone to take possession of the estates willed to him. "You've come just at the right time," he said, "to help me and the Abbé. Lothario has entrusted us with important business regarding the purchase of estates in the neighborhood, a matter that has been brewing for quite a time—and now we have the requisite funds and credit. The only matter of concern is that another business house, not in this area, has designs on these estates also. But we have finally decided to go partners with them, otherwise each of us would have driven up the price unreasonably and unnecessarily. We seem to be dealing with a shrewd businessman. So we are working out calculations and proposals, and we must consider from a farming point of view how best to divide up the land so that each receives a good piece of property." The documents were produced, and the fields, pasturelands and buildings were carefully surveyed; but Wilhelm expressed the desire that Therese should also be consulted. They spent several days on all this, and Wilhelm had little time at first to tell his friends about his adventures—nor to inform them of his doubtful paternity which, though important to him, was treated lightly and received indifferently by them.

He had noticed that when the others were engaged in private conversation, at table or on walks, they would sometimes stop short and change the subject, thereby revealing that they had secrets amongst themselves. He remembered what Lydie had said, and gave it ever more credence because the whole side of the castle in front of him remained always inaccessible. Up till now he had sought in vain to find a passage and entry to certain galleries and above all to the ancient tower.

One evening Jarno said to him: "We can now justly consider you as one of us, and therefore it would be unreasonable not to introduce you further into our mysteries. When a man makes his first entry into the world, it is good that he have a high opinion of himself, believes he can acquire many excellent qualities, and therefore endeavors to do everything; but when his development has reached a certain stage, it is advantageous for him to lose himself in a larger whole, learn to live for others, and forget himself in dutiful activity for others. Only then will he come to know himself, for activity makes us compare ourselves with others. You will soon come to know the small world that exists right here, and how well known you are in it. Be dressed and ready tomorrow morning before sunrise."

Jarno came at the appointed hour and conducted him through familiar and unfamiliar rooms in the castle, then through several galleries, until finally they arrived before a huge old door strengthened with iron bands. Jarno knocked and the door opened just wide enough for a man to slip through. Jarno pushed him through, but did not follow behind. Wilhelm found himself in a narrow dark space, everything was darkness around him and when he tried to take a step forward he stumbled. A voice, not entirely unfamiliar, called out to him: "Enter!" He then realized that the walls were covered with tapestries through which shone a dim light. "Enter!" it said once more. He lifted the tapestry and went in.

The hall in which he now found himself seemed at one time to have been a chapel. Instead of an altar there stood, at the top of some steps, a large table covered with a green cloth, and over it a drawn curtain which seemed to cover some painting or other. Off to the sides were some finely wrought cupboards, with wire grilles as in libraries, behind which were, instead of books, a large number of scrolls side by side. There was nobody else in the room. The light of the rising sun shone through the stained-glass windows directly into his face, and welcomed him.

"Be seated!" said a voice which appeared to come from the altar. Wilhelm sat down on a small armchair standing against the partition by the entrance. There was no other seat in the room, so he had to make do with this one, despite the fact that the morning sun was blinding him. But the chair was good and steady, so he could shield his eyes with his hand.

Then there was a slight sound and the curtain above the altar opened showing an empty dark space inside a frame. A man in ordinary clothes stepped forward and greeted him, saying: "Don't you recognize me? Don't you, amongst all the other things you would like to know, wish to find out where your grandfather's collection of works of art now is? Don't you remember the painting that especially appealed to you? Where do you think the sick prince is languishing at the moment?" Wilhelm had no difficulty in recognizing the stranger who on that momentous night had talked with him in the hostelry. "And perhaps this time," the man continued, "we could come to some agreement on fate and character."

Wilhelm was about to say something in reply, when the curtains quickly closed. "How strange!" he said to himself. "Can there be some pattern in chance events? Is what we call 'fate,' really only chance? Where can my grandfather's collection be; and why am I reminded of it in this solemn hour?"

He had no time for further reflection, because the curtain opened again, and there before his eyes stood a man whom he immediately recognized as the country priest of the boat trip with his jolly companions. He looked like the Abbé, but did not seem to be him. The man spoke with dignity and with a certain radiance on his face. This is what he said: "The duty of a teacher is not to preserve man from error, but to guide him in error, in fact to let him drink it in, in full draughts. That is the wisdom of teachers. For the man who only sips at error, can make do with it for quite a time, delighting in it as a rare pleasure. But a man who drinks it to the dregs, must recognize the error of his ways, unless he is mad." The curtain closed again, and this time Wilhelm did have time to reflect. "What error can the man be referring to," he asked himself, "except that which has dogged me all my life: seeking cultivation where none was to be found, imaging I could acquire a talent to which I had no propensity."

The curtain opened more quickly this time and an officer stepped out, saying in passing: "Learn to become acquainted with persons one can trust!" The curtain closed; and Wilhelm needed little time to recognize this officer as the one who had embraced him in the park of the count's castle, the man who was responsible for his thinking that Jarno was a recruiting officer. How he got here and who he was, were a complete mystery to Wilhelm. "If so many people have been taking an interest in you, knew what your life was and what was to be done about it, why didn't they guide you more firmly, more seriously?" he said to himself. "Why did they encourage your pastimes instead of deflecting you from them?"

"Do not remonstrate with us!" a voice declared. "You are saved, and on the way to your goal. You will not regret any of your follies, and not wish to repeat any of them. No man could have a happier fate." The curtain opened again, and there stood the old King of Denmark in full armor. "I am your father's ghost," said the figure in the frame, "and I depart in peace, for all I wished for you has been fulfilled more than I myself could imagine. Steep slopes can only be scaled by bypaths; on the plains, straight paths lead from one place to another. Farewell, and remember me when you partake of what I have prepared for you." Wilhelm was dumbfounded: he thought he heard his father's voice, and yet not; so confused was he by present reality and past memories.

He had not been musing long when in came the Abbé and stationed himself behind the green table. "Step forward!" he said to his astonished friend. Wilhelm stepped forward and mounted the steps. On the cloth covering the table lay a small scroll. "These are your Articles," said the Abbé. "Cherish them well, their content is important." Wilhelm took the scroll, opened it and read:

Certificate of Apprenticeship

Art is long, life is short, judgment difficult, opportunities fleeting. Action is easy, thinking is hard: acting after thinking, uncomfortable. Every beginning is joyous, every threshold a point of expectation. The boy stares in wonder, impressions condition him, he learns in playing, seriousness takes him by surprise. Imitation is natural to us all, but what to imitate is not easily ascertained. Rarely is the best discerned, still more rarely appreciated. Height attracts us, not the steps upwards; with the mountaintop in our eyes we linger lovingly on the plain. Only a part of art can be taught, an artist needs the whole. Those who know only half of it, are always confused and talk a lot; those who have the whole, act and talk little, or long afterwards. The former have no secrets and no strength, their teaching is like freshly baked bread, tasty and satisfying for one day; but flour cannot be sown and the fruits of the grain should not be ground. Words are good, but they are not the best. The best is not made clear by words. The spirit in which we act, is what is highest. Action can only be grasped by spirit and portrayed by spirit. No one knows what he is doing when he acts rightly, but we are always conscious of what is wrong. He who works only with signs, is a pedant, a hypocrite or a botcher. There are many such, and they get on well together. Their gossiping impedes the student, and their persistent mediocrity alarms those who are best. The teaching of a real artist opens up sense; for where words are lacking, action speaks. A true pupil learns how to unravel the unknown from the known, and thereby develops toward mastery.

"That's enough!" said the Abbé. "Save the rest for some other time. Now look around in these cupboards."

Wilhelm walked up to them and looked at the names on the scrolls. To his amazement he found there Lothario's apprenticeship, Jarno's apprenticeship, and his own, in amongst many others with names unknown to him.

"May I hope some time to take a look at these scrolls?"

"Nothing is closed to you in this room anymore."

"May I ask one question?"

"Of course you may! And you can expect a decisive answer if it concerns a matter that is close to your heart and should be so."

"Very well, then! You strange wise men, whose sight can pierce so many mysteries, tell me if you will: is Felix really my son?"

"Praise be to you for asking that question!" exclaimed the Abbé, clapping his hands with joy. "Felix is your son! I swear it by all our most sacred mysteries. Felix is your son, and in spirit his deceased mother was not unworthy of you. Take unto yourself this lovely child from our hands, turn around, and dare to be happy."

Wilhelm heard a noise behind him, turned round, and saw the face of a child peering mischievously through the tapestries covering the entrance: it was Felix. The boy hid himself laughingly, once he was seen. "Come out!" said the Abbé. He came, his father rushed toward him, folded him in his arms and pressed him to his heart. "Yes, oh yes," said Wilhelm, "you are indeed mine! What a gift this is from Heaven that I have to thank my friends for! Where have you come from at this moment, my child?"

"Don't ask," said the Abbé. "Hail to you, young man. Your apprenticeship is completed, Nature has given you your freedom."

Book Eight

Chapter One

Felix ran out into the garden, and Wilhelm followed him in a state of exhilaration. It was the most beautiful morning, everything around him looked lovelier than ever, he was sublimely happy. Felix was a newcomer in this world of freedom and beauty, and his father was not much better acquainted with the things that the boy repeatedly and tirelessly asked about. They finally went up to the gardener, who could tell him names and uses of various plants. Wilhelm was observing nature through a new organ, and the child's curiosity and desire to learn made him aware how feeble his interest had been in the things outside himself and how little he knew, how few things he was familiar with. On this day, the happiest of his entire life, his own education seemed also to be beginning anew: he felt the need to inform himself, while being required to inform another.

Jarno and the Abbé had not reappeared, but in the evening they came with a visitor. Wilhelm was so astonished he could not believe his eyes. Werner hesitated a moment before recognizing him. They embraced each other affectionately, and neither could conceal the fact that he found the other changed. Werner thought that his friend was taller, stronger, more upright, more cultivated in manner and more pleasant in behavior. "I miss something of your earlier spontaneity, however," he added. "That will come back once we have recovered from our initial amazement at seeing each other again," said Wilhelm.

The impression that Werner made on him was by no means so favorable. The good fellow seemed to have regressed rather than advanced. He was much thinner, his pointed face seemed sharper and his nose longer, he was bald, his voice was loud and strident and his flat chest, dropping shoulders and pallid cheeks showed quite clearly that this was a sickly creature with a mania for work.

Wilhelm did not go out of his way to comment on this change, but Werner gave full vent to his delight in his friend. "My goodness!" he exclaimed, "you may have spent your time poorly and, as I suspect, made little profit, but you have become a man of parts who will, in fact is bound to, make his own fortune. Don't squander or dissipate it this time; with your figure you should be able to get yourself a rich heiress." "You haven't changed a bit," said Wilhelm with a smile. "You've just seen your friend again after a long interval, and you are already treating him as a commodity, a source of speculation, from which profit may be gained."

Jarno and the Abbé seemed in no way surprised by this recognition scene, and left the two friends to expatiate at will on both past and present. Werner looked at Wilhelm from all sides, twisting and turning him to the point of making him embarrassed. "I've never seen anything like this," said Werner, "and yet I know I am not deceiving myself. Your eyes are more deep set, your forehead is broader, your nose is more delicate and your mouth is much more pleasant. Look at how you stand! How well everything fits together! Indolence makes one prosper, whereas I, poor wretch," he said, looking at himself in the mirror, "if I had not spent my time earning a mint of money, there wouldn't be anything to say for me."

Werner had never received Wilhelm's last letter. It was his firm with which Lothario intended to accomplish the joint purchase of the estates; and this was the occasion of Werner's visit. He had no idea that he would find Wilhelm there. The magistrate came, the papers were produced, and Werner found the conditions reasonable. "If you, as it seems, are well disposed towards this young man," he said, "see to it that our part of this is not reduced. It depends on my friend whether he wants to acquire the estate and expend part of his funds on it." Jarno and the Abbé assured him that they did not need to be reminded of that. They quickly settled their business and then Werner wanted to play a game of cards, in which the Abbé and Jarno joined him, for he was by now accustomed to spending every evening in this way.

When dinner was over and the two friends were alone together, they spent their time in eager questionings and discussion, each informing the other what he wished him to know. Wilhelm was full of praise for his present situation and his good fortune at being received into the company of such excellent persons. Werner, however, shook his head and said: "One should only believe what one sees with one's own eyes. Some of my most obliging friends have told me that you are consorting with a loose-living young nobleman, provide him with actresses, help him squander his money, and are responsible for his being on such bad terms with all his relatives." "I would be very distressed, both on my own account and on that of those good people, if actors were so misjudged," Wilhelm replied. "But my theatrical career has accustomed me to all kinds of slanderous defamation. How is it possible for people to judge our actions, when all they see is bits and pieces, a small part of something that contains both good and bad, and in its appearances is neither one nor the other. Put actors and actresses before them on an elevated platform, light the lamps, the whole thing is over and done with in an hour or so, and nobody really knows what to make of it."

He then asked about the family, his old friends, and his home town. Werner told him very quickly all that had changed, what was still there, and what was happening. "The women in the house are happy and content, for there is no lack of money. They spend half their time preening themselves, and the other half displaying themselves. They devote a reasonable amount of time to household affairs. My children are growing into sensible boys. I can already envision them sitting and writing, doing accounts, running errands, bargaining and selling things off. I want them all to have their own business as soon as possible. As for our capital, you will be delightfully surprised. As soon as we have settled about these estates, you must come back with me, for it seems as if you, by exercising some degree of reason, could take an active part in our affairs. Your new friends are to be complimented for putting you on the right path. I'm a silly fool to find out only now how fond I am of you, and I'm unable to take my eyes off you when you look so fine and well. Your appearance is quite different from the picture you once sent your sister, which caused quite a furor in the house. Mother and daughter thought the young man was charming, with his open-neck shirt, chest half bared, big ruff, loose hanging hair, round hat, short vest and baggy trousers — but I thought that outfit was pretty close to a clown's. But now you look like a man, except that I urge you to have your hair done in a pigtail, else you will be taken, with that loose hairstyle, for a Jew, and have to pay tolls."

Felix had come into the room while they were talking, and since no one was taking any notice of him, he had sat down on the sofa and fallen asleep. "Who's that brat?" Werner asked. For the moment Wilhelm did not have the courage to tell him the truth, nor the inclination to relate the whole story to someone who was by nature disinclined to believe him.

They then went off to inspect the estates and conclude their business. Wilhelm kept Felix close by him and, for his sake, took great pleasure in the property they were looking at. The child's eagerness for cherries and berries that would soon be ripe, reminded him of his own youth and his father's dutiful way of preparing, creating and preserving pleasures. He examined the plantings and buildings with great attention, actively considering how to restore and rebuild. He surveyed the world around him, but not like a bird of passage; a building was for him no longer a rapidly assembled shelter that would wither away before one left. Everything he planned was now to mature for the boy, and everything he built was to last for several generations. His apprenticeship was therefore completed in one sense, for along with the feeling of a father he had acquired the virtues of a solid citizen. His joy knew no bounds. "All moralizing is unnecessarily strict," he exclaimed. "Nature turns us, in her own pleasant way, into what we should be. Strange indeed are those demands of middle-class society that confuse and mislead us, finally demanding more from us than Nature herself. I deplore all attempts at developing us which obliterate the most effective means of education by forcing us towards the endpoint instead of giving us a sense of satisfaction along the way."

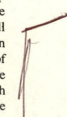

Much as he had seen in his life already, he now understood human nature through the eyes of the child. The theater, like the world as a whole, had appeared to him like a throw of dice, each of which counted for more on one face and less on the other, and only added up to a whole when they were counted together. But here in the child was, so to speak, one single die, on whose various faces the worth and worthlessness of human nature were clearly marked.

The child's demand for distinctions grew daily: once he had learnt that things have names, he wanted to hear them all. He believed his father must know everything, pestered him constantly with questions, and gave him cause to inquire after objects that he had never paid much attention to. A native impulse to find out the origin and end of everything soon became apparent. When he inquired where wind came from and where flames went to, his father became all too aware of his own limitations. He wondered how far human curiosity can extend and how much he could hope to satisfy it. The child's anger when it saw a living creature maltreated, pleased his father, who saw in it the sign of superior character. Felix set about the kitchenmaid when she was cutting up pigeons. However, this admirable disposition of his was counteracted by his merciless destruction of frogs and butterflies, and Wilhelm was reminded that there are many people who appear quite righteous when their passions are not aroused or when they are observing the actions of others.

The pleasant feeling that the boy was having a really good influence on his life was dispelled in a trice when he realized that the boy was educating him more than he the boy. He had nothing to object to in the boy, he was not capable of giving him a direction that he was not taking of his own accord, and even those bad habits that Aurelie had worked so hard to eradicate seemed to return after her death. He would still not close the door behind him, he still would not finish what was on his plate, and he was never more delighted than when people observed that he ate from the platter rather than his plate, left his glass standing, and drank out of the bottle. He was also quite charming when he sat in the corner with a book, and said, very earnestly: "I must study this learned stuff!" even though he couldn't as yet (and wouldn't) distinguish the letters of the alphabet.

When Wilhelm thought of how little he had done for the child and how little he was able to do for him, he was overcome by a sense of uneasiness, and this well-nigh outweighed his happiness. "Are we born so selfish," he said to himself, "that we are unable to care for someone other than ourselves? Here you are at the same point with this boy as you were with Mignon. You took charge of the poor child, her companionship delighted you, and yet you have cruelly neglected her. What have you done to give her the development she longed for? Nothing! You left her to her own devices, and to all the mischance she was necessarily exposed to in an uncultivated society. And now with this boy, who attracted you even before he was so precious to you—has your heart ever impelled you to do the slightest thing for him? It is high time that you stopped wasting your time and that of others: pull yourself together and just think what you have to do for yourself and for those dear creatures that nature and affection bind so closely to you."

Actually, this soliloquy was just a prelude to his recognition of all that he had been thinking, worrying about, looking for, and finally decided on. He could no longer put off admitting to himself that, after repeated outbursts of sorrow at the loss of Mariane, he must now find a mother for the boy, and he could not find a better one than Therese. He now knew this excellent woman completely, and a wife and companion like her seemed the only possible person to whom he could safely entrust himself and his loved ones. Her noble affection for Lothario did not cause him any qualms, for the two of them were separated forever by a strange train of events. Therese thought of herself as free, and had spoken of marriage with a certain indifference, though also as something that was self-evident.

Having reasoned with himself for some time, he finally decided to tell her as much as he knew about himself. She should get to know him as well as he knew her, and he began to work over his own life story; but it seemed so totally lacking in events of any significance, and anything he would have to report was so little to his advantage that more than once he was tempted to give up the whole idea. Finally he decided to ask Jarno for the scroll of his apprenticeship from the tower, and Jarno said this was just the right time. So Wilhelm got possession of it.

It is a terrifying feeling for any worthy person to find himself in a situation where he is about to be informed about himself. All transitions are crises, and is not crisis a form of sickness? How unwilling we are, after we have been sick, to look at ourselves in a mirror! One feels better, but sees only the evidence of one's illness. Wilhelm was by now sufficiently prepared for the occasion, circumstances had given him the lead, his friends had not been sparing in their opinions, and although he unrolled the parchment with a certain hastiness, he found that he calmed down the more he read in it. The account of his life was related in every detail and with great incisiveness. His attention was not distracted by the report of individual events or momentary emotions, sympathetic comments enlightened him without embarrassing him, and he saw a picture of himself, not like a second self in a mirror, but a different self, one outside of him, as in a painting. One never approves of everything in a portrait, but one is always glad that a thoughtful mind has seen us thus and a superior talent enjoyed portraying us in such a way that a picture survives of what we were, and will survive longer than we will.

As the manuscript recalled every detail of Wilhelm's life, he began to compose in his mind his story for Therese, feeling almost ashamed at having nothing to match her own fine qualities, nothing that testified to any active purpose in his life. Detailed as the survey was in his thoughts, when he came to write it down in a letter, this turned out quite short: he asked for her friendship, if possible for her love, offered her his hand in marriage, and asked for a speedy reply.

After some inner doubt whether to seek the advice of his friends, especially Jarno and the Abbé, on this important matter, he decided not to. His mind was too firmly made up; the whole matter was too important for him to submit to the judgment of the best or most reasonable person in the world, and he was judicious enough to see that his letter went out with the very next post. Perhaps it was the feeling that, as emerged quite clearly from the scroll, there had been so many occasions in his life when he thought he was acting freely and unobserved, only to discover that he had indeed been observed, even directed; perhaps it was this that made him now unburden his heart freely, at least to Therese's heart, and let his fate depend on her decision alone. And so he had no qualms of conscience about circumventing his guardians and overseers on this important issue.

Chapter Two

He had just dispatched his letter when Lothario returned. Everyone expressed satisfaction that the important business in hand would soon be concluded, and Wilhelm awaited with eager anticipation for many different threads to be severed or joined and his future prospects be decided. Lothario greeted everyone most cordially. He was by now fully recovered, cheerful, and looking like a man who knows what he has to do, which nothing will prevent him from doing.

Wilhelm was not able to return his greeting with equal cordiality. "This," he had to admit to himself, "is the friend, the lover, the bridegroom of Therese, whom you intend forcibly to replace. Do you really think you can ever erase or banish the impression he has made on her?" If the letter had not already been on its way, he would probably never have dared to send it. But fortunately the die was cast, perhaps Therese had already decided, and perhaps only the distance between them was delaying a happy resolution. It would soon be decided whether there was to be gain or loss. He tried to find solace in such thoughts, but his heart was filled with feverish agitation. He had difficulty in giving much thought to the important business transactions on which to a certain extent his future prosperity depended. In such emotional moments as this, nothing else has much importance for any man, neither what is outside him nor what belongs to him.

It was fortunate for him that Lothario dealt with the matter nobly and Werner speedily. Werner, in his eagerness to acquire the splendid property, showed great delight at this gain to himself or rather to his friend Wilhelm, whereas Lothario for his part seemed to have quite other thoughts. "I cannot be pleased at acquiring such property unless it be honestly gained," he said. "Is that not the case here?" asked Werner. "Not exactly," Lothario replied. "Didn't we give them ready money for it?" "That we did," said Lothario, "and perhaps you will consider what I must remind you of as being unnecessarily scrupulous. I do not consider any acquisition of property an honest deal unless the State is accorded that part which is due to it." "What do you mean?" said Werner. "Would you prefer that our freely bought lands were subject to taxation?" "Yes, I would," said Lothario, "up to a certain point. Our land will only be secure if it is treated like everybody else's. What reason should a farmer have in these times to consider his land as a less firmly established possession than that of a nobleman, except that the latter is not encumbered but encumbers him?"

"And what about the return on our capital investment?" said Werner.

"That will not be adversely affected if the State, in return for reasonable and regular tax payments, continues to allow us the feudal hocus-pocus by which we have complete right of disposal over our property, are not obliged to maintain it in such large units, and can divide it up more equally among our children, so that all of them may indulge in free vigorous activity instead of being restricted by hereditary privileges to justify which we have to invoke the spirits of our ancestors. And how much happier would men and women be, if they could have the free opportunity of advancing some worthy young woman or promising young man to a better position in life, without any further considerations. The State would acquire more and better citizens, and not be so often lacking in heads and hands."

"I can assure you," said Werner, "that in all my life I have never thought about the State, and only paid my dues and taxes because that was customary."

"Well," said Lothario, "I hope to be able to make a good patriot out of you. A good father is one who at mealtimes serves his children first; and a good citizen is one who pays what he owes the State before dealing with everything else."

These general reflections facilitated rather than delayed the completion of their business transaction, and when things were pretty well in order, Lothario said to Wilhelm: "I must now send you to a place where you are more urgently needed than here. My sister requests that you come to her as soon as possible. Poor Mignon seems to be wasting away and they think your coming may perhaps check her decline. My sister has sent me this letter from which you will see how important your coming would be to her." Lothario handed him the letter and Wilhelm, who had been listening to him in a state of great perturbation, recognized the countess's handwriting in the hastily written lines, and did not know what answer to give.

"Take Felix with you," Lothario added, "so that the two children may cheer each other up. My sister's carriage, in which my servants came back, is still ready. I'll give you horses to take you halfway; then you can take the posthorses. Goodbye; give my greetings to my sister, and tell her I will be coming to see her soon, and she should be prepared for a number of guests. My greatuncle's friend, the Marchese Cipriani, is on his way here. He was hoping to find the old man still alive so that they could entertain each other with recollections of past experiences and their mutual love of art. The Marchese is much younger than my uncle, to whom he owed the greater part of his education. We must do all we can to try to fill the gap for the Marchese, and that is best done by assembling a fairly large group of people."

Lothario then went to his room, accompanied by the Abbé, Jarno having already left. Wilhelm rushed off to his own room, with no one to confide in, no one to dissuade him from embarking on what he anticipated with such trepidation. The young servant boy came and urged him to start packing, because they wanted to load up the horses that night, so as to be able to start out at dawn. Wilhelm did not know what to do, and finally said to himself: "Just see to it that you get away from this house; then you can decide what to do as you go along. You could stop at the halfway point and send a message back, putting in writing what you did not dare to say, and then just let things take their course." Despite having reached this decision, he spent a sleepless night; but the sight of Felix peacefully asleep encouraged him. "Oh!" he cried. "Who knows what tests still lie in store for me; who knows how much my past mistakes will return to torment me, and my good, sensible plans for the future miscarry! But the treasure I have here, may this never be taken from me, by inexorable, or beseechable, Fate! If this very best part of me were ever to be destroyed, this heart be torn from my heart, then farewell reason and sense, farewell care and caution, farewell every impulse of preservation! Be gone, all that sets us off from the animals! And if I am not permitted to put an end to all my misery, may early madness obliterate my consciousness before death's dark night dissolves it forever!"

He grasped the boy in his arms, kissed him, pressed him to his breast, and covered him with copious tears. The boy woke up. His bright eyes and friendly glance affected his father deeply. "What a scene it will be," he cried, "when I present you to the lovely countess, and she presses you to her bosom, that bosom which your father so deeply wounded! Must I not fear that she will thrust you from herself with a cry, when your touch reawakens her real, or imaginary, pain!"

The coachman did not allow him time for further reflection or choice, constraining him to get into the carriage before daybreak. Wilhelm saw to it that Felix was well wrapped up, for the morning was cold, though bright. The child saw the sun rise for the first time in his life. His astonishment at the first fiery glow, the increasing brightness of the light—his whole joy, and the strange remarks that accompanied this, were a delight to the father, who gazed into the child's heart, a calm, clear lake over which the sun rose and hovered.

The coachman unharnessed the horses in a small town, and rode back. Wilhelm secured a room in the inn, then asked himself whether he should go on, or stay there. Undecided, he took out the letter again, which he had not yet dared to reread, and saw that it contained the following words: "Send your young friend to me very soon. Mignon's condition has taken a turn for the worse these last two days. Sad as the occasion is, I would very much like to meet him."

Wilhelm had not paid attention to those final words when he first looked at the letter. He was frightened by them, and now firmly determined not to go. "Why is it," he cried, "that Lothario, who knows the whole story, did not tell her who I am? She can't be calmly expecting someone she already knows and would rather not see again; she is expecting a stranger — and who should walk in but me! I can see her recoiling, see her blushing. No; I cannot possibly face such a scene!" The horses had just been readied, but Wilhelm was determined to unload and stay where he was. His mind was in a state of complete turmoil. Hearing a girl coming upstairs to tell him all was prepared, he quickly tried to think up a reason that made it necessary to delay his departure. His eyes glanced through the note in his hand. "Heavens! what is this?" he cried. "This is not the countess's handwriting; it is the Amazon's!"

The girl came into the room, urging him to go down, and taking Felix with her. "How is this possible?" he said. "Can this be true? What am I to do? Stay and wait for an explanation, or get there quickly and plunge into whatever ensues? You are on your way to join her; why do you hesitate? This evening you will see her; why voluntarily shut yourself up in here? It is her hand, of course it is; her hand summons you, her carriage is ready to go and take you to her. The mystery is now solved: Lothario has two sisters. He knows about my relationship to one of them, but he does not know how much I owe the other. And she doesn't know that the wounded traveler, who owes his recovery, if not his very life, to her, has been received with such unmerited generosity in the house of her brother."

Felix, rocking to and fro down there in the carriage, called up to him: "Father, come down here and look at these beautiful clouds with their lovely colors!" — "I'm coming," said Wilhelm, racing down the stairway. "And let me tell you that the heavenly phenomena you so much admire, are nothing compared to what awaits me!"

While he was seated in the carriage, he went over everything in his mind. "So this Natalie is the friend of Therese! What a discovery, what hopes, what prospects! How strange that my fear of hearing about the one sister had completely obscured the fact that the other existed!" He looked at Felix, full of joy, hoping that he and the boy would be well received.

Evening drew on, the sun went down, the road was not of the best, and so the coachman drove slowly. Felix fell asleep, and new cares and doubts rose in Wilhelm's mind. "What crazy ideas these are that are occupying your mind," he said to himself. "A dubious resemblance of handwriting removes all your doubts and gives rise to the wildest fancy." He took out the letter again, and in the fading light again thought he recognized the countess's hand. His eyes persisted this time in not finding what his heart had been telling him. "So these horses are dragging you toward the most frightful scene! Who knows whether they will not bring you back here in a few hours! And suppose you find her there alone! Suppose her husband is there, or the baroness! Will she be much changed? Shall I be able to remain upright before her gaze?"

Only a vague hope of seeing the Amazon pierced the gloom of these melancholy reflections from time to time. Night had fallen, the carriage rumbled into a courtyard, and halted. A servingman with a wax candle came out through a splendid portal and down a flight of broad steps to the carriage. "We've been expecting you for quite a while," he said, opening the carriage door. Wilhelm stepped out, holding the sleeping Felix in his arms, and the servant called to another man standing in the doorway with a light, saying, "Take this gentlemen straight to the baroness."

In a flash Wilhelm thought to himself: "What luck! The baroness is here, whether by chance or by design. I shall see her first. Perhaps the countess is already sleeping. Kindly protective spirits, grant that this moment of extreme embarrassment may pass without mishap!"

He went into the house, and found himself in the most solemn and, for him, sacred place he had ever seen. A low-hanging lantern gave light to the stairway opposite him, which was wide and rose gradually until it divided into two arms at a landing. There were marble statues and busts standing on pedestals and in niches. Some of them seemed familiar to him. Youthful impressions never fade away entirely. He recognized a muse which had belonged to his grandfather, not by its shape or quality, but because one arm had been restored along with various sections of the drapery. He felt as though he were in a fantasy world. The child began to weigh heavy on him, so he paused and knelt down on the steps, as if to get a better hold of him, but really just to relax a minute. He had difficulty in getting up again. The servant with the light offered to take the child from him, but he did not want to let go of it. They then went into an anteroom where, to his utter amazement, he saw the picture of the sick prince hanging on the wall. He had no time for more than a fleeting glance at it, because the servingman ushered them through a series of rooms into a small chamber where, beneath a lampshade and partly obscured, a woman sat reading. "If only it were she!" he said to himself in this decisive moment. He put down the child who seemed to be waking up, and was about to move toward the woman, when, as the child sank back into sleep, she stood up and came toward him. It was the Amazon! He could not control himself, fell on his knees, and cried: "It is she!" He clasped her hand and kissed it with rapturous delight. The child lay between them both on the carpet, fast asleep.

They lifted him on to the sofa, Natalie sat down beside him and asked Wilhelm to take a seat on a nearby chair. She offered him some refreshment, which he declined, being far too busy making sure that this was really she, looking closer at her features shaded by the lamp and finally deciding for sure that it was. She spoke to him in general terms about Mignon's illness, telling him that the girl was becoming more and more the prey of strong emotions, and, highly sensitive as always, concealed the fact that she often suffered from violent cramps around the heart, but so dangerously severe that sometimes this prime organ of life stopped beating suddenly when she was unexpectedly excited, and there seemed to be no sign of life in the dear child's body. Once this frightening convulsion had passed, the strength of her nature returned in strong pulse beats which now frightened the child by the intensity of what before had been completely lacking.

Wilhelm remembered one such scene, and Natalie referred him to the doctor, who would explain things further and give the reason why they had summoned the child's friend and protector just now. "You will notice a peculiar change in her; she now wears only women's clothes, which formerly she utterly despised."

"How did you get her to do that?" Wilhelm asked.

"One might say it was pure chance. Let me tell you what happened. You perhaps know that I always have a group of young girls around me with the purpose of encouraging in them, by letting them grow up in close proximity to me, a sense of what is good and right. From me they never hear anything that is not true, but I cannot prevent them — nor would I wish to — from acquiring from others errors and prejudices current in the world at large. If they ask me about these, I try my best to show the difference between such undesirable ideas and what, for me, are correct attitudes, so that these errors, though never useful, may at least not become harmful to them. Recently my girls had been hearing from some peasant children about angels, and about Santa Claus and the Christ Child, who come every now and then to reward good children and punish the naughty ones. The girls suspected that these were real persons dressed up; I encouraged them in this belief and, without offering any explanation, decided to organize such a spectacle on the first appropriate occasion. It so happened that two of them, twin sisters and always well behaved, had a birthday coming; I promised them that an angel would bring the presents they had so well deserved. They looked forward to this with great excitement. I chose Mignon to play the part of the angel, and on the appointed day, she was clothed in a long, thin white garment with a girdle of gold around her chest and a golden crown in her hair. I first thought I would omit the wings, but the women who dressed her insisted on a pair of big golden wings with which she could demonstrate her skill. And so this miraculous vision appeared, a lily in one hand and a little basket in the other, right in the midst of the girls, and surprised me as well. "Here comes the angel!" I said. All the children made as if to withdraw, but then finally shouted: "It's Mignon!" though still not venturing any closer to the wondrous sight.

"'Here are your presents,' she said, handing them the basket. They gathered around her, gazed, touched her, and then one of them asked: 'Are you an angel?' 'I wish I were,' Mignon replied. 'Why are you holding a lily?' 'My heart should be open and pure as a lily, then I would be happy.' 'What are the wings for? Let me see!' 'They stand for lovelier wings which are not yet opened.'

"She continued to give these remarkable answers to their simple questions. When their curiosity was satisfied and the first impressions of her appearance began to fade, they wanted to undress her. But she would not allow this. She took up her zither, climbed up on this high desk, and sang with unbelievable grace and appeal this song:

> So let me seem till I become:
> Take not this garment white from me!
> I hasten from the joys of earth
> Down to that house so fast and firm.
>
> There will I rest in peace a while,
> Till opens wide my freshened glance.
> Then I will cast my dress aside.
> Leaving both wreath and girdle there.
>
> For all those glorious heavenly forms,
> They do not ask for man or wife,
> No garments long or draperies fine
> Surround the body now transformed.
>
> I lived indeed untouched by care.
> And yet I felt deep sorrow there,
> Sorrow has made me old too soon,
> Now make me young for ever more!

"I decided immediately," Natalie went on, "to let her keep the dress, and had others made that were similar. These she is now wearing, and in them, it seems to me, her whole being appears quite different."

Since it was already late, Natalie bade Wilhelm leave, which he did in a state of some anxiety. "Is she married, or not?" he wondered. When he heard a noise he feared that a door might open and a husband come in. The servant who conducted him to his room, left him before he had summoned up the courage to ask about Natalie's circumstances. His uncertainty kept him awake for a time, which he spent comparing the image of the Amazon with his new friend. The two would not coalesce: the former had been fashioned, as it were, by him, the latter seemed almost to be refashioning him.

Chapter Three

The next morning, while everything was still peaceful and quiet, he walked around looking at the house. The building had clean lines and was the finest and noblest he had ever seen. "Good art," he said to himself, "is like good society: it obliges us, in the most pleasing way, to recognize form and limitations like those which govern our being." His grandfather's statues and busts gave him unusual pleasure. He returned eagerly to the picture of the sick prince, still finding it as moving and affecting as ever. The servant opened the doors to several other rooms: there was a library, a collection of natural history specimens, and another of stones and metals. He felt quite strange, standing in front of all these objects. Felix had by now woken up and was following him around. Wilhelm was concerned to know when and how he would receive a reply from Therese. He felt some trepidation at seeing Mignon — also, in a way, at seeing Natalie. How different his present mood was from when he sent the letter to Therese, joyfully entrusting his whole self to such a noble being!

Natalie asked him to come to breakfast. He went into a room where several neatly dressed girls, all apparently less than ten years old, were laying the table while an older person was bringing various beverages.

Wilhelm's attention was drawn to a picture that hung over the sofa. He took it for a portrait of Natalie, but not a very satisfying one. At this point she entered the room, and the resemblance seemed to disappear entirely. However, he noticed that she was wearing the cross of some order, just like the woman in the picture.

"I've been looking at that portrait," he said, "and am amazed that the artist could be so true and so false at the same time. It is a good general likeness of you, a very good one really, but it does not capture either your features or your character."

"What is still more amazing," Natalie replied, "is that it is such a good likeness, for it is not a picture of me, but of an aunt who, even as an old lady, resembled me as a child. It was painted when she was about the age I am now, and most people, when they first see it, think it is a picture of me. I wish you had known this splendid person, for I am indebted to her for so much. Her delicate health, along with perhaps too much concern about herself, and in addition an extreme moral and religious reserve, prevented her from becoming for the world what, in other circumstances, she might well have been. She was a light that shone on just a few friends — and especially brightly on me."

"Can it be possible," said Wilhelm after a moment's reflection on how strangely so many different circumstances seemed to be combining in this moment, "can it be possible, that the noble, beautiful soul whose private confessions I was privileged to read, was your aunt?"

"You have read what she wrote?" asked Natalie.

"Yes, I have!" said Wilhelm. "I did so with sympathetic understanding and it has had a great effect on the course of my life. What emerged for me most clearly was, I would say, the purity of her life and of everything that surrounded her, her independent spirit and her inability to make anything part of herself which did not conform to her noble loving nature."

"You are more liberal and more just toward her fine character than many others who have read her manuscript. Every cultured person knows how hard one has to struggle with a certain degree of coarseness in oneself and others, how costly self-cultivation is, and how often one thinks solely of oneself and forgets what one owes to others. Every good human being reproaches himself occasionally for not having acted gently enough; and yet if such a fine person becomes too gentle, too considerate, too cultivated, if you will, the world shows no tolerance, and no consideration for what such a person is. Persons like her are outside us what ideals are inside us, models not to be imitated, but to be striven after. People laugh at the cleanliness of Dutch women, but would my friend Therese be what she is, if she did not have some such ideal of cleanliness in her mind when she is engaged in domestic activities?"

"So you, Natalie, are the friend of Therese to whom she is so devoted, the precious relative who, as a young girl and since, has always been so affectionate, sympathetic, and helpful! A person like you could only come from such a family, and now that I know your heritage and the whole circle you belong to, I feel immense vistas opening up before me!"

"Indeed," said Natalie, "you could not have been better informed about us all than from my aunt's account. One must admit that her affection for me presumed too much good in me as a child, but when one talks about children, it is one's hopes for them rather than what they actually are which one has in mind."

Wilhelm was now informed about Lothario's origins and early youth. He could picture the charming countess as the child with her aunt's pearls around her neck. And he had been so near these pearls when her delicate, loving lips had pressed themselves on his. He tried to dispel these memories with other thoughts. He ran through all the people he had become acquainted with from the manuscript. "So here I am," he declared, "in the house of that remarkable uncle; yet, it isn't a house, it's a temple, and you are its noble priestess, indeed, its presiding genius. I shall remember all my life the impression I had yesterday evening when I came in here, and there in front of me were those old treasures from my youth—there once more. I remembered the sorrowing statues in Mignon's song; but these objects have no need to sorrow for me, they looked at me in solemn seriousness, linking my earliest memories to this present moment. Here I have rediscovered the family treasures, the joys of my grandfather, set between so many other noble works of art. And I, whom nature made the favorite child of that good old man, I, unworthy as I am, find myself in such worthy company, such a wealth of relationships!"

The young girls had left the room one by one, in order to get on with their various jobs. Now that he was alone with Natalie, Wilhelm had to offer some explanation of what he had just been saying. The discovery that a notable part of these works of art had belonged to his grandfather, put him in a cheerful, sociable mood. The manuscript had made him acquainted with this house, and he now found himself reunited with his own inheritance. He wanted to see Mignon, but Natalie asked him to be patient and wait until the doctor, who had been summoned away to somewhere in the neighborhood, should return. It will come as no surprise that this was the same busy little man whom we already know, the same we met in the *Confessions of a Beautiful Soul*.

"Well, here I am in the midst of your family," said Wilhelm, "and so I suppose that the Abbé who is mentioned in your aunt's narrative, is that strange, mysterious man whom I rediscovered after a train of peculiar circumstances in your brother's house? Perhaps you would give me some more information about him?"

To this Natalie replied: "There would be a great deal to say about him. What I am best informed about, is his influence on our education. He was convinced, at least for a time, that all education should build on inclination. What his present opinion is, I do not know. He used to say that the most important thing is to be active, but one cannot engage in any activity without the necessary predisposition or the instinct impelling us in that direction. 'It is agreed,' he would say, 'that poets are born, not made; and this claim is made for all the arts. But if one considers the matter more closely, we are only born with minimal ability, and there is no such thing as indeterminate ability. It is only our piecemeal, vague education that makes us uncertain of ourselves; it arouses desires rather than active impulses, and instead of helping to develop predispositions, it directs our activity toward objects, which are often out of line with the minds that are so taken up with them. A child or young person who goes astray on his chosen path is, in my opinion, preferable to many of those who pursue uncongenial paths. When the former do find the right path, either by themselves or under direction, it will be the path suited to their nature, and they will never depart from it; but the latter will constantly be in danger of casting off an alien yoke and abandoning themselves to complete freedom of action.'"

"It is strange that this extraordinary man has taken an interest in me too," said Wilhelm, "and if he has not precisely guided me according to his fashion, he has at least encouraged me for a time in my mistakes. How he will in future account for the fact that, in company with several others, he has almost made a fool of me, is something that I can only wait patiently to discover."

"I can't complain about this peculiarity of his, if indeed it is a peculiarity," said Natalie. "For, of all my siblings, I am the one who has least suffered from it. I cannot imagine that my brother Lothario could have been better educated. Perhaps my dear sister, the countess, might have been treated differently—they could have tried to give more seriousness and strength to her character. And what is to become of my brother Friedrich, I haven't the least idea. I'm afraid that he may well be the victim of these pedagogical experiments."

"So you have a second brother?" said Wilhelm.

"Yes I do," she replied, "and he is the merriest, most lighthearted creature. Since he has never been prevented from wandering about the world, I do not know what will come from his frivolous, carefree nature. I haven't seen him for a long while. My only consolation is that the Abbé and all my brother's friends always know where he is and what he is doing."

Wilhelm was about to inquire further of Natalie about these paradoxes, and try to obtain more information about the secret society, when at that very moment the doctor came into the room and, having greeted them briefly, began to talk about the condition of Mignon. Natalie took Felix by the hand, saying that she would bring him to Mignon and prepare her for Wilhelm's coming.

The doctor, now that he and Wilhelm were alone, began as follows: "What I have to tell you, is stranger than you could possibly expect. Natalie has given us an opportunity to speak openly about matters that I have learnt only from her but which cannot be discussed freely in her presence. What we are concerned with is the strange personality of that dear child Mignon. It consists almost entirely of a deep sort of yearning: the longing to see her motherland again, and a longing, my friend, for you—these, I may say, are the only earthly things about her, and both of them have an element of infinite distance about them, both goals being inaccessible to her unusual nature. She may have come originally from near Milan. She was taken from her parents when she was very young by a company of acrobats. No further details could be ascertained from her, partly because she was too young at the time to remember exact names and locations, and partly because she made a vow never again to reveal her home and origins to a living soul. For she did give an exact account of her home to the persons who found her wandering about, begging them earnestly to take her back there, but they dragged her away with them and joked at night, when they thought she was asleep, about the good catch they had made, resolving that she should never be allowed to find her way back. The poor creature was overcome by utter despair, in the midst of which the Mother of God appeared to her and promised to take care of her. So she swore a sacred oath that she would never again trust anyone, never tell anyone her story, and live and die in the expectation of direct divine sustenance. What I have been telling you, was not something she conveyed in so many words to Natalie, but what Natalie has pieced together from occasional remarks, from songs and childish indiscretions which revealed what they intended to keep secret."

Wilhelm could now account for many a song, many an utterance of the poor girl. He beseeched his friend not to withhold from him anything else that he had gathered from the songs and confessions of this extraordinary child.

"Well then," said the doctor, "be prepared for a strange revelation concerning an event in which you had an important part, though you may not remember, and which, I fear, became decisive for the life and death of this dear creature."

"I am very eager to hear about it," said Wilhelm.

"Do you remember the night after the performance of *Hamlet* when you had a mysterious female visitor?"

"Of course I do," said Wilhelm with some embarrassment, "but I wasn't expecting to be reminded of that at this particular moment."

"Do you know who it was?"

"You scare me! Surely not Mignon? Who was it then? Tell me!"

"I do not know myself."

"Not Mignon, then?"

"Certainly not! But: Mignon was on the point of coming to you secretly, when with horror she observed from a corner that a rival had anticipated her."

"A rival!" exclaimed Wilhelm. "Do go on. You are completely bewildering me."

"Be thankful," said the doctor, "that you shall quickly learn what we found out. Natalie and I, though only indirectly involved, were greatly distressed by the troubled state of the girl whom we desired to help, until we obtained some clearer insight. From some frivolous remarks of Philine and the other girls, as well as from a certain song, Mignon conceived the idea of how delightful it would be to spend a night with her beloved, without any further thought than fond, peaceful nestling. Her affection for you, my friend, was so strong; she had already recovered from many a sorrow in your arms, and now she wanted to enjoy her happiness to the full. Her first impulse was to ask you quietly, but inner anxiety made her desist from that. It was the hilarity of the evening and the mood induced by frequent drafts of wine that finally gave her the courage to creep up to your room that night. She went ahead in order to conceal herself in your room, which was not locked, and had just ascended the staircase when she heard a noise. She took cover, and saw a woman in white enter your room. Then you yourself arrived and she heard you bolt the door.

"Mignon was deeply distressed. Violent jealousy combined with the unrecognized urgency of latent desire to take its toll of her only half-developed nature. Her heart, which up till then had been beating with expectation and yearning, suddenly stopped. It was like a dead weight, she could not breathe, she didn't know what to do. Then she heard the sound of the old man's harp, rushed to his room, and spent the night at his feet, in terrible convulsions."

The doctor paused for a moment, but since Wilhelm remained silent, he went on: "Natalie assures me that nothing scared her so much in her whole life as when the child told her all this. In fact, she reproached herself for eliciting by her questions these confidences and so cruelly reviving the memory of all that the dear child had suffered. Natalie told me that when the girl reached this point in her story, she suddenly fell down at her feet, clasped her breast and complained that the pain of that terrible night had come back again. She rolled about on the ground, and Natalie had to concentrate all her efforts on deciding, and using, the best means she knew of dealing with such a state of mind and body."

"You put me in a very painful position by making me feel my injustice toward the poor creature, just at the moment when I am to see her again," said Wilhelm. "If I am to see her again, why do you take away from me the courage to meet her freely and openly? And how can my being here help her if she is in that state of mind? Are you convinced, as a doctor, that the twofold yearning you have described has so undermined her nature that she is in danger of dying? If that is the case, why should I aggravate her misery by my presence and perhaps bring on her death?"

"My dear friend!" the doctor replied, "even if we cannot help, we have an obligation to appease. And I know several notable instances where the physical presence of what one loves can relieve the imagination of its destructive tendencies and transform longing into calm contemplation. Everything should be undertaken with moderation and purpose. For it is also possible that such encounters may revive flagging emotions. Go and see her, be kind to her, and let's see what happens."

Natalie came back into the room and asked Wilhelm to accompany her to Mignon. "She seems to be quite happy with Felix, and I hope she will also be pleased to see you," she said. Wilhelm followed her with some trepidation: He was deeply disturbed by what he had heard and was afraid of a highly emotional scene. But when he arrived, he found exactly the opposite.

Mignon, in a long white dress, her thick brown hair partly hanging loose and partly arranged, was seated with Felix on her lap, pressing him to her breast. She looked like a departed spirit, and the boy like life itself: it seemed as though heaven and earth were here conjoined. She smiled and, stretching out her hand to Wilhelm, said: "Thank you for bringing back the child. You stole it from me, I don't know how. And since then I could not live. As long as my heart has any needs on earth, this child shall fill them."

The tranquillity with which Mignon greeted Wilhelm was a source of great satisfaction to the rest of the company. The doctor insisted that Wilhelm should go and see her often, and that they should all try to restore her physical and mental equilibrium. He himself departed, but promised to return soon.

Wilhelm was now able to observe Natalie in her own environment. One could not imagine anything better, he thought, than living in her proximity. Her presence had a most salutary influence not only on the young girls but on women of various ages, some of whom lived in her house and others came to visit her from nearby.

One day Wilhelm said to her: "The course of your life seems always to have been very even. For the description your aunt gave of you as a child still seems to be apposite. One feels that you never lost your path; you were never obliged to take a step backward."

"For that I am indebted to my uncle and to the Abbé," said Natalie, "for they had such a clear sense of my personal inclinations. I remember that the strongest impression of my youth was that of human need everywhere; and I had an irresistible urge to do something about this. A child that could not yet stand on its feet or an old man who could no longer do so, a rich family's longing to have children or a poor family's inability to support theirs, one man's search for a trade and another's to develop some talent—all such situations were what I seemed by nature predisposed to discover. I saw things that nobody directed my attention to; I saw them because I seemed born to do so. The delights of inanimate nature, so meaningful to others, left me unmoved, and art appealed to me even less. My greatest delight was, and still is, to be presented with some deficiency, some need in others, and be able to think of some way of repairing or alleviating it.

"If I saw someone poor and in rags, I thought of the unnecessary garments hanging in the closets of my friends. If I saw children languishing for lack of care and attention, I remembered this or that woman consumed by boredom in the midst of wealth and comfort. If I saw a crowd of people crammed into a tiny room, I thought how they might be better housed in the vast halls of many a fine residence. This way of seeing things came quite naturally to me; I never had to think twice about it, and I sometimes did the oddest things as a child, embarrassing people on more than one occasion by the strangest requests. Another peculiarity of mine was that I rarely thought of money, and then only later as the means to satisfy needs; my generosity consisted in the giving of natural objects, and I know I was often laughed at for this. The Abbé was the only one who seemed to understand me, and he assisted me by making me better acquainted with myself, my desires and inclinations, and by teaching me the most effective way of fulfilling these."

"Did you, in the instruction of your women charges, carry out the principles of these extraordinary men?" asked Wilhelm. "Do you allow each human being to develop by itself? Do you let them search and lose their way, make mistakes, and either happily reach their goal or lose themselves miserably in the process?"

"No, I do not," said Natalie. "To treat people thus would be quite contrary to my convictions. If someone does not provide help when it is needed, he will, to my mind, never be of any help; if he does not come up with advice immediately, he will never provide any. It seems to me of the utmost importance to enunciate certain principles and inculcate these into children— principles that will give their lives some stability. I would almost be inclined to say that it is better to err because of principles than to do so from arbitrariness of nature, and my observation of human beings tells me that there is always some gap in their natures which can only be filled by a principle expressly communicated to them."

"Your procedure, then, is radically different from that followed by our friends?" said Wilhelm.

"Yes it is!" Natalie replied. "But you should respect their tolerance in letting me go my own way, just because it is my own."

We will postpone a more detailed account of how Natalie operated with the children under her supervision.

Mignon constantly asked to join the company, which was gladly permitted because she was gradually becoming accustomed to Wilhelm again, opening up her heart to him and generally seeming to be recovering her good spirits and her love of life. She liked to put her arm in his as they walked, for she easily got tired. "Well," she would say, "Mignon can't jump and climb anymore, but she still feels the urge to walk over the tops of mountains, from one house to another, from one tree to the next. How I envy the birds, especially when they are building their nests nicely and quietly."

Mignon frequently took occasion to ask Wilhelm to go with her into the garden. If he was busy or somehow not to be found, Felix had to take his place, and if the girl seemed at times quite detached from the earth, there were others when she clung to father and son, fearing more than anything that she might be separated from them.

Natalie seemed puzzled and concerned. "We have tried," she said, "to open up her poor dear heart by bringing you here; but whether we did right, I do not know." She stopped, and seemed to be waiting for Wilhelm to say something. It occurred to him that, as things were at present, Mignon would be greatly upset if he married Therese, but he was uncertain whether he should mention what he had in mind to Natalie. He did not suspect that she knew about it already.

He also could not listen with an open mind when she spoke about her sister, praising her good qualities and lamenting her situation. And he was quite ill at ease when she announced the impending arrival of the countess. "Her husband," she said, "has now only one thought in his head; he is determined to take over the position of the late Count Zinzendorf in the community, and support and develop that great undertaking by his insight and activity. He is coming here with his wife to take a sort of leave from us. He will then visit the various places where the community has established its settlements. It seems that his intentions are generally approved of; and it could be that he will venture on a journey to America with my poor sister, so as to emulate his predecessor. Since he seems almost convinced that he lacks little to acquire sainthood, he may be inspired as well by the desire to be a shining martyr."

Chapter Four

They had often talked about Therese, or mentioned her in passing, and time and time again Wilhelm was about to tell Natalie that he had offered his heart and his hand to that excellent woman. But he was restrained from doing so by a certain feeling, which he could not account for. He hesitated so long that Natalie, with that radiant, serene, and gentle smile so characteristic of her, finally said to him: "So it is I who must eventually break the silence and force my way into your confidence. Why, my friend, do you keep secret from me a matter that is so important to you, and also affects me closely? You have offered your hand to my friend Therese. I am not willfully interfering in your affairs, here is my justification—here is the letter she has written to you and sends you through me."

"A letter from Therese!" he cried.

"Yes! And your fate is decided. You are a happy man. Allow me to congratulate both you and my friend."

Wilhelm lapsed into silence, staring in front of him. Natalie looked at him, noticing that he had turned pale. "Your happiness is so extreme," she said, "that it has taken the form of fright and robbed you of speech. My pleasure is not less because it still permits me to speak. I hope you will be grateful when I tell you that my influence on Therese's decision was not inconsiderable. She asked for my advice, and strangely enough you were here at the time. I was easily able to dispel the few doubts she still had as messengers went quickly back and forth between us. Here is her decision! Here's the solution! And now you shall read all her letters and look freely and directly into her noble heart."

Wilhelm opened the letter, which she handed to him unsealed, and read these kindly words:

"I am yours—just as I am, and as you know me. And I shall call you mine—just as you are, and as I know you. Whatever is changed by marriage in us and our relationship, we will accept with good will, intelligence and happy hearts. Since it is not passion, but mutual inclination and trust that brings us together, we run a lesser risk than thousands of others. You will surely forgive me if I sometimes still think about my former friend; and I, for my part, will clasp your son to my bosom as a mother. If you would like to share my little house with me right now, you shall be lord and master, and that will give time for the purchase of the estate to be concluded. I do not want any changes to be made in the estate without me, so that I may show that I deserve the trust you are placing in me. May things fare well with you, my dear, dear friend! Beloved bridegroom, honored spouse! Therese clasps you to her heart in hope and joy. My friend Natalie will tell you more—indeed everything."

Wilhelm, for whom this letter revived his whole image of Therese, had by now completely recovered himself. As he read, various thoughts were coursing through his mind. With some alarm he became aware of definite signs of a growing affection for Natalie within him; he reproved himself, terming all such thoughts pure madness, recalled Therese in all her perfection, read the letter again, brightened up—or rather recovered sufficiently to appear bright. Natalie then showed him the other letters from which we will select some passages.

Therese, having described Wilhelm in her own fashion, had gone on to say: "This is how I see the man who is offering me his hand. How he sees himself, will become clear to you when you read the frank account he has given me of himself. I am convinced I will be happy with him."

"As far as social status is concerned, you know what my opinions have always been. Some persons suffer acutely from disparity in external conditions and cannot adjust to this. I never try to convince anybody, but I act according to my own convictions. I never try to set an example, though I do myself act according to an example. It is only disparities in inner conditions that trouble me, vessels unsuited to what they are to contain, external show without inner satisfaction, riches combined with miserliness, nobility with vulgarity, youth with pedantry, neediness with ceremoniousness. Such combinations are enough to destroy me completely, no matter what the world calls them or how it values them."

"When I say that I have hopes we will suit each other, my belief is based primarily on his similarity to you, dear Natalie, whom I treasure and respect so greatly. Like you he has that noble seeking and striving for betterment which enables us to do good where we think we perceive the possibility. I have often blamed you in my mind for treating this or that person differently and reacting to this or that situation differently from how I would have; and yet the outcome usually showed you were right. 'If we just take people as they are,' you once said, 'we make them worse; but if we treat them not as they are but as they should be, we help them to become what they can become.' I can't think or act like that—this I know all too well. Insight, order, discipline, commands—that is my way. I remember Jarno once saying to me: 'Therese trains her pupils, whereas Natalie cultivates hers.' He even went so far as to deny me completely the three primary virtues of faith, love, and hope. 'Instead of faith,' he said, 'she has insight; instead of love, persistence; instead of hope, confidence.' Before I met you, I believed there was nothing of greater value than clarity and common sense, but knowing you has convinced me, given me new life, overcome my previous belief, and now I yield the palm to your finer, loftier spirit. I respect my friend Wilhelm in the same terms. His life has been continuous searching and failure to find. But his searching has not been just idle seeking; it is sustained by the well-intentioned but curious belief that he will receive from without what can only come from within. And so, my dear, this time my belief in the importance of clarity has been beneficial to me, for I know my future husband better than he does, and respect him all the more for that. I see him, but I do not oversee him, and all my powers of insight do not suffice to estimate what he is capable of achieving. When I think about him, his image is always merging with yours; and I do not know how I have deserved the association with two such remarkable people. But I will try to deserve this by doing my duty in fulfilling what is expected and anticipated from me."

"Whether I ever think about Lothario? A great deal, and every day of my life. He is never absent from my mind. How sorry I am that, related to me by an error of his youth, this excellent man should also be so closely related to you. For someone like yourself would be more worthy of him than I. I could and would gladly let him be yours. Let us be everything to him that we possibly can, until he finds a suitable wife, and even then let us remain together as close friends."

"Now, what will our friends have to say?" Natalie began. "Your brother knows nothing about it?" Wilhelm asked. "No more than your family does," she replied. "This time the whole thing was a matter between us women. I don't know what ideas Lydie has put into Therese's head, for she seems to mistrust both the Abbé and Jarno. Lydie has made her somehow mistrust certain secret plans and arrangements of theirs, which I know about in a general way but have never involved myself with, and so, at this decisive point in her life, Therese sought no other opinion than mine. She had agreed with my brother that when either of them got married, they would simply announce this without seeking each other's advice beforehand."

Natalie thereupon wrote to her brother, inviting Wilhelm to add a few words, as Therese had asked her to do. They were just about to seal the letter when Jarno unexpectedly arrived. He was received very warmly, seemed extremely cheerful and jocular, and finally said: "I have actually come here today to bring you the strangest piece of news, though a very pleasant one. It concerns our friend Therese. You have often blamed us, Natalie, for busying ourselves with so many different things; but now you will see how useful it is to have spies everywhere. Guess what has happened—and let's see how sagacious you are!"

He said this in a very self-satisfied way, and his malicious expression as he looked at both Wilhelm and Natalie led them to believe that their secret was discovered. Natalie smiled and said: "We are much more skillful than you think, for we have put the solution to the riddle on paper before you told us what the riddle was."

She then handed him the letter to Lothario, pleased by this means to be able to counter the surprise and embarrassment he had prepared for them. Jarno received the letter with some amazement, skimmed it through, was astonished, let it fall from his hands, and looked at them both wide-eyed, with an expression of stupefaction, indeed of horror, such as one was not used to with him. He did not say one word.

Wilhelm and Natalie were distinctly puzzled. Jarno paced back and forth in the room. "What am I to say?" he exclaimed. "Shall I tell them? It can't remain a secret, and some confusion is unavoidable. All right: a secret in exchange for a secret! Surprise for surprise! Therese is not her mother's daughter! The obstacle is removed. I have come here to ask you to prepare her for union with Lothario."

Jarno observed the consternation of both of them. Their faces dropped. "This is one of those cases that is difficult to tolerate socially," he said. "Whatever we may all think, we would best pursue our thoughts in private. I at least will ask for an hour's respite." He hurried off into the garden. Wilhelm followed him instinctively, but at a distance.

After about an hour they met again. Wilhelm was the first to speak, and said: "While I was living an easy, one might say frivolous life, friendship, love, affection and trust came to me with open arms, pressed themselves upon me; but now, when things are serious, fate seems to be taking a different course with me. My decision to offer Therese my hand in marriage was perhaps the first that came to me entirely from within myself. I made my decision after careful consideration, my mind was completely made up, and my fondest hopes were fulfilled by her acceptance. But now the strangest turn of fate casts down my outstretched hand, Therese extends hers from afar, as in a dream, and my whole image of bliss is gone forever. Farewell then, beauteous image, and with you all those happy scenes I had associated with you!"

He stopped for a moment, stared in front of him, and Jarno was about to speak. "Let me just say something else," Wilhelm added, "for at this moment my whole destiny is being decided. I remember now the first impression I had of Lothario, an impression that is still firmly planted in my mind. That man deserves every sort of friendship and affection, and no friendship is conceivable without readiness to sacrifice. For his sake it was easy for me to fool an unhappy girl; therefore it should also be possible for me to renounce the worthiest of brides for his sake. Go to him and tell him the whole extraordinary story; and tell him what I am prepared to do."

Jarno answered: "In such instances as this, I think the ultimate solution is not to act too hastily. Let's do nothing without Lothario's approval. I will go to him, but you stay here quietly and wait either for my return or a letter from him."

He rode off, leaving Wilhelm and Natalie in a melancholy mood. They now had time to look at the situation from various angles and make some observations to each other. First of all, it struck them as strange that they had heard this extraordinary news from Jarno, but had not inquired about the circumstances surrounding it. Wilhelm even began to have some doubts about it; and the next day their astonishment and bewilderment were raised to a peak when a messenger arrived from Therese with this peculiar letter to Natalie: "Strange as it may seem, I must follow up on my last letter immediately and ask you to send Wilhelm to me as quickly as possible. He shall be my husband, no matter what plans others are making to steal him away from me. Give him the enclosed letter! And in private, no matter who else is at your house."

The letter to Wilhelm ran as follows: "What can you be thinking of your Therese pressing suddenly and passionately for an immediate union, whereas it was initiated in such cool consideration? Let nothing stop you from coming here instantly on receiving this letter. Come, my dear, dear friend, my thrice beloved, for they are trying to rob me of having you, or at least making that difficult."

"What is to be done?" exclaimed Wilhelm after reading the letter.

"Never," said Natalie after some thought, "have my heart and my mind maintained such silence. I don't know what to do, or what to advise you to do."

"Could it be possible," exclaimed Wilhelm somewhat angrily, "that Lothario himself knows nothing about this, or if he does, that he and we are the victims of some secret machinations? Did Jarno, when he read our letter, make the whole thing up on the spur of the moment? Would he have told us something else if we had not been so precipitate? What do they want? What are they up to? What plan is Therese referring to? It can't be denied that Lothario is surrounded by secret activities and alliances. I myself have experienced such activities, and learnt that these persons are trying to influence and control the actions, the whole lives of others. I do not understand what the ultimate goal of these clandestine operations is, but this latest attempt to separate me from Therese is clear enough. On the one hand I am regaled with the good fortune awaiting Lothario, though perhaps that is only a pretense; on the other hand I find my beloved, my honored bride urgently calling me to come to her. What shall I do? What shall I leave undone?"

"Just have a little patience," said Natalie, "just take a little time for reflection. In this strange concatenation of circumstances there is one thing I am certain about: We should not act hastily, when what is at stake is irrecoverable. Our defense against idle fictions and secret machinations is to be sensible and maintain patience, for everything will soon be cleared up, and we shall know whether there is any truth in all this or not. If my brother really has hopes now of being united with Therese, it would be cruel to deprive him of that happiness in the very moment it seems so inviting. Let us therefore wait and see whether he knows anything about it, whether he really believes it, and has hopes."

A letter arrived from Lothario which fortunately added further justification to her advice. "I am not sending Jarno back to you," he wrote. "A few words from me will mean more to you than all those of an intermediary. I am quite sure that Therese is not her mother's daughter, and I cannot abandon hope of winning her until she herself is also convinced and can make a considered choice between me and our friend. Don't, I beg you, let him leave you; a brother's happiness, his whole life, is in the balance. I promise you that this state of uncertainty will not continue much longer."

"You see how things stand," said Natalie gently to Wilhelm. "Give me your word that you will not leave the house."

"I will not leave this house against your will," he said, extending his hand to her. "I thank God and my good angel that this time I am being guided, and by you."

Natalie wrote to Therese telling her all that had happened, assuring her she would not let Wilhelm leave, and enclosing Lothario's letter.

Therese replied: "I am quite surprised that Lothario is convinced. He would not pretend that he was, to his sister, not to this extent anyway. I am very upset, and it is best if I say nothing further, but come to you as soon as I have provided for poor Lydie, who is being cruelly treated. I fear we are all being deceived, and in such a manner that we shall never straighten things out. If Wilhelm thought as I do, he would slip away from you and throw himself on the bosom of his Therese, whom no one would then deprive him of; but I am afraid I shall lose him, and yet not regain Lothario. They are snatching Lydie away from Lothario by giving him the distant hope of winning me. I won't say any more; the confusion will get worse. Time alone will decide whether good relationships are becoming so twisted, so undermined, even destroyed, that once everything is cleared up, it will be too late to repair them. If my friend Wilhelm does not break loose, I will come in a few days to see him at your house and keep him there. You will be surprised at such passion taking hold of your Therese; but it is not passion, it is the conviction that, since Lothario could not be mine, this new friend will make my life happy. Tell him this on behalf of the little boy who sat beneath the oaktree with him and cherished his affection! Tell him in the name of Therese, who received his proposal with such honest delight! My first dream—living together with Lothario—is now far removed from my mind; my dream of a life with my new friend is, however, everpresent in it. Have they so little respect for me that they believe it is so easy to exchange one for the other again, on the spur of the moment?"

"I trust you not to run away," said Natalie to Wilhelm, handing him Therese's letter. "Do realize that my whole happiness lies in your hands. My life is so intensely bound up with that of my brother, that when he suffers pain, so do I, and the joys he experiences are what gives me happiness. I can truly say that only through him have I learnt that the heart can be moved and uplifted, that there is joy and love in the world, and feeling which brings contentment beyond all need . . . "

She paused; and Wilhelm took her hand and said: "Do go on! This is the time for confiding in each other. We have never needed more urgently to know each other better."

"Yes, my friend," she said with a smile of indescribably gentle and calm dignity. "And perhaps it will not be the wrong time to tell you that what we read in books about love, and what the world shows us of what it calls love, has always seemed to me idle fancy."

"You have never been in love?" Wilhelm asked.

"Never—or always!" she replied.

Chapter Five

They had been walking to and fro in the garden as they talked. Natalie had picked various strangely shaped flowers quite unfamiliar to Wilhelm, and he asked her for their names.

"You will never guess for whom I am picking these. My little bouquet is for my uncle, whom we are going to visit. The sun is shining so brightly on the Hall of the Past, that I would like to take you there. And I never go without taking some of the flowers my uncle particularly liked. He was a strange man with strong inclinations of his own. He had a decided affection for certain plants and animals, people and places, even stones, and this was often not easy to account for. 'If I had not resisted myself from youth on,' he would say, 'if I had not striven to extend my mind outward from myself into wider vistas, I would have become a very constricted and thoroughly insufferable person. For nothing is more unbearable than isolation and idiosyncrasy in someone who could be expected to indulge in some unselfish, useful activity.' Yet he had to admit also that life would lose its savor if he did not sometimes consider himself and passionately indulge in what he could not always approve of or make excuses for. 'It is not my fault,' he used to say, 'if I have not completely been able to harmonize my mind with my instincts.' He would make fun of me, and say: 'Natalie can truly be said to be in a state of bliss on this earth, for her nature never demands anything but what the world desires and needs.'"

They had now arrived. She conducted him through a wide corridor up to a portal guarded by two granite sphinxes. The portal itself was narrower at the top than at the bottom, after the Egyptian fashion, and its solid iron doors led one to expect a somber, perhaps gruesome, interior. It was therefore a pleasant surprise to find this gloomy anticipation replaced by a world of brightness and light, when one entered a hall in which art and life dispelled all thoughts of death and the grave. Arches were inset in the walls and in them stood large sarcophagi. In the pillars between them there were niches with funeral urns and caskets. The remaining surface of the walls and the vault were divided up into regular spaces, and bright, imposing figures painted on backgrounds of various sizes, surrounded by a whole variety of bright borders, garlands and other decorative motifs. The architectural elements were fashioned from fine yellow marble, which shaded over into reddishness, blue stripes of an ingenious chemical composition reproduced the effect of lapis lazuli, and, pleasing the eye by the contrast, gave coherence and unity to the whole. All this splendor and decoration was achieved by purely architectural means, and everyone who entered felt uplifted by the design of the whole, showing what man is and what he can be.

Across from the entrance, on a magnificent sarcophagus, stood the marble effigy of a distinguished man, his head resting against a pillow. He was holding a scroll in front of him which he appeared to be reading attentively. The scroll was so placed that one could read the words written upon it. These were: *Remember to live.*

Natalie removed some withered flowers from her uncle's tomb (for his it was) and replaced them by those she had brought with her. The effigy was full-length, and Wilhelm thought he recognized the features of the old man he had once seen in the forest. "We used to spend many hours here together," said Natalie, "while the hall was being constructed. In his last years he brought several skilled artists here, and his favorite occupation was to plan and decide on the drawings and cartoons for these paintings."

Wilhelm was overjoyed at everything he saw around him. "What life there is in this Hall of the Past!" he cried. "One could just as well call it the Hall of the Present, and of the Future. This is how everything was, and this is how everything will be. Nothing perishes except him who observes and enjoys. The picture of this mother clasping her child will survive many generations of happy mothers. Some father in a future century will delight in this bearded man casting aside all seriousness and joking with his son. Bashful brides will sit like that for all time, silently asking to be consoled and persuaded; impatient like this one, all bridegrooms will stand, listening to find out when they may enter."

Wilhelm's eyes wandered from one picture to another. In a splendid sequence of vivid representations, ranging from the first childish impulses to employ all one's limbs in play, to the calm, grave detachment of wise old age, showing that there is no inclination or faculty innate in man that he does not need or use. From that first delicate awakening of self with which the maiden delays drawing water while she gazes admiringly at her own reflection, to the grand festivities at which kings and nations call on the gods to sanction their alliances—everything was there in all its power and significance. A whole world, heaven itself, surrounded the observer in this place, and aside from the thoughts and feelings aroused by these images, something else seemed to be there that took hold of the whole man. Wilhelm felt it without being able to account for it. "What is it," he cried, "that, apart from all meaning, aside from the sympathetic interest that all human events and fortunes evoke in us, what is it that affects me so strongly and at the same time so pleasantly? It speaks to me from the whole without my comprehending the whole, and from each of the parts without my being able to relate these especially to myself! What is the magic that for me pervades these surfaces, lines, height and breadth, masses and colors? What is it that makes these shapes, even though only decoration, so appealing? That one could remain here, reflect on all one sees, be happy, and yet feel and think things quite different from what one sees with one's eyes."

If we could only describe how admirably everything was arranged, how everything appeared as it should, by combination or contrast, uniformity or variety of color, and thereby produced a perfect as well as clear effect—if we could do that, we would be transporting the reader to a place he would never wish to leave.

Four large marble candelabras stood in the corners of the Hall, and four smaller ones in the center were ranged around a sarcophagus of exquisite workmanship which, from its size, would seem to have contained the body of a young person of medium height. Natalie stood for a while beside this monument and, placing her hand upon it, said: "My dear uncle had a special love for this classical work. He often said that it is not only the first fruits that wither—and can be preserved up there in those smaller spaces—but fruits that hang on the bough, full of promise for many a day until a hidden worm causes their premature ripening and decay. I fear," she continued, "that he was thinking of the dear girl who is step by step withdrawing from our care and seems to have a yearning for this peaceful resting place."

As they were about to leave, Natalie said: "I must draw your attention to one other thing. Do you see these semicircular openings up there on both sides? Those are for the choirs of singers, so that they may remain unseen, and these metal ornaments below the cornice are for hanging tapestries on, which, according to my uncle's disposition, are to be hung at all funerals. He could not have lived without music, especially vocal music, but he had the peculiarity of never wishing to see the singers. He would say: 'We have been spoilt too much by theaters, where music only serves the eye, accompanying movements, not feelings. In oratorios and concerts the physical presence of the singer is disturbing. Music is only for the ear. A lovely voice is the most universal thing one can think of, and if the limited individual producing it is visible, this disturbs the effect of universality. When I am talking to someone, I need to see him, for he is an individual whose character and figure determine the value of what he says; but when someone is singing, he should be invisible, his appearance should not prejudice me in his favor or distract me. With singing it is a case of one organ addressing another, not one mind speaking to another, not a manifold world to a single pair of eyes, not heaven to a single man.' He also wanted players in an orchestra concealed as much as possible, because one is only distracted and disturbed by the laborings and necessary strange gestures of musicians. He therefore listened to music with his eyes closed, so as to concentrate entirely on the pleasure of the ear.'"

They were about to leave the Hall when they heard the children running hurriedly toward them and Felix shouting: "No, me! Me!"

Mignon came hurtling through the door, panting for breath and unable to get a word out, while Felix followed some distance behind, saying: "Mother Therese is here!" The children apparently had raced to see who could bring the news first. Mignon lay in Natalie's arms, her heart beating wildly.

"You naughty child!" said Natalie. "Haven't you been forbidden all violent movement? Look how your heart is beating!"

"Let it break!" said Mignon with a deep sigh. "It has been beating long enough!"

They had hardly recovered from their confusion and alarm when Therese entered. She rushed up to Natalie, embraced her, and then the child. She turned to Wilhelm, looked at him with her clear eyes, and said: "Well, my friend, what's the situation? I hope you haven't let yourself be deluded." He took one step toward her, she moved toward him and fell into his arms. "Oh, my Therese!" he cried. "My friend! My beloved! My husband! Yours for evermore!" she replied amidst passionate kisses.

Felix tugged her coat and said: "Mother Therese! I'm here too!" Natalie stood gazing in front of her, when all of a sudden Mignon shot up, clasped her heart with her left hand, flung out her right arm, and fell with a cry at Natalie's feet, as if dead.

Everyone was greatly alarmed. There was no sign of any movement in heart or pulse. Wilhelm took her into his arms and quickly lifted her up, her body hanging lifeless over his shoulders. The doctor came but gave little hope, though he and the young surgeon whom we already know did all they could — but in vain. The poor dear creature could not be brought back to life.

Natalie motioned to Therese, who took Wilhelm by the hand and led him out of the room. He was speechless, and did not have the courage to look her in the eyes. He sat beside her on the same sofa where he had first seen Natalie. In quick succession he thought about the fates of several people — or rather he did not think at all, he simply let his mind be invaded by what he could not repel. There are moments in our lives when events, like winged shuttles, flit backwards and forwards before our eyes, weaving continuously at a tapestry which we have more or less designed and spun for ourselves. "Dear friend! Beloved Wilhelm!" said Therese, breaking the silence and taking his hand, "let us keep a firm hold on this particular moment, as we will often have to do at other times. Events like these need two people to tolerate them. Do realize that you are not alone, please feel that; show that you love me by sharing your sorrow with me!" She embraced him, pressing him gently to her breast; he clasped her in his arms, and pressed her against him. "That poor child," he said, "in her moments of sadness would look for refuge and protection in my uncertain bosom. May your certainty strengthen me in this terrible hour." They remained in each other's arms. He could feel her heart beating, but his mind was empty and desolate. Only the forms of Mignon and Natalie hovered like shadows before his imagination.

Natalie entered the room. "Give us your blessing!" said Therese. "Let us be united in your presence at this sad moment." Wilhelm's face was buried in Therese's breast; he was fortunate enough to be able to weep. He did not hear Natalie come, did not see her; but at the sound of her voice his tears redoubled. "What God has joined together, I will not put asunder," said Natalie with a smile. "But I cannot unite you, nor can I approve of the fact that sorrow and affection should erase all memory of my brother from your hearts." Wilhelm broke loose from Therese's arms. "Where are you going?" both women asked. "Let me see the child that I have killed," he cried. "Misfortune seen with our own eyes is a lesser evil than when our imagination forces it upon our minds. Let us go and see the departed angel. Her radiance will tell us that all is well with her." Since they could not restrain him, so deeply was he affected, they both followed him, but the good doctor, accompanied by the surgeon, dissuaded them from approaching the dead girl, and said: "Stay away from this mournful sight and let me use my art to give some permanence to the remains of this unusual person. I will start immediately to employ the delicate art of embalming, and also preserve an appearance of life in this beloved creature. Since I foresaw that she was dying, I have made all preparations, and my assistant and I will see that we succeed. Grant me but a few days and don't ask to see her until we have brought her into the Hall of the Past."

The young surgeon again had with him the instrument case they had noticed earlier. "Where did he get that case from?" Wilhelm asked the doctor. "I am very familiar with it," said Natalie, "he got it from his father who bound your wounds that day in the forest."

"So I was not mistaken," Wilhelm said. "I recognized the ribbon immediately. Give it to me! That ribbon first put me on the track of my benefactress. Inanimate objects like this outlast so much joy and sorrow! It was present at so much suffering, and yet its threads still hold. It was there at the last hours of many persons, but its colors have never faded. It was there at one of the most precious moments of my life, when I lay wounded on the ground and you came to my aid, while that poor child with blood on her hair was tenderly caring for my life, that girl whose own untimely death we now are mourning."

They did not have much time to acquaint Therese with the probable cause of the child's unexpected death; for visitors were announced, who turned out to be Lothario, Jarno and the Abbé. Natalie went up to her brother while the others stood in silence. Therese smiled and said to Lothario: "You hardly expected to see me here, and it is hardly suitable for us to seek each other out at this particular moment. But I am glad to see you after so long an absence."

Lothario grasped her by the hand and said: "If we must suffer and forebear, then let us do so in a spirit of love and goodwill. I do not demand any influence on your decision, and my confidence in your heart and mind and your good sense, is as strong as ever; so I gladly entrust to you my fate and that of my friend."

The conversation then turned to more general and less important matters. They divided up into pairs. Natalie walked with Lothario, Therese with the Abbé, and Wilhelm stayed in the house with Jarno.

The arrival of the three friends at that moment when Wilhelm was weighed down with sorrow, in no wise distracted him; it irritated him and made his mood worse. He was ill-tempered and suspicious, and made no attempt to conceal this when Jarno asked him to account for his sullen silence. "What more do we need?" said Wilhelm. "Lothario arrives with his supporters, and it would be a miracle if the mysterious forces of the Tower, always so busy at something, did not work on us to achieve heaven knows what strange purpose. Those holy men, so far as I can make out, seem always to have the laudable intention of breaking up alliances and bringing together again what has been separated. What sort of pattern will eventually emerge from this, that will always remain a mystery to our unholy eyes."

"You're ill-tempered and bitter," said Jarno. "That's all well and good. But when you get angry, that will be still better."

"That can be easily managed," Wilhelm replied, "for I am very much afraid that delight is being taken in driving my native and my assumed patience to extremes."

"In that case I would like, while we are waiting to see how our adventures turn out, to tell you something about this Tower that you seem so much to distrust."

"It's up to you," Wilhelm replied, "if you feel like risking it when I am so distracted. My mind is occupied with so many things that I do not know whether I will be able to give the attention I should to your worthy adventures."

"I will not be dissuaded by your pleasantry from informing you about this matter. You take me for a shrewd fellow, but I will also show you that I am honest — and what's more, I have been instructed to give you this information." "I could wish," Wilhelm replied, "that you let your feelings speak with the intention of enlightening me. But since I cannot listen to you without mistrust, why should I listen to you at all?" "If all I have to do is to spin yarns for you, then you will surely have time to attend to those," said Jarno. "Perhaps you will be more inclined to do so, if I first tell you that everything you saw in the tower was the relics of a youthful enterprise that most initiates first took very seriously but will probably now just smile at."

"So they are just playing games with those portentous words and signs?" Wilhelm exclaimed. "We are ceremoniously conducted to a place that inspires awe, we witness miraculous apparitions, are given scrolls containing mysterious, grandiose aphorisms which we barely understand, are told we have been apprentices and are now free—and are none the wiser." "Do you still have the document?" asked Jarno. "There's much that is good in it. Those general maxims have real solid foundation, though they may seem obscure, perhaps even meaningless, to someone without experience of his own. Would you please give me the so-called Certificate of Apprenticeship, if you have it at hand?" "Indeed I do," Wilhelm replied. "One should carry an amulet like that always on one's chest." "Well," said Jarno with a smile, "maybe someday its contents will enter your heart and your head."

Jarno skimmed through the first half of the manual. "These remarks refer to the cultivation of our artistic sense—other persons will talk to you about that; the second part deals with life, and here I feel more at home."

He then began to read certain passages, interspersing them with remarks, comments and stories. "Young people have an unusually strong hankering after mysteries, ceremonies and grandiloquence: this is often the sign of a certain depth of character. For at that time a person wants to feel, albeit dimly and indefinitely, that his whole being is affected and involved. A young man who is full of presentiments believes that he can account for much and discover even more in mysteries, and that he must work by means of mysteries. The Abbé encouraged a group of young people in this way of thinking, partly because it corresponded to his own principles, partly out of inclination and habit, for he had previously been connected with people who worked in this mysterious way. But I was the least able to conform to this; I was older than the others, had seen things clearly from early on, and valued clarity more than anything else. My sole interest was to know the world as it was, and I infected the best of the others with this passionate concern. As a result I almost deflected our whole pedagogic efforts on to a wrong track, for we began to see only the faults and limitations of others and consider ourselves as perfect. The Abbé came to our assistance, instructing us that we should not observe others except in order to show interest in their cultivation of themselves, and that we are only really able to observe or eavesdrop on ourselves when we are engaged in activity. He advised us to return to earlier forms of social life. As a result there was a certain adherence to laws in our meetings and a perceptible mysticism in our whole organization, which thereby, so to speak, transformed itself from craft into art. That's why we evolved the appellations of Apprentice, Assistant, and Master. We wanted to make our own observations, and establish our own archive of knowledge. That is how the various confessions arose, written sometimes by ourselves and sometimes by others, from which the records of apprenticeship were subsequently put together. Not all are equally concerned with their self-cultivation—many want merely panaceas for contentment, or recipes for wealth and happiness. Those who did not want to be set on their feet, were obstructed or deflected by mystifications and all sorts of hocus-pocus. We assigned freedom of action only to those who felt deeply and saw clearly what they were born to, and had enough experience of their own to pursue their chosen course with ease and gladness."

"Well then," said Wilhelm, "you were much too precipitate with me, for since that moment of liberation I know less than ever what I can do, or what I desire, or should do." "It is not our fault that we got ourselves into this muddle," said Jarno. "Let us hope that good fortune will get us out of it. Meanwhile let me say this: A person who has great potentiality for development will in due course acquire knowledge of himself and the world. Few people have the understanding and simultaneously the ability to act. Understanding extends, but also immobilizes; action mobilizes, but also restricts."

"Do desist from giving me any more of these wondrous observations," Wilhelm interjected. "Such verbiage has confused me quite enough." "Very well then, let me go on with my story," said Jarno, half rolling up the scroll and only glancing at it occasionally. "I myself have been very little use to the Society or mankind. I am a very bad teacher, for I find it unbearable to observe someone making clumsy attempts to do something. When someone is off the track, my inclination is always to alert him, even if it were a sleepwalker in danger of breaking his neck. I always had trouble on this score with the Abbé, who claimed that error can only be cured through erring. We often disagreed about you: he was very favorably disposed toward you, and it means a great deal to earn his approval. Whenever I encountered you, I always told you the honest truth." "You certainly didn't treat me with any indulgence," said Wilhelm, "and you always remained true to your principles, so far as I can see." "What indulgence is needed," Jarno replied, "when it is simply a case of a young man with many a talent, embarking on the wrong course?" "Pardon me!" said Wilhelm, "you were severe enough to tell me that I had no talent for acting. But I must confess that, although I have given that up entirely, I cannot agree that I had absolutely no gift for it." "My view is quite definitely that a man who always plays himself is not an actor," said Jarno. "No one deserves to be called an actor who cannot transform his personality and appearance into that of many other persons. You, for example, played Hamlet quite well and a few other roles, where your character, your physical appearance and your mood of the moment assisted you. That would be good enough for an amateur and someone without higher aspirations. But," said Jarno, with a quick look at the scroll, "one should be wary of any talent that one cannot hope to bring to perfection. However much one may achieve, one finally must regret the expenditure of time and energy on such dabbling when one is brought face to face with the achievements of a master."

"Don't start reading again!" said Wilhelm. "I would urge you just to go on talking: tell me more, give me more information! Am I then right in thinking that it was the Abbé who helped me in *Hamlet* by providing the Ghost?"

"Yes, because he was sure that was the only way to cure you, if you were curable."

"And that is why he left the veil with me, and urged me to flee?"

"Yes; he hoped that the performance of *Hamlet* would be sufficient to satisfy your desire, and that you would never go on stage again. But I thought the opposite, and I was right. We argued about this that same evening after the performance."

"So you saw me act?"

"Yes, indeed I did."

"Then who was it who played the Ghost?"

"That I cannot say. Either the Abbé or his twin brother— probably the latter, for he is a shade taller."

"So you too have secrets amongst yourselves?"

"Friends can—and must—keep secrets from each other, for they are not secrets to each other."

"The very recollection of that confusion is enough to confuse me," said Wilhelm. "Do tell me some more about the man I am so indebted to and have so much to reproach for."

"What makes him so respected by us," said Jarno, "and what gives him supremacy over all of us, is the clear untrammeled perception Nature has given him into all human faculties, and how each is to be best developed. Most persons, even the best of us, are somehow limited. Each one of us values certain qualities in himself and the same in others, and it is only these qualities that we favor and wish to develop. But the Abbé takes an entirely different view; he is interested in everything, takes pleasure in acknowledging and furthering everything. I must now look at the scroll again," he went on, quoting: 'All men make up mankind and all forces together make up the world. These are often in conflict with each other, and while trying to destroy each other they are held together and reproduced by Nature. From the faintest active urge of the animal to the most highly developed activity of the mind, from the stammering delight of the child to the superlative expression of bards and orators, from the first scuffles of boys to those vast undertakings by which whole countries are defended or conquered, from the most meager desire and most fleeting attraction to the most violent passions and deepest involvements, from the clearest sense of physical presence to the dimmest intimations and hopes of distant spiritual promise—all this, and much else besides, lies in the human spirit, waiting to be developed, and not just in one of us, but in all of us. Every aptitude is significant and should be developed. One man cultivates the beautiful and another what is useful, but only the combination of both constitutes the true man. Usefulness cultivates itself, for it is cultivated by the general mass of people, and no one can do without it; but beauty must be expressly cultivated, for few people embody it and many need it.'"

"Stop!" said Wilhelm, "I've read all that already."

"Just a few more lines!" Jarno responded. "Here is the Abbé speaking again: 'One force controls another, but none can create another. In every predisposi- tion, and only there, lies the power to perfect itself. Very few people who want to teach and affect others, understand that.'"

"I don't understand it either," said Wilhelm.

"You will often have the opportunity to hear the Abbé on this subject, so let us perceive quite clearly what we are and how we can develop ourselves, and be just toward others, for we only deserve respect if we respect others."

"Heavens! No more maxims, please! I feel they are inadequate balm for a wounded heart like mine. Tell me rather, with your customary cruel clarity, what you expect from me, and how you intend to victimize me."

"You'll be apologizing to us later for all your suspicions, I can assure you. Your job is to test and to choose; ours to assist you. No one is ever happy until his unlimited striving has set itself a limitation. Don't be guided by me; go to the Abbé. Don't think of yourself, but of those around you. Learn to appreciate Lothario's fine qualities, see how his farsightedness and his activities are indissolubly bound up with each other; he is always moving forward, always expanding and taking others with him. He always has a world around him, no matter where he may be, and his very presence invigorates and instigates. On the other hand, look at our dear doctor with his totally different disposition. Where Lothario always works in wide perspectives for the whole, the doctor directs his clear-sighted attention on the most immediate concerns, providing the means for activity rather than stimulating activity itself. His work is like good housekeeping, his influence consists in gentle encouragement of each in his own particular sphere, his knowledge is a continual process of collecting and transmitting, receiving and bestowing on a small scale. It may well be that Lothario could destroy in one day what the doctor has built over a period of years, but it may also be true that Lothario can impart to others in a single moment the power to restore a hundredfold what has been destroyed."

"It is a sad business," said Wilhelm, "to have to think about the excellent qualities of others at a moment when one is so divided within oneself. Such reflections are appropriate when one is calm, but not when one is tormented by passion and uncertainty."

"Calm rational reflection is never harmful," said Jarno, "and by accustoming ourselves to think about the virtues of others, our own good qualities will imperceptibly find their place, and every wrong line of action that our fancy inclines us toward will be gladly abandoned. Free your mind if you can from all suspicion and fear. Here comes the Abbé. Be polite to him until you have had time to find out how much you have to thank him for. Just look at the old rogue walking between Natalie and Therese! I bet he's up to something. He likes to try his hand at playing the role of Fate, and sometimes he cannot resist indulging in the pastime of arranging marriages."

Wilhelm's petulant, wrought-up mood had not been alleviated by Jarno's fine, sensible words, and he found it extremely indelicate of his friend to mention such a subject at this particular moment. So he said, smiling but with some bitterness: "I would think one should leave the pastime of arranging marriages to those who are in love with each other."

Chapter Six

Since the others had now joined them, our two friends found it necessary to break off their conversation. A courier was announced with a letter to be delivered directly into Lothario's hands. He looked sturdy and reliable, and was dressed in a livery that was sumptuous and in very good taste. Wilhelm had the feeling that he had met this man somewhere before, and he was not mistaken, for it was the same man that he had dispatched after Philine and the presumed Mariane, and who had never returned. He was about to speak to him when Lothario, having read the letter, asked him sternly and somewhat angrily who his master was.

"That is a question I am totally unable to answer," said the courier somewhat bashfully, "I hope the letter will tell you, for I was given no verbal instructions."

"Be that as it may," Lothario replied with a smile. "Since your master has the face to write to me so impudently, we will be glad to see him."

"He won't keep you waiting long," said the courier, as he bowed and retired.

"Just listen to this crazy, absurd communication," said Lothario. "He writes as follows: 'Since good humor is always the most welcome guest, and since I am always accompanied by this wherever I go, I am convinced that the visit I intend to pay your Graces will not be ill received. I hope to arrive with the whole noble family of Absolute Contentment, and then in due course depart, etcetera. Signed: Count Snail's Pace.'"

"That's a new family to me," said the Abbé.

"Maybe he has been temporarily elevated to the rank of Count," said Jarno.

"The mystery is easily solved," said Natalie. "I bet this is our brother Friedrich who has been threatening us with a visit ever since our uncle's death."

"Bull's eye! o wise and beauteous sister," said a voice from a nearby bush, and out came an attractive, lively young man. Wilhelm could not suppress a cry. "Why!" he said, "Is our blond little rogue here too?" Friedrich became attentive, looked hard at Wilhelm, and then said: "My goodness, I would have been less surprised to find in my uncle's garden the famous pyramids that stand so solidly in Egypt, or the tomb of King Mausolus which I am assured no longer exists, than you, my old friend and manifold benefactor. I am very glad to see you again!"

Once he had greeted and embraced everybody, he rushed back to Wilhelm, and said to the others: "Take good care of this hero, this chieftain, this dramatic philosopher! At our first meeting I really hackled him fiercely, yet he saved me from many a blow after that. He is as noble as Scipio, generous as Alexander, at times also in love but always without hating his rivals. Not only does he never heap coals on his enemies' heads, which is said to be a disservice, but he even sends trusty servants after those friends who have run off with his girl, to see that she doesn't come to any harm."

He went on and on in this fashion, with no one able to stop him; and since none of them could answer him in the same vein, he was the only one talking. "Don't be amazed," he said, "at my learning in sacred and profane matters. You will soon find out how I achieved it." They wanted to know how things were with him and where he had come from; but he was so full of moral tags and rusty anecdotes that he was unable to give them any precise information.

"His brand of merriment makes me uncomfortable," said Natalie quietly to Therese. "I bet he is not so happy as he pretends to be."

Since Friedrich's tomfoolery, apart from a few jokes parried by Jarno, did not elicit any response from the company, he said: "Well, it seems the only thing for me to do is to be serious in this most serious company, and since all my sins weigh heavily upon me in such sober circumstances, I must resign myself to making a general confession, but you, noble ladies and gentlemen, shall hear nothing of it. Only my worthy friend here, who is already familiar with some of my doings, shall be treated to this, for he has more cause than anybody to want to know. Aren't you curious," he said to Wilhelm, "to find out the how and the where, the who, the when and the why? And how the conjugation of the verb 'to love' went, and what all the derivatives of that delightful verb were?"

He took Wilhelm's arm and led him away, hugging and kissing him the while.

When Friedrich arrived in Wilhelm's room, the first thing he saw was a powder knife lying in the window, with the inscription: "Remember me!" "You take good care of your things," he said. "That is Philine's, and she gave it to you on the day I roughed you up so badly. I hope it made you think about that girl a lot; I can assure you that she has not forgotten you. If I had not long since removed any trace of jealousy from my heart, I would still view you with envy."

"Don't talk to me about that creature," Wilhelm replied. "I will not deny that for a long time I could not get rid of the impression her agreeableness made on me—but that was all there was to it."

"Shame on you!" said Friedrich. "Who can ever disavow that he loved someone? And you loved her as completely as one could possibly wish. Not a day passed without your giving her some present or other—and when a German gives presents, then he is certainly in love. There was nothing left for me to do but snatch her away from you, and the little red officer finally succeeded."

"How so? Were you the officer we saw at Philine's she went off with?"

"Yes, indeed—the one you took for Mariane. How we laughed at that mistake!"

"How cruel it was to leave me in such a state of uncertainty," said Wilhelm.

"And as for the courier you sent after us—we simply took him into our service! He's a fine fellow and never left us. And I still love the girl as madly as ever. She has so bewitched me that I find myself almost in a mythological situation, expecting every day to be transformed into something or other."

"But do tell me," said Wilhelm, "where have you got your learning from? I am astonished at your habit of referring constantly to ancient tales and fables."

"I became learned — indeed, very learned — in the most amusing way. Philine is living with me, we have rented an old castle, and there we sit like a couple of hobgoblins, having a most amusing time. We have a large, but also very choice, library which includes a huge old folio bible, a world history from the beginnings, two volumes of European history, a collection of anecdotes culled from the best Greek and Roman authors, the works of the celebrated poet Andreas Gryphius, and other titles of lesser importance. Sometimes when we had our fling and felt bored, we had the urge to read something, and before we knew it, were more bored than ever. Then Philine lit on the splendid idea of piling all the books on to the table and opening them up. We sat across from each other and read to each other, always bits and pieces, from one book and then from another. This was the greatest fun! We really thought we were in high society where it is deemed improper to stick to one topic for too long or go into it too deeply; and we felt we were in lively company where no one lets anyone else speak. We entertained ourselves day after day in this fashion, and thereby became so learned that we were astonished at each other. We soon found there was nothing under the sun that our knowledge could not account for. We varied our means of instructing ourselves, sometimes reading against an hourglass that would run out in a few minutes, then be reversed by Philine as she began to read from another book, and when the sand reached the bottom glass, I would begin my piece. And so we studied away in true academic fashion, except that our lessons were shorter and our studies more varied."

"I can understand such a crazy way of doing things when two such merry people as you are sitting side by side; but that you could stay so long together, I find not so easy to understand."

"There's a good and a bad side to that," said Friedrich. "Philine can't let herself be seen, doesn't even want to look at herself, for she is pregnant. You can't imagine anything more shapeless and ridiculous than she is. Shortly before I left she happened to catch sight of herself in a mirror. 'Oh, my god!' she said, turning her face away, 'the living image of Madame Melina! How hideous, how vulgar one looks!'"

"I must confess, " said Wilhelm, laughing, "that it is pretty funny to think of you two as father and mother."

"It's a crazy trick that I should finally have to accept being the father. She says I am, and the timing seems to be right. But at first I was somewhat uncertain because of that visit she paid you after the performance of *Hamlet*."

"What visit?" said Wilhelm.

"You surely haven't forgotten it? If you don't know already, I can tell you that the delightfully palpable ghost that night was Philine. This was hard for me to accept as a dowry, but if one can't accept something like that, one shouldn't love at all. Fatherhood rests only on conviction; I am convinced, therefore I am the father. So you see: I can use logic in the right circumstances. And if the child doesn't die laughing as soon as it is born, then it will be a pleasant citizen of the world, if not a useful one."

While these two were conversing with such gaiety about light-hearted matters, the rest of the company had embarked on a serious conversation. As soon as Friedrich and Wilhelm had gone off together, the Abbé led the others into the conservatory and, once they were seated, he delivered the following oration.

"We have made the general assertion that Therese is not the daughter of her mother, and it is now necessary for us all to be informed of the specifics. Here is the story, and I will document and corroborate it in every way possible.

"During the first years of their marriage Madame *** had a very good relationship with her husband, but the children they were hoping for, were all born dead, and on the third such occasion the doctors almost expected the mother to die and told her that the next time this would certainly happen. The two of them therefore had to reach certain decisions, but did not wish to dissolve the marriage because, from a domestic point of view, they were very happy. Mme. *** sought some kind of compensation for childlessness in the cultivation of her mind, in social activities, and vain pleasures. She was joyfully indulgent toward her husband when he developed an interest in a woman who took over the whole running of the household—a woman of beauty and good solid character. She soon came to approve this arrangement, according to which the good woman entrusted herself to Therese's father, continued the supervision of the household, and showed even more devotion than before to the lady of the house, and readiness to serve her.

"Some time later the woman announced that she was pregnant, and the couple arrived at the same idea, though for different reasons. The husband wanted to claim the child of his mistress as his own legitimate offspring, and his wife, annoyed that her doctor had been indiscreet enough to broadcast her situation, thought that she could regain her social status by accepting a substitute child, and by such an agreement maintain her control over her house, which she feared she might otherwise lose. She was more reticent than her husband, but realized what he wanted and knew how, without accommodating herself to his point of view, to make some explanation easier. She made her conditions, obtained almost everything she demanded, and that is how the terms of the will were established, which made very little provision for the child. The old doctor had died in the meantime, and so they turned to a young, intelligent physician who was well rewarded and extremely flattered to have the opportunity of revealing his deceased colleague's lack of skill and patience, and of putting things right. The natural mother agreed to all this, the deception was successfully accomplished, Therese came into the world, and was entrusted to a stepmother because her real mother fell victim to the deception by getting up from childbed too soon, died, and left the poor man disconsolate.

"Madame *** had, however, achieved her purpose. In the eyes of the world she now had a delightful child whom she displayed everywhere with excessive pride, and she had got rid of a rival whose relationship with her husband she regarded jealously and whose influence in the future she secretly feared. She showered the child with affection, and, in moments of intimacy, found ways to win her husband òver by expressing great sympathy at his loss, so that he abandoned himself to her completely, placed the fortunes of himself and his child entirely in her hands, and only shortly before his death, and then only through his grown daughter, did he once again become master in his own household. This, my dear Therese, was probably the secret that your ailing father was trying to tell you; this is what I wanted to tell you about in detail while our young friend, your future bridegroom by a strange concatenation of circumstances, was not with us. Here are papers which prove the truth of what I have been telling you. You will see how long I have been on the track of all this and that I have only recently become certain about it. I did not dare suggest to my friend earlier that the achievement of a happy union with Therese was possible, for if this had turned out to be wrong a second time, he would have been utterly despondent. Now you will understand Lydie's suspicions; for I must confess that I never encouraged his affection for that girl, once I contemplated again the possibility of his marrying Therese."

Nobody expressed any reaction to what he had told them. The women returned the papers after a few days, without any further mention of the matter.

There was plenty in the neighborhood to keep the assembled company diverted, and the country was so delightful that they made frequent excursions alone or in groups, either by foot, on horseback or in carriages. On one such occasion Jarno explained to Wilhelm his proposal, showing him the relevant documents, but not pressing for a decision on Wilhelm's part.

Wilhelm's reaction was as follows: "Given the strange situation in which I find myself, I can only repeat what I said earlier with all sincerity in Natalie's presence. Lothario and his friends can legitimately demand every kind of renunciation from me, and so I hereby abandon all claim to Therese's hand. Please secure me the formal permission to leave. I can assure you, my friend, that my decision requires no further reflection. I have felt these last days that Therese is having difficulty in preserving that appearance of delight with which she first greeted me. Her affection is estranged from me; or perhaps I have never had it."

"Such situations resolve themselves better over the course of time, gradually, and in silence, rather than by a lot of talking, which only produces ferment and embarrassment," said Jarno.

"I would have thought," Wilhelm replied, "that just such a situation as this should be resolvable by an act of clear, quiet decision. I have so often been reproached with dilatoriness and indecision; why then, when I am firmly decided, should I be expected to indulge in a failing I have so often been charged with, this time to my own disadvantage? Does the world take such trouble to educate us, merely to show us that it cannot educate itself? Just allow me the satisfaction of ridding myself of a fruitless relationship which I entered into with the best intentions in the world—and that right soon."

Despite his request, several days passed without his hearing any more about the matter or noticing any change in the attitudes of his friends, for all the conversation tended to be general and unconcerned.

Chapter Seven

Natalie, Jarno and Wilhelm were sitting together, when Natalie said: "You have something on your mind, Jarno. I've been noticing that for quite a while."

"Yes I have," he replied. "There is an important venture we have been planning for a long time, and it seems to me that now is the time for it to get started. You," he said to Natalie, "already know about it in general terms, and I must tell our young friend about it, because it will depend on him whether he wishes to take part. You will not be seeing me here much longer, for I am about to embark for America."

"America?" said Wilhelm, with a smile. "I would not have expected such a wild idea from you, still less that you would choose me to accompany you."

"Once you know our whole plan," said Jarno, "you will not consider it a wild idea and might well be taken with it. Let me explain. One does not have to know much about the present state of the world to realize that great changes are impending and property is no longer safe anywhere."

"I have no clear sense of that," said Wilhelm, "and have only recently concerned myself about my possessions. Perhaps I would have done better to neglect them still longer, for concern about their preservation seems to make people gloomy."

"Let me finish what I have to say," said Jarno. "Concern befits age, whereas youth can well do without it for a while. Balanced activity can unfortunately only be achieved by counterbalancing. At the present moment it is highly inadvisable to have all one's property and all one's money in one place, but on the other hand it is difficult to manage them if they are in different places. We have therefore worked out a new plan: from our ancient Tower a Society shall emerge, which will extend into every corner of the globe, and people from all over the world will be allowed to join it. We will cooperate in safeguarding our means of existence, in case some political revolution should displace one of our members from the land he owns. I am now going to America in order to take advantage of the good connections that Lothario made when he was over there. The Abbé will be going to Russia, and you shall have the choice, if you wish to join us, of either staying with Lothario in Germany or coming with me. I would imagine that you would choose the latter, for a long journey can be very advantageous for a young man."

Wilhelm collected himself and replied: "Your proposal is certainly worth consideration, for my motto in the immediate future will be: The farther away, the better. I hope you will give me more details about your plan. It may be due to my insufficient knowledge of the world, but it seems to me that there are insuperable difficulties in establishing such an organization."

"Most of which will be overcome," said Jarno, "because so far there are a few of us honest, intelligent, determined persons, with a broad enough vision to establish such a Society."

Friedrich, who had been listening but said nothing till now, exclaimed: "If you will put in a good word for me, I will go with you."

Jarno shook his head at this.

"Why not?" said Friedrich. "What do you object to in me? A new colony will need young colonists: those I will bring you, and amusing ones at that, I can assure you. And then there is a fine young girl I know, who has no place over here any longer: I mean that sweet, charming Lydie. Where shall the poor girl go with all her sorrow and pain, except into the depths of the sea unless some worthy fellow takes charge of her. I would have thought," he said, turning to Wilhelm, "that since you are good at consoling abandoned women, you would decide to let everyone take his girl along, and then we could all follow this old gentleman."

This made Wilhelm angry. He answered, with seeming composure: "I don't even know whether Lydie is free, and since I do not seem to be very lucky in wooing, I would not want to try that."

"Friedrich," said Natalie, "when you yourself act so frivolously, you imagine that others share your point of view. Our friend here deserves a woman's heart that belongs only to him and is not beset by extraneous memories. Only with someone as sensible and pure in heart as Therese would such a risk have been advisable."

"What do you mean by 'risk?'" said Friedrich. "Love is always a risk, whether under the trees or before the altar, in embraces or wedding rings, when crickets are chirping or drums and trumpets playing, everything is a risk, everything is decided by chance."

"I have always thought," said Natalie, "that our principles are merely supplements to our existence. We are all too ready to give our faults the semblance of valid principles. Look out for the path that pretty girl, who at the moment attracts and claims you so strongly, will lead you."

"She herself is on a very good path," said Friedrich, "the path to sanctity. It is a detour, for sure, but all the more amusing and secure. Mary Magdalene went the same way—and who knows how many others. When the talk is of love, my dear sister, you really shouldn't intervene. I don't believe you will marry until some bride or other is missing, and you, with your customary generosity, will provide yourself as a supplement to someone's existence. So let's conclude our business with this seller of souls, and agree on who is to join the travelling party."

"You're too late with your proposal," said Jarno. "Lydie is already provided for."

"How so?" asked Friedrich.

"I have offered her my hand in marriage," Jarno replied.

"Old man," said Friedrich, "you are embarking on something which, as a substantive, invites various adjectives, and as a subject all sorts of predicates."

"I must honestly confess," said Natalie, "that it seems to me a dangerous venture to take over a girl at the moment when she is desperate because of love for another."

"I have taken the risk," said Jarno. "She will be mine under one condition. There is nothing in the world more precious than a heart capable of love and passion. Whether it has loved, or still loves—that's not what matters. The loved bestowed on another is for me almost more appealing than that with which I may be loved. What I perceive is the power and strength of a loving heart, and my self-love will not cloud this perception."

"Have you spoken to Lydie recently?" she asked.

Jarno nodded with a smile. Natalie shook her head and, getting up, said: "I no longer know what to make of you all. But I can tell you that I myself will not be led astray by you."

She was about to leave when the Abbé came in with a letter in his hand, and said to her: "Don't leave! I have here a proposal that I would like your opinion on. The Marchese, your late uncle's friend, whom we have been expecting for some time now, will be here in a few days. He writes that he is not so much at ease in the German language as he thought, and he needs a companion who is at home in that language and in several others. Since he wishes to establish scholarly rather than political connections, an interpreter of this kind is essential to him. I cannot think of anyone more suited for this than our young friend here. He knows his own language and is informed about many things, and it will be a great advantage for him to get to know Germany in such good company and under such favorable conditions. He who does not know his own country has no yardstick with which to measure others. What do you say, my friends? What do you say, Natalie?"

Nobody could think of any reason to object to this proposal. Jarno did not seem to see in it an obstacle to his plan of going to America; he was not intending to depart immediately. Natalie was silent. Friedrich recited various tags about the usefulness of travel.

Wilhelm was so enraged at this new proposal that he could hardly contain himself. He saw in it an arrangement to get rid of him as quickly as possible, an all too obvious stratagem and, what was worse, one that was announced publicly without any consideration for him. The suspicions that Lydie had aroused in him, together with all that he himself had experienced, came alive in his mind, and the unpretentious way that Jarno had explained things to him now seemed to him false and contrived.

But he controlled himself sufficiently to say: "Your proposal certainly deserves consideration."

"A speedy decision might be necessary," said the Abbé.

"I am not ready for that," Wilhelm replied. "Let us wait until the man arrives. Then we can see whether we are suited to each other. But one condition must be agreed on in advance, that I take Felix with me and that he shall accompany us everywhere."

"That condition will hardly be acceptable," said the Abbé.

"I don't see why I should allow conditions to be dictated to me by anybody, nor why, if I am to see my native land, I need an Italian to accompany me."

"Because a young man, " said the Abbé with impressive solemnity, "always has cause to seek the company of other people."

Wilhelm, realizing full well that he was unable to control himself much longer and that his temper was restrained only by the fact that Natalie was present, replied somewhat hastily: "Allow me a little time to think this over; I believe it will not take me long to decide whether I really need to seek further company, or whether my heart and mind will not irresistibly impel me to liberate myself from so many bonds that threaten to produce a state of wretched, lasting imprisonment."

That he said with deep feeling. A glance at Natalie assuaged him somewhat, her person and all it meant for him affecting him more strongly than ever in this moment of anguish.

"You might as well admit it," he said to himself when he was alone again. "You are in love with her; once again you are experiencing what it means to love someone with your whole being. It was like this when I loved Mariane, and things went so terribly wrong. I was in love with Philine, but could not respect her. I respected Aurelie, but could not love her. I revered Therese, and my paternal feelings led me to feel affection for her. But now when all those emotions which should make one feel happy fill my heart—I am being forced to leave! Oh, why must the irresistible desire to possess her associate itself with what I am now experiencing, and why without the certainty of possession, do these feelings, these convictions destroy all else that makes me happy? Will I ever again be able to enjoy the sun and world, the company of others, or any other pleasures? Will I not always say to myself: 'But Natalie is not here!' And yet, unfortunately, she will always be there. If I close my eyes, she will appear before me; if I open them, she will dominate everything like the effect produced by a blinding image in the eye. Was not the fleeting vision of the Amazon always present in my imagination, though I had only seen her, but did not know her? And now that you do know her and have been close to her, now she has shown such interest in you—now all her qualities are as clearly impressed on your mind as her image was formerly on your senses. It is always troublesome to seek, but more troublesome to find and have to do without. What else should I ask for from the world? Why should I look around any longer? What country, what town contains a treasure equal to this? Why should I travel all over the place just to discover something of lesser value? Is life nothing but a racecourse, where one must turn round immediately once one has reached the outmost limit? Are goodness and excellence a firmly established, immovable goal which one must hastily retreat from just when one believes one has reached it, whereas those who only strive for earthly possessions can acquire them in various places, even at markets or fairs?"

"Come, dear boy," he said to his son who had just run up to join him, "may you be and remain everything for me. You were given to me in place of your dear mother, you shall replace that second mother I had intended for you; now you have a larger gap to fill. Your beauty and charm, your thirst for knowledge and your developing abilities shall totally occupy my heart and mind."

The boy was busy playing with a new toy. His father tried to make it work. But while he was doing this, the child lost interest. "You're just like the rest of us," said Wilhelm. "Come, son! Come, brother-man, let's saunter about in the world, without any particular goal, as well as we can!"

His decision to leave, taking the child with him, and to distract himself by seeing what the world had to offer, was now firmly established. He wrote to Werner, asking him for money and letters of credit, and sent this by Friedrich's courier, instructing him most specifically to return soon. However much he was irritated with all his other friends, nothing clouded his relationship with Natalie. He confided to her what he intended to do, and she accepted it as self-evident that he could, indeed had to, do that; and although her apparent indifference to his decision caused him pain, her kindness and her very presence did much to comfort him. She advised him to visit various cities, where he could get to know some of her friends, both men and women. The courier returned, bringing what Wilhelm had asked for, despite the fact that Werner did not approve of this new venture at all. "I had hoped you were becoming sensible at last," he wrote, "but that seems to have been put off for a while. Where will you all be drifting to? And where will the woman be whose help in domestic affairs you gave me reason to think you had hopes of? None of the others will be around, so the whole burden of the business arrangements will have to be borne by me and the magistrate! Thank goodness he's as good a lawyer as I am a businessman, and we are both accustomed to shouldering responsibilities. Goodbye for the present. Your aberrations are forgivable, for without them we would not have gotten along so well in this part of the world."

As far as external conditions were concerned, Wilhelm could have left immediately, but his mind was preoccupied with two obstacles to this. First: They had refused to allow him to see Mignon's corpse, except at the funeral exequies, which the Abbé was determined to hold, though the preparations were not yet completed. Secondly, the doctor had been called away by a strange letter from the pastor, which had some reference to the Harper, and Wilhelm wanted to find out more about his situation.

In these circumstances neither his mind nor his body could be at rest, by night or by day. When everyone else was sleeping, he was pacing up and down in the house. The presence of those old familiar paintings partly attracted and partly repelled him. He could neither accept nor reject what surrounded him, everything reminded him of something else, he could see the whole chain of his life, but at the moment it lay in pieces which would not join together again. These works of art, the ones his father had sold, seemed to him a symbol of the fact that he too was partly excluded from calm, solid possession of what was desirable, and partly deprived of this by his own fault or that of others. He became so lost in these lugubrious reflections that he sometimes seemed to himself like a ghost, and even when he was feeling and touching objects outside himself, he could hardly resist the sense of not knowing whether he was alive or not.

It was only the stab of pain that he sometimes felt at so wantonly and yet so necessarily having to abandon what he had found and refound, only his tears that gave him once more the sense that he was indeed still alive. In vain did he remind himself of the fortunate state he was in. "Everything is worthless," he said to himself, "if that one single thing is lacking which makes everything else worthwhile."

The Abbé announced the arrival of the Marchese. "It seems," he said to Wilhelm, "that you are determined to go off alone with your son, but do at least make the acquaintance of this man, for wherever you may encounter him on your travels, he could be useful to you." The Marchese appeared, a man not far advanced in years, one of those handsome, agreeable Lombard types. He had made the acquaintance of the uncle, who was much older than he, when he was a young man in the army, and then through business transactions. Later they had traveled together through a great part of Italy, and the works of art that the Marchese rediscovered here, had been largely acquired while he was present, and on various happy occasions which he vividly remembered.

The Italians have a deeper sense of the value of art than other nations. Anyone who does anything wants to be an artist, a master or professor, and acknowledges through this craze for titles that acquiring things by inheritance is not enough, nor is achieving skills by practice. Italians concede that one should be able to think about what one does, establish principles and elucidate for oneself and others the reasons why this or that should be done.

The guest was touched to rediscover these beautiful objects without their owner, and delighted to find the spirit of his friend pervading his admirable descendants. They looked at the various works, and experienced great comfort at being able to relate to each other. The Marchese and the Abbé led the conversation; Natalie, feeling once again in the presence of her uncle, found it easy to agree with their thoughts and opinions. Wilhelm had to translate everything into theatrical terminology, if he was to understand what they said. It was hard to restrain Friedrich's joking. Jarno was rarely present.

In consideration of the fact that fine works of art are rare in modern times, the Marchese said: "It is not easy to contemplate what part circumstances have to play in an artist's activity, and the endless demands an outstanding genius, a person of remarkable talent, has to make on himself, and the immense effort he must expend on his training and development. If external conditions do little for him, if he concludes that the world is easily satisfied and only desires a pleasing and comforting illusion, it would be surprising if convenience and self-satisfaction did not commit him to mediocrity, and it would be strange if he did not prefer to acquire money and praise by producing fashionable wares than by pursuing a course that will more or less result in impoverishment and martyrdom. Therefore the artists of our age are always offering instead of giving. They always aim at attracting rather than satisfying. Everything is suggested, with no solid foundation and no proper execution. One only needs to spend a short while quietly in a gallery, observing what works of art appeal to the multitude, which of them are praised and which are ignored, to lose all joy in the present age and have little hope for the future."

"Yes," said the Abbé, "and as a result the artist and the lovers of art have a mutual influence on each other. The lover of art looks for some general indefinite pleasure: the work of art is to appeal to him just like a natural object. People tend to believe that the faculty of appreciating art develops as naturally as the tongue or the palate, and they judge a work of art as they do food. They do not understand that a different type of culture is required to attain a true appreciation of art. What I find most difficult is the separation a man must achieve within and for himself if he is ever to attain self-cultivation. That is why we encounter so many one-sided cultures, each of which presumes to speak for all."

"I am not quite clear what you mean," said Jarno, who had just joined the others.

"It is difficult," said the Abbé, "to speak briefly and definitively about this matter. All I would say is this: When a person sets himself a goal of manifold activity or experience, he must be capable of developing manifold organs in himself which are, in a manner of speaking, independent of each other. Anyone who aims at acting or experiencing with his total self, or tries to embrace everything outside himself into one total experience, will spend his time in constantly unfulfilled striving. How difficult it is to do what may seem so natural, to consider a fine statue or a superb painting in and for itself, music as music, acting as acting, a building for its own proportions and permanence! Nowadays most people treat finished works of art as if they were soft clay. The finished marble shall modify its shape according to their inclinations, their opinions and whims, the firmly established building expand or contract; a painting shall offer instruction, a play be morally uplifting, everything become something else. But because most people are themselves without form, since they cannot give a shape to their own self, their personality, they labor away at depriving objects of their form, so that everything shall become the same loose and flabby substance as themselves. They reduce everything to what they term 'effects,' to the notion that everything is relative; and so the only things that are not relative are nonsense and bad taste which, in the end, predominate as absolutes."

"I understand what you are saying," Jarno replied. "Or rather, I can see that what you are saying conforms to the principles you always firmly advocate.

But I cannot be so hard on those poor devils, those human beings you speak of. It is true that many of them are reminded of their own wretched deficiencies when they are in the presence of great works of art and of nature, that they take their conscience and morality with them to the opera, do not discard their loves and hates before a noble colonnade, and their comprehension necessarily diminishes the grandeur and splendor of what comes to them from outside, so that they may be able to relate it somehow to their own paltry selves."

Chapter Eight

In the evening the Abbé summoned everyone to the funeral rites for Mignon. The whole company repaired to the Hall of the Past, and found it strangely decorated and illuminated. The walls were almost entirely draped with tapestries of azure blue, so that only the base and the frieze remained uncovered. Huge wax candles were burning in the four big candelabras at the corners of the room, and others of appropriate size in the four smaller ones surrounding the sarcophagus in the center. Four boys were standing beside the bier, dressed in silver and blue, fanning with sheaves of ostrich feathers a figure that lay on top of the sarcophagus. The assembled company all took their seats, and two invisible choruses intoned in gentle strains: "Whom do you bring to those at rest?" The four boys answered, with love in their voices: "A weary comrade we bring unto you; here let it stay and rest till joyful comrades in heaven shall wake it once more."

CHORUS. Child so young for this our realm, welcome, be welcome in sorrow! Nor boy, nor girl shall follow thee! Old age alone shall wend its way, eagerly, calmly, here to this silent hall, but thou, dear child, shalt rest here too, rest in solemn company.

BOYS. Sadly we brought her here, here shall she stay. We too will stay, weep and mourn, shed our tears above her corpse.

CHORUS. See now the mighty wings, see the light unspotted robe, the golden circle gleaming in her hair; see the beauty and grace of her repose.

BOYS. They lift her not, those mighty wings. Her garments float no more in easy play. Her head we crowned with roses, sweet and friendly was her gaze.

CHORUS. Lift the eyes of the spirit! May in you dwell the power that transports what in life is finest, loveliest, up aloft, beyond the stars.

BOYS. Down here she is lost to us now. In gardens she wanders no more, flowers she gathers no more. Let us weep and leave her here, let us weep and stay with her.

CHORUS. Children, return to life! Your tears shall be dried in freshness of air circling water's edge. Flee the night! Daylight and joy and continuance — those are the lot of the living.

BOYS. We rise and turn to life again. The day shall give us labor and joy, till evening brings us rest, and night refreshing sleep.

CHORUS. Hasten back to life anew! And beauty clothed in raiment pure shall bring you love, the sight of heaven, and the crown of immortality.

The boys moved away, and the Abbé rose from his seat and stepped behind the sarcophagus. "The man who prepared this silent dwelling-place," he said, "left instructions that each new arrival should be received with due ceremony. The designer and builder of this hallowed place came first; now we have brought here a young stranger, so that this one room encloses two very different victims of the solemn, arbitrary and inexorable goddess of death. Fixed laws govern our entry into life and the number of our days, our maturing in countenance of the light, but there is no law that prescribes the length of our life. The feeblest lifethread may stretch into unexpected length, and the strongest may be forcibly severed by Fate, which seems to delight in inconsistency. The child that we bury here, we know little about. We know not from where it came, nor who its parents were; and we can only guess at the length of its life. Its firmly locked heart gave us no inkling of what was going on inside it; nothing was clear or apparent about her except her love for the man who rescued her from the clutches of a barbarian. This tender affection and her intense gratitude seemed to be the flame that consumed the oil of her life. The doctor's skill could not preserve the beauty of her life, nor could friendship and care prolong it. But if art could not give permanence to her spirit, it could employ every skill to preserve her body and save it from decay. Balsam has been introduced into all her veins and, instead of blood, this colors those cheeks that faded so early. Draw near, my friends, and observe the wonders of art, the sum of solicitude!"

He lifted the veil, and there lay the child in its angel costume, as if sleeping, in the most pleasing position. They all stepped up, and marveled at this semblance of life. Only Wilhelm remained seated. He could not bring himself to do otherwise, he could not think about what he was feeling, for every thought seemed to shatter what he felt.

The Abbé had spoken in French, for the benefit of the Marchese, who stepped up with the others and looked attentively at the figure before him. The Abbé went on to say: "This good heart that was so closed to us, was always open to its God, in whom it had sacred trust. Humility, even a tendency toward self-debasement, seemed to be natural to her. She adhered fervently to the Catholic religion, in which she had been born and raised. She often expressed the desire to be interred in consecrated ground, and we have, according to the custom of her church, consecrated this marble coffin and the small amount of earth it contains, which is concealed in her pillow. In her last moments she fervently kissed the image of the Crucified One, which was delicately traced in hundreds of dots on her little arms." As he said this, the Abbé lifted the sleeve from her right arm, and there on her white skin they saw a bluish crucifix, together with various letters and signs.

The Marchese observed this very closely. "Oh God!" he cried, standing up straight and extending his arms to Heaven, "oh, you poor child, my unhappy niece – it is here that I find you at last! What painful joy it is to find you again, when we had so long abandoned all hope of doing so, to find your dear, sweet body that we thought was snatched by the fish of the lake, to find you again – dead, but preserved! I have witnessed your burial, glorified by its surroundings and even more by the good friends who accompanied you on your road to this place of rest. And when I am able to speak again," he said with a broken voice, "I will thank them all."

Tears prevented him from saying more. Pressing a spring, the Abbé lowered the corpse into the depths of the marble sarcophagus. Four young men, dressed like the boys, came from behind the hangings, placed the heavy, beautifully decorated lid on to the sarcophagus, and began to sing:

THE YOUTHS. The treasure now is well preserved, the beauteous image of the past. Unconsumed, in marble it rests; in your hearts it lives and works. Guide your steps back into life once more! With you take this solemn zeal, for zeal is sacred, it alone transforms life into eternity.

The invisible chorus joined in these final words, but no one heard their fortifying message, so absorbed were they all in the strange revelations and their own feelings. The Abbé and Natalie walked out with the Marchese; Therese and Lothario followed with Wilhelm. Only when the singing had completely died away, were they once more overcome with sorrow, reflection, consideration and curiosity, and longed to be back in the peace of what they had just left.

Chapter Nine

The Marchese avoided saying anything further openly, but he did have some long private conversations with the Abbé. When they were all together, he often asked for music, a request willingly granted because everyone was pleased to be relieved of the necessity of making conversation. Time passed, and he was making preparations to leave. One day he said to Wilhelm: "I do not wish to disturb the remains of that dear child. Let her stay where she loved and suffered. But her friends must promise to visit me in her homeland, in the place where she was born and raised. They must see the columns and statues she remembered in her song, the coves where she gathered pebbles. You, young man, will not decline the thanks of a family that is so indebted to you. I am leaving tomorrow. I have confided the whole story to the Abbé and he will communicate it to you. As an outsider he will be able to relate it more coherently than I could under the stress of my sorrow, for which he has already forgiven me. If you still wish to accompany me on my travels through Germany, as the Abbé has suggested, I would be delighted. And do bring your boy along with you; and if he should cause some occasional inconvenience, we will remember the care and consideration you gave my poor niece."

That same evening they were surprised by the arrival of the countess. Wilhelm was trembling in every limb when she came into the room, and she, though not unprepared, kept close to her sister who showed her to a seat. How simple was now her dress, how changed her appearance! Wilhelm could hardly bear to look at her. She greeted him, and a few general remarks sufficiently revealed her thoughts and feelings. The Marchese had retired early, but the rest of the company had no desire to disperse. The Abbé produced a manuscript, saying he had committed to paper the strange story he had been entrusted with, and that pen and ink had not been spared in recording the details of such a remarkable sequence of events. The countess was informed of what they were referring to, and the Abbé began to read what the Marchese had told him:

"Much as I have seen of the world, I must consider my own father as one of the oddest men I ever knew. He was of noble, upright character, his ideas were broad and, one could well say, big; he was strict toward himself, in all his plans there was unflinching purposefulness, in all his actions, steadiness and consistency. Productive as it was, on the one hand, to consort and do business with him, he himself had difficulty in being at ease in the world, because he demanded from the state, his neighbors, his children and his servants conformity to the same laws that he imposed on himself. His most modest demands became aggrandized by his strictness, and he was never entirely satisfied, because nothing turned out as he had wanted it to. I have seen him when he was building a palace, planning a garden, or acquiring a fine new estate, inwardly resentful at the conviction that fate had condemned him to self-denial and toleration. He maintained great dignity in his behavior: when he joked, it was to show his superior intelligence, he could not bear criticism and I only once saw him lose his temper, which was when he heard someone refer to one of his undertakings as ridiculous. It was in this spirit that he treated his children and handled his wealth. My elder brother was brought up to become the lord of huge estates, I was to enter the church, and my younger brother the army. I was vigorous, fiery, active, quick and good at all bodily activities. My younger brother was more inclined to a life of reflective repose, and devoted to study, to music and to poetry. It was only after a great struggle, when my father became ultimately convinced of the impossibility of his intentions for our future, that he agreed, though even then unwillingly, that my younger brother and I should switch professions; but although he saw that this was what we wanted, he was never resigned to it and foretold that no good would come of it. The older he became, the more cut off he felt from all society, till finally he lived almost entirely alone. Only one old friend, who had served in the German army, lost his wife during a campaign, and had a daughter about ten years old, provided my father with companionship. This man acquired a pleasant property in the neighborhood, visited my father regularly at certain times each week, often bringing his daughter with him. He never opposed my father, who came to consider him finally as the only company he could put up with. After my father's death we noticed that this man had been well provided for by my father—in fact he had not wasted his time. He enlarged his property holdings and his daughter had expectations of a fine dowry. She grew up to be an exceptionally beautiful girl, and my elder brother often teased me by saying I should seek her hand.

"Meanwhile, my brother Augustin was spending his time at the monastery in the most peculiar way: he gave himself over to indulgence in ecstasies of both spiritual and physical nature, which at times transported him into a seventh heaven, but at others plunged him into depths of weakness and a void of misery. While my father was still living, any change for my brother was unthinkable; even so, what could we have wished to propose? After my father's death, Augustin came to see us frequently. His condition, which we had pitied at first, became more tolerable, for he himself had become more reasonable. But the more his reason promised him health and contentment by following the course of nature, the more urgently did he implore us to liberate him from his vows. And he told us that his intentions were directed toward Sperata, the girl in our neighborhood.

"My elder brother had suffered too much from my father's severity to remain unmoved by the condition of his youngest brother. We both spoke with the family confessor, a fine old man, and revealed to him our brother's intentions, urging him to initiate and facilitate the matter. He expressed hesitation such as was unusual for him, but when our brother pressed us further and we advocated the matter more ardently to the confessor, he had to reveal to us a very strange story.

"What he told us was that Sperata was our sister, the child of both our father and mother. Affection and heat of the senses had come over my father once more in those later years when conjugal rights usually have abated. There had been much amusement recently over a similar case in the neighborhood, so my father, in order not to incur ridicule, decided to conceal this late, legitimate fruit of his love with the same care that other people conceal accidental products of their early affections. Our mother's delivery took place secretly, the child was taken into the country, and my father's old friend, who apart from the confessor was the only other person who knew the secret, pretended the child was his own daughter. The confessor had agreed not to reveal the secret except in dire emergency. My father's friend died, the young girl was placed in the care of an old woman. We knew that love of singing and music had led to my brother visiting her, and when he repeatedly demanded that we should release him from his former bonds in order to forge a new one, it became necessary to tell him as soon as possible of the danger with which he was beset.

"He looked at us with wild, scornful eyes. 'Spare me such outlandish tales,' he said, 'they are only for children and credulous ninnies. You will never tear Sperata away from me. She is mine. Dismiss this terrifying phantom with which you vainly try to scare me. Sperata is not my sister, she is my wife!'—He then ecstatically described how this heavenly girl had led him out of his state of unnatural isolation into what is truly life, how their minds had joined like two throats in harmony, and how he even came to bless his former pain and aberration for depriving him of the company of woman so that he could now devote himself entirely to this lovely girl. We were horrified at this discovery, pitied him, but did not know what to do. He assured us quite definitely that she was carrying a child by him. Our confessor did everything his duty required, but that only made matters worse. My brother vehemently opposed all he said about the demands of nature, of religion, morality and social order; nothing was sacred to him save his relationship to Sperata, no names more worthy than those of father and wife. 'Such designations,' he said, 'are natural, all else is fancy or opinion. Haven't there been great nations that have sanctioned marriage with one's sister? Don't talk about your gods, you only refer to them when you want to fool us, lead us away from nature, distort our noblest instincts into crimes by infamous coercion, committing your victims to utter distraction of mind and disgraceful misuse of their bodies, burying them alive. I should know, for I have suffered more than anybody, falling from the highest pitch of rapture and ecstasy, down into the terrible waste of insensibility, emptiness, destruction and despair, from the loftiest sense of the existence of supernatural beings into the depths of disbelief, disbelief in oneself. I had drunk the terrible dregs of the cup whose lip had been so enticing, and every part of my being was poisoned. And now, when benevolent Nature has healed me by its greatest gift—the gift of love—now that I feel once again, at the bosom of this lovely girl, that I exist, that she exists, that we are one, that from our living union a third person will come and smile at us—now you loose the fires of hell and purgatory, which can only singe morbid imaginations, and hurl them at the unassailable certainty of the experience of true, living, pure love! Come and meet us beneath those cypresses that extend gravely into the sky, visit us in those groves where lemons and pomegranates surround us, and the tender myrtle unfolds its delicate blossoms—and then try to frighten us with your dismal, gray, man-made entrapments!'

"He persisted for a long time in not believing what we had told him, and even when we assured him of its truth, and the confessor confirmed this, he would not be deflected. On the contrary, he cried out: 'Don't listen to the echoes of your cloisters, don't consult your musty parchments, your crotchety and quirky regulations: ask Nature and your hearts. Nature will tell you what you have to tremble at: she will solemnly point to what she has irrevocably laid her lasting curse upon. Consider the lilies: Do not husband and wife grow on one and the same stem? Does not the blossom they bear unite them? And is not the lily the image of innocence? Is not its sibling union fruitful? Nature clearly indicates what it abhors: a creature that should not exist, cannot exist, develops wrongly, or is soon destroyed. The marks of her curse, the signs of her severity are: barrenness, stunted growth, premature decay. She metes out her punishments right away. Look around you: You will not see anything that is forbidden, anything that bears her curse. In the silence of the cloister and the bustle of the world, thousands of actions are honored and sanctified which bear Nature's curse. She regards with sadness both easy leisureliness and overstrained activity, free choice and abundance as well as compulsion and neediness; she advocates moderation. Her terms are valid, her workings gentle. He who has suffered as I have, has the right to be free. Sperata is mine; only death shall take her from me. How am I to keep her? How am I to be happy? That is for you to worry about. I'm going to her now, and never will I be parted from her.'

"He was about to board the ship to join her, but we dissuaded him, urging him not to do what might have the direst results. He should remember, we said, that he was not living in the free world of his own thoughts and ideas but in a state whose laws and customs had the inviolability of natural law. We had to promise the confessor that we would not let our brother out of our sight, and certainly not out of our castle. Augustin left us, promising to return in a few days. What we expected, occurred: His mind was strong, but his heart was weak, his earlier religious feelings revived, and he was overcome by terrible doubts. He spent two fearful days and nights, the confessor tried to help him, but in vain. His reason, when left to itself, absolved him of all blame, but his feelings, his religion, all customary concepts, declared him a criminal.

"One morning we found his room empty. There was a letter on the table telling us that, since we were restraining him by force, he was justified in seeking his freedom; he was going to Sperata, hoping to flee with her, and was prepared for all eventualities, should we try to separate them.

"We were much afraid, but our confessor constrained us to remain calm. Our poor brother had been closely watched, and the boatmen, instead of ferrying him across the water, returned him to his monastery. Tired from two days of wakefulness he fell asleep as soon as the boat began to rock in the moonlight, and did not waken until he was in the hands of his spiritual brothers. He did not recover until he heard the monastery gate closing behind him.

"Painfully affected by our brother's fate, we heaped reproaches on the confessor. But this worthy man soon persuaded us with medical arguments that our sympathy for the poor sick fellow was mortally dangerous. He said he was not acting on his own account but under orders from the bishop and the consistory. The intention was to avoid all public unpleasantness and cover up this sad case with the veil of secret ecclesiastical discipline. Sperata should be spared; she should never discover that her lover was her brother. She was referred to a priest to whom she had previously confided her physical condition. Her pregnancy and delivery were kept secret. She was happy to be the mother of the little creature. Like most of our young girls she could neither read nor write; and therefore she told the priest what he should say to her lover. The priest thought he owed a nursing mother some pious deception; so he brought her news of our brother without ever seeing him, told her in his name to be at peace, take good care of herself and the child, and leave the future to God.

"Sperata was by nature inclined to be religious. Her condition and her lone-liness only increased this tendency, and the priest encouraged it so as to pre-pare her for a lasting separation. As soon as the child was weaned, and she had regained sufficient bodily strength, the priest began to present to her in ter-rifying colors her offense in giving herself to a priest, which he termed a sin against nature, a form of incest. For he had the strange idea of making her repentance like to that she would have felt if she had known the true nature of her transgression. By this means he brought great grief and misery into her mind, stressing the importance of the church and its high authority, depicting the terrible effects on the salvation of souls if clemency were exercised in such cases and the guilty rewarded by approving such a union. He indicated to her the saving grace of temporal atonement and the consequent attainment of the crown of glory. And in the end, like a poor sinner, she gladly sacrificed her-self, imploring them to separate her forever from our brother. Since they had now achieved this much, they allowed her the freedom, though under supervi-sion, to stay in her own dwelling or in the cloister.

"The child grew and soon revealed strange characteristics. It began very early to run and develop great skill in bodily movements, it would sing very pleasingly, and soon learned by its own efforts to play the zither. But it could not express itself in words, and the obstacle seemed to be in its mind rather than in its speech organs. The poor mother had a sad relationship with the child, the priest having so confused her that, without being mad, she found herself in the strangest state of mind. Her crime became ever more fearful and impious to her, and the reference to incest had impressed itself so strongly on her, that she was overcome by repulsion, as if she had known the true nature of their relationship. The confessor often wondered about the image he had used, which had broken the girl's heart. It was pitiful to see how a mother's love, delighting in the living presence of the child, fought with the ghastly thought that the child should not be there at all. The conflict between these two feelings became intensified, but repulsion soon won out over love.

"Quite early on they took the child away from her and gave it to some good people living down by the lake, and with this greater freedom it developed a special delight in climbing. The child made her way up the highest hills, clam-bered along the sides of ships, and imitated the feats of ropedancers who sometimes came to these parts—all this quite naturally.

"In order to be able to move more freely in all this bodily exercise, she wore boys' clothing, and although her foster parents thought this improper and undesirable, we tried to be as indulgent as we could. Her strange walks and climbs often led her far afield: she would get lost, stay away, but then reappear. When she returned, she would usually seat herself between the columns of the portal of a nearby villa. Nobody searched for her anymore, she was always to be found there, resting on the steps, running into the great hall, peering at the statues and then, unless she was detained by someone, running home.

"But our trust was deceived and our indulgence paid its price, for one day she did not return, her hat was found floating on the water not far from the place where a mountain torrent gushed into the lake. It was assumed that she had fallen whilst clambering over the rocks. Extensive searches were made, but the body was never found.

"Through the thoughtless gossip of some of her companions, Sperata soon learned of the death of her child. She seemed calm and serene and gave it to be understood that she was clearly pleased that God had taken the poor little creature unto Himself and thereby spared it from experiencing or creating even greater misfortune.

"In this connection all sorts of wild tales began to be bruited about regarding our lakes. For example: Every year a lake must have an innocent child, it will not tolerate a dead body and will sooner or later cast it up on the bank, even the very last bone will come up from the bottom. A story was told of one disconsolate mother whose child had drowned in the lake and who implored God and all the saints to allow her at least to bury the bones. The next storm cast up the skull, the next the rump, and when everything was together she carried all the bones in a cloth to the church. But then a miracle happened! As she was entering the building, the package got heavier and heavier, and finally, when she laid it on the steps of the altar, the child began to cry and to everyone's astonishment broke out of the cloth. Only one bone of the little finger of its right hand was still missing, which the mother sought and found, and this was preserved as a memorial amongst other relics in the church.

"These tales had a great effect on poor Sperata. Her imagination awakened and intensified the desire of her heart. She assumed that the child had atoned for itself and its parents, that the curse and punishment which had previously lain upon it were now entirely removed, and that what she had to do now was to find the bones and take them to Rome; then the child would appear before the people, in its fresh white skin, on the steps of the high altar of St. Peter's. It would once again look upon its father and mother, and the Pope, convinced of the approval of God and the saints, would forgive the parents their sins, to the loud acclaim of the assembled throng, absolve them and join them in marriage.

"Her eyes and attention were now always directed toward the lake and its shores. When at night the waves rolled in the moonlight, she would believe that every one of them was casting forth her child, and someone ought surely to run down there and pick it up on the bank.

"During the daytime she tirelessly visited those places where the stony shore ran into shallow parts of the lake, gathering into a little basket all the bones she could find. Nobody dared tell her these were animal bones. She buried the large ones, but kept the smaller ones. She continued relentlessly in her search. The priest who, impelled by an irresistible urge of duty, had brought about her condition, began to devote himself to her in every way he could. Influenced by him, people in the neighborhood began to consider her as someone in a state of religious rapture, not as someone out of her mind. They would stand with folded hands when she passed by; the children would even kiss her hand.

"Her old friend and foster mother was absolved by the confessor of her sin in bringing the two together, on the condition that she stay always with the poor unhappy creature, an obligation which she patiently and faithfully fulfilled until the very end.

"Meantime we had not lost touch with our brother. Neither the doctors nor the monastery authorities would let us visit him; but to convince us that he was well enough in his way, they allowed us, as often as we wished, to observe him in the garden or the cloister, even through a window in the ceiling of his room.

"After many terrible and peculiar periods, which I will not pause to describe, he entered on a strange state of mental repose and bodily restlessness. He hardly ever sat down except when playing his harp, which he often accompanied with song. Most of the time, however, he was restless, though easily guided and glad to follow, for all the violence and passion of his nature seemed now to focus on one thing—the fear of death. One could get him to do anything by threatening him with mortal illness or death.

"Apart from his habit of continually walking about in the monastery and asserting, in no uncertain terms, that it would be still better to be traversing hills and valleys, he spoke about an apparition that was constantly tormenting him. What he said was that every time he woke up, no matter at what hour of the night, he would see a handsome boy standing at the foot of his bed, threatening him with an open knife. They put him in another room, but he said the boy was there waiting for him. His walking back and forth became more and more restless, and people remembered afterwards that at that time he could be frequently seen at the window, looking out over the lake.

"Meantime our poor sister seemed to be steadily more and more worn down by her single preoccupation and her limited activity. So our doctor proposed that the bones of a child's skeleton should gradually be intermingled with those she already had, to increase her hopes. The idea seemed somehow dubious, but what might possibly be achieved, was that, when everything was put together, she might at least be persuaded to cease her endless searching and look forward to a journey to Rome.

"And so it was: her companion secretly exchanged what she had acquired with what Sperata herself had gathered, and a great joy spread over the poor woman's face when the parts gradually fitted together and she was told which were still lacking. She had fastened every part where it belonged with ribbon and thread, and had filled in the gaps with silk and embroidery as is done to honor the remains of saints.

"Everything was by now assembled, except for a few extremities. One morning, when she was still asleep, the doctor came to inquire how she was, and her old companion took the pieces out of the casket in the bedroom in order to show him what she had been busying herself with. Soon after this they heard her getting out of bed, lifting up the cloth, and, finding the box empty, falling on her knees. They came into the room and heard her fervent joyful prayer. 'It is true!' she cried. 'It wasn't a dream, it is true! Rejoice, my friends!

I have seen the dear, lovely creature alive again. It rose up, threw off the veil, its radiance filling the room, its beauty transfigured, its feet unable to touch the ground, even had they wished to. It was lifted up lightly into the air and could not even touch me with its hand. Then it called to me, showing me the path I had to follow. I will follow my child, and soon. I feel this, and my heart is easy, so easy. My sorrow is departed; and the sight of my risen child has given me a foretaste of heavenly bliss.'

"From this time on, her whole soul was filled with joyful prospects. She no longer paid attention to earthly things, took little food, and her spirit gradually freed itself from the weight of the body. One day they found her unusually pale and without feeling, she never again opened her eyes, she was what is called dead.

"The report of her vision soon spread amongst the people, and the reverence she had aroused while she was still alive, gave way when she died to the conviction that she was to be considered blessed, maybe even holy.

"When she was carried to her grave, people thronged around to touch her hand or at least her garment. In the experience of passionate exaltation many sick people no longer felt the torments that had afflicted them; they thought they were cured and acknowledged this, praising God and his new saint. The priests were obliged to place her body in a chapel, and the people demanded to worship there. Large numbers came: miners (who always tend toward strong religious feeling) flocked from their valleys; reverence, adoration and miracles increased from day to day. Episcopal ordinances to restrict, and finally discredit, this new form of religious worship, could not be implemented: any attempt to curb it was vigorously opposed by the populace, who began to take active steps against any disbelievers. Did not the saintly Borromeo appear in these parts among our forefathers? Did not his mother experience the joy of his canonization? Does not that great statue on the rock of Arona portray in visible form his spiritual greatness? Do not his own descendants still live amongst us? Has not God agreed to renew his miracles amongst a people of believers like ourselves?

"When, after several days, the body showed no signs of corruption, was whiter than ever, and almost transparent, the people's faith increased and there were several cures, which no attentive observer could explain or dismiss as false. The whole district was in a state of excitement, and even those who did not come to see, heard about nothing else for a long time.

"The monastery where my brother was was filled with reports of these marvels, like the rest of the district, but no one took pains to conceal these things from my brother, since he paid so little attention to anything and his relationship with Sperata was not known to anyone there. But this time he seemed to listen very carefully to what he heard, and engineered his escape so craftily that no one could understand how he managed it. It was later ascertained that he got himself ferried across the lake with a group of pilgrims, and implored the boatmen, who did not notice anything odd about him, to take extreme care that the boat should not capsize. Late at night he came to the chapel where his beloved was resting after her suffering. There were only a few worshippers kneeling in the corners, and her old companion was seated by her head. He went up to the woman, greeted her and asked how her lady was. 'You can see for yourself,' she said, with some embarrassment. He looked at the corpse, but only from the side. After some hesitation he took Sperata's hand but, horrified at its coldness, let it drop immediately, looked around distractedly, and said to the old woman: 'I cannot stay with her now. I still have a long way to go. But I will come back soon. Tell her that, when she wakes.'

"And so he left. We were only told about this later, tried to find where he had gone to, but with no result. How he managed to make his way over mountains and valleys, we do not know. He finally left traces in the canton of Grisons in Switzerland, but it was too late for us to follow them up. After that he disappeared completely; we believed that he was somewhere in Germany, but the war completely obliterated any signs of his whereabouts."

Chapter Ten

The Abbé finished reading. They had all wept as they listened. The countess was still wiping her eyes; finally she stood up and left the room with Natalie. The others were silent. Then the Abbé said: "The question now arises whether we should let the Marchese leave without telling him what we know, but he does not. For how can there be the slightest doubt that Augustin and our Harper are one and the same person? We ought to consider what we should do, both for the sake of that poor unfortunate man and for the family. My advice would be to do nothing hastily, to wait and see what news the doctor will bring us."

Everyone agreed; so the Abbé continued: "There is another question that can perhaps be dealt with more quickly. The Marchese is deeply moved by the kindness his niece has enjoyed from us, and particularly from our young friend. I have told the Marchese all about it, and he has warmly expressed his gratitude. 'That young man,' he said, 'declined to accompany me on my travels before he knew the bond that exists between us. But now I am no longer a stranger for him, one whose moods and temperament he might well feel uncertain about: I am his associate, his close relative as it were, and since the main obstacle to his joining me was his son, may this child now become a finer, firmer bond to knit us together. In addition to what I owe him, his companionship on the journey would be extremely useful to me. Let him return with me, my elder brother will receive him gladly, and let him not despise the inheritance of his foster child, for, according to a private agreement between my father and a friend of his, the money he set aside for his daughter reverts to us, and we will certainly not deny the benefactor of our niece what he has so amply deserved.'"

Therese took Wilhelm by the hand, and said: "We are experiencing once again one of those happy occasions when unselfishness and generosity earn the best interest. Follow this strange call, and while making yourself doubly valuable to the Marchese, hasten toward that beautiful country that has more than once engaged your heart and your imagination."

"I consign myself entirely to my friends and their direction," said Wilhelm, "for it is useless trying to act according to one's own will in this world. What I most wanted to keep, I have to let go, and an undeserved benefit imposes itself upon me."

He pressed Therese's hand and withdrew his. "I leave it entirely to you, what you decide about me," he said to the Abbé. "So long as I do not have to separate myself from Felix, I am ready to go anywhere or undertake anything that is appropriate."

Having heard this, the Abbé unfolded his plan: the Marchese should take his leave, Wilhelm should wait for the doctor's report, and then, when they had considered what should be done about the Harper, Wilhelm should follow with Felix after the Marchese. The Abbé suggested to the Marchese that their friend's preparations for his journey should not prevent him from examining the monuments of the town. The Marchese departed, but not without repeated assurances of his gratitude, which the various presents he left—jewels, gems, fabrics—amply attested.

Wilhelm was now all ready to leave, but everyone was concerned that no news came from the doctor. They feared that some misfortune might have befallen the poor old Harper just when there were good expectations of an improvement in his condition. They dispatched the courier; but the doctor arrived that same evening accompanied by a man of impressively grave appearance, whom nobody recognized. Neither of them said anything at first, then the stranger walked up to Wilhelm, stretched out his hand, and said: "Don't you recognize your old friend?" His voice was that of the Harper, but his appearance was totally different. He was dressed like a normal traveler, clean and tidy, the beard was gone, his hair was cared for, and what made him quite unrecognizable was that there were no signs of age in his features. Wilhelm eagerly and joyfully embraced him, and introduced him to the others. His behavior was completely rational, but he was quite unprepared for how well they knew him. "I must ask you," he said calmly, "to be patient with someone who may look grown-up but, after a long period of suffering, has re-emerged into the world as an inexperienced child. I owe it to this fine man here that I can once more appear in the company of others."

They welcomed him into their midst, and the doctor immediately suggested a walk, in order to break off the conversation and turn it into more neutral channels.

Once he was alone with the others, the doctor gave this account of what had happened: "It was the strangest chance that enabled us to effect his cure. For a long time we had been treating him morally and physically as we thought fit, things were going pretty well, but his fear of death was still intense, and he would not give up his beard or his long cloak. Otherwise, he was taking more interest in the things of this world, and his songs as well as his mental reactions seemed to indicate that he was drawing closer to life again. You will remember that strange letter from the pastor, which caused me to rush away last time. I went home and found the man completely changed: he had voluntarily had his beard removed and his hair dressed in a normal fashion, he asked for ordinary clothes, and seemed suddenly to have become a different person. We were curious to find out what had caused this, but did not dare to ask him about it.

"Then by pure chance we discovered a strange chain of events. A glass of liquid opium was missing from the pastor's medicine cabinet, and it was thought necessary to conduct a thorough search. Everyone was eager to absolve himself from suspicion, and there were some violent altercations amongst the persons in the house, until one day the Harper admitted that he had it. He was asked whether he had taken any of it, and said no. But he continued: 'I owe the return of my wits to this. You have the power to take it away from me, but if you do, you will see me lapse back into my former condition. It was the sense that it would be desirable to see one's earthly suffering terminated by death that first put me on the way to recovery. Soon after this the idea occurred to me of terminating it myself, and it was for this reason that I took the flask of opium. The possibility of ending my suffering gave me the strength to bear my suffering, and now that I have this talisman, I have forced my way from the presence of death back into life again. Do not be concerned that I shall make use of it,' he said. 'Satisfy yourselves, as persons with knowledge of the human heart, that you have made me attached to life by allowing me the means of detaching myself from it.' After mature consideration we decided not to press him any further, and he now carries on his person, in a secure glass bottle, this poison, the strangest of antidotes."

They informed the doctor of everything they had discovered, and it was decided not to reveal any of this to Augustin. The Abbé undertook never to let him out of his sight, and to guide him further along the path to recovery.

Meanwhile it was decided that Wilhelm should undertake his tour of Germany with the Marchese, and if it seemed possible to revive in Augustin the desire to see his native land of Italy, this would be communicated to his relatives and Wilhelm could return him to them.

Wilhelm had by now made all preparations for his journey, and if at first it seemed strange that Augustin was glad to hear that his old friend and benefactor was setting out again, the Abbé soon discovered the reason for this unexpected reaction. Augustin had never overcome his fear of Felix, and was therefore glad to see the boy depart as soon as possible.

By now so many guests had arrived that there was no longer any room in the castle and the adjoining buildings, especially since arrangements had not been made in advance for their accommodation. They breakfasted and dined together, and would have liked to persuade themselves that they were living in a delightful state of harmony, were it not for the fact that in their minds they were quietly veering away from each other. Therese had gone riding several times with Lothario, even more frequently on her own, and had made the acquaintance of all the landowners, male and female, in the neighborhood. This was her particular concept of domesticity, and she may well have been right in believing that one should be on the very best footing with neighbors and cultivate mutually helpful relationships. There seemed to be no talk of a marriage between her and Lothario. Natalie and the countess had a great deal to say to each other, the Abbé was always watching out for the Harper, Jarno having frequent conferences with the doctor, Friedrich clinging to Wilhelm, and Felix turning up wherever he could have a good time. They tended to walk in pairs when the company dispersed, and when they had to come together again, they took refuge in music so that they could be together and also alone with themselves.

An unexpected addition to the company was the count, who came to fetch his wife and, apparently, take formal leave of his worldly relations. Jarno ran to meet his carriage, and when the count asked who the company consisted of, Jarno said, in one of those fits of crazy humor that always came over him when he saw the count: "You will find the whole nobility here: Marcheses, Marquises, Mylords and Barons. All we lacked was a Count." They walked upstairs, and Wilhelm was the first person to meet them in the anteroom. "Mylord!" said the count to him in French, after inspecting him for a moment, "I am delighted to be able to renew our acquaintance so unexpectedly, for I must be gravely mistaken if I did not meet you in the prince's entourage when he was in my castle." "I did have the good fortune, Your Grace, to wait on you at that time," said Wilhelm, "but you show me too high a regard in considering me an Englishman, and, in addition, one of high rank. For I am a German and . . ." "A real good fellow," said Jarno, breaking in immediately. The count smiled at Wilhelm, and was about to say something, when the rest of the company came in and greeted him cordially. Excuses were made for not giving him suitable accommodation at once, but a promise was made to remedy this situation as soon as possible.

"Well, well!" he said, laughing. "I see the quartering arrangements have been left to chance, whereas foresight and planning can achieve marvels! But don't move a single thing, otherwise I can see there will be absolute bedlam. Everybody will be uncomfortable, and that shouldn't happen to anybody on my account, not even for one hour. You were witness," he said to Jarno, "and you too, Mister," turning to Wilhelm, "to the large number of people I comfortably housed that time in my castle. Give me a list of the guests and their servants, show me where everyone is housed at present, and I will rearrange things so that, with the least expenditure of effort, everyone gets comfortable quarters and there is still room left for the guest who turns up unexpectedly."

Jarno acted straight away as though he were adjutant to the count, brought him all the necessary information and had the greatest fun, according to his fashion, in leading the old gentleman astray. The latter, however, soon achieved a tremendous triumph. The whole rearrangement was completed, he had the names put over all the doors, and nobody could deny that the goal had been achieved with a minimum of reorganization and fuss. In addition to this, Jarno had so arranged things that persons with a particular interest in each other at the moment were accommodated in adjoining rooms.

When this was all settled, the count said to Jarno: "Help me to get clear about that young man you call Meister, who is said to be a German." Jarno said nothing for the moment, because he was well aware that the count was one of those people who, when they ask to be informed, really want to inform you themselves. Anyhow, the count, without waiting for an answer, went on to say: "It was you who introduced him to me then and commended him to me in the prince's name. If his mother was German, then I would vouch for it that his father was an Englishman, and of high station. The amount of English blood flowing in German veins during the last thirty years is considerable. I won't press the point further; everyone has family secrets. But I can't be hoodwinked in such matters." He then went on to recount various episodes involving Wilhelm at that time in his castle, to which Jarno said nothing, although the count was quite wrong and several times confused Wilhelm with a young Englishman in the prince's retinue. The old gentleman had once had an excellent memory, and was always proud at being able to recall the most insignificant details of his youth. But now he confidently imposed the stamp of truth on the wildest combinations of fancy that his imagination created out of failing memory. He had become very gentle and agreeable, and his presence had a salutary effect on the company. He requested that they should read something useful together, and even arranged little entertaining pastimes with great care, though not participating in them himself. And when people expressed their amazement at his condescension, he would say that it was incumbent on anyone who withdraws from the world in major matters, to consort with the world on minor matters.

More than once Wilhelm had an anxious moment during these entertainments, and frivolous Friedrich irritated him by hinting at an interest in Natalie on Wilhelm's part. How did he arrive at that idea? What gave him the justification for thinking this? And, since he and Wilhelm were much together, would not the company conclude that Wilhelm had slipped him an incautious and unfortunate confidence?

One day when they were amusing themselves and merrier than usual, Augustin appeared at the door, tore it open, and rushed in. His whole appearance was frightening—his face deathly pale, his eyes wild, his attempts to speak, fruitless. They were all alarmed: Lothario and Jarno, suspecting a recurrence of his madness, grabbed him and held him fast. First he stuttered indistinctly, but then shouted loud and clear: "Don't stay here holding me! Hurry up! Help! Save the child! Felix is poisoned!"

They let go of him, and he rushed out of the door with the whole company following in horror. The doctor was called. Augustin directed his steps to the room of the Abbé, where they found the child, frightened and ill at ease when they called to him as they drew nearer, asking him what he had done.

"Father!" said Felix, "I did not drink out of the bottle, I drank from the glass. I was so thirsty."

Augustin wrung his hands and said: "He is lost!" He pushed his way through the others and ran away.

On the table they found a glass of almond milk and beside it a half-empty carafe. The doctor arrived, heard what they had been told, and then observed to his horror the bottle that had contained the opium lying empty on the table. He gave him some vinegar to drink, and used all his skill to help the child.

Natalie had Felix carried to her room, where she anxiously took care of him. The Abbé had run off to find Augustin and elicit more information from him. The unhappy father had done the same, but without success, and when he returned he found consternation on everyone's face. The doctor had examined the drink in the glass and found that it contained a strong admixture of opium. The child was lying on a sofa and seemed very ill. He asked his father not to make him drink any more for it hurt him. Lothario sent people to discover where Augustin had gone, then himself went in search of him. Natalie sat by the child, who crept on to her lap, asking her to protect him and give him a piece of sugar because the vinegar was much too sour. The doctor agreed to this, saying that the child, who was in a very troubled state, should be allowed to rest for a while. All that should be done, had been done; as for the rest, he himself would do everything that was humanly possible. The count came in — somewhat unwillingly, so it would seem — looking grave and ceremonious. He laid his hands on the child, turned his eyes to Heaven, and remained for some minutes in this posture. Wilhelm, who had been stretched out disconsolate in a chair, jumped up, looked despairingly at Natalie, and left the room. The count left soon afterwards.

"I do not understand," the doctor said after a while, "why there are no signs of a dangerous condition in the child. Even if he only took one gulp, he must have absorbed a massive dose of opium, but his pulse shows no acceleration, except that caused by my medication and the state of fright we have put him in."

Jarno then brought the news that Augustin had been found in the attic lying in a pool of blood. There was a razor beside him, so he had probably cut his throat. The doctor rushed off and met the persons bringing down the body. It was placed on a bed and carefully examined. The cut had penetrated the windpipe, and he had fallen unconscious after a severe hemorrhage. But it soon became clear that there were still signs of life, and hope. The doctor placed the body in the proper position, dealt with the laceration, and put a bandage over the place. The night passed uneasily and sleeplessly for everyone. The child would not be separated from Natalie. Wilhelm sat in front of her on a stool, with the child's feet on his lap and its head and chest on hers. So between them they shared the pleasing burden and the pain of anxiety, and remained in this uncomfortable position until daybreak. Natalie had stretched out her hand which Wilhelm was clasping, neither of them said a word, they both looked at the child, and then at each other. Lothario and Jarno were sitting at the other end of the room, engaged in a very important conversation, which we would have gladly communicated to our readers if we were not so preoccupied with the rapid course of events. The boy slept peacefully, and woke quite happy in the early morning, jumped up, and asked for something to eat.

As soon as Augustin was somewhat recovered, they tried to get some more information out of him. What they did find out, was only extracted with difficulty and piece by piece. For instance: when as a result of the count's unfortunate rearrangements Augustin found himself in the same room as the Abbé, he discovered the manuscript with his life story, read it with horror, and became convinced that he could not live any longer. He then took his usual refuge in opium, poured some of it into a glass of almond milk, but recoiled at the moment he lifted it to his lips. He then left it standing while he went into the garden to look at the world once more. When he returned, he found the child about to refill the glass from which it had been drinking.

They urged the poor unhappy man to compose himself, but he grasped Wilhelm's hand frantically. "Oh!" he cried, "why did I not leave you long ago! I knew perfectly well that I would kill the child, and he me." "But the boy is alive," said Wilhelm. The doctor, who had been listening carefully to what Augustin said, asked him if all the drink had contained poison. "No," he said, "only the glass." "Then it was a lucky chance," said the doctor, "that the boy drank only from the bottle. Some good angel guided his hand so that he did not clutch the death that awaited him." "No, no!" cried Wilhelm, covering his eyes with his hands. "What a dreadful thing to say! The boy specifically said that he did not drink from the bottle, only out of the glass. He only seems not to be ill; he will wither away!" —And with these words he hurried out of the room. But the doctor went up to the child, stroked its head, and said: "Tell me, Felix; didn't you drink from the bottle, and not from the glass?" The little boy began to cry. The doctor spoke quietly to Natalie, telling her how matters stood. She then in turn tried to get the truth out of the child, but in vain. He cried bitterly, and continued to cry until he fell asleep.

Wilhelm watched over him, and the night passed peacefully. The next morning Augustin was found dead in his bed. He had deceived the watchful eyes of those attending him by feigning sleep, then quietly taken off the bandage, and bled to death. Natalie went for a walk with the child who was as cheerful as in his happiest days. "You are so kind," he said to her. "You never get angry, you never beat me. So I will tell you: I did drink out of the bottle. My mother Aurelie always slapped my fingers when I reached for the carafe. My father looked so fierce, I thought he was going to hit me."

Natalie flew with winged steps to the castle. Wilhelm came to meet her, still full of anxiety. "Happy father!" she cried, lifting up the child and placing it in his arms, "Here you have your son back! He did drink out of the bottle; his bad habit saved him."

The count was told the fortunate outcome, but he received the news with a smile and that modest, quiet sense of not being surprised, which enables us to tolerate the mistakes of well-meaning persons. Jarno, attentive to everything, could not understand such lofty self-satisfaction, till after much searching he found out that the count was convinced the child really had taken poison but had been miraculously preserved by the count's prayers and his laying-on of hands. The count now decided it was time for him to leave, his packing was as usual done in a trice, and on their departure the countess took Wilhelm's hand with one hand while still holding Natalie's in the other, pressed all four together, turned away quickly and leapt into the carriage.

This large number of terrible and strange events following one upon the other, brought about such a change in everyone's life, such continual disorder and confusion, that a kind of feverish agitation came over the whole household. Times for sleeping and waking, eating, drinking and social gatherings were delayed or reversed. Apart from Therese, everyone was thrown off course. The men tried to regain their normal good spirits by drinking intoxicating liquors, and while they acquired thereby a certain artificial enlivenment, they lost that spontaneity that alone can produce true good spirits and actions.

Wilhelm was disturbed, and disorganized by strong emotions. His whole being became totally bereft, through all these terrible unexpected happenings, of any power to withstand the passion that had taken such a strong hold over his heart. Felix had been restored to him, and yet everything seemed to be wrong. The letters with final arrangements were there from Werner, and all he needed for his journey was the courage to leave. Everything was pressing him to start out. He could well imagine that Lothario and Therese were simply waiting for him to leave, in order to get married. Jarno was unusually quiet; one might even say he had lost some of his usual brightness. Fortunately the doctor helped Wilhelm out of his quandary, by declaring that he was sick and giving him medicine.

The company came together every evening and Friedrich, that uninhibited fellow who usually drank more wine than he should have, monopolized the conversation, making them laugh in his usual way with hosts of quotations and waggish allusions, but often disconcerting them by his habit of saying exactly what he thought.

He seemed not to believe in Wilhelm's "sickness." One evening, when everyone was present, he said: "What's the name of the sickness afflicting our friend, Doctor? Which of those three thousand names would you select to cloak your ignorance? There is no lack of similar cases. There is one," he added ominously, "in Egyptian, or Babylonian, history."

They all looked at each other, and smiled.

"What was the king's name?" he said, pausing for a moment. "If you don't prompt me, I'll know where I can find out." He opened the doors and pointed to the large painting in the anteroom. "What's the name of that old goatee with the crown, pining away at the foot of the bed of his sick son? What's the name of the beauty who enters with poison and antidote simultaneously in her demure, roguish eyes? Who is that botcher of a doctor who suddenly sees the light and for the first time in his life can prescribe a sensible remedy, give medication which is a complete cure and is as tasty as it is effective?"

He went on swaggering in this tone. Everyone present did their best to control themselves and concealed their embarrassment behind forced smiles. A light flush came over Natalie's cheeks and betrayed the feelings she was harboring. Fortunately for her she was walking with Jarno, and when she reached the door, she skillfully managed to slip out, paced to and fro a few times in the anteroom and then went to her own room.

The others were all very quiet. But then Friedrich began to dance, and sing:

Ah what wonders you shall see!
What's done, is done,
What's said, is said.
Before day breaks,
Wonders shall you see.

Therese had followed Natalie, and Friedrich led the doctor up to the painting, delivered a ridiculous encomium on medicine, and crept away.

Lothario had been standing motionless in a bay window, looking out into the garden. Wilhelm was in a sorry state. Being at last alone with his friend, he nevertheless remained silent, quickly surveying his life up to that point and finally shuddering at his present situation. Suddenly he jumped up and said: "If I am responsible for what is happening to you and me, then rebuke me! My suffering is now aggravated by your withdrawing your friendship, leaving me without this consolation to go out into the wide world I should long have been part of. If, however, you regard me as a victim of the cruel enmeshment of chance, from which I was unable to disentangle myself, do give me the assurance that your friendship and love will accompany me on a journey I can no longer postpone. The time will come when I can tell you what has been going on within me these last days. Perhaps I do deserve a rebuke for not unbosoming myself to you earlier, for not revealing my whole self. If I had, you would have stood by me and helped me out. Time and time again my eyes have been opened to what I am, but always too late and always to no purpose. How I deserved that dressing down by Jarno! I thought I had understood it well enough to embark on a new life! Could I? Should I? There is no sense in blaming either fate, or ourselves. We are all miserable creatures, destined for misery; and is it not a matter of complete indifference whether it is our own fault or the workings of some higher force, or chance, virtue or vice, wisdom or madness, that plunges us into destruction? Farewell! I will not stay a moment longer in a house where unwittingly I have so grievously abused such gracious hospitality. Your brother's indiscretion is unpardonable, it drives me to the utmost desperation."

"Well," said Lothario, taking him by the hand, "just suppose that your marrying my sister was the secret condition for Therese's agreeing to give me her hand? This was the compensation that noble girl designed for you: she swore that both pairs should go to the altar on the same day. 'His mind chose me,' she said, 'but his heart demands Natalie, and my mind will go to the assistance of his heart.' We agreed to observe you and Natalie, we confided in the Abbé and had to promise him not to take any steps to further your union but rather let things run their own course. This we have done. Nature did the job, and my crazy brother only shook down the ripe fruit. Since we encountered each other in such an extraordinary way, let us not live ordinary lives, let us work together in a worthy enterprise. It is beyond belief what a cultivated man can achieve for himself and others, if, without trying to lord it over others, he has the temperament to be the guardian of many, helping them to find the right occasion to do what they would all like to do, and guiding them toward the goals they have clearly in mind without knowing how to reach them. Let us then join together in a common purpose—that is not mere enthusiasm, but an idea which can quite well be put into practice, and is indeed often implemented, though not always consciously. My sister Natalie is a living example of this. The ideal of human activity which Nature has prescribed for her beautiful soul will always remain unattainable. She deserves this name more than many others—more even, if I may say so, than our noble aunt, who, when our good doctor assembled that manuscript, was the most beautiful personality we knew. But since then Natalie has developed, and everybody must rejoice at such a person."

He was going to continue, but Friedrich came running into the room, shouting: "What sort of garland have I earned? How will you reward me? Bind together myrtle, laurel, ivy, oak leaves—the freshest you can find. There are so many merits in me for you to crown. Natalie is yours! And I'm the sorcerer who raised the treasure!"

"He's crazy," said Wilhelm. "I'm leaving."

"Have you authority to speak?" Lothario asked Friedrich, keeping a firm hold on Wilhelm.

"Yes, on my own behalf, and by the grace of God, if you will; I was the intermediary, and now I'm the emissary. I listened at the door; she revealed it all to the Abbé."

"How disgraceful!" said Lothario. "Who told you to eavesdrop?"

"Who told her to shut herself in?" replied Friedrich. "I heard it all very clearly. Natalie was in quite a state. During that night when the child seemed so ill and was lying half on her bosom, with you sitting glumly there in front of her and sharing the precious burden, she made a vow that if the child should die, she would acknowledge her love and offer you her hand in marriage. Now the child is alive, why should she change her intentions? A promise once made should be kept under all conditions. Here comes the parson to surprise us with the news!"

The Abbé entered. "We know everything," said Friedrich. "Make it short. Your appearance is just a formality, we don't need you gentlemen anymore!"

"He eavesdropped," said Lothario.

"How improper!" exclaimed the Abbé.

"Hurry up!" said Friedrich. "How are the ceremonies to be? Pretty thin; you can count them on five fingers." And turning to Wilhelm, he said: "You have to start on your journey: the Marchese's invitation is very timely! Once you are on the other side of the Alps, everybody will be here, thanking you for all the wonderful things you will be doing, which will provide them with free entertainment. It's as if you were giving an open party to which persons of every station in life can come!"

"You have certainly had great success with the public in providing popular entertainment," the Abbé replied. "It seems as if I shall never get to speak today."

"If everything doesn't turn out as I say," said Friedrich, "then suggest something better. Come here and look at them—and let's be happy!"

Lothario put his arm around his friend. He led him up to his sister, who came toward them with Therese. Nobody said a word.

"Don't delay!" said Friedrich. "You can be ready to leave in a couple of days. Did you ever imagine, my friend," he said, turning to Wilhelm, "when we first met and I asked you for that lovely bouquet, that you would ever receive such a flower as this from me?"

"Don't remind me of those days at this happiest of all moments," Wilhelm replied.

"But you should no more be ashamed of those days than you should be of your parentage. Those times were good times: and I must laugh when I look at you now. You seem to me like Saul, the son of Kish, who went in search of his father's asses, and found a kingdom."

"I don't know about kingdoms," said Wilhelm, "but I do know that I have found a treasure I never deserved. And I would not exchange it for anything in the world."

Notes

P. 9, *Professor Gottsched*. Johann Christoph Gottsched (1700–66), professor of poetry at Leipzig since 1730, published (1740–45) an anthology in six volumes of German plays by himself and his friends. His preface stressed the importance of the rules derived from Greek and Roman drama.

P. 11, *Tasso's* Jerusalem Delivered. Torquato Tasso's romantic epic *Gerusalemme Liberata* (1581), which celebrates the First Crusade, was a cardinal text for the cultivated German and European reader. Goethe read it as a boy in the famous German translation by Johann Friedrich Kopp (1742). The characters mentioned later by Wilhelm are all figures in the poem. *Clorinda* is a warrior maiden, initially a pagan; *Armida* is the beautiful niece of a pagan enchanter; *Tancred* and *Rinaldo* are crusaders, the poem's main protagonists; *Godfrey* of Bouillon is the leader of the Christian forces.

P. 47, *Guarini*. Italian playwright (1537–1612). *Pastor fido* was a popular pastoral play.

P. 77, *"Who never with hot tears ate his bread."* An unrhymed, more literal translation (by E.A.B.) of the poem reads:

Who never ate his bread with tears,
Who never sat upon his bed,
Weeping through anguished nights of grief:
He knows you not, ye heavenly powers.

You lead us into life, and then
Let each poor man his guilt acquire
And then you leave him to his pain:
For all guilt takes its toll on earth.

P. 83, *"Know you the land where lemon blossoms blow."* In E.A.B.'s translation:

Knowst thou the land where lemons bloom,
Through darkest leaves the golden orange glows,
And gentle breezes blow from bluest sky,
The myrtle still, the laurel proudly stands,
Knowst thou it well?
                              O there, o there,
Beloved, would I gladly go with thee!

Knowst thou the house? Columns support its roof,
The hall is gleaming, glittering the rooms,
And marble statues stand and gaze at me
"What have they done to you, you poor dear child?"
Knowst thou it well?
                              O there, o there,
Protector, would I gladly go with thee!

Knowst thou the mountain and its cloud-clad path?
The mule in swirling mists seeks out the way,
In caverns dwell the dragons' ancient flood!
Knowst thou it well?
                              To there, to there,
Our path doth lead us. Father, let us go!

For another rhymed translation (by Christopher Middleton) of the poem,
see Vol. 1 of this series, *Selected Poems*, p. 133.

P. 99, Montfaucon. Bernard de Montfaucon (1655–1741), author of *L'anti-
quité expliquée et representée en figures*, 15 vols., 1719–24.

P. 104, Racine. Racine's tragedies *Britannicus* and *Bérénice* were much
praised by Gottsched.

P. 104, Shakespeare. At the end of the 18th century, Shakespeare's plays
became among German writers the epitome of dramatic art, replacing the
admiration for the French playwrights. See also Vol. 3 of this series, *Essays on
Art and Literature*, especially "Shakespeare: A Tribute" (pp. 163–65).

P. 113, this present war. The Seven Years' War (1756–63).

P. 127, national stage. The first German "national theater" was actually not
founded until in 1767, in Hamburg; it offered Lessing the material for his
Hamburg Dramaturgy (1767–68).

P. 142, "Only they know my pain." Another translation (by E.A.B.) of the
poem reads:

Only the one who yearns,
Knows what I suffer!
Alone and separate
From joy and pleasure,
Into the firmament,
Upward I gaze!

For he who loves and knows
Me, is far distant.
Dizzy my eyes, my heart
Burns deep within me.
Only the one who yearns,
Knows what I suffer!

P. 179, Wieland. Wieland's *Hamlet* translation appeared in 1766.

P. 186, Grandison. Grandison, Clarissa and Pamela are the chief figures of Richardson's novels (1753–54; 1748; 1740). Oliver Goldsmith's *Vicar of Wakefield* appeared in 1766, Henry Fielding's *Tom Jones* in 1749.

P. 191, best remark. Hamlet says to Ophelia in *Hamlet* III,2: "That's a fair thought to lie between maids' legs."

P. 191, "Do not sing in tones depressing." In E.A.B.'s translation, the poem reads:

Do not sing in sombre tones
Of the loneliness of night;
No, oh no, my pretty ones,
Night is made for company.

Once was woman given to man
As his lovely, better half,
Night is half of life itself,
And the better half, for sure.

How can daytime please you so,
Since it breaks your pleasures?
As a respite it can serve,
With no further uses.

But when in the depth of night
Twilight flows from sweetest lamp,
Mouth approaches close to mouth
Spreading joy and merriment;

When the wanton speedy boy,
Wild and fiery oftentimes,
Dallies now with gentle play
When, as now, the gift is small;

When the nightingale her song
Sings to lovers, lovingly,
Sounding like a tale of woe
To fettered hearts and troubled minds;

Gentle stirrings of the heart,
When you listen to the clock,
Twelve momentous strokes ring out,
Peace and safety promising.

Therefore when the day is long,
Mark my words, o loving heart:
Every day its sorrows has
Every night its rapture sweet.

P. 211, Moravians. Protestant community founded in Herrnhut in 1722.

P. 213, Lessing's Emilia Galotti. That much-admired play appeared in 1772. An open copy was found on Werther's desk after his suicide.

P. 217, Confessions of a Beautiful Soul. For Susanna von Klettenberg's (1723–74) influence on Book VI, see *Poetry and Truth*, Vol. 4 of this series, p. 253 f. and passim.

P. 218, Christian German Hercules. Title of a Baroque novel by Andreas Heinrich Buchholtz (1669).

P. 218, Roman Octavia. Title of a Baroque novel by Anton Ulrich von Braunschweig-Wolfenbüttel (1677).

P. 236, pietist theologians. The doctrines of August Hermann Francke (1663–1727), the founder at Halle of "pietism," were expanded by his disciples to form a system of modes of conversion.

P. 238, Agathon. Allusion to Wieland's *Agathon*, the first German *Entwicklungsroman* (1766–67) — literally "novel of development" — a prototype of the *Bildungsroman*, but putting less emphasis on the influence of the environment on the development of soul and mind. Agathon, though educated in the most moral manner, becomes susceptible to temptations, which he ultimately overcomes.

P. 239, David. David committed adultery after observing Bathsheba bathing. See 2 Sam. 11.

P. 241, Zinzendorf. Nikolaus Ludwig von Zinzendorf (1700–60), the founder of the pietist community at Herrnhut.

P. 241, Moravian hymnal. Pietist hymnal put together in 1742 for the community of Ebersdorf.

P. 248, Danaids. The daughters of Danae who murdered their husbands during the bridal night. — In the netherworld Sisyphus had to atone for his ruthless life by pushing a rock to the top of a hill, from which it rolled down, only to repeat the hopeless task ad infinitum.

P. 307, pigtail. Orthodox Jews followed the biblical injunction not to cut or arrange their hair. Jews had to pay a personal tax when crossing a border.

P. 311, subject to taxation. In this discussion of economic policy, Lothario advances principles of universal taxation, which were unknown in the feudal society of the 18th century.

P. 321, a certain song. See Philine's song, p. 191.

P. 331, Remember to live! In contrast to the medieval injunction, "Memento mori" (Remember death), Goethe here states the human (or social) obligation to follow a life of purposeful activity.

P. 342, Andreas Gryphius. Silesian poet and most important German playwright of his century (1616–64).

P. 362, Borromeo. Arona at the southern end of Lago Maggiore was the birthplace of Borromeo (d. 1584), the archbishop of Milan. In 1697, a large statue of him was erected at the southern end of the Lake.

P. 373, Saul. According to 1 Sam. 9 and 10, Saul, chosen by God to be king, comes, in search of his father's asses, upon the prophet Samuel, who anoints him as king.

Afterword

Novels tend to be more closely connected than some other forms of literature with the conditions of life at the time they were written. *Wilhelm Meister's Apprenticeship* could only have been written in the late eighteenth century, and it has been frequently and adequately interpreted in these terms. But that is not my purpose here, because the audience I am envisaging is not one made up primarily of students of the transition from the *ancien régime* to the new configurations of the nineteenth century. Some broader perspective is surely required in presenting this novel to a twentieth-century audience of general readers. The reader whom I would term "specialist," that is to say, someone with knowledge of conditions in Germany at the time the novel was written, and possibly some familiarity with the language in which it was written, will interpret various features of the book from this historically grounded standpoint, and quite justifiably. But generalists will necessarily approach it differently. They may know that it is a historically important novel, sometimes claimed as the prototype of the *Bildungsroman*; but that is unlikely to be foremost in their minds as they read it, reading it as a novel like (but very unlike) any other novel, predominantly concerned with its qualities as a work of art and what it has to say to readers of all generations. How does it stand up as a work that, though of its time, transcends the special concerns, extends beyond the confines of that time? What does it mean to us?

To bring out the difference between presenting this novel to a general audience and interpreting it to "specialists," let me start by indicating some of the problems that it presents. The main difficulty is the apparent disunity of the book, which seems to begin as one thing—a novel of theatrical life?—and end as something different—a novel about social or communal integration? about finding one's way in life? Related to this is the change between the predominantly realistic tone of the earlier part of the novel, and the rather stylized nature of the last two books. Add to this that there are elements in the first five books which are hardly encompassable by realistic criteria—the two Strangers, Mignon, and the Harper—characters that seem to be at odds with the generally realistic atmosphere and tone, yet are described realistically. Where does Book Six fit in? Can it be conceived as a transition to the last two books; if so, in what sense? And those last two books: predominantly concerned with ideas and debates about ideas, and yet shot through with elements that seem to fit uneasily into a novel on the ideational plane, such as the character of Lydie, Lothario's love affairs or Felix drinking out of the bottle. What does this all add up to? What is Philine doing in a novel of ideas or the Harper in a realistic novel? What is Mignon doing in either?

The "specialist" will probably reply that we happen to know that Goethe's original intention was to give a broad picture of theatrical life at the time — a realistic purpose. But coupled with this was an idealistic theme, to present the theater as an educative institution. Goethe got to a certain point in the composition of the novel, then stopped, probably because these two purposes got in each other's way. When he returned to it several years later, he had changed his mind about what was to be the general import of the novel, for one thing was clear: it was to have an import, though now a different one. In other words: the specialist will account for the "disunity" by the fact that the novel was written at two different periods in Goethe's development. But that will not satisfy the general reader. For the novel does not fall so neatly into two halves. The second half is not devoid of realities, nor the first of abstractions. There is no clean break: most of the characters of the first half are still there, relatively unchanged, in the second. Goethe radically revised the first five books, excising incidents and personages that no longer belonged in his final conception of what his novel should be; he was also careful to link the first half with the second by certain judicious additions. The great themes of the last books are there from the start. The novel expands; it does not divide.

Second problem: The plot line abounds in coincidences, in incursions of the rationally improbable or unacceptable (such as the unknown person who appears to play the Ghost at the appropriate moment in the performance of *Hamlet*), with all sorts of hocus-pocus that few self-respecting modern readers can be expected to swallow. The specialist will point out that this sort of thing occurs all over the place in eighteenth-century popular novels that catered to the lust for mysteries, which lurked very close to the surface of rationalist self-satisfaction in the age of the later Enlightenment, which was also the age of the Secret Societies. True, but once we realize that a major theme in the novel is Chance, which we blithely interpret or misinterpret as Fate or Providential Guidance, all this becomes meaningful as a form of irony. For this is a highly ironic novel and all the talk about education by the Society of the Tower, together with all the moralistic hocus-pocus of guidance by error, is, to some degree, blarney as Jarno confirms and Natalie, more indulgently, accepts as well-meaning but mostly mistaken. For she is the moral center of the book, a focus of all the differences and disagreements, with her sublime smile that advocates toleration.

What I am trying to demonstrate is that the novel has a general validity that transcends its period significance. The ideas on education that it contains are period-bound; but the theme of education, self-cultivation, or rather of finding one's self, combines with the theme of chance to produce a complex amalgam of tolerant irony which, as a pattern, has lasting validity. Much else in the novel is easily explicable biographically or historically. Take the references to Tasso, Shakespeare, and Lessing, for instance. The specialist will refer us to Goethe's reading of the *Gerusalemme Liberata* at his father's encouragement, the discovery and first translations into German of Shakespeare in the 1760s and 1770s, the fact that Lessing's *Emilia Galotti* was the first native tragedy of importance. But the generalist, perhaps devoid of such information or at least unconcerned about it, will see these differently in the total texture of the novel. Tasso's epic is particularly notable for three women characters, Clorinda, Erminia, and Armida, who have their counterparts, as types, in the novel. *Hamlet* stands for an idea that Wilhelm tries to identify with, and represents art disconcertingly invading life. Lessing's *Emilia Galotti* is closely associated with Aurelie: like the Countess Orsina in the play, she too is a cast-off mistress, she too wields and cherishes a dagger, and her last great performance on the stage is, appropriately enough, as Orsina. That she also plays Ophelia and works so hard at understanding that character, is also significant; but she is more Orsina than Ophelia. In all these instances the reference to another work of literature is both metonymic and metaphoric.

Similarly, the sixth book is rightly seen by the specialist as an expression of German eighteenth-century pietism; and the community to which the count and countess retire after the culminating disaster of Book Three is depicted in terms of piestically grounded Moravian communities such as Count Zinzendorf had founded. Goethe himself referred to the sixth book as "the religious book," and the general reader is fully justified in seeing it as the expression of the religious life in general, and as a testimony to the presence of religious feelings and aspirations in the texture of human experience—not simply religion of a particular eighteenth-century type. It presents the viability, but also the limitations, of an entirely inner-oriented existence.

So too the details of theatrical life, though drawing on contemporary practices—for instance, the prologue that Wilhelm composes in honor of the visiting prince, or the cuts he makes in *Hamlet*—will, for the general reader, be representative of broader issues rather than offer specific reflections of the times. And the contrasting of aristocracy and bourgeoisie, easily and justifiably referable to social conditions in the Germany of the 1790s, is also open to wider interpretation. Aristocrats with landed estates, such as those in the last two books of the novel, are obviously meant to contrast with the aristocrats of the count's castle in Book Three—the ones responsible, the others dangerously frivolous—and although the feudal aristocrats of Books Seven and Eight now hardly exist anymore (and that, of course, can be said if we are thinking historically), what they represent still has, and always will have, a certain validity, namely the maintenance of lasting values, the inheritance of traditions, and the responsibilities of leadership.

I would therefore appeal for an approach that is neither historical nor biographical. Consider first the theme of the theater. We know that Goethe had been interested in the theater since childhood; we know that he was actively involved in theatricals almost immediately after his arrival in Weimar in 1775, and that the first reference to work on this novel is two years later. Also, history tells us that there was a movement afoot to establish standing professional theaters in Germany to compare with those of England and France. The theater was very much in people's minds, not merely as cultural entertainment, but as an educative force toward raising the level of culture. All this might explain why Goethe decided to write a novel about the theater. On the other hand it might not. He was not the first nor the last to write a novel on this subject. The appeal of such a subject rests most obviously on the fact that by choosing a group of actors as his personages, a novelist can present a variety of individuals who nevertheless make up a community. More important: Acting implies the assumption of a personality other than one's own, and usually several such roles. All this gives breadth and constant variety, with characters changing according to the demands of performance. Performance and personal life, public and private existence and appearance, fictive and real selves, illusion and reality, art and ordinary living, all these become natural concomita of the theme. Also, a theatrical company is a close community apart from the various strata of society and therefore able to interact with and react to all classes of society. As we have already suggested, Goethe's original plan broke down thematically because there was a conflict within it between a lofty concept of the theater as moral institution and the desire to present a true picture of the life of actors, which was often immoral, that is to say, between an idealistic and a realistic purpose. Perhaps because he realized this, he stopped writing it soon after he went to Italy in 1786, but when he took it up again in 1794, he adopted a consistently ironical attitude toward this subject. Whether the Wilhelm Meister of the 1770s and 1780s was to find his fulfillment as actor-manager and dramatist is uncertain. By 1794, he was definitely not to do so. What he thought was to be his destiny is now shown to be a mistaken objective. A mistaken objective *for him*, for there was nothing wrong with the objective itself. The conflict that I referred to earlier, between idealistic and realistic strains within the subject as originally conceived, is now transformed into a dichotomy of much broader implications and more general interest.

The idealistic motif of the theater as educative, and therefore moral, force remains an important element in the book, *but* its idealism is now not merely ironized by being contrasted with the real life of the actors, but is itself ironized as illusory and deluding *because* of its very idealism. The actress Aurelie tells Wilhelm at an important point in the action that for him theater has supplanted life, that he can talk magnificently about Shakespeare but is an absolute greenhorn when it comes to relationships with people. For him, theater has supplanted life; for her, it has suppressed it. She is a tragic actress of some stature, but she lives in her roles and is consumed by them. Her hysteria is histrionic: she is always acting even when off stage. So what Wilhelm comes to realize is the artificiality, the ersatz-quality of what he once declared to be man's fullest and highest expression. Drama and art are not decried as deceit, the passages on Shakespeare show that is not the case. But we are not all Shakespeares, and Wilhelm is not. We are not all Aurelies, and Wilhelm is not. He persuades himself that his life is to be the theater, and talks beautifully about the noble function of theater as being the reason for his persuasion, but in fact the real impetus is his desire to marry an attractive actress. He eventually rejects the acting life, ostensibly because he finds actors beneath his intellectual sights, but in fact because he is not gifted enough to be really first-rate. So now the realistic and idealistic strands no longer obstruct each other; they complement each other in ironic interplay.

The irony goes even deeper: How can something that essentially presents illusion-as-reality, the theater, be an educative force to dispel illusion? Both Wilhelm and Aurelie, in different ways, labor under the illusion that the illusionist world of the theater is truer than the bleaker world of non-illusion, not to say disillusion. Yet Wilhelm, unlike Aurelie, is disillusioned by the theater – disillusioned by his own illusion of it as an educative force, something that he has arrogated to the theater in particular (to justify his going after it, though the reason is also sexual), and which the theater may sometimes have (Goethe never denies that), but which is not solely the prerogative of the theater. Any community can be a moral educative force – school, church, feudal establishment, non-feudal communities that have their own principles of order. This is how the novel broadens out. It is a broadening process, not disunity, that characterizes its structure. Its structure is truly organic.

That first unfinished version, of which we have a contemporary copy, was characterized by disunity, and by discomfort. Goethe was not happy with it. His narrator ironizes à la Fielding, but sporadically. You never know where you are in relation to Wilhelm. But in the final version the irony is consistent from the very first pages, where his actress falls asleep while Wilhelm is telling her about his idealistic passion for the theater, to the very last where, having for so long thought of himself as the Prince of Denmark (and made cuts in the text to facilitate this reflected self-portrait), he ends up like Saul, the son of Kish, who finds his kingdom when looking for something quite different, namely, his father's asses. Wilhelm never inherits the kingdom of Denmark any more than Hamlet does, and what he is to make out of the kingdom he has found remains uncertain – and will depend entirely on him. There is a lot of talk in the book – and very good talk at that – about the effect of outer circumstances on development, on the benefits and disadvantages of being born to comfortable circumstances, also on the greater importance of what one has within, the *ingenium*. A good deal is also said about guidance, about the value, and the infuriating nature, of those who would direct us and save us from error, on fate and chance, on the whole dubious concept of education, especially in the form of pedagogy, on the advantages of gregariousness and of avoiding it, on being guided by reason (but ending up a narrow rationalist like Jarno) or being guided by nature (and committing incest and eventually going mad like the Harper). But it is Jarno who introduces Wilhelm to Shakespeare, which he reads in a room normally only entered by Mignon and the Harper, the two characters that Jarno expressly disapproves of. Confusion on Goethe's part? No: presentation of a complex tissue of mutually balancing concepts and approaches. It is Mignon, the spirit of poetry, who tries on two separate occasions to dissuade Wilhelm from joining the theater, and later dissuades him from marrying the all-too-practical and extrovert Therese. In a way, Mignon is the guiding force in the book, though this is not generally recognized. At her funeral the spectators are bidden back into life and she is described as the formative power, "die bildende Kraft." It is she who brings Wilhelm into closer contact both with the Harper and with Friedrich, who represent extremes of dark and light. She is his symbolic child. Hence the central importance given to the ritual of her obsequies in the Hall of the Past. Her spirit survives as the true guiding force, even when her body is lowered to its final resting place.

The verses that Wilhelm wrote as a young man are justly committed to the flames, for his image of the poet as a bird apart from and soaring above humanity is false and leads nowhere. But if poetry means what is immeasurable by ordinary linear-rational standards—mysteries, transcendent moments of experience, intimations, unaccountable insights of understanding—then the poetry he *lives* through his association with, and symbolic fathering of, Mignon— "Beloved . . . Protector . . . Father"—is far more real than the illusions of the theater. When, at the climax of the initiation scene, he asks the crucial question whether Felix is really his son, and is told that Nature has declared his apprenticeship completed, this means that the most important thing is to recognize what is of one's own, what is one's own fruition. Mignon, Friedrich, and the Harper are all part of this too. It has been said that the *Apprenticeship* describes the discovery of self. It does so by charting the rejection of illusions about what we are or should be. The theme is therefore of universal, general interest, and the novel is in no wise an old-fashioned book.

The very breadth of this theme means that within the novel is contained almost everything one could hope for: marvelously vital characters acutely perceived and presented with great psychological understanding, especially the women; a romance-structure with plenty of surprises and unexpected twists and turns that never stray into sheer fantasy; logical sequences of cause and effect broken by incursions of the inexplicable; classical control and romantic states of uncontrolment; a good dose of Enlightenment ideas (though sometimes ironized); humor and tragedy, prose and poetry, and a superbly anticlimactic climax. When Schiller complained that Goethe had not sufficiently explained the ideas represented by certain elements of the plot, Goethe referred, with apologetic irony, to his "realistic tick." He was too great an artist to *explain* what this or that in the book *meant*. He was vigorously opposed to didacticism in art. So we must be careful if we talk in terms of a *Bildungsroman*. A true *Bildungsroman* should contain, or at least imply, a concept of what the author conceives culture to be. The term, if properly used (and it rarely is nowadays), is not synonymous with a "novel of development," nor even with a novel of education. *Wilhelm Meister's Apprenticeship* contains no such statement of what culture is, nor, from what I have just said about Goethe, would we expect one. It offers us all sorts of ways of ordering one's life. Take your choice, it may be saying. What fits one, doesn't fit the other. The end is high comedy, which is why Friedrich leads the dance. To find what is best, one must discover one's self. And this sometimes comes upon us unawares. We talk of feeling that our destiny lies in a certain direction. We talk of "fate," but it was chance that gave Saul, the son of Kish, his kingdom and therewith his fulfillment. Or was it?

E.A.B.